Case Studies in
ORGANIZATIONAL
COMMUNICATION

This book is dedicated to Geriel,
whose integrity is constant.

Case Studies in
ORGANIZATIONAL
COMMUNICATION
Ethical Perspectives and Practices

2nd Edition

Edited by Steve May

The University of North Carolina at Chapel Hill

Los Angeles | London | New Delhi
Singapore | Washington DC

Los Angeles | London | New Delhi
Singapore | Washington DC

FOR INFORMATION

SAGE Publications, Inc.
2455 Teller Road
Thousand Oaks, California 91320
E-mail: order@sagepub.com

SAGE Publications Ltd.
1 Oliver's Yard
55 City Road
London EC1Y 1SP
United Kingdom

SAGE Publications India Pvt. Ltd.
B 1/I 1 Mohan Cooperative Industrial Area
Mathura Road, New Delhi 110 044
India

SAGE Publications Asia-Pacific Pte Ltd.
33 Pekin Street #02-01
Far East Square
Singapore 048763

Acquisitions Editor: Matthew Byrnie
Associate Editor: Nathan Davidson
Editorial Assistant: Stephanie Palermini
Production Editor: Catherine M. Chilton
Copy Editor: Megan Markanich
Typesetter: Hurix Systems Pvt. Ltd.
Proofreader: Annette R. Van Deusen
Indexer: Julie Grayson
Cover Designer: Karine Hovsepian
Marketing Manager: Liz Thornton
Permissions Editor: Karen Ehrmann

Printed in the United States of America

Case studies in organizational communication : ethical perspectives and practices / Steve May, editor. — 2nd ed.

p. cm.

Includes bibliographical references and index.

ISBN 978-1-4129-8309-9 (pbk. : acid-free paper)

1. Communication in organizations—Case studies.
2. Communication in organizations—Moral and ethical aspects. I. May, Steve (Steve Kent), 1961-

HD30.3.C37155 2013

302.3'5—dc23

2011031163

This book is printed on acid-free paper.

Certified Sourcing
www.sfiprogram.org
SFI-00453

11 12 13 14 15   10 9 8 7 6 5 4 3 2 1

Contents

List of Figures and Tables

Preface

I first considered editing a case study book on organizational ethics nearly a decade ago. As an instructor of organizational communication, I was frustrated by two features that were lacking in most textbooks in the field. First, I found that many of the primary textbooks in organizational communication included few, if any, case studies. By contrast, Business and Management programs had a long and successful history with case-based teaching and, as a result, cases were widely available. Yet, they did not necessarily offer the range and variety of perspectives I wanted my students to learn.

Although I had developed many of my own cases over the years, including a semester-long consulting case, I wondered why there was such a lack of cases in organizational communication textbooks. Most textbooks included discussion questions and even the occasional homework or fieldwork assignment, but these features never provided the extensive application of organizational theory that in-depth cases provided for my students. When cases were included in textbooks, they were typically short and general in their description of organizational phenomena. Until recently, there was even a lack of supplemental case study books to use in introductory or advanced organizational communication courses. I wanted more for my students.

Second, it also became clear that few, if any, textbooks included an extensive discussion of organizational ethics. Given the range and scope of organizational misconduct over the past several decades, it struck me as a glaring omission in our teaching. Based on conversations with other colleagues around the world, I knew that many instructors were, at least implicitly, discussing organizational ethics in their classrooms. But I found that many were reluctant to explicitly identify organizational ethics as an issue in their courses. Textbooks were not much help. When they included ethics, it was often relegated to a concluding chapter. Business ethics books have been available for years, but they seemed to define "organizations" and communication very narrowly. For example, rarely were nonprofit organizations, government agencies, universities, churches, or other collectives discussed in them. In addition, they often included classic, historical cases of ethics rather than recent emerging ethical issues most relevant to today's students.

The confluence of these two pedagogical frustrations was further set in motion with the series of organizational scandals (e.g., Enron, Arthur Andersen, Tyco, WorldCom) that have received such attention in the past decade. For this second edition, they have been further compounded by the ethical misconduct in the financial sector that has produced the worst economic downturn since the Great Depression. For years, my former students had contacted me about their own personal ethical dilemmas in organizations, but now my current students were asking important but challenging questions: What went wrong with these organizations? Why? How common are such unethical practices in organizations? Is this a new phenomenon? What should I do if I belong to an organization that engages in unethical behavior? What if I observe a boss or coworker engaging in such behavior? What changes are necessary in order to improve the ethical conduct of organizations and the people in them? What can I do to help?

Their questions led to informative, instructive, and wide-ranging discussions of organizations and ethics, but I wanted a framework for discussing ethical issues with them in both a theoretical and a pragmatic way. This book, then, is an attempt to focus and structure a meaningful and productive dialogue about organizational ethics with students. It is designed to integrate ethical theory and practice in order to strengthen students' ethical awareness, judgment, and action in organizations by exploring ethical dilemmas in a diverse range of cases. For this, the second edition of the book, the need to improve our ethical behavior in organizations seems even more pronounced.

USES FOR THE BOOK

The book may be used in a variety of ways. Ideally, its availability will prompt some instructors to begin teaching courses on organizational ethics. In such courses, it may be used as a primary textbook. Or it may be used as a supplemental text for an introductory or advanced course in organizational communication. The book will serve as an excellent companion to a primary textbook in order to bring ethics to the foreground of students' attention. As such, the book not only includes discussions of ethical perspectives and practices but the case studies also cover a range of topics typical in many organizational communication courses such as leadership, teamwork, organizational culture, work–family balance, gender, new technologies, organizational change, crisis communication, decision making, power/resistance, and conflict, as well as emerging topics such as telecommuting, offshoring, and social media, among others. In addition, instructors will notice that many of the cases can be easily applied to common theories of organizational communication such as classical management, human relations, systems theory, critical theory, and postmodern theory.

WHY TEACH ORGANIZATIONAL ETHICS?

This ethics case study book is based on the belief that organizational theory and practice have become increasingly wide ranging and diverse in the past two decades. Similar to the emergence of new, diverse theories to understand organizations, organizations themselves are growing more and more complex. Their size, mission, function, structure, and processes all seem increasingly fluid as organizations become more "emergent" and adaptable. As a result, books on organizational dynamics cannot necessarily present singular, simplistic explanations of "the way organizations are." Rather, they must provide students with a range of organizational examples that best approximate the current and future evolution of organizations—and the practices among and between them.

One of the most recent shifts in organizations is a renewed interest in ethics, partly in response to recent scandals but also in response to the desire to rethink the role of organizations in our lives. Members of organizations are asking themselves the following questions: What are our mission, vision, and goals? What do we value? What principles should guide our behavior with our multiple stakeholders? No longer is it accepted wisdom that "business ethics" is a contradiction in terms. Instead, questions of ethics are being taken seriously by many organizations around the world, particularly now that executives and boards of directors have realized that ethics may actually enhance individual and organizational performance. Rather than being viewed as merely a compliance or crisis issue, ethics is now seen as part of the bottom line.

The intent of this book, then, is to raise students' awareness regarding ethics and to provide them with the tools to evaluate situations and conduct themselves ethically. It introduces students to a broad, yet context-specific range of ethics-oriented issues in organizations that will supplement and extend their understanding of organizational communication. The book is based on the belief that students are best engaged when they can directly address the challenges and opportunities they will encounter in their own organizational lives. Often these challenges and opportunities converge around ethical dilemmas that workers experience, as they seek to negotiate their interests with those of their organization.

As a pedagogical tool, this book is designed to encourage students' critical thinking skills about ethics through analysis, reflection, and dialogue. Organizational ethics cases do not present easy, linear answers to organizational problems and, as a result, students will learn to explore complex, contextual, and conflicted questions about organizational life in ways that integrate theory and practice. A primary purpose of the book, then, is to further develop students' understanding of organizations by stimulating analysis and discussion of specific organizational practices that enable or constrain ethical action, thereby provoking multiple alternatives or solutions that are made more accessible to them. Additional features of the book include the following:

- An introductory chapter that explores multiple perspectives of ethics
- An innovative discussion of the most common practices of ethical organizations
- Timely case studies that examine a range of ethical dilemmas in diverse organizations
- Discussion questions at the end of each case study to prompt dialogue regarding the opportunities for, and challenges of, ethical behavior in today's organizations
- An afterword that raises new, challenging questions for ethical behavior in today's organizations

WHY USE CASE STUDIES?

All too often I have overheard students in the buildings and on the sidewalks of universities describing courses in the following fashion: "It's a theory course" or "It's a practical course." On the one hand, students are dissatisfied when courses belabor what is common sense. On the other hand, they are even more dissatisfied when courses have no clear bearing on everyday life. One of the ways to bridge this dichotomy is to recognize that understanding is the joint product of theory and common sense. As Karl Weick (1987) aptly explained, "Theory and research should focus on what people routinely overlook when they apply common sense. Theory should not be redundant with common sense; it should remind people of what they forget" (p.106).

Ideally, then, this book should combine theory and practice as it relates to organizational ethics. My assumption is that the two are mutually dependent. For instance, we all use implicit theories of the world around us to guide our behaviors. When those theories do not seem applicable to everyday life, then we adjust them accordingly. The same should hold true for the theories and practice of organizational ethics. Through this book, students will examine various theories of organizational ethics. Yet each ethical perspective should also be judged according to its applicability to the cases in this book. By studying these specific organizational cases, students should develop the critical thinking skills to determine which theories are applicable and which theories are not. They should also gain an appreciation for what "works" and what "doesn't work" in organizations when it comes to ethics.

Yet, this appreciation—and the knowledge that derives from it—cannot simply be told in a lecture. It is based on doing. According to Thomas Donaldson, the "case method," as it is often called, builds on the Socratic method of teaching, which involves the active involvement of students who explore, question, and discover in the give and take process with an instructor and fellow students.

In my teaching career, I have found that one of the primary teaching challenges is to provide students with concrete, context-specific knowledge that will supplement their past work experiences, which vary widely from student to student. Many college students often need supplemental materials that ground their theoretical understanding in a practical understanding of organizational life. This is particularly true in terms of ethical challenges that students may face once they enter (or reenter) the full-time workforce.

Many instructors draw upon their own research and/or consulting experience to help supplement students' work experiences. Or they utilize the short, limited case studies that are often found at the end of chapters in textbooks. However, many instructors complain that such cases provide neither the detail nor the full range of organizational opportunities/challenges that will develop the critical thinking skills necessary for students to comprehend the complexities of organizations. Finally, instructors often question whether a primary text, alone, allows students to confront—in a safe, classroom environment—the ethical dilemmas that many workers face in their careers.

In the future, then, I believe that students will need to understand both the theoretical developments in organizational communication and also how those developments are enacted in ethical organizational practice. This book, then, is designed to address this focus on praxis in a manner that clarifies the rapidly changing organizational environment—as well as the diversity of organizational practices that has followed these changes. In short, students need an explicit mechanism by which they can compare and contrast a growing number of developments in organizations. In addition, students need to understand and appropriately act upon the various ethical dilemmas and challenges they will confront in the workplace. Case studies of ethical and unethical organizational practices are one of the primary means to accomplish these goals.

Through case studies, students and instructors are able to directly assess ethical and unethical decision making in a rich, diverse, and complex manner that moves beyond only theoretical discussions of ethics (e.g., duty, rights, utility, virtue, relationships). In short, this case study book explores "ethics in action" and, as a result, is both theoretical and practical in its focus.

OVERVIEW OF THE BOOK

The Introduction provides the context for organizational ethics and an overview of ethical perspectives and practices. It explores current and past examples of ethical and unethical conduct in organizations. It also introduces students to some of the most important challenges for enhancing the ethics of organizations, as well as a means for analyzing ethical dilemmas they may face in organizations. Finally, the Introduction provides the theoretical foundation for students and is divided into two primary sections: (1) ethical perspectives and (2) ethical practices. The section on ethical perspectives gives students an overview of common ethical theories such as duty, rights, utility, virtue, and relationships. These theories provide one means for students to assess the case studies. Any—or all—of the theories may be applied to each case study, although students may find that one theory is either more prominent or more relevant in a case. The section on ethical practices explores several behaviors that are most common among ethical organizations, including alignment, dialogic communication, participation, transparency, accountability, and courage. Each practice is then applied to both ethical and unethical organizations.

Parts I through VI include 23 case studies that represent a range of organizational types and ethical dilemmas. Cases include not only business but also nonprofit organizations, universities, and government agencies. The cases are organized according to the ethical practices discussed in the Introduction. However, students may find that several of the ethical practices may be relevant to each case. As a result, instructors should use the structure of this section only as a preliminary guide for exploring the case studies. For example, the cases could also be discussed according to topic (e.g., leadership, organizational culture, decision making) or according to theory (e.g., classical management, human relations, systems theory). At the least, though, students should also be prepared to discuss each case according to the ethical perspectives (e.g., duty, rights, utility, virtue, relationships).

The book ends with the Afterword, which reminds students why our discourse around ethics matters. It also extends ethics to broader organizational and cultural issues and proposes a revised ethical theory. Finally, it offers several alternative directions for students interested in further pursuing organizational ethics.

My hope is that the book will stimulate not only dialogue about but also action on issues of organizational ethics. The recent scandals have brought public attention to the practices of both unethical and ethical organizations and, as a result, we have a rare opportunity to help our students create organizations of the future that are simultaneously productive and ethical. Whether as employees, citizens, consumers, or stakeholders, our students will hopefully make that difference in their own organizational lives.

BENEFITS OF CASE STUDIES

Case studies are one of the best ways to engage in dialogue about the real, day-to-day ethical dilemmas in organizations. They are also an ideal way to apply theories learned in the classroom, whether they are ethical theories or organizational theories (e.g., see Donaldson & Gini, 1996; Keyton & Schockley-Zalaback, 2004; Sypher, 1997). This case studies book is based on the assumption that you need to not only understand the theoretical developments in organizational studies but you also should know how they are enacted in ethical organizational practice.

This book, then, is designed to address this focus on praxis in a manner that clarifies the rapidly changing organizational environment—as well as the diversity of organizational practices that has followed these changes. In short, you need an explicit mechanism by which you can compare and contrast a growing number of developments in organizations. In addition, you will need to be prepared to understand and appropriately act upon the various ethical dilemmas and challenges you may confront in your organizational lives. Case studies of ethical and unethical organizational practices are one of the primary means to accomplish these goals.

Case studies, in general, offer several benefits:

- Case studies provide an opportunity to explore the real-world functioning of organizations in context.
- Case studies stimulate reflection on others' actions.
- Case studies provide exemplars of appropriate and inappropriate, productive and unproductive, useful and irrelevant behaviors.
- Case studies prompt lively discussion regarding alternative courses of action.
- Case studies provide an opportunity to apply theoretical knowledge to practical situations.
- Case studies serve as an impetus for future action.

More specifically, the case studies in this book may also be used to develop skills in these primary areas:

- Ethical engagement—You should develop the desire to pursue ethical issues in greater detail and establish your own independent thinking about ethics.
- Ethical reasoning and decision-making—You should develop greater confidence in your judgments and in your ability to understand and appreciate others' points of view regarding ethics.
- Ethical practice—You should develop the ability to respond to and proactively address ethical challenges that may arise in your life.

Case studies, then, should increase your motivation and interest in ethical issues, should improve your analytical and critical thinking skills around ethical challenges, and should provide you with a foundation for making organizations more ethical.

CASE STUDIES OF ORGANIZATIONAL ETHICS

My hope is that this book will motivate you to think more critically about organizational ethics in your own life and also in the lives of others. More specifically, the book will (1) introduce you to a range of ethical theories based on duty, rights, utility, virtue, and relationships and (2) explore case studies of organizations that either enable or constrain common elements of ethical practice such as alignment, dialogic communication, participation, transparency, accountability, and courage.

One of the reasons I was motivated to edit this volume is because many organizational case study books tend to be both atheoretical and ahistorical in their focus and typically marginalize ethics. By contrast, this book seeks to conceptualize and historicize ethics-oriented cases by (1) providing a theoretical foundation of ethical perspectives that can be applied to them, (2) identifying sets of ethical practices that might serve as examples for future organizational behavior, and (3) drawing upon their relationship to other cases (e.g., within an industry, a nation-state, a profession) within a particular period of time. The contributors to the book were encouraged to utilize their own scholarly strengths and expertise to develop fuller, richer cases, while also supplementing their expertise with additional historical and current resources. As such, the cases should be seen merely as a starting point for a more thorough and complex understanding of the cases themselves—and others that may be related to them by topic, issue, ethical perspective, or practice.

The cases in this volume were selected because they focus on organizations that have confronted challenging ethical dilemmas and, as a result, have acted ethically or unethically in response to them. That is, the cases in the book represent a full range of organizational practices, from overt violations of the law to exemplars of responsible behavior. Each case, however, is written to direct you to ethical dilemmas that present tensions, contradictions, challenges, and/or opportunities for the organization and others that it affects. You will also notice that, in contrast to some other case study books, these cases are about real—rather than hypothetical—organizations. I believe it is important for such organizations to be included in a case study book, first to present you with a realistic account of organizational life and second to hold unethical organizations accountable and to praise ethical organizations.

As you will see when you read the cases, contributors were asked to define organization broadly to include not only businesses but also other types of organizations (e.g., educational institutions, religious institutions, political organizations, nonprofit organizations) and organizing, in general. This is in stark contrast to most business ethics case study books that focus exclusively on corporations. Contributors were also encouraged to write cases that examined broader cultural constructions of work (e.g., work and identity, work–family balance, welfare-to-work programs, health care and work, globalization) that are so relevant to our everyday lives. The book, then, not only explores ethical issues within organizations but also within the social, political, economic, ideological, and technological contexts that affect, and are affected by, organizations.

Each case also examines a unique dimension of organizational communication. Some cases focus on the communication response of organizations after a product or service has failed. Other cases in the book explore the communication strategies of leaders who have produced ethical organizations. Or, in some cases, communication is discussed as a means to "frame" organizational decisions. Still others explore how gender, race, and family are constructed in and through communication within organizations.

You will also notice that a variety of sources were used in constructing these cases about organizational ethics, including observations, interviews, questionnaires, and documents (e.g., company documents, media coverage, legal materials, legislative hearings, professional association studies/reports). As a result, some cases are organized chronologically to follow a timeline of events while others are structured in a narrative form.

Regardless of the structure of each case, though, you should first identify the ethical dilemmas that are raised in the case. Once you have identified the ethical dilemmas, use the ethical perspectives and practices in combination with outside resource materials to fully understand, appreciate, and discuss their complexities. You should be able to understand the context of the case, the evolution of the ethical dilemmas, and the key actors facing them. Finally, as you develop your own opinions about the cases, be sure to consider alternative views that may be presented by your instructor or by other students. Doing so strengthens your "ethical agility" and better prepares you for the variety of ethical dilemmas you may confront in the future.

Although I will not recount all of the cases here, you will find a wide array of organizations and ethical issues in this volume. Here are some of the cases:

- Walmart—The case examines criticisms of the company that its economic impact "limits the ability of local businesses to survive." The case study also examines how Walmart has responded to charges that it negatively affects local businesses.

- British Petroleum (BP)—The case examines the range of decisions that led to the country's largest oil spill that damaged not only natural resources in southern states but also the livelihood of many workers there.

- Mitsubishi—The case addresses a class action sexual discrimination lawsuit by several female employees of the company and explores their claims, as well as the company and union responses to them.

- Aon Hewitt—The case considers the degree to which single and married employees with families should be treated similarly or differently.

- Enron—The case explores the ways in which overidentification of employees can cause them to overlook, if not misrepresent, unethical behavior in an organization.

- Toyota—The case discusses how Toyota sought to manage a product recall crisis in ways that maintained its reputation for safe vehicles.

- Google—The case explores the extent to which Google negotiated policies with the Chinese government that allowed broader access to users' data and content.

- College Athletics and Integrity—The case examines scandals and fraud in several university athletic departments that have increasingly focused on the financial benefits of sports programs at the expense of academic integrity.

- Wyeth—The case discusses how human health can be negatively affected when a pharmaceutical company ghostwrites articles for prestigious medical journals, without the general knowledge of physicians and patients.

As students of organizations, it is particularly important that you be able to first identify current trends regarding ethics and then, second, to intervene in the emergence, development, and acceptance (or rejection) of those trends. The case studies should help you in that process. Before we move to the cases themselves, though, it is important for you to have some additional background information regarding a range of ethical perspectives and ethical practices. The Introduction will provide that theoretical and practical foundation for you to thoroughly explore the case studies. The Introduction should give you the tools to understand, critique, and apply theoretical and practical material to the cases and, ultimately, to consider alternative, ethical futures for organizations.

REFERENCES

Donaldson, T., & Gini, A. (Eds.). (1996). *Case studies in business ethics* (4th ed.). Upper Saddle River, NJ: Prentice Hall.

Keyton, J., & Schockley-Zalaback, P. (Eds.). (2004). *Case studies for organizational communication: Understanding communication processes*. Los Angeles: Roxbury.

Sypher, B. D. (Ed.). (1997). *Case studies in organizational communication 2: Perspectives in contemporary work life*. New York: Guilford Press.

Weick, K. E. (1987). Theorizing about organizational communication. In F. M. Jablin, L. L. Putnam, K. H. Roberts, & L. W. Porter (Eds.), *Handbook of organizational communication: An interdisciplinary perspective* (pp. 97–122). Newbury Park, CA: Sage.

Acknowledgments

As in the case of all scholarly endeavors, this book could not have been completed without the guidance, assistance, and support of numerous other individuals. So although I take full responsibility for any of the limitations of the book, I also recognize that its strengths are the culmination of many conversations with friends, family, colleagues, and students over the course of several years.

At the least, the book is a creative collaboration that required the contributions of many colleagues who produced the cases contained in it. Although I will not name each of the case authors here, I do want to acknowledge their efforts to produce cases that, hopefully, will stimulate students' ethical awareness, judgment, and decision making. The case authors' own varied interests and perspectives have helped represent an incredibly wide-ranging and diverse set of ethical dilemmas in today's organizations.

I am also grateful for the strong support of SAGE in the original development of this book. In particular, I want to thank Todd Armstrong, senior acquisitions editor, for his initial encouragement, insight, patience, and good humor in the development of the first edition. He is, in many respects, the ideal editor. I have enjoyed the opportunity to work with Matthew Byrnie on the changes that have been made in this second edition. Nathan Davidson, associate editor, helped guide the book's progress throughout the revision process. I also want to thank Elizabeth Borders, editorial assistant, for her professionalism, promptness, and thoroughness throughout the process. In addition, Catherine Chilton and Megan Markanich were detailed and responsive in their work on the final stages of the volume.

The early stages of the book emerged while I served as a leadership fellow at the Institute for the Arts and Humanities at the University of North Carolina at Chapel Hill. Ruel Tyson's direction of the institute and his advocacy of ethical academic leadership served as a motivator to follow through with the project. In addition, the leadership fellows offered continual encouragement and support regarding the relevance and the significance of the book. A year later, I served as an ethics fellow at the institute, supported by the direction of Martha Crunkleton. My participation in that program further strengthened the intellectual and theoretical foundations of the book. I would like to acknowledge the ethics fellows for their engagement with the project and for their feedback regarding the teaching of case study on organizational ethics.

I would also like to thank the Kenan Institute for Ethics at Duke University for ongoing opportunities to both discuss organizational ethics and to put theory and research into action through ethics training in a range of organizations. I am especially grateful to Alysson Satterlund, who first established my connection to Kenan and who championed my work to them. Elizabeth Kiss graciously accepted my offer to make a praxis-oriented contribution by entering into an already productive and thought-provoking dialogue with members of the institute. Noah Pickus has extended and expanded that role in a manner that continues to stretch and challenge those of us committed to ethical organizational change. Finally, members of the Ethics at Work team—John Hawkins, Deborah Ross, Catherine LeBlanc, Amy Podurgal, Kathy Spitz, Morela Hernandez, and Doris Jordan—have played an integral role in my own ethical learning and development as we tested theory "in the field." I would like to acknowledge that the ethical practices in the book are based not only on my own research and teaching notes but also on a series of conversations with my friends and colleagues at Kenan.

Similarly, many students in my Organizational Ethics and Corporate Social Responsibility courses offered feedback on the first two chapters, as well as the cases themselves. Their willingness to assist me and their insightful suggestions consistently affirmed my faith in public higher education. In particular, I would like to thank Stephanie Evans, who gathered and synthesized much of the material that became the foundation for the discussion of ethical perspectives. Her dedication and professionalism helped move the project forward.

I would be remiss if I didn't also acknowledge, albeit briefly, my own teachers—each of whom motivated my interest in producing organizations that are not only productive but that are also ethical. Those ideas first emerged at Purdue University under the guidance of Linda Putnam, Cynthia Stohl, Phil Tompkins, and Jennifer Slack. Later, my interest and expertise in the topic were further developed and honed at the University of Utah through the intellectual support of Len Hawes, Mary Strine, Connie Bullis, Buddy Goodall, and Jim Anderson. At each of my academic homes, I was fortunate to have many thoughtful and thought-provoking mentors. I can only hope that I have motivated my own students in the same manner.

My closest colleagues at the University of North Carolina at Chapel Hill have always provided an enriching scholarly community that fosters intellectual engagement, collegiality, and mutual respect. I am particularly indebted to Bill Balthrop, whose leadership of the Department of Communication Studies combined wisdom, wit, and commitment. Bill and other faculty members there have created a context for both intellectual curiosity and rigor. My colleagues in organizational communication have also been long-standing sources of ideas and support. Ted Zorn, now at the University of Waikato in Hamilton, New Zealand, has been my model editor. He taught me the art and grace of editing while I served as the forum editor under his guidance as the editor of *Management Communication Quarterly*. His thoroughness, sense of humor, integrity, and compassion for authors and their work is an ethical template in its own respect. Dennis Mumby, Patricia Parker, and Sarah Dempsey, always generous with their time and kind with their words, have been wonderful colleagues who have been willing to further stimulate and stretch my thinking.

Finally, and most importantly, I could not have completed this book without the enthusiastic and loving support of my family. In so many respects, my parents provided the early and solid ethical foundation for me. They taught me the lessons of hard yet honest work, fairness, and respect. Hopefully, this book will, in some small measure, serve as a testament to their care of our family. My wife, Geriel, has been a steadfast source of support, a sounding board, an analytical guide, a practical problem solver, a tension reliever, and a loving companion. In addition, her business sense has frequently served as a reality test for my work. She, more than any other person, helped bring this project to its completion. During the final stages of the first edition, our daughter, Arcadia, was born. Her birth has brought me boundless joy and wonder and has provided me with a new and broader sense of perspective. Ultimately, her entry into the world has also produced a sense of urgency and a profound commitment to further strengthen ethical conduct in our "organizational society." As she has grown during the development of this second edition, the need for ethical engagement of our organizations has only intensified.

SAGE Publications would like to thank the following reviewers:

Rocci Luppicini
University of Ottawa

Kristin Froemling
Radford University–Radford

Paul E. Madlock
Texas A&M International University–Laredo

Ed Brewer
Appalachian State University–Boone

Introduction

Ethical Perspectives and Practices

The business of the modern world, for better or worse, is business. Unless we learn to conduct business in ways that sustain our souls and the life supporting web of nature, our future as a species is dim.

—Peter Barnes, Former President, Working Assets Long Distance
(now CREDO Long Distance)

THE CHALLENGE OF ORGANIZATIONAL ETHICS

If ethics were easy and straightforward in our organizations, there would be no need for books such as this one. However, this is rarely the case. Ethical decision making and practice are fraught with difficulties and challenges. Ethics often stretches us and moves us to think beyond our own self to consider others: our family, our work group, our organization, our country, our culture. At the least, when we consider our own ethics, we have to ask ourselves these questions: What is my own ethical position or stance? How is that similar to, or different from, others? Will my actions have the intended consequences? What unintended consequences might arise from my actions?

These are challenging questions to ask at a personal level. We must consider what we deem appropriate and inappropriate, acceptable and unacceptable, right and wrong for ourselves—but also in relation to others. At an organizational level, such issues can become complex if not daunting. Given the rise of organizational power and influence, the potential impact of decisions is, in some cases, profound and far reaching. Stan Deetz (1992) reminded us that, by many standards, the business organization has become the central institution in modern society, often eclipsing the state, family, church, and community in power. Organizations pervade modern life by providing personal identity, structuring time and experience, influencing education and knowledge production, and directing news and entertainment. From the moment of our birth to our death, organizations significantly influence our lives in ways that often go unnoticed.

1

That is, over time, we have developed naturalized, taken-for-granted ideas about how organizations should function and the role that they should play both in our personal lives and in our culture. One of the goals of this book, then, is to raise your awareness regarding many of our commonsense assumptions about organizations, particularly when it comes to ethics. After you have read this book, I hope that you will have developed the awareness to pursue ethical questions and establish your own views on organizational ethics. A second goal of the book is to strengthen your ethical reasoning and decision making. It is not enough to be aware of organizational ethics; it also requires strong critical thinking skills to understand ethical situations and possible courses of action. After you have read this book, you will have developed these skills as you learn about ethical theories, in general, and ethical practices, specifically. Hopefully, you will have greater confidence in your own decision making, and you will better understand the decisions of others. Finally, a third goal is to motivate you to respond to—and proactively confront—ethical dilemmas that may arise in your organizational life. Overall, then, it is my hope that, after reading this book, you will believe that "organizational ethics matters" and that you will use your knowledge, skill, and motivation to enhance the ethics of our organizations today—and in the future.

The stakes in organizational decisions can be particularly high: How safe is a particular product or service? Does it have negative effects on its users? How should employees be hired, trained, developed, compensated, and/or fired? How should wealth be developed and distributed? What effect does the accumulation of wealth have upon social, economic, political, and technological disparities with others? How do organizations impact our values, our families, and our communities? Whose definition of ethics is dominant in an increasingly global economy? These questions are certainly not exhaustive, and you may come up with many others that are relevant to you.

Regardless of the question, it is clear that the consequences of organizational actions can be great for all of us. Yet, at the same time, the ethical demands on organizations are neither extraordinary nor excessive, according to Al Gini (2005):

> A decent product at a fair price; honesty in advertisements; fair treatment of customers, suppliers, and competitors; a strong sense of responsibility to the communities [they] inhabit and serve; and the production of a reasonable profit for the financial risk-taking of its stockholders and owners. (p. x)

It is worth noting, however, that not all organizations seek to produce a profit for stockholders and owners. Others are more interested in the social welfare of citizens across the world (Bonbright, 1997; Bornstein, 2004). For example, Ashoka, founded by Bill Drayton, is a nongovernmental organization that operates in 46 countries and has assisted over 1,400 social entrepreneurs interested in improving human rights, education, environmental protection, rural development, health care, and poverty, among others.

It is also important to remember that our "organizational lives" are not separate or distinct from other realms of our lives. Increasingly, it is hard to distinguish between our public and private lives, work and family, labor and leisure (May, 1993). As a result, it is crucial that we keep in mind that organizations are a part of life. They are not silos that function in a vacuum without direct effects on all of us. For better or worse, they are part and parcel of us.

THE CURRENT STATE OF ORGANIZATIONAL ETHICS

In an era of widespread organizational scandals, it is appropriate that we study organizational ethics more closely. This edited volume is not the first to explore organizational ethics (Conrad, 2003; Donaldson & Gini, 1996; Malachowski, 2001; Michalos, 1995; Parker, 1998; Peterson & Ferrell, 2005; Seeger, 2002) nor will it be the last (Cheney, Lair, Ritz, & Kendall, 2010). But it is a volume that seeks to capture a unique historical moment as citizens have begun to seriously rethink and reevaluate the role of organizations in our lives.

Even a limited list of recent organizational misconduct should be enough to raise concerns:

- Pfizer, the producer of Viagra, Zoloft, and Lipitor, was fined a record $2.3 billion by federal prosecutors for illegal drug promotions that plied doctors with free golf, massages, and resort junkets. Similarly, Allergan, the maker of Botox, settled for $600 million on charges that it illegally promoted and sold the drug for unapproved uses.

- Bernie Madoff pleaded guilty to 11 federal felonies and admitted to turning his wealth management business into a massive Ponzi scheme that defrauded thousands of investors of $65 billion.

- The U.S. Securities and Exchange Commission (SEC) won court approval to levy a $550 million penalty against Goldman Sachs, the largest ever against a Wall Street firm, over claims the bank misled investors in collateralized debt obligations linked to subprime mortgages.

- Former WorldCom CEO Bernard Ebbers was convicted of fraud and conspiracy charges for his role for reporting false financial information, with losses estimated at over $100 billion. Until the Madoff scheme was discovered, it had been the largest accounting scandal in U.S. history.

- Adelphia founder John W. Rigas and his son Timothy Rigas were accused of looting the company and cheating investors out of billions of dollars. Both were convicted of conspiracy, bank fraud, and securities fraud.

- Martha Stewart was convicted of conspiracy, obstruction of justice, and making false statements about her sale of ImClone Systems stock.

- Former Tyco CEO Dennis Kozlowski and former CFO Mark H. Swartz were found guilty on 30 counts of stealing more than $150 million from the company.

- Former Qwest CEO Joseph Nacchio and six other executives were charged with orchestrating a massive financial fraud that concealed the source of billions of dollars in reported revenue. He was convicted on 19 counts of insider trading.

- Fannie Mae and Freddie Mac, both government-assisted entities (GAEs), face scrutiny regarding questionable accounting practices that could place millions of mortgages of U.S. homeowners at risk.

- Several pharmaceutical companies, including Merck and GlaxoSmithKline, have had to withdraw drugs that have been deemed unsafe for public use. Most were found to have hidden drug-related risks from physicians and the public. In addition, the Food and Drug Administration (FDA) is facing questions that its regulatory control over drug safety has been jeopardized by close relationships with the industry.

Even this limited list does not include scandals among nonprofit organizations (NPOs), the military, churches, athletic teams, journalists, and the U.S. government. For example, the national director of programs for the Boy Scouts of America was charged with receiving and distributing child pornography. Guards at Abu Ghraib prison in Iraq have been accused of engaging in physical and mental abuse of prisoners. Congress is currently conducting hearings on steroid use in baseball, although its use appears common in many other sports, as well. Individuals in the Catholic Church were not only aware of child sexual abuse among some of its priests but they also covered it up. Several well-known journalists plagiarized articles, and the Bush administration "purchased" favorable reporting from journalists in order to "sell" its programs to the public.

More recently, we have witnessed the meltdown of our global economy as a result of unethical behavior within the financial industry. In the pursuit of greater profit, many of the leaders of U.S. banks, financial service firms, and mortgage lenders, among others, risked not only their own companies (note the failure of Bear Stearns, etc.) but also the homes and livelihood of citizens in the United States and abroad. First identified as a series of poor financial decisions, it has become increasingly obvious that these leaders externalized their financial risks onto others for personal and corporate gain, while not recognizing the potential, systemic, negative impact on the global economy. Their unethical behavior has produced the worst economic downturn since the Great Depression, with no end in sight.

Given these historical events, reconsidering organizations and their place in our lives affords us the opportunity to even reflect on some of our common beliefs about organizations "as we know them": choice of consumers, the value of market mechanisms, the benefits of free trade, and the desire for ongoing growth and development (Cheney & Frenette, 1993).

Undoubtedly, there is growing, if not renewed, interest in organizational ethics. For a time, the recent scandals intensified the media scrutiny of organizations and their leaders. Each new scandal seemed to produce additional clamor for organizational change, with strategies that included improved legal compliance, stronger sentencing penalties for white-collar crime, more rigorous professional codes of conduct, and more stringent government oversight and regulation. The scandals also raised serious questions about our trust in corporate America, in particular (Lorsch, Berlowitz, & Zelleke, 2005), and have produced lawsuits, criminal trials, and legislation (e.g., the Sarbanes-Oxley Act). In several cases, the scandals have produced the decline, if not the destruction, of several well-known organizations—most notably Arthur Andersen.

However, even as I prepare this volume in mid-2011, I wonder whether media coverage of the scandals—and the organizational ethics issues related to them—has begun to wane. Has the public's interest in organizational ethics already faded? Will the highly visible scandals overshadow less overt misconduct, as well as some of the more subtle but substantive ethical questions of today about "market forces," consumerism, and globalization? Will the recent economic meltdown continue to be viewed as an example of system-wide, unethical behavior, or will it be attributed to "a few bad apples"?

Over the years, attention to such ethical scandals "appears to ebb and flow between the well-publicized, most egregious acts of misbehavior and the mundane, naturalized, and often overlooked practices of everyday organizational life" (May & Zorn, 2003, p. 595). Recently, however, several authors have noticed a renewed focus on organizational ethics, among them Lynn Sharp Paine (2003), a noted Harvard professor of business ethics. In her book, *Value Shift*, Paine explained that ethics has found its way back onto the agenda of organizational leaders. Executives at businesses, for example, have launched ethics programs, mission-driven strategies, values initiatives, and cultural change efforts. In addition, companies have created ethics officers, high-level ethics committees, ethics ombudspersons, codes of ethics, and ethics task forces. Finally, companies have attempted to strengthen their relationships with various stakeholders, developing programs on the environment, human rights, work–family balance, corporate volunteerism, community assistance, product safety, customer service, and philanthropy, among others.

This shift in focus has left many observers asking the following questions: What is happening? Why the recent emphasis on ethics? The obvious answer is that organizations have realized that a lack of legal compliance can produce disastrous results, similar to many of the scandals mentioned earlier in this introduction. But organizational scandals alone don't explain the change. According to Paine (2003), there are several additional reasons for the shift in focus toward ethics among organizational leaders:

- Reasons related to risk management
- Reasons related to organizational functioning
- Reasons related to market positioning
- Reasons related to civic positioning. (p. 7)

In effect, many leaders have learned that ethics improves organizational performance and, ultimately, the bottom line. Still others have decided that it is the right thing to do; they have concluded that organizations should be fair, honest, respectful, responsive, trustworthy, accountable, and responsible, regardless of whether it serves the organization's self-interest.

I hope that this edited volume of case studies—and others like it—will produce a visible and sustained recommitment to organizational ethics, as Paine has noted. Although ethical scandals are not unique to our time, the confluence of ethical misconduct in so many different realms and institutions provides a rare opportunity for organizational change. To create such change, though, requires that we delve deeper into the fundamental issues that enable and constrain the opportunities and challenges of creating organizations that are simultaneously productive and ethical, responsive and responsible (see, for example, Ihlen, Bartlett, & May, 2011). What can we learn from past eras of organizational misconduct? What, if any, relationship exists between organizational ethics and broader conceptions of ethics in our culture, as a whole? What are the prospects and limitations of changing organizational ethics? To what extent are ethical failures based on individual, group, organizational, or cultural phenomena? This volume is hopefully a first, limited step toward answering some of these questions.

HAVE WE LEARNED ANYTHING FROM THE PAST?

Occasionally, it can be helpful to consider some of these questions by learning from ethical and unethical behavior of the past. In many respects, the recent organizational scandals may seem somehow different from those of the past. They seem larger, more significant, and of greater consequence. Yet, in fundamental ways, they are similar in that they involve greed, corruption, arrogance, and power. In the 1950s, it was the wealth and power of corporations to create domestic oligopolies prior to international competition. In the 1960s, it was the rise of unwieldy and often mammoth conglomerates that expanded without regard to consumers' needs. Hostile takeovers were the ethical concern of the 1970s. By the late 1980s, figures such as Ivan Boesky and Michael Milken became icons in the insider trading scandals. In the 1990s, executive compensation, downsizing, and the transition to global labor concerned us. The most recent "corporate meltdown," according to Charles Conrad (2003), was the result of "massive financial and status-related incentives combined with declining external constraints combined to create a fraud-inducing system, which in turn provided organizational actors with ready rationalizations/legitimations of practices that 'pressed the envelope' or worse" (p. 16). Somehow, each decade seems to have its own ethical crises. Is history repeating itself? Have we learned anything from the past?

Charles Redding, considered by many to be a central figure in modern organizational communication, may help us answer these questions. Back in 1982, he noted that "the preponderance of everyday problems that plague all organizations are either problems that are patently ethical or moral in nature, or they are problems in which deeply embedded ethical issues can be identified" (p. 2). Prominent author Robert Jackall (1983, 1988) argued in his book *Moral Mazes* that businesses (bureaucracies, in particular) are vast systems of "organized irresponsibility." Similarly, two social psychologists, Sabini and Silver (1982) claimed that businesses have a "genius for organizing evil." These comments came at a time when prominent business authors were extolling the importance of ethics and numerous centers and institutes for business ethics were emerging around the United States. One observer even called ethics "the hottest topic in corporate America" (Sarikelle, 1989).

Redding also bemoaned that there seemed to be no sustained interest in organizational ethics. He likened the lack of attention to organizational ethics to "wandering in a lonely desert," asking the question of any interested observers who might listen: "When will we wake up?" At that time, over two decades ago, Redding explained that he noticed increased talk about the ethical dimensions of organizational life, as managers and executives were attending numerous conferences, seminars, and workshops that focused on ethical problems in organizations. Yet he wondered whether all of the ethical talk was backed up by ethical action.

Redding's question regarding an ethical "awakening" could be asked today, as well. No doubt, many persons have awakened to issues related to organizational ethics (see, for example, May, Cheney, & Roper, 2007). One can hardly pick up a newspaper or listen to the evening news without some new ethical scandal in the business world. Ethics centers and institutes have proliferated in the last two decades. The conferences and training programs that Redding noted in the early 1980s still continue today and, in many respects, have grown. Yet, organizational scandals—in both the for-profit and not-for-profit sectors—appear rampant. This time I hope we will learn from our mistakes and misdeeds.

ETHICAL DILEMMAS

One of the ways to learn from the past—and also to enhance our ethical action in the future—is to think about the nature of ethical dilemmas that organizations and their members have faced. Throughout my discussion of organizational ethics in this introduction—as well as the remainder of the book—it is important to remember that it is people who make decisions in and about organizations. Organizations don't make decisions, per se. People do, albeit within the accepted norms and standards of organizations. At one level, then, any book on organizational ethics needs to account for the actions of individuals. So, although I frequently refer to organizational ethics, it is merely a shorthand way of referring to the numerous individual and collective decisions that are made within and between organizations.

In an accessible and popular book, *How Good People Make Tough Choices: Resolving the Dilemmas of Ethical Living*, Rushworth Kidder (1995) explored the personal dimension of ethical decision making. Each of us faces a multitude of ethical decisions throughout our lifetime, even if they are not readily apparent to us. Those decisions shape our sense of self, as well as others' sense of us.

Kidder explained, though, that some of our attention to ethics is misdirected. He claimed, for example, that right/wrong ethical dilemmas gain much of the public attention. On the one hand, we denounce persons who have engaged in organizational misconduct. On the other hand, we praise the courage and integrity of those persons who have engaged in "right action." The former are often shunned while the latter are sometimes idolized. But, in the end, right/wrong dilemmas tend to be fairly clear-cut and straightforward. By contrast, Kidder argued that "right/right dilemmas" are much more challenging and merit more attention. Kidder (1995) explained his premise this way: "The really tough choices . . . don't center on right versus wrong. They center on right versus right. They are genuine dilemmas precisely because each side is firmly rooted in one of our basic core values" (p. 18).

Although any number of right/right dilemmas is possible, Kidder noted that several are most common:

- Justice versus mercy
- Truth versus loyalty
- Individual versus community
- Short-term goods versus long-term goods

According to Kidder, each of the preceding dilemmas—and others like them—pose the most difficult challenge for us since they represent pairs of values, both of which we tend to accept. For example, in organizational terms, should a boss show mercy on an employee who has made a costly blunder, or should the boss punish the employee? When an employee finds out that a significant downsizing is imminent and a friend will be fired, should the employee tell the friend the truth or remain loyal to the company? When an employee conducts a safety study that suggests a product is unsafe for public use, should the employee remain loyal to her/his company by staying silent or should the employee inform the public? Should a company executive make a financial decision that will benefit stockholders and employees in the short term but may have a negative impact in the long term? We struggle with such ethical dilemmas because we are torn between two values, both of which seem right, but we are forced to decide between them.

In most cases, we choose the action that is "the nearest right"—the one that best fits our own ethical perspective of the world. As you will see later in this introduction, we may be more or less oriented to duty, rights, utility, virtue, or relationships when it comes to ethics. However, Kidder (1995) also encouraged us to explore whether there is a "third way" that might enact both values, the "trilemma solution":

> Sometimes that middle ground will be the result of a compromise between the two rights, partaking of each side's expansiveness and surrendering a little of each side's rigidity. Sometimes, however, it will be an unforeseen and highly creative course of action that comes to light in the heat of the struggle for resolution. (p. 167)

A trilemma solution may be a "compromise between the two rights, partaking of each side's expansiveness and surrendering a little of each side's rigidity" (Kidder, 1995, p. 167). Ideally, though, the resolution is not so much a compromise or middle ground position so much as it is a creative means to move beyond the ethical dilemma by appreciating the tension between the two values.

COMMUNICATING ABOUT ETHICS

Since organizations are so "close" to us, it can be challenging to talk about the ethical dilemmas that arise from them. Before we continue further, then, we should explore how we talk about ethics and how ethics is structured within our culture (see, for example, Willmott, 1998).

For example, it is worth considering how ethical issues are communicated in contemporary life. Are ethical issues framed in a particular way? Are there particular persons or groups who have greater (or lesser) opportunities to speak regarding ethical issues? Are there ethical issues that are rarely, if ever, discussed publicly? That is, are some ethical issues marginalized? How do persons tend to respond to ethical violations of the law or cultural norms and expectations? How do persons who have violated them explain their behavior? Noticing such patterns of discourse should provide you with interesting insights regarding the place of ethics in our culture today.

For anyone interested in constructive conversations regarding organizational ethics, it is important to consider the distinctions between descriptive ethics, normative ethics, and analytical ethics (Goodpaster, 1995). The goal of descriptive ethics is to represent, in a neutral and empirical manner, the "facts" of an ethical situation, as well as the values of the persons and organizations involved. There is no attempt to make an ethical judgment regarding the situation since the emphasis is on attaining accuracy, as best as possible. In effect, the purpose of descriptive ethics is to "map the terrain" of the ethical situation. No personal judgment is presented.

Normative ethics, by contrast, according to Kitson and Campbell (2001), "seeks to develop and defend judgments of right and wrong, good and bad, virtue and vice" (p. 11). It involves exploring points of view and presenting one's position. It introduces this question: Given the situation, what is my ethical judgment about it? As an extension of the first two, analytical ethics is interested in whether an ethical judgment is appropriate, in comparison to other ethical judgments. It functions at a metaethical level by comparing and contrasting different ethical perspectives, decisions, and practices. Therefore, analytical ethics provides the justifications for a normative ethical judgment.

During discussions of ethics-based case studies of organizations, it is important to distinguish the type of statement being made. Am I describing the ethical situation in the case? Am I presenting a normative position or point of view in response to the case? Or am I analytically arguing for a position or point of view in contrast to others? In everyday conversation, it is all too common for us to describe situations in a normative or analytical manner, reflecting our own personal values or biases. However, it can often be a helpful exercise to bracket our comments in these three steps, beginning with description and moving to defense of a position, based on an evaluation of multiple points of view. However, we should keep in mind that the assumption that we can accurately describe an ethical situation rests on the belief that the factual content can be separated from our values (Willmott, 1998). While descriptive ethics claims to describe "what is," some critics question whether such an approach actually privileges one way of viewing an ethical situation over another—in effect, presenting what is ultimately a value-laden description of a situation as if it is natural or taken-for-granted. As you discuss these cases with others, you may find, for example, that what you consider to be clear-cut and factual may be questioned by others.

Using the concepts of descriptive, normative, and analytical ethics as a conversational guide, class discussions of organizational ethics may be conducted around some of the following questions:

- How should organizational ethics be defined? That is, what constitutes responsible and irresponsible action?

- Why should students, owners, employees, consumers, and citizens be interested in organizational ethics?

- What are the prominent meanings and discourses surrounding ethics, in general, and organizational ethics, specifically?

- How has ethics evolved historically?

- What is the relationship between organizational ethics and specific social, political, economic, ideological, and technological conditions?

- How, if at all, has ethics changed the nature of management and organizational communication?

- What is/should be the role of ethics in our emerging, global economy?

- How, if at all, has ethics changed organizing processes?

- From your perspective, how do ethics enable and/or constrain today's organizations?

- How might a renewed emphasis on ethics change management and organizational communication in the future?

- How, if at all, has recent attention to ethics affected management practices?

- What are the agendas for research, teaching, and practice that are relevant to persons interested in organizational ethics?

ETHICAL PERSPECTIVES AND PRACTICES

Over the past two decades, we have seen the historical, social contract between employers and employees change, raising a series of ethical questions regarding the role of organizations—and businesses, in particular—in our culture. In the era of corporate mergers, downsizing, restructuring, offshoring, and temporary work, it is now common to observe that the old social contract, which guaranteed or implied lifetime employment in exchange for employee competence and good behavior, has expired. Taking its place is a new social contract in which employees are sent a mixed message, in which they are expected to work more for less pay and limited employment stability and yet still remain loyal to the company.

This new social contract is the result of multiple cultural forces, including global competition, domestic deregulation, and technological change, as well as executive mismanagement and corruption. Regardless of the reasons for the change, however, the impact will be especially profound on management and labor relations in the years ahead. For example, the dramatic changes in the workplace are being blamed for escalating workplace violence, exploding workplace litigation, and growing numbers of employees seeking medical and psychological help for work-related stress.

The range and scope of these organizational changes pose serious questions for persons interested in ethics. Can organizations, in fact, be ethical? If not, what social, political, economic, and technological conditions limit this possibility? If so, what would constitute an ethical organization? Do our organizations have a unique ethical responsibility to employees? Customers? Shareholders? Citizens? The environment? What ethical perspectives and best practices within organizations might assist us in developing and sustaining ethical organizations? In order to produce a dialogue about these responsibilities and their implications for "managing" a new ethical agenda in organizations, this book includes case studies that are drawn from diverse types of organizations. It is my hope that these diverse readings will further your understanding of the multiple ways that organizations address (or do not address) ethics.

As a means to further stimulate discussion regarding the cases in the book, you will need additional background to raise ethical questions about the cases. The remainder of this introduction explores two primary ethical tensions that are common in many organizations. It also briefly summarizes some of the primary ethical perspectives. Finally, it identifies several "best practices" of ethical organizations, providing both positive and negative examples of each organizational practice.

The purpose is not necessarily to provide a comprehensive overview of ethical theory and practice. Several other books (Dienhart, 2000; Donaldson & Werhane, 1999; Gini, 2005; Johannesen, 1996; Shaw & Barry, 2001; Snoeyenbos, Ameder, & Humber, 2001) may serve that purpose. Rather, it is to provide you with an additional foundation for analyzing the cases, reflecting on them, and discussing them with your instructor and your fellow students. It is hoped that the result will be your ethical competencies will be improved and that you will be better able to confront and respond to ethical dilemmas that you face in your own organizational life.

ETHICAL TENSIONS

Different ethical perspectives lead to quite different conclusions regarding what constitutes ethical behavior (Cheney, May, & Munshi, 2011). These differences are based on fundamental assumptions about the character of reality, the nature of individuals, and the obligation of individuals to one another (May & Mumby, 2005). The differences in these ethical perspectives may be described as tensions—or oppositions—and can be plotted on axes in order to locate one's own perspective. These tensions are likely to either enable or constrain ethical action, and the most commonly noted tensions, according to Anderson and Englehardt (2001) include foundational/situational, individual/community, and essence/existence. However, we could also consider any number of additional tensions that are found in most organizations such as centralization/decentralization, collaboration/competition, control/autonomy, strategies/tactics, specialization/differentiation, and flexibility/structure, among others.

For our purposes, the two most relevant tensions are (1) foundational/situational and (2) individual/community. Briefly exploring these tensions will allow us to not only apply them to the case studies but it will also enable us to better understand our own ethical assumptions.

Foundational/Situational Tension

The first tension considers whether ethics is foundational or situational. As you read the case studies, you should consider whether you believe that ethical behavior is based on a set of actions that are constant or whether it is based on actions that are context-specific. Foundational—or universal ethics—persists while situational ethics shifts over time.

Foundational ethics suggests that reality is given, self-evident, objective, and neutral while situational ethics views reality as socially constructed, subjective, and interpreted.

If, for example, you were to develop ethics training for an organization from a foundational approach, you might argue for a core set of values that the organization and its members must adhere to in order to be ethical. Most likely, these values would be long standing and widely accepted (e.g., telling the truth, respecting others). In my experience, ethics training for organizations often draws on a foundational approach, since it frequently focuses on a core set of principles that are applied to every organization, regardless of size, structure, or industry.

For example, professional codes of ethics are expected to create a degree of stability and consistency regarding ethical behavior across organizations in a profession, such as medicine, accounting, psychology, or journalism.

As you think about this approach, ask yourself the following questions: Are there any foundational values or principles that you believe all organizations should follow? If you were working with an organization to improve its ethics, would you be willing to accept your client's values even if they contradicted your own? The answers to these questions may help you determine if you take a foundational approach to ethics in your organizational life.

If, by contrast, you developed ethics training from a situational approach, you might prefer to tailor ethics services to the specific needs of a particular organization. You might argue, for example, that it is not enough to only "follow the rules" of legal compliance or a formal code of ethics. Instead, you might focus on the distinct organizational culture of your client and seek to adapt your training to meet the needs of that organization. As a result, you might try to learn as much as possible about the organization itself, drawing on member knowledge and experience, before you offer recommendations for improving the organization's ethics. Such an approach would attempt to facilitate organization member's development of their own ethical behaviors, based on a collaborative process.

Individual/Community Tension

The second tension considers whether the individual (libertarian approach) or the community (communitarian approach) should be primary. For our general purposes, we may define community in terms of the organizations in the cases. To better understand this tension, we may ask three questions. First, is the advancement of the individual good for the organization or is the advancement of the organization good for the individual? Second, is the individual the source of ethics, or is the collective wisdom of the organization the basis of ethical judgment? Third, is ethics better served by justice or by compassion (Anderson & Englehardt, 2001, p. 47)?

To extend the ethics training example a bit further, an ethics training program might integrate personal and organizational ethics. However, a more individual-oriented ethics initiative might focus more exclusively on the ethical reasoning and action of organizational members. As a trainer, you might ask yourself this question: How can I best develop ethics-based skills that are relevant and useful to every member of the organization? You might assume that individual change among the members is likely to produce organizational change.

Or, by contrast, you might develop training tools that extract the collective wisdom of the organization, since it is considered the basis of ethical judgment. For example, you might be more focused on the advancement of the organization by improving its ethical culture (May, 2009). In effect, you would be assuming that the organization and its leaders should be the ethical guides for members of the organization, setting the ethical tone for personal behavior.

As you consider the differences between the individual and community approaches when you read the cases, also think about how the tension raises some challenging questions for all organizations. What happens when there are contradictions between the interests of the individual member and the organization? How can you best negotiate the needs of the individual and the organization? Are their needs and interests inherently divergent or are there ways to find convergence among them?

WHAT IS THE ETHICAL RESPONSIBILITY OF AN ORGANIZATION?

Thinking about the preceding ethical tensions leads us to a broader, more practical question. What *is* the ethical responsibility of an organization? How should it behave toward its various stakeholders, such as members, customers, suppliers, distributors, governing/regulatory agencies, and its community? Can/should an organization be separated from its members when ethical matters are considered (see, for example, May, 2011)?

To begin thinking about these questions in more depth, it may be helpful to refer to one of the best known and widely cited commentators on organizational ethics, Milton Friedman. Although there is widespread debate regarding whether Friedman's classic 1970 essay, "The Social Responsibility of Business Is to Increase Its Profits," is an appropriate or an inappropriate guide for ethical action, his views are still widely accepted and used with the curriculum of many business schools.

Friedman was interested in exploring duties, and in his essay, he considered the responsibilities of business. Given the recent corporate scandals and a renewed interest in organizational ethics, Friedman's essay is very timely. His essay was in response to a growing interest at that time in the new term *corporate social responsibility* (CSR). Taking a largely economic perspective on business responsibility, Friedman critiqued arguments of the time that businesses have responsibilities beyond making money. Because of their increasingly significant role in political, social, and economic realms, critics had raised questions about the broader role of businesses in society. According to Friedman (1970), the doctrine of CSR required accepting that "political mechanisms, not market mechanisms, are the appropriate way to determine the allocation of scarce resources" (p. 122). For Friedman, such an approach was more firmly grounded in socialism than capitalism; therefore, he was highly critical of expanding the responsibilities of business beyond making money.

Friedman, then, was primarily concerned with the economic outcomes of business decision making. He believed that the greatest good would occur for all if businesses made decisions based on increasing shareholder value. His essay has been widely used to support the common business adage that one's first duty is to increase shareholder value. For example, in the case of Enron, Friedman might argue that its executives' mistakes were not that they misled employees but that they misled the shareholders—who should have been their primary responsibility. Friedman (1970) did suggest, though, that an executive should try "to make as much money as possible, while conforming to the basic rules of society, both those embodied in the law and those embodied in ethical custom" (p. 32). Aside from this minor caveat, though, he explained that acting in a socially responsible manner—at the expense of shareholders—is akin to spending someone else's money for the social interest. The person is, in effect, imposing a tax of his/her choice in the process.

He argued that it is best to trust market mechanisms when making decisions. A focus on social responsibility, according to Friedman, is a "fundamentally subversive doctrine" in a free society.

While accepted by many in the business world, Friedman's arguments have also created widespread criticism regarding economic justice (Schaefer, Conrad, Cheney, May, & Ganesh, 2011). According to some, his essay raises many unanswered but important questions. What criteria should executives use in deciding which actions are acceptable and which actions are unacceptable? Is a cost-benefit analysis of responsible behavior the only way to decide how to act in a business? What about the role of companies in creating (e.g., lobbying) and resisting (e.g., violations, paying fines) laws? That is, to what extent does Friedman address the relationship between economics and politics in today's society? How are we best able to determine the rules of society, based in "ethical custom"? Have ethical customs changed enough since 1970 to support CSR? How would Friedman respond to corporate volunteerism? Philanthropy? Do executives only have a duty to serve their shareholders? If shareholder value is improved by reducing labor costs by downsizing, outsourcing, or offshoring, is that a responsible decision?

ETHICAL PERSPECTIVES

Beyond Friedman's well-known and oft-repeated arguments, a more extensive understanding of the following ethical perspectives will allow us to understand that Friedman's arguments themselves are based on ethical perspectives: in this case, duty-based and utilitarian ethics. That is, he is speaking from a particular perspective. Regardless of whether we agree or disagree with his views, we should understand the basis for his arguments. However, we are not only interested in Friedman's arguments. We are also interested in your views, as well. So a brief exploration of ethical perspectives will also allow you to better identify your own assumptions regarding ethics as you read the cases and as you move forward in your own careers.

Duty

In general, a duty perspective is concerned with the individual's obligations to others (often, the collective). Duties are often viewed as natural, universal, rational, and self-evident. In some examples of duty ethics—such as moral law—one performs an action because of an obligation to follow a set of standards or rules. From this perspective, persons have a duty to obey moral guidelines; therefore, it is often considered to be a form of foundational ethics.

In other examples of duty ethics—such as deontology—actions are judged on the intrinsic character of the act rather than on its effects. Kant, for example, used the "categorical imperative" to specify the universal character of duty: "One ought only to act such that the principle of one's act could become a universal law of human action in a world in which one would hope to live." In effect, if an action is right for one person, then it should be right for everyone. In addition, he stated that "One ought to treat others as having intrinsic value in themselves and not merely as means to achieve one's ends." So Kant argued that "right actions" should be those that are done without qualification. From this perspective, even some seeming "goods" such as intelligence and happiness can be suspect because they can have negative effects for others, in some cases. He believed that the categorical imperative was within the grasp of all rational humans to discover and, ultimately, come to agreement—causing one's own goodwill and rationality to benefit the collective as a consensus develops on the right actions.

As an Enlightenment philosopher, Kant also believed that a good action is one done by free will and motivated by the right reasons. Thus, reason should guide the will of a person and intentions are considered a part of ethical decision making. When reason guides the will, the actions are done from duty, despite one's personal inclinations. In effect, "good will" is everything for Kant. In that respect, Kant is suggesting that an ethical action is one that lies in the worth of the act itself and not in the consequences or outcomes of the act—even if they are positive. Ethical decisions, from a Kantian perspective, then, require each person to have respect for other rational humans. As a result, he focuses on the quality—or intrinsic merit—of others in order to develop his universal principles of ethics. Following religious rules and/or government laws, for example, is not ethical if the inherent dignity and free will of others are harmed in the process.

From this perspective, improving the ethics of an organization might require developing ethical, universal principles—rationally derived—that are enacted out a sense of duty or responsibility. Members of an organization might ask themselves these questions: What universal, ethical principles would I be willing to follow that would also become guides for behavior throughout the entire organization? What are the "right actions" in this organization that should be done without qualification? What behaviors are inherently "good," without considering their outcome or effect on the organization and its members? Organizations that tend to focus on these questions seem most likely to address acceptable and unacceptable behavior by a universal code of ethics since such documents often explicitly identify duties to various stakeholders. At a more personal level, this perspective would encourage organizational members to also choose the right action, even when their inclination (often out of self-interest) is to do otherwise.

Rights

A rights perspective focuses on the obligation between self and other, based on the duty that the collective owes the individual. The duty of the collective is owed to the individual in the form of rights (e.g., equality). Similar to the duty perspective, a rights approach also universalizes ethics; as a result, rights are often considered unalienable, such as in the U.S. Constitution. From this perspective, then, the rights of all humans are granted, naturally, and cannot be altered because they are rationally self-evident. The goal is to establish a social compact, or contract (hence, often called the contractarian alternative to deontology), of rights that are maintained between individuals and the community.

This covenant creates agreed-upon behaviors that are derived from natural law, according to Hobbes. For Hobbes, all humans are bound to such agreements because they can be understood through human reason which, itself, is a fundamental part of human nature. Natural law, according to Hobbes, reminds us that our behaviors—and our laws—should be consistent with our nature as reasoning persons. Similarly, Locke claimed that all persons are born with, and possess, basic natural rights. They are possessed by everyone equally and, therefore, cannot be taken away. Rights, then, become the basis by which we judge not only the action of others but also those of institutions. The social contract between people, he argued, can only be preserved if human rights or developed, maintained, and preserved.

For Rawls, in contrast to Locke, the standard for ethical action is based on a "reasonable position." Rights, for him, can be determined by placing persons behind a "veil of ignorance" or in "the original position," where persons have a limited sense of past, present, and future. In this position or behind this veil, one cannot anticipate how s/he be might be affected by her/his own actions. For example, no person can expect to either benefit or be harmed any more than others. From this perspective, then, an ethical person can uphold the basic rights necessary to maintain a minimum level of dignity and justice that, for example, produces fairness for all. Organizations, from this perspective, are obligated to address injustices and resolve inequities. Regardless of the differences between them, though, both Locke and Rawls sought to create principles and practices of justice through rights. No society can be just if it is devoid of rights for its people, according to them.

From this perspective, improving the ethics of an organization might involve an emphasis on compliance and legally sanctioned rights such as U.S. Equal Employment Opportunity Commission (EEOC) guidelines, the Americans with Disabilities Act (ADA), the Family and Medical Leave Act, and the National Labor Relations Act, among others. These laws—as well as company policies—might be used to create equity or fairness in organizations as a means to preserve human rights. For example, ethics training could be devoted to issues such as gender equity, diversity, and/or the fairness of performance appraisal processes. Members of an organization might ask these questions: How can we best preserve the human rights and dignity of employees, owners, shareholders, suppliers, distributors, customers, and communities? How might the diverse rights afforded to each group be protected? What policies and procedures are just in this organization? Unjust? What is our current social contract between one another and how can it be improved? How might organizations behave so that no particular group benefits at the expense of others?

Utility

A utility perspective is based on the outcomes or consequences of an action and, therefore, is considered "consequentialist." Ethical actions should be judged according to whether they produce positive effects, often in relation to other alternatives. Jeremy Bentham, for example, noted that a principle of utility is necessary in order to evaluate whether an action creates the greatest pleasure or happiness in relation to other alternatives. He also believed that any actions should be considered in terms of not only their immediate consequences but also their long-term effects, as well. What produces benefits in the short term may not produce positive consequences over a longer period of time.

A utility perspective also suggests that the good of the collective is primary. According to John Stuart Mill, the purpose of ethical action is to achieve the "greatest overall happiness for the greatest number," and actions are evaluated by the extent to which they contribute to that end. However, not all pleasures are necessarily considered equal and he valued intellectual pleasure over physical pleasure. In addition, the good of an individual may be sacrificed for the good of many. By extension, then, followers of a utilitarian perspective are also interested in the long-term consequences of any action, as previously noted.

Other (pluralistic) utilitarians do not necessarily equate the good with happiness and focus on other goods, such as knowledge, maturity, and friendship. In addition, act utilitarians believe that every specific, individual action should be measured according to whether it maximizes good. Finally, rule utilitarians believe that one must weigh the consequences of adopting a general rule that would follow from that action.

From this perspective, improving the ethics of an organization might mean creating change that will have positive consequences for the organization and its stakeholders. An organization would need to have tools or mechanisms in place to evaluate its effects on others. However, an ethical approach to utility would require moving beyond traditional economic models of cost-benefit analysis to consider which decisions benefit the greatest number with the greatest good. As a result, organizations might have to consider the unintended and long-term consequences of their actions. Members of an organization drawing on utility-based ethics may ask these questions: Have we considered all alternative actions and selected the one that produces the greatest good or pleasure? How can we best serve the ends of the collective rather than the individual? What specific actions or general rules will either maximize or minimize "good"?

Virtue

In some respects, virtue ethics represents a middle ground between duty and rights. Persons have the duty to self-actualize and, therefore, should be granted the right to accomplish that self-actualization. This perspective suggests that all humans are born with inherent potential, and as a result, human development is the struggle for self-actualization. An action is judged based on whether it allows for expression of full potential, thus creating benefits for both the individual and the community. Ethical virtue focuses on realizing one's social, spiritual, and intellectual potential—or other habits that are considered important to society. The development of virtue, then, requires the cultivation of good habits. These habits occur within a social realm because humans are, according to Aristotle, "social animals," thereby suggesting that ethics involves being a contributing member of a community. Doing so satisfies one's natural constitution, particularly when we use our intellect and contemplate before we make decisions. Society, then, has an obligation to develop educational and learning opportunities for citizens to develop their full potential.

A virtue (e.g., prudence, temperance, justice, fortitude) is often seen as an internal feature of humans that produces ethical behavior. For the Greeks, virtue also included not only individual attributes but also societal attributes. Aristotle, for example, also argued that virtue should be connected to the good of a society and can be developed not by following principles but by living a harmonious, balanced life. In *The Nicomachean Ethics,* he described ethics as the process of both doing good works and living well and, therefore, also connected virtue to happiness.

Plato, a student of Socrates, is perhaps best known as an advocate for virtue-based ethics. He identified courage, temperance, wisdom, and justice as the most important virtues. However, Plato considered justice to be the central virtue, and as a result, a primary question in *The Republic of Plato* is as follows: What is the nature of justice? Ultimately, Plato's aim was to create social and political stability on a foundation of moral and spiritual absolutes by which every person might live. Plato, for example, suggested that the shepherd's responsibility is to consider those under his/her care, thereby articulating an early principle of ethics and authority. For Plato, authority is always used for the benefit of the subordinate. Authority, properly understood, serves as a trustee for the interests of those over whom authority is wielded. In this respect, Plato has been used to better account for the multiple stakeholders that any one leader—or organization—might serve. Implied in his comments is the belief that "reluctant leaders" tend to be more virtuous because decent people accept power "because they can find no one better than themselves, or even as good, to be entrusted with power."

From this perspective, an organization's ethics might be improved by strengthening personal and institutional virtues in order to maximize human potential—both within and outside the organization. The organization would need to address the unrealized potentials of others. Or, more specifically, members might focus on improving the organization's culture or strengthen a person's character—particularly his/her ability to learn. Appropriate questions might include the following: What personal and organizational values are most important to us? Can they be aligned? How can we infuse the organization's culture with ethics and facilitate the full potential of its members? What are the best means to help others self-actualize and develop to the best of their abilities? How can we emphasize responsibility, reflection, courage, collaboration, and commitment, among other virtues? What is the most virtuous way to use one's authority in an organization? Should the authority of a particular person or group be presumed in an organization? What strategies might be used to develop balanced, harmonious, and happy lives among the collective?

Relationship

As a relatively new perspective, relationship ethics focuses on the care that emerges in and through communication. Proponents of this perspective believe that dialogue is the basis of successful relationships and that, ultimately, productive relationships are the foundation for ethical action among individuals and within (and across) cultures. Via communication, organizational relationships among various stakeholders (e.g., employees, stockholders, executives and managers, customers, suppliers, community members) are built, developed, maintained, transformed, repaired, and, on occasion, dissolved. This perspective is interested in the processes that enable productive and satisfying relationships, such as a willingness to listen and engage others in interaction and a desire to establish trust through openness. Ongoing care and attention to relationships, then, is important to consider from this perspective. Attention is focused on the evolution and negotiation of relationships—and the adaptations that may be necessary to successfully sustain them. Further, relationship ethics seeks to create a dialogic community that uses "power with" others rather than "power over" others. As a result, our attitudes toward each other become an important foundation for ethical action.

This emphasis on the "other" is important in the work of Martin Buber. He suggested that interaction with others provides the opportunity for the development of personality, self, and reflection. In effect, our "self" arises in and through our dialogue with significant others such as family, friends, and coworkers. Each person in a communicative situation, then, should be cognizant of his/her effect in the development of others. Such attention requires a sense of responsibility for others through respect, honesty, spontaneity, and genuineness. It also requires that all of us engage in "perspective-taking" as we se fully understand and appreciate another person's views and experiences. Ethical prac then, emphasizes authentic communication that fosters a sense of equality, interest, and commitment between people. In addition, each participant in a conversation is expected to be fully present.

Mikhail Bakhtin also suggested that, through dialogue, persons produce centripetal (change) or centrifugal (stability) forces in a relationship. That is, the specific speech acts of each person may either sustain or alter the status quo in a relationship. These micropractices of communication may also have an iterative effect; they are repeated, expanded, and altered in new relationships with others. This partially explains why some organizations find it difficult to change their ethical cultures since sets of communicative practices become embedded and sedimented in everyday talk.

As a related ethical perspective that focuses on relationships, feminists such as Carol Gilligan propose an "ethic of care." Drawing on the female voice and critiquing traditional notions of moral development, she suggests that interdependence is central to ethical behavior. As a component of interdependence, people should nurture others and be compassionate toward them. In an ethic of care, then, mutuality and reciprocity become central principles. Ethical actions sustain the caring relationship between self and others, and as a result, bonds of trust, loyalty, affection, and engagement are essential to an emphasis on care.

Efforts to create positive ethical change in organizations, from this perspective, would focus not surprisingly on relationships of all types: superior/subordinate, employee/customer or client, owner/worker, coworker/coworker, and so on. However, relational dimensions of ethics and care would not only be limited to employees within an organization but they would also likely include relationships with regulators, government agencies, and communities, among others. From this ethical point of view, an organization might emphasize the importance of dialogue, participation, and collaboration in order to build and strengthen relationships. In addition, an organization might shift its focus from engaging in dialogue *about* stakeholders to engaging in dialogue *with* stakeholders. Members of such an organization might ask these questions: With whom do we have important relationships? How can we foster those relationships to the benefit of all? In what ways can we develop perspective-taking regarding others' points of view and experiences? How can we best care for others in and through dialogic communication? See Table 1.1.

ETHICAL PRACTICES

I suspect that your reaction to many of the questions at the end of each theoretical perspective is that they seem overly idealistic and unrealistic. While I may agree with you to a certain extent, the seeming irrelevance of some of the questions merely confirms how far many of our organizations have drifted from ethics. As you read through the case studies, seriously consider how the actions of the organization—and its members—might be changed if one or more of the ethical perspectives were applied in a rigorous manner.

TABLE 1.1   Ethical Tensions and Ethical Perspectives

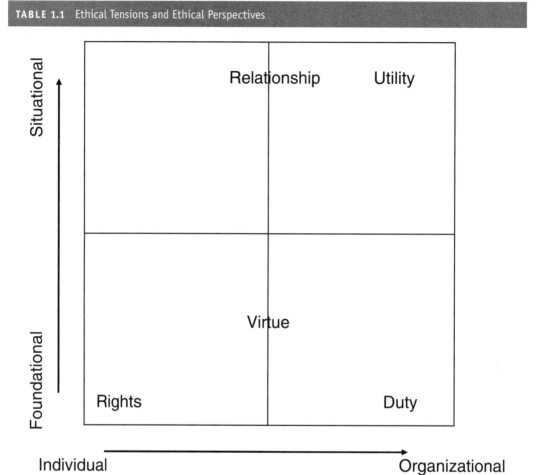

Note: Each ethical perspective may be plotted on two axes, based on the foundational/situational and individual/
   community tensions.

I hope that the preceding brief summary of the various ethical perspectives helps you to better understand and evaluate the ethical dilemmas common to organizations and their members. But it is also important to consider how we act in response to those dilemmas. In many respects, each of the cases in this book is designed to test the strengths and limitations of the ethical perspectives. As you read the cases, you should also think about how decisions were made—or might have been made—based on the perspectives. You may find, for example, that a particular ethical perspective is presented in a case. You may discover that several seemingly contradictory ethical perspectives can coexist in a single case. Or you may realize that an ethical perspective raises a set of questions that cut across cases.

However, you should not feel limited to merely applying the perspectives to the various cases in the book. You should also feel free to evaluate your comfort (or discomfort) with the ethical perspectives themselves, as a result of reading the cases. That is, how can we rethink the appropriateness of each ethical perspective, based on the current organizational issues discussed in the cases? Are there some perspectives that are more or less suited to today's organizational life? Turning to the future, we might also ask this question: Which ethical perspective provides the best opportunity for ethical behavior for the future? The cases, then, can also serve as a means to "test" the appropriateness of the ethical perspectives, while simultaneously taking into account the past, present, and future of organizations and their members.

This book—and the cases in it—should be read, then, not as an argument for either a foundational or a situational approach—or a community or individual approach—to organizational ethics. Rather, I hope that reading about both general principles and specific behaviors will allow you to think about both the foundational (i.e., ethical perspectives) and the situational (i.e., specific cases) dimensions of ethics, as well as the community and the individual. Keeping both of the tensions in mind, simultaneously, means that the cases may be used to evaluate and adapt the perspectives, and in turn, the perspectives may be applied in specific situations or cases. This integration of theory and practice—often referred to as "praxis"—provides a more thorough (and challenging) method for both evaluating others' actions and considering our own actions (see Cheney, 2004).

Ultimately, then, although each of you will have differing views of the ethical perspectives and the cases, you share at least one common ethical challenge: All organizations and their members must balance a variety of competing demands and conflicting values in determining how to negotiate a range of common ethical dilemmas, such as justice versus mercy, individual versus community, cost versus quality, competition versus collaboration, flexibility versus structure, and long term versus short term, among others. Balancing these demands and managing among these values requires not only ethical vigilance but also ethical insight, combining ongoing analysis and reflection.

Although I have suggested that ethics, as presented in this book, should be viewed neither as singular nor relativist, I would be remiss if I did not offer at least some ideas regarding practices that seem common to most ethical organizations. Without attempting to necessarily create a universal list, we should then ask this: What practices do ethical organizations share in common?

In my experience, an ethical organization does the following:

- *Alignment* occurs in personal, professional, and organizational aspirations and behaviors
- Fosters *dialogic communication*
- Encourages *participation* in decision making
- Establishes *transparency* in structures, policies, and procedures
- Emphasizes *accountability* for anticipating and responding to ethical crises
- Promotes *courage* to identify and resolve ethical dilemmas

Alignment

One of the common practices among ethical organizations is that they tend to align formal policies and procedures (e.g., ethics code, employee handbook, training and development, performance appraisal) with the organization's informal culture (e.g., norms, rituals, narratives). While the former prescribes an organization's ethics, the latter describes the day-to-day experience of the organization's ethics. In order to develop, maintain, and refine ethical practice, an organization—and its members—will need to, in effect, "walk the talk." In order to sustain a culture of ethics, an organization needs more than an ethics code. It needs the will to engage in the myriad behaviors that keep informal and formal dimensions aligned, ethically. For example, Enron had a widely accepted, formal code of ethics.

In retrospect, however, we now realize that such formal and very visible features of Enron's culture hid an informal set of unethical practices. Similarly, Tyco's code of ethics also masked a reality different from its public image.

In each of these ethics codes—and many others like them—the question is whether the codes' prescribed practices are deeply embedded in the everyday life of the organization's members—whether they "stick" ethically. That is, ethical organizations have both high aspirations and realistic, practical means to meet those aspirations.

ENRON

Our Values

Communication

We have an obligation to communicate. Here, we take the time to talk with one another . . . and to listen. We believe that information is meant to move and that information moves people.

Respect

We treat others as we would like to be treated ourselves. We do not tolerate abusive or disrespectful treatment.

Integrity

We work with customers and prospects openly, honestly, and sincerely. When we say we will do something, we will do it; when we say we cannot or will not do something then we won't do it.

Excellence

We are satisfied with nothing less than the very best in everything we do. We will continue to raise the bar for everyone. The great fun here will be for all of us to discover just how good we can really be.

Why We Exist and the Essence of Our Business

We will increase the value of our company and our global portfolio of diversified brands by exceeding customers' expectations and achieving market leadership and operating excellence in every segment of our company.

What We Seek to Achieve

Governance

Adhere to the highest standards of corporate governance by establishing processes and practices that promote and ensure integrity, compliance, and accountability.

Customers

Fully understand and exceed our customers' needs, wants, and preferences and provide greater value to our customers than our competition.

People

Attract and retain, at every level of the company, people who represent the highest standards of excellence and integrity.

Operating Excellence

Implement initiatives across our business segments to achieve best-in-class operating practices and leverage company-wide opportunities, utilizing six sigma measurements.

Financial Results/Liquidity

Consistently achieve outstanding performance in revenues, earnings, cash flow, and all other key financial metrics. Establish a capital structure that meets both long- and short-term needs.

Aligned work—work that is both excellent and responsive to the needs and wishes of the broader community in which it takes place—is most readily carried out when an organization's mission, its members, and its various constituencies share some common ground, work collaboratively, and engage in activities that advance mutual goals. Or, at the least, they acknowledge differences and seek to negotiate their competing interests in ways that will benefit all. In contrast, when there are wide disparities within and across these groups, aligned work is elusive. As a current example, some of the recent scandals among journalists (e.g., plagiarism, contrived stories, accepting money to "sell" government programs to the public) indicate that their personal and professional goals often conflict with their employers. Given the competitive nature of the information and news business today, journalism is faced with a credibility crisis as it seeks to balance objectivity with profits—particularly since the industry is increasingly dominated by media conglomerates.

To successfully align the formal and informal dimensions of organizational life, then, ethical organizations find ways to keep ethics "alive." Beyond ethical alignment, ethical organizations do so by fostering dialogic communication, confronting difficult realities by promoting participation to meet the highest ethical standards, establishing trust through transparent operations, emphasizing accountability for anticipating and responding to crises, and promoting the ethical courage to identify and resolve ethical dilemmas.

Dialogic Communication

Alignment is best facilitated by dialogic systems in which communication is open and decentralized. A dialogic organization values the perspective of all employees and facilitates their ability to voice their opinions and concerns. It also promotes the ability of all stakeholders to have a substantial influence on the organization's decisions. Employees of dialogic organizations understand the perspective of others in ways that promote understanding among different departments, make managing diversity possible, and acknowledge the need for "collective mindfulness." In order to establish dialogue, all parties understand that they are interdependent and, therefore, are responsible for effective, responsible communication. Leaders are better able to communicate their goals to employees, and in turn, employees are better able to provide useful feedback to leaders. A dialogic organizational culture also limits employees' desire to take concerns to the media, courts, or others outside the organization.

There are a number of organizations that foster dialogic communication, including Levi Strauss & Co., Hanna Andersson Clothing, and Patagonia, among others. However, one company has developed an ethics training program that is quite extensive and might be considered dialogic: BellSouth (now AT&T). For example, the company has integrated its ethics and compliance training materials into multiple delivery sources to demonstrate to employees that ethics is integral to every part of the business and to leverage existing infrastructure. Using media such as CD-ROMs, videos, and the company's Intranet, BellSouth has blended its ethics and compliance training into new employee orientations, general management courses, sales training, and other learning modules. The ethics and compliance team sees human resources (HR) as a key partner in its work and continually looks at ways to include ethics and compliance topics in other employee training programs. In addition, each operations unit has a compliance executive and a coordinator responsible for ethics and compliance oversight in that operating division. These managers draw information from "the bottom up," conduct risk assessments, and report back to the compliance office when gaps in training or communication are discovered. If the subject can best be handled on a small scale, the compliance coordinator will take care of it. However, if the corporate compliance office sees that many areas are addressing similar issues, time and money can be saved by creating cross departmental programs. Examples of this include antitrust and environment training. While the company uses technology to deliver the message, it views that the most productive work comes from face-to-face meetings, where employees are given the time to sit and discuss the nuances of various ethical dilemmas.

By contrast, there are many organizations that still suffer from monologic communication that limits candor, fosters secrecy, and manages communication and information in a top-down manner. One well-known example includes the Sears Auto Center scandal in the early 1990s. In June of 1992, the California Bureau of Auto Repairs (BAR) revoked the operating permits of 72 auto centers in that state. The decision was based on 18 months of undercover investigation into repair practices at 35 centers. The California BAR accused Sears of fraud and willful departures from accepted trade standards and launched a sting effort in 1990 after receiving 250 customer complaints. According to BAR, in 42 of 48 visits, Sears employees performed unnecessary services or repairs. On average, customers were bilked of $250 when Sears unnecessarily replaced new parts, and in some cases, cars emerged in worse condition. The problem was caused by the company's efforts to improve lagging profits after the recession of the 1980s that had hurt Sears. As a result, a new compensation policy was created to give commissions to auto mechanics that, in effect, provided an incentive for the mechanics to provide additional services. Employees were instructed to sell a certain number of services in an 8-hour day. If they failed to meet the goals, employees received a cutback in their hours or were transferred. When confronted with the allegations, however, Sears communicated an angry denial. It was not until the story became news that the company began to communicate more directly and honestly with its customers, placing full-page ads to apologize to them. Even then, though, the chairman of Sears only admitted that "mistakes may have occurred." Similar claims might be made about Nike and secrecy surrounding its sweatshops in Asia, as well as both Ford and Firestone in the case of the rollover deaths of drivers of Ford Explorers, which included each company blaming the other.

Participation

Ethical organizations are, by their very nature, participatory—both internally and externally. Participatory organizations empower their employees to engage in decision making through delegation. Such organizations develop skills among employees by enabling and motivating them. They produce organizational commitment by encouraging a culture of trust that rewards and recognizes high performance and responsibility. As a result, participatory organizations are well known for their ability to recruit, develop, and retain talented employees. Externally, participatory organizations listen to their stakeholders' concerns and are responsive to their feedback, using their knowledge and skills to improve organizational performance. In response to the opportunity to participate, stakeholders tend to be particularly loyal to and invested in such organizations.

One of the classic examples of a participatory organization is W. L. Gore & Associates. Best known as the maker of GORE-TEX, Gore is well known for its ability to motivate its employees through participation. Gore has developed a variety of rules that focus on providing the resources and opportunities for a work environment in which employees participate and, as a result, take greater responsibility for their work. For example, Gore has become a successful innovator in its field by requiring managers to act more like coaches than bosses by (1) listening to employees' concerns, (2) avoiding close supervision, (3) trusting employees to work within a framework of clear direction, and (4) being responsive to employees' feedback. In addition to Gore, companies such as 3M, the Grameen Bank, the RR Donnelley Corporation, Ashoka, CREDO Long Distance, and the Mondragon Corporation in Spain have been praised for their participatory workplace cultures.

As noted in one of the cases in this book, NASA has been less successful in its efforts to involve employees in important decisions—even those that affect the safety of its astronauts. For years, NASA was well known for a variety of its successes, particularly the Apollo missions. However, in recent years, they have been better known for the visible, public failures in the Challenger and Columbia disasters. Although NASA has blamed technological problems (e.g., the O-rings) for the disasters, oversight commissions have indicated that a lack of participation in decision making is at least one of the causes. Still fairly hierarchical in its structure, NASA employees were aware of the technical problems with both shuttles. However, there were few, if any, mechanisms in place for persons with the knowledge to fully participate in launch decisions. This lack of participation at all levels of NASA is particularly troubling since the Rogers Commission (in its review of the Challenger disaster) had noted that experienced engineers were discouraged from providing negative feedback about the O-rings. The Columbia disaster suggests that although feedback mechanisms were later put in place they were not used. Other well-documented cases include the Ford Pinto and its exploding gas tanks and A.H. Robins and its Dalkon Shield contraceptive IUD, which resulted in sepsis and sometimes death for the women who used it (Anselmi, 1994).

Transparency

Ethical organizations engage in decision making that is transparent to their employees and other stakeholders. Transparent organizations have clear and visible governance, mission, policies, procedures, and guidelines. The actions of transparent organizations allow others to fully comprehend processes such as hiring, performance appraisal, and promotion, among others. In addition, transparent organizations are candid, thereby producing greater trust, respect, and fairness. Employees of transparent organizations better understand the rationales for decision making and more fully support them and learn to make effective decisions themselves. As a result, employees of transparent organizations are more likely to accept the decisions of leaders, even when the decisions do not necessarily benefit the employees themselves. Such benefits are particularly common in industries or organizations with strained labor/management relations. For other stakeholders—such as shareholders—transparency provides greater confidence that the organization is being managed effectively, thereby increasing its perceived value.

Although companies such as Ben & Jerry's, Fair Trade Coffee, and Tom's of Maine are best known for their transparency, there are less visible examples, as well. One example is Baxter International, which is discussed later in one of the cases. The company's medical therapies are used by health care providers and their patients in more than 100 countries. Because Baxter's 40,000 employees are located throughout the world (with more than half outside the United States), the company has approached the challenge of communicating its business practice standards to a global workforce by decentralizing its ethics training programs. All new employees—and in many cases, prospective employees—are given a copy of the company's business practice standards, which have been translated into 14 different languages. Each new employee takes part in mandatory training conducted by managers who have been designated as ethics trainers. Additional training programs and training schedules are left up to each region and business unit, with headquarters providing resources. For example, the team responsible for the company's Asian operations has developed a yearly training program, based on real-life scenarios, that is designed to encourage group discussion and participation. In Latin America, the company's employees develop and present their own scenarios as part of the training. In addition to the large library of case studies, Baxter is developing web-based vehicles to supplement existing communication channels of ethical standards. These efforts suggest that, at least internally, Baxter is seeking to infuse ethics in a transparent manner.

A much more visible case, Enron, is evidence of the risks of a nontransparent organization when it comes to ethics. The level of secrecy (and related risk) upon which Enron was built, and upon which it failed, cost the jobs and retirement incomes of thousands, contributed to a slump in the stock market, and may have exacerbated California's 2000 to 2001 energy crisis. The collapse of the company, the largest bankruptcy in U.S. history, was followed by several criminal and civil lawsuits against the executives of the company. These lawsuits have suggested that the arrogance and greed of Enron's leaders was related to the lack of transparency in decisions made at the highest level of the company. In short, since rank-and-file employees did not necessarily realize their jobs and the company were at risk, they could not hold leaders accountable for their decisions. It appears that they had limited information about the specific decisions that were being made, and when criticisms were raised within the company, employees were reprimanded for making their concerns public. Similar, related examples include R.J. Reynolds and the tobacco industry, the Catholic Church, and WorldCom.

Accountability

Ethical organizations are accountable to their multiple stakeholders in a responsible and responsive manner. This accountability is evident in the high quality of products/services offered by such organizations. Accountable organizations view legal and industry compliance as important but have minimum expectations. Rather, they accept direct responsibility for any actions that negatively affect their stakeholders, and they seek to maximize their positive contributions to those stakeholders. Ethical organizations are also accountable to broader sets of stakeholders, including both local and global communities. Employees of accountable organizations take "automatic responsibility" for ethical challenges and strive to promote aspirational, ethical opportunities. Accountable organizations have a bias toward action that prompts member involvement and learning. As a result, employees develop better problem-solving skills and are less likely to blame others for mistakes. Employees in such organizations are less likely to view business units as "silos" that operate independently of one another. They learn how their decisions affect others in the organization.

The Body Shop, created by Dame Anita Roddick, is known for its accountability to its employees, its suppliers and, ultimately, the environment. The Body Shop has grown worldwide and is an example of a company that "does good business by doing good." Believing that both employees and customers are hyped-out, The Body Shop seeks to educate both employees and customers, producing greater accountability for decision making. In addition, The Body Shop is well known for its stewardship of the environment and its support of local, indigenous groups through programs such as "Community Trade." Through a series of interrelated programs, Roddick sought to be responsible to various stakeholders throughout the supply chain. As a result, employees are able to hold one another accountable for their actions and to hold the company accountable for its decisions, as well. As she explained, "I think you can trade ethically. . . . It's showing that you forsake your values at the cost of forsaking your work force."

Arguably the worst corporate disaster provides a stark contrast to The Body Shop. In 1984, the Union Carbide pesticide plant in Bhopal, India, released a dangerous chemical, methyl isocyanate (MIC) gas, creating the worst industrial accident in history. As a result of the accident, at least 10,000 people were killed, over 300,000 became ill, and nearly 500,000 were displaced. In time, it became clear that the plant was neither safe nor efficient and had been located in India to take advantage of cheap labor and limited regulations. In addition, most employees and citizens had not been told that they would be working and living amidst toxic chemicals. Once among the top 50 companies in the United States, Union Carbide's reputation was further tarnished when it fought lawsuits against it to compensate the victims of the disaster. Although the lawsuits have been settled, the Indian government and citizens still seek the full compensation required under the law. Another example during the 1980s was the Manville Corporation and its use of asbestos in various products, consistently denying accountability for its negative health effects on persons exposed to it. A more recent example of a lack of executive accountability, in particular, can be found in Adelphia.

Courage

Ethical organizations have employees who have the courage to identify, assess, and resolve ethical dilemmas that may negatively affect the organization or its stakeholders. Courageous organizations have the courage to admit mistakes, reject conformity, respond to injustice, and defy standard industry practices or laws that may be unethical. In addition, courageous organizations seek not only to respond to ethical challenges but also to anticipate them; they exhibit the positive courage to be ethical. Such an organization facilitates effective problem identification and problem solving in ways that also foster innovation and creativity. They also produce cultures that are safe and supportive for employees, thereby strengthening organizational identification. The result is that employees are more likely to identify problems when they arise and communicate those concerns to their superiors. In addition, they are also more likely to offer new ways to resolve the problems.

Johnson & Johnson is perhaps best known for its ethical courage. In response to tainted Tylenol capsules, Johnson & Johnson strengthened its standing as one of the leading health care companies by pulling the capsules off the shelves and addressing consumers' concerns about the capsules, truthfully and quickly, via the media. Although the company suffered short-term financial losses, it also affirmed its commitment to patient health and consumer safety, which have remained features of its organizational culture. As a result, it has been lauded as one of the country's most ethical and successful companies. Similarly, the owner of Malden Mills suffered financial loss in order to retain jobs for his employees. In addition, various whistle-blowers at Enron, in the tobacco industry, in the FBI and CIA, and in numerous attorneys general offices across the country have showed ethical courage to protect the public.

As a contrast to Johnson & Johnson, accounting firm Arthur Andersen made one of the quickest and most devastating falls from grace in corporate history. Despite a long-standing reputation as one of the most objective and responsible accounting firms, Arthur Andersen employees signed off on earnings statements for Enron (and other clients such as Waste Management) that were, according to industry observers, "aggressive and unique at best," "misleading or irresponsible" at worst. The failure of Arthur Andersen came after a series of reports in the 1990s by the Government Accounting Office that noted the growing conflict of interest between auditor/client relationships in the accounting industry. In response to numerous concerns expressed over auditor independence, Arthur Andersen argued before the SEC that "a broad scope of practice" was necessary and that "the future of the accounting profession is bright and will remain bright—as long as the commission does not force us into an outdated role trapped in the old economy" (quoted in Bazerman & Watkins, 2004, p. 49). Court documents filed in a 2002 trial for "deceptive practices" indicated that Arthur Andersen had been warned about its practices and that many employees were aware of the practices and the warnings. The response of many mid-level managers was to shred company documents. The result has been the unexpected and incredibly fast decline of one of the most well-known and successful companies in the United States. An additional example, as of this writing in 2011, include new pressures placed on the pharmaceutical industry and the FDA to come forward with more details regarding drug risks for patients.

THE FUTURE OF ORGANIZATIONAL ETHICS

There is no question that, over the past 20 years, there have been a growing number of organizations who have sought to foster the ethical practices that were previously noted. Here are some examples:

- The Ford Motor Company has developed initiatives in South Africa to fight HIV/AIDS.
- UPS has established welfare to work programs, in partnership with various government, social service, community, and NPOs.
- BankBoston has established a community banking group that focuses on economic development efforts that target an entire community of moderate income and inner-city markets, while avoiding industry norms for predatory lending.
- Levi Strauss & Co. has sustained a long-standing antiracism initiative.

Certainly, each of these organizations may not meet stringent standards of ethical practice in all areas, but at the least, they have sought to make a positive impact on local and global communities.

In addition, in a speech to the United Nations titled "Globalization's Next Frontier: Principled Codes of Conduct that Bolster the Rule of Law" Deloitte CEO William G. Parrett challenged multinational organizations to establish codes of behavior that go beyond minimum legal compliance through principled ethical behavior that bolsters the rule of law and would, therefore, create expanded economic opportunities around the world. Speaking to global business executives, representatives from nongovernmental organizations (NGOs), and academic scholars, he claimed that globalization and world security itself could be jeopardized unless multinational organizations develop ethical practices that adhere to values and principles rather than merely the law. Although his comments may be self-serving, Parrett nevertheless identified the potential stakes for organizations that do not think about and practice business ethics. So, even within the context of national security concerns, ethics is located as a pivotal international issue.

At the same time, it seems that a growing number of organizations also fall short when it comes to ethical practices. In this introduction, I noted some of the recent examples of organizational scandals such as WorldCom, Adelphia, and Tyco, among others. In some respects, then, there appears to be a bifurcation among organizations that pride themselves on their ethics and social responsibility and organizations that seek to mislead employees, stockholders, and the public for short-term profit (May, in press).

I am hopeful that this introductory chapter has prepared you for the realization that our ethical challenges are significant but that our ethical opportunities are perhaps even greater. Given the widespread influence of today's organizations, there is tremendous potential for rethinking, reframing, and reproducing organizations that can be not only productive but also ethical. It is my hope that this book—and the cases included in it—will cause you to take a long, hard look at organizational practices and the positive or negative effects they have on various groups.

George Cheney (2004) aptly challenged us to consider the future of organizational ethics and our own responsibility within it:

> Today we should consider an ethics of being and not just an ethics of regulation; an ethics that embraces how we are and who we are with others; an ethics that engages pressing and compelling issues of today; an ethics that challenges people yet begins with the tensions they experience in everyday life; an ethics that joins personal happiness with public integrity; and an ethics that recognizes the role of public discourse in extending or pulling back our ethical horizons. (pp. 35–36)

It is my strong conviction that the ethical scandals of the past decade and the recent economic meltdown provide both the motivation and the means to expand our ethical horizons. I think all of the contributors to this book would agree that as future leaders of organizations—for profit or otherwise—we expect you to fully engage with and participate in the important ethical issues of the day. It is time to remove organizational ethics from the margins and to stimulate broader, public dialogue about the often difficult and challenging questions regarding the role of organizations in our culture. Whether it is as an

organizational owner, employee, stockholder, customer, or concerned citizen, w
that this book will encourage you to do so.

REFERENCES

Anderson, J. A., & Englehardt, E. E. (2001). *The organizational self and ethical conduct.* Fort Worth, TX: Harcourt.

Anselmi, K. K. (1994). *Women's response to reproductive trauma secondary to contraceptive iatrogenesis: A phenomenological approach to the Dalkon Shield case* (Paper AAI9427493). Retrieved from http://repository.upenn.edu/dissertations/AAI9427493

Bazerman, M. H., & Watkins, M. (2004). *Predictable surprises: The disasters you should have seen coming and how to prevent them.* Boston: Harvard Business School Publishing.

Bonbright, D. (1997). *Leading public entrepreneurs.* Arlington, VA: Ashoka.

Bornstein, D. (2004). *How to change the world: Social entrepreneurs and the power of new ideas.* Oxford: Oxford University Press.

Cheney, G. (2004). Bringing ethics in from the margins. *Australian Journal of Communication, 31,* 35–36.

Cheney, G., & Frenette, G. (1993). Persuasion and organization: Values, logics, and accounts in contemporary corporate public discourse. In C. Conrad (Ed.), *The ethical nexus* (pp. 49–74). Norwood, NJ: Ablex Publishing Company.

Cheney, G., Lair, D., Ritz, D., & Kendall, B. (2010). *Just a job?: Communication, ethics, and professional life.* New York: Oxford University Press.

Cheney, G., May, S. K., & Munshi, D. (Eds.). (2011). *The handbook of communication ethics.* New York: Routledge.

Conrad, C. (2003). The corporate meltdown. *Management Communication Quarterly, 17,* 5–19.

Deetz, S. (1992). *Democracy in an age of corporate colonization.* Albany: State University of New York Press.

Dienhart, J. W. (2000). *Business, institutions, and ethics: A text with cases and readings.* New York: Oxford University Press.

Donaldson, T., & Gini, A. (Eds.). (1996). *Case studies in business ethics* (4th ed.). Upper Saddle River, NJ: Prentice Hall.

Donaldson, T., & Werhane, P. H. (1999). *Ethical issues in business: A philosophical approach.* Upper Saddle River, NJ: Prentice Hall.

Friedman, M. (1970, September 13). The social responsibility of business is to increase its profits. *New York Times Magazine,* pp. 32–33, 122–126.

Gini, A. (2005). *Case studies in business ethics* (2nd ed.). Upper Saddle River, NJ: Prentice Hall.

Goodpaster, K. E. (1995). Commentary on "MacIntyre and the manager." *Organization, 2*(2), 212–216.

Ihlen, O., Bartlett, J., & May, S. (Eds.). (2011). *Handbook of communication and corporate social responsibility.* Boston, MA: Wiley-Blackwell.

Jackall, R. (1983). Moral mazes: Bureaucracy and managerial work. *Harvard Business Review, 61*(5), 118–130.

Jackall, R. (1988). *Moral mazes: The world of corporate managers.* New York: Oxford University Press.

Johannesen, R. J. (1996). *Ethics in human communication* (4th ed.). Prospect Heights, IL: Waveland Press.

Kidder, R. (1995). *How good people make tough choices: Resolving the dilemmas of ethical living.* New York: Fireside.

Kitson, A., & Campbell, R. (2001). Case studies in business ethics. In A. Malachowski (Ed.), *Business ethics: Critical perspectives on business and management* (Vol. IV, pp. 7–12). London: Routledge.

Lorsch, J. W., Berlowitz, L., & Zelleke, A. (2005). *Restoring trust in American business.* Cambridge, MA: American Academy of Arts and Sciences.

Malachowski, A. (Ed.). (2001). *Business ethics: Critical perspectives on business and management* (Vol. IV). London: Routledge.

May, S. K. (1993). *Employee assistance programs and the troubled worker: A discursive study of knowledge, power, and subjectivity.* Unpublished doctoral dissertation. University of Utah, Salt Lake City.

May, S. K. (2009). Transforming the ethical culture of organizations. In J. Friedman (Ed.), *Doing well and good: The human face of the new capitalism* (pp. 87–112). Charlotte, NC: Information Age Publishing.

May, S. K. (2011). Activating ethical engagement through communication in organizations: Negotiating ethical tensions and practices in a business ethics initiative. In L. Frey & K. Carragee (Eds.), *Communication activism* (Vol. 3, pp. 325–365). New York: Hampton Press.

May, S. K. (in press). *Corporate social responsibility.* New York: Polity Press.

May, S. K., Cheney, G., & Roper, J. (Eds.), (2007). *The debate over corporate social responsibility.* New York: Oxford University Press.

May, S. K., & Mumby, D. (2005). *Engaging organizational communication theory and research: Multiple perspectives.* Thousand Oaks, CA: Sage.

May, S. K., & Zorn, T. (2003). Communication and corporate social responsibility. *Management Communication Quarterly, 16,* 595–598.

Michalos, A. C. (1995). *A pragmatic approach to business ethics.* Thousand Oaks, CA: Sage.

Paine, L. S. (2003). *Value shift: Why companies must merge social and financial imperatives to achieve superior performance.* New York: McGraw-Hill.

Parker, M. (Ed.). (1998). *Ethics and organization.* Thousand Oaks, CA: Sage.

Peterson, R. A., & Ferrell, O. C. (Eds.). (2005). *Business ethics: New challenges for business schools and corporate leaders.* Armonk, NY: M.E. Sharpe.

Redding, C. W. (1982). *Ethics and the study of organizational communication: When will we wake up?* Lecture presented to The Center for the Study of Ethics in Society, Kalamazoo, MI, Western Michigan University.

Sabini, J., & Silver, M. (1982). *Moralities of everyday life.* New York: Oxford University Press.

Sarikelle, P. (1989, February). Going by the book. *BFG Today,* 4–5.

Schaefer, Z., Conrad, C., Cheney, G., May, S., & Ganesh, S. (2011). Economic justice and communication ethics: Considering multiple points of intersection. In G. Cheney, S. K. May, & D. Munshi (Eds.), *The handbook of communication ethics* (pp. 436–456). New York: Routledge.

Seeger, M. W. (2002). *Ethics and organizational communication.* Cresskill, NJ: Hampton Press.

Shaw, W. H., & Barry, H. (2001). *Moral issues in business* (8th ed.). New York: Wadsworth.

Snoeyenbos, M., Ameder, R., & Humber, J. (2001). *Business ethics,* (3rd ed.). Amherst, MA: Prometheus Books.

Willmott, H. (1998). Toward a new ethics? The contributions of poststructuralism and posthumanism. In M. Parker (Ed.), *Ethics and organizations* (pp. 76–121). Thousand Oaks, CA: Sage.

PART I

Alignment

Ethical Dilemmas in the Financial Industry

Katherine Russell, Megan Dortch, Rachel Gordon, and Charles Conrad

This case explores the recent global financial meltdown as an example of unethical behavior among U.S. corporations. The case notes that such corporate scandals are much more common and cyclical than the general public might believe. It challenges the commonly held notion that a few individuals are responsible for the misconduct. This case, by contrast, offers a more complicated interpretation, both of financial crises and of organizational ethics in general. While the home mortgage ideology and related systems did provide opportunities for exploitation by excessively greedy individuals, it also created impossible situations for honest actors who were struggling to meet the contradictory needs of multiple groups of stakeholders.

> If a reward system is so designed that it is irrational to be moral, this does not necessarily mean that immorality will result. But, is this not asking for trouble?
>
> —Kerr (1975, p. 770)

Since 1900, the United States has repeatedly experienced a cycle that begins with the development of an investment "bubble" in the financial industry, which eventually explodes. It is quickly followed by a government (taxpayer) bailout of the organizations whose members took on far too much risk in pursuit of massive individual rewards and organizational profits.[1] Almost every generation has lived through one of these cycles, but

---

[1] A "bubble" is a precipitous rise in the value of an asset that cannot be explained by fundamental economic principles. Prices paid for the asset rapidly increase, based almost wholly on the belief that they will continue to increase. Cautionary responses are dismissed through a rhetoric claiming that the economy has entered a "new era of growth" in which the "fundamentals of investing" have changed (Posner, 2010).

today's "twentysomethings" have experienced two—the savings and loan (S&L) crisis of the late 1980s and the financial industry meltdown of 2007 and beyond. Young adults, who are notoriously uninterested in economics and only sporadically interested in politics, now have trillions of reasons to be interested in these seemingly esoteric topics. This is because *they* will be paying for the current crisis and bailouts for decades to come in increased taxes, limited economic growth, frustrated career aspirations, and reduced retirement income. And that picture is becoming even bleaker. The modest regulatory reforms enacted after the 2008 crash (usually called the Dodd–Frank Act) did very little to change the underlying factors that created it (Blake, 2010; Cohan, 2010). Banks that were "too big to fail" are even larger now; the campaign contributions and industry lobbying efforts that undercut meaningful regulatory reform have grown astronomically, and the processes that create cycles of economic bubbles, crashes, and bailouts still are in place (Cohan, 2010; Johnson, 2010; Morgenson, 2011b; Posner, 2010; Stiglitz, 2010). Regulators charged with implementing the Dodd–Frank act are doing so in ways that exacerbate those problems (Davidoff & Henning, 2010; Johnson, 2011; Krugman, 2011; Puzzanghera, 2011), and leaders of the Congress elected in 2010 have vowed to roll back regulatory reforms and cut the budgets of regulatory agencies (Fram, 2011; *New York Times* Editorial Board, 2011). Of course, politicians now claim that they will never again bail out financial institutions, but they made the same claims after the bailouts of 1907 (J.P. Morgan), 1974 (Franklin National Bank), 1984 (Continental Illinois Bank and Trust), and the S&L crisis.

The easy response to these events is to condemn all of the individuals who were involved—that is, to criticize the ethics of homeowners who took on loans they eventually could not afford, financial officers who persuaded them to do so, Wall Street operatives who found innovative ways to obscure the level of financial risk contained in the products they were selling, lobbyists who persuaded Congress to weaken regulations and hamstring regulators, and politically appointed regulators who actively suppressed dissent by some of their employees and ignored warnings from others (see Fox, 2010; Jackall, 2009; Posner, 2010). Of course, this response is easy to understand. In highly individualistic cultures such as the United States, "morality" is treated as an attribute of each person, and "ethics" is viewed as a process through which *individuals* draw upon their *own* moral codes to make decisions about how to act in concrete life situations. But, as noted in the introduction to this book, this individualistic, "foundational" perspective is problematic in a number of ways.

First of all, it ignores the need to carefully and realistically examine the contexts within which people make ethical choices—to "walk a mile in their shoes" as the old adage suggests. All cultures strive to teach their members the difference between right and wrong. They also teach their members how to interpret the situations they face and how to act ethically in response to them. But many situations are ethically ambiguous, and others reward people for acting unethically and/or punish them for acting ethically. Individuals *are* responsible for the ethicality of their choices, but they make those choices within situations that were constructed over long periods of time through choices made by other people. Expecting individuals to make ethical choices within unethical systems and situations is unrealistic and unfair. In addition, individualizing organizational ethics shifts attention away from situational factors, making systemic reform less likely, and ensures another round of bubbles and bailouts.

The second ethical dilemma in "foundational" views involves the disparate interests of multiple stakeholders. Because stakeholder interests often conflict with one another, making an *ethical* choice usually requires a decision maker to privilege the interests of some stakeholders and violate the interests of others—for example, a choice that treats workers in an ethical manner may unfairly penalize stockholders and vice versa. From a purely legal perspective, this is not a problem—a manager's *legal* responsibility is to maximize the income of the organization's owners (individuals, or stockholders if the organization is a publicly owned corporation) through maximizing the firm's profits. Privileging any other stakeholders' interests violates this fiduciary responsibility and thus is "unethical" from a purely legal perspective (Friedman, 1970). Moreover, engaging in socially responsible activities (that is, privileging the interests of other stakeholders) costs money so it puts the firm at a disadvantage compared to competitors that only seek to maximize profits. Doing so threatens the survival of the firm, which punishes its owners/stockholders, employees, and the communities within which the firm operates.[2] Even if the firm survives, applying "multiple stakeholder" models of organizational ethics can lead decision makers to violate their employment contracts and impose their own ethical values on the firms they have been hired to manage. Both of these dilemmas are illustrated powerfully by recent crises in the financial industry.

CONSTRUCTING THE ETHICAL SYSTEM FOR HOMEOWNERSHIP

Recent financial industry crises were grounded in an assumption that has been taken-for-granted in the United States for more than a half century—that homeownership is virtuous. The concept may have been part of the "American dream" from the country's beginnings, although early immigrants wanted to own property more as a *means* of escaping the abusive landlords and debtors' prisons of their countries of origins than as an *end* in itself (Cawelti, 1974). Owning *land* also was a *means* of gaining financial independence through farming and ranching. But homeownership as a desired *end* in itself was an alien concept. In fact, when historian James Trulow coined the phrase "the American Dream" in 1931, it did not include homeownership at all, much less depict it as *the* key component. But by the early 1900s, politicians of all stripes, as well as spokespersons for the home construction and sales industry, were elevating the concept to a core cultural value—an *end* in itself—and creating structures to encourage it.

Over time, the rhetoric of homeownership has been remarkably persuasive. Almost all U.S. residents now see it as *the* most important element of the American dream, an investment that will enhance the quality of their lives and the lives of their children. However, statistical correlations between homeownership and its purported positive effects—increased citizen involvement in politics and civic organizations, better educational systems, lower rates of crime, fewer school dropouts, and reduced teen pregnancy—are weak, and there is even less evidence supporting the inference that homeownership causes those outcomes. Family auto ownership is more strongly related to dropout rates than homeownership,

---

[2] The rhetorical appeals underlying this position are analyzed superbly by James Arnt Aune (2007) and Cheney, Roper, and May (2007).

and all of these outcomes are correlated more strongly with time spent in a community than with homeownership *per se*. Furthermore, both the outcomes and homeownership are better predicted by other factors (having a stable family life and average neighborhood income) than by one another (Kiviat, 2010).

Furthermore, the mythology ignores a number of disadvantages to homeownership, the most important of which is the "illiquidity" of housing. It is hard to turn a house into cash, especially during recessions when people most need to be mobile in order to relocate to areas with better job prospects. As a result, the areas with the highest levels of homeownership also tend to have the highest levels of unemployment—during recessions the "stability of homeownership" is transformed into "being trapped in a house you cannot sell" (van Praet, 2011). But, in spite of all these data, Americans *believe* the mythology of homeownership and do so without questioning it. Cultural assumptions are sustained by perceptions and rhetoric, not by data and statistical analysis.

The homeownership mythology also has led to the creation of a number of supportive systems. For individuals, the most important of these are subsidies and deductions that are built into the federal tax code, something that almost half of homeowners cite as a primary reason for buying a home instead of renting (Hiber & Turner, 2010). There is no question about the size of these incentives—in 2010, the federal government lost more than $100 billion in revenue to them, more than double the loss in 1995, and it is estimated that the total loss from 2010 through 2013 will exceed $500 billion (Harrop, 2011). But to get tax advantages, taxpayers must itemize their deductions, an option that largely benefits wealthier households. In 2009, the 2.8 million home-owning families with incomes above $250,000 (the top 2% or so) saved $15 billion a year in federal income taxes (about $15 a day each), while the 19 million families making $40,000 to $75,000 (middle income) saved only $10 billion (about $1.50 a day) (Peterba & Sanai, 2010). In addition, being able to deduct interest paid to purchase *second* homes exclusively benefits wealthier taxpayers (this deduction alone was worth $800 million in 2010). Being able to deduct property taxes increases these effects.[3] Of course, a tax and subsidy system that primarily rewards wealthy taxpayers but is justified in terms of the rhetoric of homeownership *for all* raises some important ethical questions.

For financial institutions, the homeownership system includes a series of government-sponsored and funded incentives and protections. Savers will not deposit their funds in financial institutions unless they believe that it is both safe and profitable to do so. Similarly, the "dream" of homeownership will be within the reach of nonwealthy families only if financial institutions can be persuaded to offer home mortgages on terms that make them affordable. In order to persuade savers that banks were safe after the economic crash of 1929, the Roosevelt administration created deposit insurance programs (the Federal Deposit Insurance Corporation [FDIC] for banks, the Federal Savings and Loan Insurance Corporation [FSLIC] for savings and loans, and so on). Funded by a combination of levies on financial firms and tax monies, there were (and still are) two rationales for these programs.

---

[3] The system also has a number of indirect costs, the most important of which is encouraging suburbanization that forces taxpayers to pay for infrastructure—highways, sewer lines, utilities, and so on—that would not be needed in an urban, more rent-oriented society.

The first is practical—persuading people to deposit their savings in a financial institution allows them to loan money to entrepreneurs who want to start businesses, small business owners who want to expand their operations, and/or families who want to purchase homes. Since society as a whole benefits, the risks taken by depositors should be spread over the entire society—that is, they should be "socialized."

The second rationale for deposit insurance is ethical. Depositors almost never have any influence over the decisions that create financial crises. Financial institutions are "limited-liability" corporations, which means that if a bank or S&L fails, the people who manage them and the stockholders who own them cannot lose more money than they have invested in the organization. For managers, this usually means that making bad decisions *might* get them fired, but they will not lose their assets. However, the *gains* that decision makers receive if things go well are not socialized—they are left in the private hands of managers and owners (usually stockholders). This *combination* of socialized risks/losses and privatized gains creates "moral hazards," situations in which it is economically rational for managers to take excessive risks (and owners to allow or encourage them to do so). They control large sums of other people's money, will benefit handsomely if their risky actions succeed, and will break even if they fail. If decision makers also believe that government (taxpayers) will bail them out when they make bad choices, the hazard is increased. So it would be unethical to put depositors' life savings at risk when the people who decide how to manage that money do not have *their own* assets at risk. Of course, while deposit insurance programs protect depositors from unwise managerial decisions, they do not protect taxpayers. To do that, governments must regulate financial institutions very tightly.

The goal of widespread homeownership also relies on persuading financial institutions to offer mortgages at a low enough interest rate and extend repayment schedules over a long enough period of time to make monthly payments affordable and predictable. The kind of mortgage that became the U.S. standard—one that has a 30-year term and a fixed interest rate—achieves this goal but creates two kinds of risk for lenders, *credit risk* and *interest rate risk*. Credit risk involves the possibility that borrowers may default on a mortgage. This is especially likely during recessions when people lose their jobs or move from full-time to part-time work. During recessions, the value of the homes that are used as collateral for mortgages also tend to fall, leaving financial institutions holding property that may be worth less than the balance left on the mortgage. In order to encourage lenders to offer these long-term mortgages, the Roosevelt administration created the Federal Housing Administration (FHA). It guaranteed that the government would pay the balance owed by borrowers who defaulted on their mortgages, as long as all parties had met a number of requirements when the mortgage loan was created. By shifting credit risk from lenders to the federal government (taxpayers), they would be able to offer home loans on terms that nonwealthy Americans could afford.

Long-term mortgages also involve interest rate risk for lenders. This kind of risk is a bit more difficult to explain. In order to attract deposits, financial institutions that offer mortgages must be safe *and* must offer a high enough interest rate on savings accounts. Since economic conditions (and thus short-term interest rates) fluctuate frequently, tying up funds in a 30-year mortgage at a fixed interest rate is incredibly risky for lenders. They cannot adjust the interest they charge on long-term mortgages to reflect the changing interest rates paid on savings deposits. So if a society really does value homeowner-ship for as many people as possible it must find a way to help lenders manage interest rate risk. This is why the federal government created Fannie Mae in 1939.[4] It purchases federally insured mortgages from the FHA, thereby encouraging lenders to offer afford-able mortgages to more people. In order to protect the government's (taxpayers') invest-ment, Congress adopted a series of very strict regulations, the most important of which were included in what was called the Glass-Steagall Act, and created the Federal Reserve System to regulate the financial industry. The Fed quickly enacted two important rules for mortgage lenders. One prohibited them from investing in risky venues such as the stock market. Another (called Regulation Q) limited the interest rates paid on savings accounts, but allowed S&Ls, which were the primary source of home mortgages, to pay a little more interest (usually 1/4% to 1/2%) than other institutions.[5] When considered *as a group*, these measures encouraged savers to place their money in mortgage-granting institutions (by socializing risk and giving savings accounts an interest rate advantage), protected those institutions from credit risk and interest rate risk, and offset moral hazards through tight regulation. But for the system to work each and every component had to be maintained—changing or weakening one would undermine the entire system.

BUBBLES AND BAILOUTS, FIRST VERSE

The policies enacted during the 1930s were remarkably successful in making homeowner-ship possible for millions of middle-income Americans. In addition, for half a century the regulations included in the Glass-Steagall Act protected taxpayers from the risks that were included in the homeownership system. But during the early 1980s, the situation changed quickly and radically. In order to deal with the economic crisis of the late 1970s, the Carter administration created 6-month savings certificates that paid higher interest rates than those allowed on regular savings accounts. It also allowed stock brokerage firms and insurance companies to offer money market mutual funds that offered savers even higher interest rates. Even though money market funds were not federally insured (something that many depositors did not realize and many money market salespersons did not make clear to them), people rapidly moved their funds out of traditional savings accounts. Suddenly, S&Ls were saddled with commitments to millions of dollars in long-term mortgages at low, fixed interest rates but could not pay enough interest to attract or keep savings account deposits. The balanced regulatory system that had been created during the 1930s was being dismantled, and interest rate risk skyrocketed.

After the election of Ronald Reagan in 1980, life rapidly became even more complicated for mortgage lenders. In order to fight inflation, Treasury Secretary Paul Volcker increased interest rates, driving the returns on 6-month certificates of deposit to more than 15%. To make matters even worse, the new administration decided to further deregulate the financial

---

[4] Freddie Mac was created later.

[5] This combination protected S&Ls against interest rate risk, but the industry continued to lobby for the right to offer adjustable rate mortgages (ARMs) whose interest rate changed along with economic conditions. Because ARMs contradicted the socially legitimized goal of encouraging homeownership by as many people as possible, Congress repeatedly rejected the proposals.

services industry. In 1980 and 1982, Congress eliminated Regulation Q, and the people who were regulating the industry allowed banks and S&Ls to *both* invest in much riskier products than before *and* to write mortgages for people who would not have qualified under previous rules.[6] Managers of S&Ls, most of whom had no training in how to deal with a volatile, highly competitive market, were suddenly faced with the *combination* of sky-high interest rates, deregulation, and interest rate competition, precisely the combination that the Glass-Steagall Act had been designed to prevent. Their cash reserves continued to plummet. In a search for higher returns, many S&L managers abandoned mortgage lending altogether and engaged in land speculation and risky commercial ventures, primarily in California, which was in the midst of an economic boom supported by a real estate bubble, and in Texas, whose economy was buoyed by high oil prices. In many cases, the riskier investments did not pay off, and thousands of honestly managed S&Ls teetered on the edge of bankruptcy. In addition, the resulting chaos was an invitation for unscrupulous figures to enter the industry and for accountants to engage in questionable auditing practices.[7]

Then, in the mid-1980s the California housing bubble burst and oil prices plummeted, with a devastating effect on the Texas economy. By 1989, half of all U.S. S&Ls were bankrupt. People who still had funds in traditional savings accounts were protected by the FSLIC, but it soon ran out of funds and had to be shored up by a $20 billion infusion from Congress. The industry eventually received the largest taxpayer bailout in U.S. history, but only after a great deal of political theater.[8] The moral hazards that Glass-Steagall had been carefully crafted to avoid had come to pass with a vengeance, and the S&L bailout solidified the perception that managers of financial institutions would be able to shift the costs of risky and/or unethical behavior to taxpayers.

BUBBLES AND BAILOUTS, SECOND VERSE

Within months, the lessons of the S&L crisis and bailout seemed to be forgotten. A new rhetoric emerged, one asserting that the debacle had resulted from the excesses of a few "bad apple" managers and not because of anything that was wrong with the changes that had been made in the regulatory system.[9] Attention quickly shifted to Iraq's invasion of Kuwait and Operation Desert Storm. By the mid-1990s, the fervor for deregulation had

---

[6] The most important steps were the Depository Institutions Deregulation and Monetary Control Act of 1980 and the Garn–St. Germain Depository Institutions Act of 1982. Individual states also began to compete with one another to attract financial corporations by weakening their regulations.

[7] Criminal misconduct and insider abuse was a "principal" or "significant contributing" factor in more than 20% of S&L bankruptcies (see the 1987 study by the House Subcommittee on Commerce, Consumer, and Monetary Affairs, summarized in Strunk & Case, 1988).

[8] Five senators were accused of interfering with regulators who were investigating fraudulent activity. Only one, Alan Cranston, was formally reprimanded by the Senate Ethics Committee, and two, who were found to have exercised bad judgment (John Glenn and John McCain) ran for reelection and won. President George H. W. Bush's son Neil was fined $50,000 for "multiple breaches of his fiduciary duties" and barred from running financial institutions. Bailout of this S&L cost the taxpayers $1.3 billion, and a federal suit against Bush and other officers was settled out of court for $26.5 million. Congress and the Bush administration arranged to have the bailout excluded from the official federal budget so that it would not increase the official budget deficit, and the bankrupt S&Ls were sold at a fraction of their prebankruptcy value, often to the same managers whose excessive risk-taking had driven them into bankruptcy.

[9] For an analysis of "bad apples" rhetoric, see Cheney, Lair, Ritz, and Kendall (2010), Conrad (2004), and McMillan (2007).

returned, and financial industry lobbyists increasingly pressured Congress to eliminate what remained of the Glass-Steagall Act. They finally succeeded in 1999.[10] At the same time, employees of financial institutions developed innovative techniques that made it easier to disguise the level of risk that was involved in the products they sold. The most important involved *derivatives*, which are complex financial instruments whose value depends on the worth of other complex financial instruments that are then sold to other investors. Derivatives have a number of legitimate purposes. For example, they provide funding for new industries that do not have access to traditional loans. But they also can be used to shift risk to unsuspecting parties, obscure the actual value of investments, and generate massive profits for financial firms that far exceed their contribution to the economy (Posner, 2010). By 2004, the global derivatives market, which was almost nonexistent just a decade earlier, was worth more than $70 trillion (Johnson & Kwak, 2010).[11] In addition, antiregulation interest groups persuaded politicians (most of whom needed very little persuasion) to further weaken accounting standards and government regulation of financial transactions (Johnson & Kwak, 2010).[12] All that was standing in the way of another financial meltdown was a period of sustained low interest rates and an investment bubble. Like the S&L crisis, the bubble came in real estate.

To explain the ethical situation involving the mortgage industry in the late "aughts" (2005–2009), we need to return to the mythology of the American dream. It legitimizes active government intervention in the mortgage market in order to make homeownership available to as many families as possible. In 1995 and 1997, the federal government took steps to make the dream accessible to low or moderate income families by encouraging lenders to approve loans for applicants who previously would have been deemed marginal. The primary mechanism for doing so was the ARM, which had long been advocated by the home mortgage industry (Cantrell, 2010). Strong economic growth and increasing home prices during the 1990s made it *seem* like borrowers' incomes were likely to rise in the future, which would allow them to manage the increased payments they would encounter when the initial interest rates on their ARMs rose. Steadily increasing home values also made it *seem* that even if borrowers did default on their mortgages financial organizations would be able to repossess their homes and resell them at a profit. So offering what came to be called "subprime" mortgages *seemed* to be safe, in part because lenders started to believe their own rhetoric about a never-ending increase in home values (Posner, 2010). Deregulation of the industry *allowed* mortgage writers to create even more "innovative" (which meant risky) kinds of mortgages, which made even more people eligible. Bringing more people into the mortgage market stimulated the construction of new homes and drove up housing prices, which made it *seem* that home values would continue to increase.

---

[10] The bill that did so was called the Financial Modernization Act but is more commonly known as the Gramm-Leach-Bliley Act.

[11] Derivatives are like packages of meat. While all of the meat in a package may be lean and free of bones and gristle, an unscrupulous butcher may have put very nice cuts on the top of a pile of low-quality ones and then sealed them up in the same package. Unless a customer looks very closely, which may be impossible if the packages already have been sealed and/or they are very large, she or he can wind up with a very bad investment.

[12] The legislation was called the Community Reinvestment Act. It also was motivated by evidence that some lenders were "redlining" minority mortgage applicants (refusing to loan them money even if they met standard financial criteria, particularly if they were trying to buy houses in traditionally white neighborhoods).

In addition, large mortgage lenders such as Countrywide Financial, Ownit Mortgage Solutions, and American Home Mortgage shifted away from using human underwriters to assess the creditworthiness of applicants to cheaper automated systems. This reduced the amount of time needed to process a loan application from about 1 week to 30 seconds but added risk to the system because automated systems cannot detect the unique combinations of risks that humans might have found. By 2007, approximately 40% of subprime loans were being accepted by automatic systems (Browning, 2007). Even after the 2007 and 2008 crises, major banks continued the practice (Krugman, 2011).

The growth of the mortgage industry meant that financial organizations were holding a very large amount of debt by historical standards. Some especially innovative employees took a cue from the derivatives market and realized that they could bundle mortgages together and sell stock using them as collateral. This would provide additional funds for their organizations to invest, garner massive bonuses for them, and shift much of the risk to the people who purchased the stocks. If all of the mortgages that were "securitized" in this way had been of high quality, it would not have created much of a problem. But some banks started packaging subprime mortgages with good ones. Since some of these packages were worth a billion dollars or more, a lot of subprime loans could be included in securities "packages" without anyone noticing. In theory, ratings agencies are supposed to protect buyers by labeling bundles as A + +, B +, etc., based on the level of risk that they contained, but for a number of reasons, they did not do an adequate job (Krugman, 2009). Bankers also suggested to insurance companies that they should create policies that guaranteed the value of these bundles. Since the insurance companies (the biggest one was AIG) thought the bundles were safe (in part because they had little incentive to examine them very closely) and knew that these insurance policies could be very, very profitable, they cooperated by creating what came to be called "credit default swaps." By 2005, the number of loans that were bundled and sold as mortgage-backed securities was almost 27 times larger than the *total* value of *all* mortgages written 10 years earlier (Cantrell, 2010). Since the banks' high-risk mortgages had been shifted to others, they could write even more subprime mortgages and take on even greater risks. If a mortgage applicant could not qualify for one type of "alternative" loan, other alternatives were created. Eventually, even applicants who had neither the savings needed for a down payment nor stable employment were routinely approved.

In addition, the federal government responded to the economic downturn after 9/11 by lowering interest rates across the board, further increasing the number of potential homeowners. As early as November 2002, Federal Reserve Chairman Alan Greenspan realized that these trends could not be sustained over the long term and told a private meeting of Fed officials that the housing boom could not continue indefinitely (Mishkin, 2008). But, Greenspan's public comments painted a very different picture. In 2003, he declared that the 2001 to 2002 recession was over (even though it would be years before unemployment returned to prerecession levels), which encouraged the "irrational exuberance" that he had previously warned against. His repeated declarations that a major drop in home prices was "quite unlikely" fed the bubble further (Johnson & Kwak, 2010; Posner, 2010). In a form of self-fulfilling prophecy, easy credit and low interest rates supported both a boom in homebuilding and increasing housing prices, which made risky loans *seem* to be secure, and a housing bubble was born and nurtured.

However, economies move in cycles. When the U.S. economy began to slow after 2004, unemployment increased and the incomes of people who still had jobs plateaued or started to decline. With reduced demand, housing prices leveled off and in some areas began to fall. By early 2005, people who had taken out ARMs saw their payments increase, sometimes significantly, as their low initial teaser rates expired. Some lost their homes—70% more people faced foreclosure in 2005 than the year before. Housing developers who had raced to build homes with subprime borrowers in mind now had fewer customers, leaving tens of thousands of homes unsold, further reducing housing prices. By June 2008, the bubble had exploded—new home sales were 33% lower than a year earlier (Mishkin, 2008; "The Wrecking-Ball Response," 2008). The declining market left many homeowners with property that was worth less than the amount they owed on their mortgages (they were "underwater" in loan speak), making it impossible for them to refinance their mortgages or sell homes they could no longer afford (Klein, 2008). Soon, the housing crisis spilled over to other parts of the economy, dragging down retail sales and making consumers less willing to spend on new cars and other items (Posner, 2010; Stiglitz, 2010). Financial organizations now were so large and so tightly interconnected that the failure of one would have ripple effects throughout the system. Since the largest firms had taken on the largest risks, the entire system was on the verge of collapse. The naysayers who had opposed deregulation and the destruction of the Glass-Steagall Act had been proven correct, and the Great Recession was born.

SUMMARY

The most popular response to both the S&L crisis and the 2007 through 2008 financial industry meltdown has been to condemn individuals and organizations for engaging in excessively risky behavior in order to make themselves rich at the expense of the rest of society. While this individualistic, good versus evil interpretation is consistent with U.S. culture, it lumps all of the people involved in the process into one of two homogeneous groups regardless of the specific situations they faced. In addition, it feeds the "bad apples" orientation that historically has absolved those who created risk-inducing systems of responsibility for them, in the process short-circuiting pressure to make meaningful changes to the system. Condemning the villains and calling it a day may feel good, but it does nothing to prevent the recurrence of investment bubble-crisis-bailout cycles. In this case study, we have offered a more complicated interpretation, both of financial crises and of organizational ethics in general. While the home mortgage ideology and related systems did provide opportunities for exploitation by excessively greedy individuals, it also created impossible situations for honest actors who were struggling to meet the contradictory needs of multiple groups of stakeholders.

In this summary, we offer an even broader perspective. These crises coincided with an era of fundamental change in the economies of the Western capitalist democracies. From the 14th century on, people have been defined by their "character," by the ethical value that they placed on their own desires and their relationships with other people (Sennett, 1998). Character was expressed through loyalty, mutual commitment, and the pursuit of long-term goals—delaying gratification for the sake of the future. But the "new economy" that started to emerge during the 1970s and became firmly entrenched after the fall of the Soviet Union in 1990 has severed links between people, their organizations, and the future. The resulting "flexible capitalism" demands nimble behavior, a focus on short-term goals, instantaneous adjustment, and independence from our organizations and our relationships. The stable foundations of our identities and our ethical systems have disappeared, creating a new kind of uncertainty that is "woven into the everyday practices of a vigorous capitalism" (Sennett, 1998, p. 31). Some of us have responded with fatalism (see Giddens, 1991); others have learned to maneuver in the moment, doing whatever is necessary to reduce the risks and uncertainties we face. Suddenly, neither morality nor security depends on honesty, long-term relationships, or a work ethic. Instead, these values are undermined by the capriciousness of a global market economy and the fleeting consent of a constantly changing group of superiors and coworkers. The new economy has created a new ethic, one that encourages us to adopt a situational view of morality, demands that we choose the course of action that maximizes immediate profits, and justifies any decision that maximizes individual economic gain. When combined with rhetoric that shifts our attention away from situations and systems, treating ethics as situation-bound triggers a loss of deeply held moral character. It may be a rational adaptation to contemporary society, but it also may mean that profit and property are the only stable anchors that we have left.

DISCUSSION QUESTIONS

1. Is it ethical for a government to act in ways that "socialize" financial *risks* or *losses*? Is it ethical to do so while *privatizing* gains/profits? Or to do so in ways that favor wealthier citizens while imposing risks on less wealthy taxpayers (or vice versa)? Or that create *moral hazards?* Why or why not? Are there social goals that are so important that they would lead you to change your answer?

2. Put yourself in the shoes of a person running a small, local S&L in the late 1980s. If you refuse to take on risk, something that you have always tried to do, depositors will move their funds to riskier investments, which offer higher interest rates. Eventually your S&L could be bankrupt. Your depositors will be protected by federal insurance, but you, your employees, family, and community will suffer. Alternatively, you could do what many of your peers are doing—make riskier investments. If you make good choices, your S&L may survive, and you could become very rich in the process. If you do not, it will go bankrupt sooner. What is the ethical thing for you to do? Why?

3. Now pretend that it is 2005 and you just graduated from college, got married, and landed an entry-level job in one of the booming economies of Southern California, Nevada, or Florida. You like your apartment but keep reading about low interest rate home loans that are available to people who have not saved up the "old-fashioned" 20% down payment. You also vividly remember messages from your childhood telling you that renting is a waste of money because it does not build equity. You

also *feel* that you won't have really become an independent, mature person until you own your home (or at least your own mortgage). Home prices are skyrocketing, and if you wait until you've saved a standard down payment, houses will be much more expensive. You find a house that both you and your partner love. Your banker shows you a way to buy the house at payments you can afford, as long as *both* of you keep your jobs. You know it's risky to commit that high a percentage of your income to housing, but you also know that interest rates may never again be this low. Would it be ethical to take the bank's offer? Will ethical considerations determine what you do? Should they? Why or why not?

4. Your new job is as a bank loan officer; your partner's job is as a construction engineer specializing in housing developments. A young couple just like you apply for a mortgage in hopes of buying a house in one of the subdivisions that your partner helped build. They don't qualify for a standard mortgage or even a standard variable rate mortgage, but they would qualify for a "subprime" package. You worry about them because you've discovered that there are a lot of hidden costs in homeownership, which have made your financial life stressful. But you need a big year-end bonus to cover those costs, and it will be based on the number and value of the mortgages you write. Turning them down would reduce your bonus and make your shaky finances even shakier. What would you do? Would ethical considerations enter into your decision making? Should they? Why or why not? What will you say when you explain your decision to your partner?

5. The Federal Debt Reduction Commission recently recommended that *both* mortgage-related subsidies and tax breaks from the federal agencies that help middle- and lower-income families buy homes be scaled back or eliminated. The Obama administration has proposed taking the latter step, eliminating Fannie Mae and Freddie Mac but doing nothing about the incentives and tax breaks that benefit wealthier taxpayers (Morgenson, 2011a; Wagner & Kravitz, 2011). Is their proposal ethical? Why or why not?

REFERENCES

Aune, J. A. (2007). How to read Milton Friedman. In S. May, G. Cheney, & J. Roper (Eds.), *The debate over corporate social responsibility* (pp. 207–218). New York: Oxford University Press.

Blake, R. (2010, July 15). Financial overhaul nothing for Wall Street to cry about. *ABCNews*. Retrieved from http://abcnews.go

Browning, L. (2007, March 27). The subprime loan machine. *New York Times*. Retrieved from http://www.nytimes.com/2007/03/23/business/23speed.html

Cantrell, A. (2010, October 29). America's biggest hedge funds control $743 billion. *Money*. Retrieved from www.money.cnn.com

Cawelti, J. (1974). *Apostles of the self-made man.* Cambridge, MA: Harvard University Press.

Cheney, G., Lair, D., Ritz, D., & Kendall, B. (2010). *Just a job? Communication, ethics, and professional life.* New York: Oxford University Press.

Cheney, G., Roper, J. & May, S. (2007). Overview. In S. May, G. Cheney, & J. Roper (Eds.), *The debate over corporate social responsibility* (pp. 3–14). New York: Oxford University Press.

Cohan, W. (2010, October 7). *Make Wall Street risk it all.* Retrieved from http://opinionator.blogs
.nytimes.com/2010/10/07/make-wall-street-risk-it-all/?hp

Conrad, C. (2004). The illusion of reform. *Rhetoric & Public Affairs, 7,* 311–338.

Davidoff, G., & Henning, P. (2010, January 12). We waited for this? *New York Times Dealbook.* Retrieved
from http://dealbook.nytimes.com/2010/01/12/we-waited-for-this/

Fox, J. (2010). *The myth of the rational market.* New York: HarperCollins.

Fram, A. (2011, July 16). Republicans nibble at Obama's overhaul. *Houston Chronicle,* p. D1.

Friedman, M. (1970, September 13). The social responsibility of business is to increase its profits. *New
York Times Magazine, 32*–33, 122–126.

Giddens, A. (1991). *Modernity and self identity.* Palo Alto, CA: Stanford University Press.

Harrop, F. (2011, February 23). Fannie Mae, Freddie Mac at fault in housing fiasco. *Houston Chronicle,*
p. B9.

Hiber, C., & Turner, T. (2010, August 12). *The mortgage interest deduction and its impact on homeownership decisions.* London School of Economics.

Jackall, R. (2009). *Moral mazes.* New York: Oxford University Press.

Johnson, S. (2010, September 23). The Fed, innovation and the next recession. *New York Times.*
Retrieved from http://economix.blogs.nytimes.com/2010/09/23/the-fed-innovation-and-the-next-
recession/?ref = business

Johnson, S. (2011, January 20). Tunnel vision, or worse, from banking regulators. *New York Times.*
Retrieved from http://economix.blogs.nytimes.com/2011/01/20/tunnel-vision-or-worse-from-
bank-regulators/

Johnson, S., & Kwak, J. (2010). *13 bankers.* New York: Pantheon.

Kerr, S. (1975). On the folly of rewarding A while hoping for B. *Academy of Management Journal, 19,*
769–783.

Kiviat, B. (2010, September 11). The case against homeownership. *Time.* Retrieved from www.time
.com/time/business/article/Q8599,2013684,00.html

Klein, A. (2008, June 15). Anatomy of a meltdown. *Washington Post.* Retrieved from www.washington-
post.com/wp-dyn/content/article/2008/06/14/AR2008061401479.html?sid = ST2008061401569

Krugman, P. (2009). *The return of depression economics and the crisis of 2008.* New York: W. W. Norton.

Krugman, P. (2011, July 19). No reason to go easy on the bankers. *Houston Chronicle*, p. B11.

McMillan, J. (2007). Why corporate social responsibility: Why now? How? In S. May, G. Cheney, &
J. Roper (Eds.), *The debate over corporate social responsibility* (pp. 15–29). New York: Oxford
University Press.

Mishkin, S. (2008, August 13). Subprime rescue hit by second mortgages. *Financial Times.* Retrieved
from www.ft.com/cms/s/0/55e670e-695a-11dd-91bd-0000779fd18c.html

Morgenson, G. (2011a, February 12). Imagining life without Fannie and Freddie. *New York Times.*
Retrieved from www.nytimes.com/2011/02/13/business/13gret.html?_r = l&ref

Morgenson, G. (2011b, July 30). *Some bankers never learn.* Retrieved from www.nytimes
.com/2011/07/31;business/do-mortgage-bankers-ever-learn.html_r = 1&ref = business

New York Times Editorial Board. (2011, February 13). Running on empty. *New York Times.* Retrieved
from http://www.nytimes.com/2011/02/14/opinion/14mon2.html

Peterba, J., & Sanai, T. (2010). *Tax expenditures for owner-occupied housing.* MIT Department of
Economics.

Posner, R. (2010). *The crisis of capitalist democracy.* Cambridge, MA: Harvard University Press.

Puzzanghera, J. (2011, June 30). Regulators give banks a break on debit cards. *Houston Chronicle*, p. 1D.

Sennett, R. (1998). *The corrosion of character.* New York: W. W. Norton.

Stiglitz, J. (2010). *Freefall.* New York: W. W. Norton.

Strunk, N., & Case, F. (1988). *Where de-regulation went wrong.* Washington, DC: United States League
of Savings Associations.

van Praet, N. (2011, January 31). Migration at all time high. *Financial Post*. Retrieved from www
.financialpost.com/news/features/Migration + year + high/4480290/story.html

Wagner, D., & Kravitz, D. (2011, February 12). White House aims to pare government mortgage role.
Houston Chronicle, p. D3.

The wrecking-ball response: How to deal with a glut of empty homes. (2008, July 10). *The Economist*.
Retrieved from http://www.economist.com/node/11708045

The Ethics of the "Family Friendly" Organization

The Challenge of Policy Inclusiveness

Caryn E. Medved and David R. Novak

This case considers the degree to which employees with different family situations should be treated similarly or differently in organizations. It raises questions regarding what, if any, ethical responsibility organizations have to help their employees manage work and family responsibilities. As a result, it explores the degree to which personal, professional, and organizational goals should be aligned. It also addresses whether (1) the virtue of self-actualization among employees should be managed by an organization, (2) organizations have a specific duty to consider the private lives of employees in decision making, and (3) single and married employees should have different rights and, therefore, different policies regarding flexible work hours.

If two people want the day off . . . if it's a married person and a single person, preference is almost always given to the married people just because their reason for taking the day off somehow becomes more justified.

—Rob, employee at Aon Hewitt

During the past four decades, organizations in the United States and around the world have adopted policies and practices designed to assist employees balance work and family obligations (Galinsky & Friedman, 1991). Types of "family friendly" work-life policies, benefits, and services include flexible work arrangements, telecommuting, day care subsidies, parental leaves, lactation rooms, as well as, occasionally, on-site day cares and concierge services. Work and family benefits can positively affect organizations' bottom lines, even during difficult economic times (A Better Balance, 2010; Galinsky & Bond, 2009), as well as provide critical assistance to employees whose needs are met through particular accommodations (Ryan & Kossek, 2008). As companies do more with less, work-life benefits can become even more essential as employees often struggle to balance the two during stressful economic times and in uncertain job markets (Kiplinger News, 2010). Further, millennial age employees just entering the workforce express the desire to balance their work and family lives even more than past generations of workers (Galinsky, Aumann, & Bond, 2008).

Yet one often overlooked ethical challenge related to work-life policies is the extent to which these benefits and the communication practices surrounding their use take into account employees' different needs and values. In other words, how inclusive or exclusive are work and life policies? For example, flextime may be critical to help employees with young children, but can employees without children use this policy to meet their nonwork obligations? Single and childfree employees may have commitments to close friends and other extended family members. Employees without biological or adoptive children often serve as "sparents," or spare parents, providing care to nieces, nephews, and friends' children. Can gay and lesbian employees take time off of work to care for a sick partner as easily as a married heterosexual employee wanting to care for an ailing spouse? And how do managers simultaneously and fairly balance workloads and also meet deadlines when one employee leaves work to attend to a sick child and their single coworker without children must take on additional responsibilities? Are managers or the organization held accountable when employees who are parents are allowed to leave work regularly at 5:30 pm while childfree employees feel obligated to work late? What if childfree employees are pressured in interactions with managers, implicitly or explicitly, to work late?

These are not easy situations to navigate for either managers or employees. Good intentions by managers to help employees can have unintended negative consequences and create some difficult choices for all concerned. So how does an organization assist employees with "traditional" family responsibilities without treating one class of employees differently than another or considering one set of employee needs as more deserving of accommodation than others? Does an organization have a responsibility to offer employees a forum to give voice to concerns related to work-life issues? All of these issues raise thorny ethical dilemmas about an organization's reach into our private lives and whether it has obligations over and above contributing to the bottom line. Rob's story[1] provides us a glimpse into these larger ethical questions by highlighting the difficult challenges that can arise related to work-life policy inclusion.

Rob began his career at Hewitt Associates, an employee benefit outsourcing company, as a business analyst in September 2008, shortly after graduating from college. In 2010, Hewitt merged with Aon Corporation to become the global leader in human capital consulting and outsourcing solutions. Many changes in Rob's personal life also have occurred during these past few years. Since beginning his first job, he got engaged, promoted, married, and purchased a house. As a result, Rob has experienced being an employee of Aon Hewitt from a number of different life perspectives: as a single employee, a married employee, and as a new husband without child. During these years, he has also faced a variety of challenges in

---

[1] This case study was developed from interviews with—at the time of the interviews—one current and one former employee at Hewitt Associates. While the employees' names have been changed, the situations and attitudes reflected in this case study represent their real experiences in the organization.

balancing his work and life responsibilities. We will begin our case study of Rob's experiences just prior to his wedding , but first, let's describe briefly the business of Aon Hewitt.

AON HEWITT: THE ORGANIZATION

Hewitt Associates was founded in 1940 as an insurance brokerage firm in Lake Forest, Illinois, a northern suburb of Chicago.[2] As a separate corporate entity, Hewitt was the world's leading provider of outsourced human resources (HR) services including benefits such as health insurance, pension, and 401(k) plans; payroll; and workforce management, along with a full complement of HR consulting services. The main line of its business is Total Benefits Administration™ (TBA), which is an integrated technology platform allowing client organizations to outsource the daily tasks of managing their employee benefit programs. In July 2010, Hewitt Associates and Aon Corporation announced a merger resulting in Hewitt becoming a subsidiary of Aon (Aon Corporation, 2010). This partnership created Aon Hewitt, which designs, implements, communicates, and administers a wide range of human capital, retirement, investment management, health care, compensation, and talent management strategies. Currently, Aon Hewitt has more than 59,000 professionals in 120 countries with $8.5 billion in combined revenue.

One of Hewitt's corporate hallmarks is its company code of conduct that "serves as a guideline for how we work with our clients, each other, and our business partners and communities." This guiding set of principles outlines the ethical standards of Hewitt regarding legal and regulatory standards as well as company values such as honesty, trust, and integrity. Included in this code is one of Hewitt's cornerstone principles: to enhance *associate engagement*. Hewitt pledges to find ways of matching employees' interests, backgrounds, and goals with comparable career opportunities at the organization. They also try to develop employee commitment through providing associates with a comprehensive benefits package that includes but is not limited to health, dental, and vision care; life insurance; retirement savings; health care spending accounts; profit sharing; 16 days of paid time off (PTO) in the first year; a volunteer program; and a tuition reimbursement plan. Hewitt is also well known for providing on-site food services where associates can eat meals whose cost is subsidized by the organization. Finally, Hewitt states a dedication to diversity. For example, the company claims a commitment to hiring and promoting a diverse workforce, recognizing the range of their clients' workforces, and promoting company diversity by engaging many community organizations, particularly those who are financially disadvantaged. They also claim to maintain a large number of diversity programs from recruiting practices to supplier diversity to business resource groups (BRGs). BRGs are forums for groups who have traditionally been underrepresented or face unique workplace challenges (Aon Hewitt, 2011). Now that you know a little bit more about what Aon Hewitt is formally about, we turn to an insider's view of work and life at the organization from Rob. We begin his story during a conversation over dinner with his coworker, Craig.

---

[2] Background information about Aon Hewitt was compiled from the Aon Hewitt website: http://www.aonhewitt.com/

WORK AND LIFE AT HEWITT: ROB'S STORY

December 1, 2010

It was a December Tuesday night in the Lincolnshire, Illinois, offices of Aon Hewitt. Rob and Craig were sitting in the cafeteria having dinner together for the second time that week. Both of them began working together just over 2 years ago after graduating from college. Rob has a degree in finance, and Craig has a degree in communication studies. Rob and Craig have had similar jobs since their arrival at Aon Hewitt, and their career paths have mirrored each other to a large degree. Both are single, but Rob recently became engaged to be married. It was 8:30 pm, and their implementation team meeting had just ended. Exhausted, they had a quick hamburger at work because it was easier than cooking at home and, more importantly, it was free.

"Craig, man, I can't believe you're quitting. You're really getting out of here?"

"Yep, tomorrow's my last day. I'm leaving you my stapler—it's all yours. It's the least I can do." Rob smiled just a bit, put some ketchup on his fries, and shook his head.

"Oh, come on Rob, what keeps you here? Why don't you look around a bit?"

Rob sighed. "Now's just not the time. I've got my wedding coming up in April, and I just got promoted. You know what's interesting, though? Before I got engaged, it was like everyone assumed that I didn't have a life. Do you know what I mean?"

"Yep, they just expect you to work late nights because you're single, like you've got nothing else to do," Craig said.

"Yeah," Rob said, "I was just expected to do stuff, right off the bat, with no thought as to what my schedule was like. Everything defaulted to me. But now it's funny. Everyone's talking about the wedding, and they are starting to take into account that I've got all of this stuff to do. It's nice but just strange."

Craig replied, "You're right. Most of the people on my client team are single, but I always noticed the married people with kids leave pretty regularly at 5:00 or 5:30 while the rest of us are there working late. Sometimes I need to leave work to do things, but I don't feel like I have a *legitimate* reason to go. What am I supposed to say? I need to get home and see my mom and dad."

Rob agreed, "Yeah, the idea that I had a personal life before this wedding never entered anybody's mind. But it's like when you get married or engaged, it trips something in your manager's head. I'm sure the slack they are giving me won't last, but spouses and kids seem to be the only responsibilities that they respect."

"You're right, Rob. Management wants to be fair, but you also have to get things done and done on time. Should be interesting to see how you are treated after you get married!"

After finishing their dinner and getting ready to head back home, Craig said, "Well, Rob, take care. I won't be too far away at school, and I'll be back here to Chicago regularly. We'll get together for that White Sox game we talked about."

"You bet," said Rob. "Take care, man. And good luck with school."

A SUMMER REUNION: REVISITING ROB

July 11, 2011

It is about 7 months later, and Craig is headed home to Chicago for part of the summer break. Craig and Rob stayed in touch, largely via e-mail. They decide to go to a baseball game and out for dinner in Chicago to catch up on Rob's experiences during these past months. After watching the White Sox lose to the Mariners 4 to 3, they head to Craig's favorite bar on the north side of Chicago, the Irish Oak, and eventually the conversation turned from baseball to Rob's recent work experiences.

"So how's work been, Rob? What does Aon Hewitt have you doing lately? How'd that promotion to the investment side work out?" Craig asked.

"For the most part, I like what I'm doing now. I analyze mutual funds. I conduct meetings and conference calls with fund managers to help clients decide what to include in their 401(k) plan. I've been doing that for about 3 months or so. And the hours are a little bit more reasonable. I don't work until 9 or 10 anymore." Rob laughed.

Craig laughed back. "That's always a good thing. It has been a busy few months for you, eh? Switching jobs, the wedding in April. . . ." said Craig.

"Don't forget we just closed on the new house, too."

"Wow. You've been busy! Good thing the new job is less stressful, huh?"

"Yeah, but one of our four group supervisors is leaving in a week. So they are in the process of chopping up his responsibilities among the rest of us, and at least for the short term, they aren't planning on any replacements. So that is looking like it might be a decent workload increase for the rest of us." Rob sighed.

"Sounds like you'll keep busy."

"It's always hectic. That's one thing that hasn't changed. You know, when Maria and I were still planning the wedding, we had to fit everything in on the weekend. And there was a lot of work picking out flowers, finding a DJ. . . ."

"I bet," said Craig. "Weddings are usually a lot of work."

"Yeah, and by time I get out of work, manage the long commute home, and eat dinner, there isn't any time to do much of anything. Even if I leave work on time, usually around 5:30, I don't get home until 7:00. And since Maria and I were married, we obviously moved into the house together, so I have to leave work by 5:30 to pick her up from the train station on her way home from work."

"Oh, well that works out kind of nice then. If you have to leave work at a certain time to pick up Maria, they can't really tell you to work late then, can they? That's got to help," Craig noted.

"Usually it's good, but it can cause problems, too. I have to be at the train station at 5:50 to pick her up, so if work is busy or traffic is bad, I'm late sometimes. There was one time in particular when Maria had to wait almost an hour because I had to finish up a report, and it caused an argument. In the end, we both knew that it wasn't my fault, but it was frustrating. And again, one of the supervisors is leaving next week, which I don't think will help."

"Probably not," Craig replied.

"You know, being in this new job is also hard. I don't feel 100% comfortable saying, 'Hey, this isn't cool how at 5:15 you always ask me to do something else and you know that I have to go pick up my wife.' They're still forming impressions of me and how I react in certain situations. I don't want to make a bad impression by saying, 'Hey, the work-life balance here isn't good.' A few of the supervisors understand. One just had a baby so he is constantly going to the doctor or things like that. He just wants to spend time with his new daughter. I completely understand, but a lot of people don't get that. They want things done—no questions asked," Rob explained.

"Yeah, when I was with Aon Hewitt, my supervisors didn't really get it either. Some of them didn't understand that you don't want to work 60 hours a week. There are other things that are important to people, and giving them time to 'have a life' might actually make them more productive, plus commuting takes time," Craig replied.

"I think the biggest thing that an employer, any employer, can do is to be understanding. They need to remember that I'll work hard when I'm here in the office but I have a life outside of work. Work isn't my life. Letting you have a life makes you a better employee instead of being bitter. I just want to be treated fairly. If my coworker can leave to pick up her son at day care, I want to be able to go get my wife on time.

"Aon Hewitt tries to have fair policies, but I think it comes down to the individual supervisor and how willing he or she is to accept that you have nonwork responsibilities. Managers need to recognize and respect that different employees have different needs and responsibilities outside of work. If you have somebody who just thinks of the short-term bottom line, you aren't going to get a lot of flexibility. But if you have somebody who *gets it,* you'll have some chance of having a life!" Rob said, exasperated.

"You're right," Craig replied.

"You know, some supervisors love working at Aon Hewitt and supposedly they do a great job. Yet in reality they aren't doing a great job. The people working under them aren't happy. You get supervisors who expect everyone under them to think and be like them. But the people who work really hard, too hard sometimes, and spend a lot of time at work are the people who get into the supervisory positions. And especially given today's economic situation, everyone's afraid to lose their jobs. There aren't too many other options out there."

"Man, it isn't easy. I don't know if I would want to be a supervisor. It would be hard. You've got people on your back pressuring you. And if you've got one employee who wants to leave early to go to a Cubs game and another who needs to take a sick kid to the doctor's office, what do you do?" Craig explained.

"You're right. You know, now I have personal stuff that I want to do. I like taking care of the new house. I like that I have the greenest lawn on the block. Getting married refocuses your personal life. You have a lot of obligations outside of work that you want to enjoy. Work is just a means to an ends. I mean I want to be successful and I enjoy my job, but your work can't be only the thing that dominates your life," Rob argued.

"I hear you, man. Well, don't you think we should probably be heading home?"

"Probably. Gotta get home to Maria!" Rob chuckled.

"All right, let's get out of here."

THE DILEMMA: THE ETHICAL CHALLENGES OF A FAMILY FRIENDLY ORGANIZATION

The ethical challenge of creating and implementing inclusive work and life policies is not an easy task for organizations, managers, and employees alike. Today, in addition to employees—married or single—with child care and elder care responsibilities, employees come to work with various personal lives and obligations. There are 96.6 million unmarried Americans over age 18, representing over 43% of the adult population (U.S. Census Bureau, 2009). Nearly 1 in 5 American women ages 40 to 44 have never had a child, compared with 1 in 10 in the 1970s (Pew Research Center, 2010). In a recent survey of 300 HR professionals conducted by the Conference Board in New York, over one quarter of respondents agreed that single employees in the United States carry more of the workload then their coworkers with children (Burn, 1998). In addition, 42% of respondents also believed that childless employees subsidize the cost of benefits for their coworkers who are parents through paying higher premiums. Yet parents and nonparents alike simply want to have both fulfilling work and personal lives.

Clearly, formal work-family programs as well as informal support from managers and coworkers are invaluable for employees with children and/or eldercare responsibilities. Yet how can work and life policy be created and implemented to be inclusive of the variety of personal obligations experienced by employees? While some organizations have experienced backlash from single or childfree employees (Flynn, 1996) and changed their previously named work-*family* programs to work-*life,* some employees and advocacy groups do not believe the changes have gone far enough or that this language change is only a "code word" for providing the same set of exclusionary family friendly benefits (Bowles, 2004).

As with all employee concerns, voicing dissent is never easy. Employees who do raise concerns about equity between single and/or childfree employees and their coworkers who are parents risk being labeled "antichild" or uncaring in today's child-centered culture in the United States (Burkett, 2000; Hays, 1996). That is, the high value our culture places on having children and raising children may serve to silence the voices of individuals who make alternative life choices. How might employees with children take advantage of organizational policies for employees with children without marginalizing employees without children? What is an organization's responsibility to its childfree workers regarding work-life policies? How can we create work environments that value all employees' personal life choices?

Rob's story asks you to consider the unintended negative consequences of well-intentioned work and family accommodations. The ethical issues raised by this case include questioning the role the organization *should* play in our private lives, equity among various employee populations, and employee power (or lack of power) to manage their work schedules in relation to their personal lives. These are complex and difficult issues to consider in relation to organizational ethics and policies. They are issues that all employees face eventually. What challenges will you face?

DISCUSSION QUESTIONS

1. What ethical responsibility do organizations have (or not have) to help their employees manage their work and family responsibilities effectively?

2. What ethical responsibility do organizations have (or not have) to help any employee, regardless of their personal relational status, to enjoy a fulfilling work and private life?

3. What ethical responsibilities do single employees without children have (or not have) to assist their coworkers when child care challenges or emergencies arise?

4. How do our definitions of what is a "legitimate" family marginalize certain employees from getting support for their work and *family* needs?

5. What ethical issues exist when organizations allow married heterosexual employees to put their spouses on their health insurance plan but do not extend this benefit to gay and lesbian employees with life partners in states where same-sex unions are illegal?

6. Is an organization acting ethically when employees with children are treated differently and more deserving of accommodation than employees who choose not to have children?

7. Should single or unmarried employees be offered work-life benefits, and if so, what options should these employees be able to choose from? Do you know of any workplaces that offer work-life benefits that appear to meet the needs of *all* employees, regardless of relational or parental status? Explain.

8. Besides employers, what other components of our society (communities, government, families) should and/or do play a role in helping individuals to have fulfilling personal and work lives?

9. Visit the website www.unmarriedamerica.org, and read about how this organization advocates for workplace rights for unmarried employees. How does this organization position the rights of unmarried employees as an ethical issue?

10. If you were an employee who had chosen a childfree lifestyle but was continually asked to work late to assist fellow employees with emergency child care responsibilities or travel at the last minute, how would you approach your supervisor or coworkers to discuss your dissatisfaction with the situation?

11. Read about some of the bottom line implications of work-life policies and how organizations can economically benefit from their successful implementation at (1) Baylin, Fletcher, and Kolb (1997), (2) A Better Balance (2010), and (3) Kossek and Friede (2005).

REFERENCES

A Better Balance. (2010). *Fact sheet: The business case for workplace flexibility.* New York: Author.

Aon Corporation. (2010, July 12). *Hewitt Associates, Inc. to merge with Aon Corporation.* Retrieved from http://www.prnewswire.com/news-releases/hewitt-associates-inc-to-merge-with-aon-corporation-98225304.html

Aon Hewitt. (2011, January 24). *Diversity.* Retrieved from http://www.hewittassociates.com/Intl/NA/en-US/AboutHewitt/Diversity/Default.aspx

Baylin, L., Fletcher, J. K., & Kolb, D. (1997). Unexpected connections: Considering employees' personal lives can revitalize your business. *Sloan Management Review, 38,* 11–19.

Bowles, S. (2004). *Single workers need work-life balance, too!* Retrieved from http://www.unmarriedamerica.org/workplace/work-life-story.htm

Burkett, E. (2000). *The baby boon: How family-friendly America cheats the childless.* New York: The Free Press.

Burn, M. (1998, April 20). Single employees: Do bosses assume that your job is your life? *Washington Post.*

Flynn, G. (1996). No spouse, no kids, no respect: Backlash, why single employees are angry. *Personnel Journal, 75,* 59–69.

Galinsky, E., Aumann, K., & Bond, J. T. (2008). *Times are changing: Gender and generation at work and at home.* New York: Work and Families Institute.

Galinsky, E. E., & Bond, J. T. (2009). *The impact of the recession on employers.* New York: Work and Families Institute.

Galinsky, E., & Friedman, B. (1991). *The handbook of work and family policies.* New York: The Conference Board.

Hays, S. (1996). *The cultural contradictions of motherhood.* New Haven, CT: Yale University Press.

Kiplinger News. (2010, September 3). *Work-life problems worsened by recession.* Retrieved from http://www.kiplinger.com/news/article.php/worklife-balance-problems-worsened-by-recession-19935764.html

Kossek, E. E., & Friede, A. (2005). The business case: Managerial perspectives on work and the family. In M. Pitt-Catsouphes, E. E. Kossek, & S. Sweet (Eds.), *The handbook of work-family: Multidisciplinary perspectives, methods, and approaches* (pp. 611–626). Mahwah, NJ: Lawrence Erlbaum.

Pew Research Center. (2010, May). *The new demography of American motherhood.* Retrieved from http://pewsocialtrends.org/files/2010/10/754-new-demography-of-motherhood.pdf

Ryan, A. M., & Kossek, E. E. (2008). Work-life policy implementation: Breaking down or creating barriers to inclusiveness? *Human Resource Management, 47,* 295–310.

U.S. Census Bureau. (2009). *American community survey.* Retrieved from http://factfinder.census.gov/servlet/DatasetMainPageServlet?_program = ACS&_submenuId = &_lang = en&_ds_name = ACS_2008_3YR_G00_&ts =

Managing the Ethical Implications of the Big Box

The Walmart Effect

Edward C. Brewer

This case examines criticisms of Walmart that its economic impact "limits the ability of local businesses to survive." The case study also examines how the company has responded to charges that it negatively affects local businesses. It raises questions regarding the effect of large businesses on other stakeholders, including whether company goals are aligned with community goals and whether the company communicates responsibly with its publics. It also addresses the utility, or consequences, of economic development and its impact on relationships with others, among other ethical perspectives.

Walmart has had a tremendous impact upon our society. Its pervasive presence has affected communities all over the United States. The first Walmart store opened in 1962 in Rogers, Arkansas. By 1970, there were 38 stores with 1,500 "associates" (employees) and sales of $44.2 million. In 1990, Walmart became the nation's number one retailer. In 2002, Walmart had the biggest single-day sales in history: $1.43 billion on the day after Thanksgiving. Today, Walmart is the world's largest retailer with 2.1 million "associates" in more than 8,800 store and club locations in 15 countries and sales of $405 billion in the fiscal year ending January 31, 2010.[1] Because of this impact, Walmart has been confronted with many ethical challenges.

One of the challenges the huge retailer has faced is to have a positive impact upon the communities it enters. Whether Walmart has acted ethically may be a matter of perspective. Certainly, Walmart does much for the communities in which it operates, but it has also faced criticism that its economic impact limits the ability of local businesses

---

Author's Note: Most of the information in this chapter was taken from the Walmart website (www.walmartstores.com) in 2004.

[1] See a complete timeline at http://www.walmartstores.com. Click "About Us" and then "History Timeline."

TABLE 3.1 The Impact of Walmart	
In 2004 Walmart claimed the following impact for the United States:	
Walmart—Economic Impact*	
Walmart Stores Inc.	
Walmart stores	1,636
Supercenters	1,093
Neighborhood markets	31
Sam's Clubs	502
Distribution centers	106
Associates employed in United States	1,043,970
Community involvement	$196 million
Total amount spent with U.S. suppliers	$107 billion
Total federal, state, and local taxes paid	$1.2 billion
Sales taxes collected and remitted	$8.5 billion

Source: http://www.walmartstores.com (Accessed April 1, 2004).

*Total state and local taxes paid include real estate, personal property, other taxes and licenses, unemployment, use, and state income taxes. Sales taxes collected and remitted are state and local sales tax collected by Walmart and remitted to government authorities.

to survive.[2] This case study will examine some of the issues and explain how Walmart has responded to them. It is up to the reader, then, to determine the ethical qualities of Walmart's communication and actions. Does Walmart show ethical consideration to the communities it enters? Do the communities have an ethical obligation to embrace Walmart or fight Walmart? Is Walmart destroying jobs and communities or helping to revitalize them? Does the big-box retail model, which Walmart has perfected, cause an ethical dilemma for local communities?

THE WALMART PHILOSOPHY

By the end of the fiscal year ending January 31, 2010, the number of stores and distribution centers had grown from 3,368 to over 3,600, and the number of associates in the United States had grown from 1.04 million to 1.4 million. Here are the figures in the United States alone: Walmart and the Walmart foundation gave more than $467 million in cash and in-kind gifts in fiscal year ending 2010 (FYE '10)—an $89 million increase over the previous year's giving. At a time when food banks are being accessed more than ever,

---

[2] See economic impact statements for all 50 states as well as the national numbers by going to http://www.walmartstores.com and searching their entire site for "economic impact" at the top right of their home page.

Walmart doubled donations to Feeding America, giving more than 127 million pounds of nutritious food to U.S. food banks, the equivalent of nearly 100 million meals (Walmart Corporate, n.d.-b).

According to their website, Walmart stores are committed to their communities:

> Wal-Mart Stores, Inc. believes each Wal-Mart store, SAM'S CLUB, and distribution center has a responsibility to contribute to the well being of the local community. Our more than 3,400 locations contributed more than $150 million to support communities and local non-profit organizations. Customers raised an additional $75 million with the help of our stores and clubs.[3]

Wal-Mart also claims that their philosophy is to do good works:

> Wal-Mart's Good Works community involvement program is based on the philosophy of operating globally and giving back locally. In our experience, we can make the greatest impact on communities by supporting issues and causes that are important to our customers and associates in their own neighborhoods. We rely on our associates to know which organizations are the most important to their hometowns, and we empower them to determine how Wal-Mart Foundation dollars will be spent. Consequently, our funding initiatives are channeled directly into local communities by associates who live there.

Walmart's approach to implementing this community involvement (again according to their website, previously noted) is as follows:

> unique, combining both financial and volunteer support. We encourage our associates to be involved in their local communities and to support the programs that are making a positive difference. In addition, associates conceive and carry out creative fundraising efforts on behalf of local charitable causes, particularly Children's Miracle Network (CMN) and the 170-plus children's hospitals nationwide that receive support from CMN.

Walmart does fund a number of programs to support communities and local nonprofit organizations. In 2004, they claimed to have given the following[4]:

- More than $88 million in community grants
- More than $265 million in 15 years for Children's Miracle Network (CMN)
- More than $184 million in 19 years to United Way chapters
- $80 million in scholarships since 1979
- $1.7 million in Environmental Grants

---

[3] You can find Walmart's philosophy concerning their commitment to communities by going to their website at http://www.walmartstores.com

[4] From this site (http://www.walmartfoundation.org/wmstore/goodworks/scripts/index.jsp), click "Recent Initiatives."

- $3.1 million in Volunteerism Always Pays grants
- $20 million raised and contributed during the 2002 holidays

Go to the Walmart website today (http://www.walmartstores.com) and click the "Community and Giving" button, and then "The Walmart Foundation" button, and you can see the myriad recipients of grants from Walmart. They have committed $2 billion cash and in-kind to hunger relief in America. You can also see a list of major contributions—65 recipients of $250,000 or more (43 recipients of over $1 million).

COMMUNITY COMPLAINTS

Clearly Walmart has participated in helping to make communities better, but there is another side to the story as well. In his book, *In Sam We Trust,* Bob Ortega (1998) suggested that Walmart is devouring America. Among other issues, Representative George Miller's (D-CA) (2004) 25-page report by the Democratic Staff of the Committee on Education and the Workforce, U.S. House of Representatives, suggests that Walmart's low wages and unaffordable or unavailable health care cost taxpayers money. In recent years, the downtown areas of many towns have been suffering as communities have become increasingly suburban. According to critics, Walmart often contributes to the decline of the downtown of small towns because they build stores at the outskirts of towns, drawing traffic away from the downtown areas.

Downtown Deterioration

For example, Wilmington, Ohio (a community of about 10,000 when Walmart moved in), saw the decline of their downtown as the traffic flow headed west of town, toward the shopping center that housed Walmart. The Kmart on the eastern edge of town eventually shut down because of the competition. Clinton Art Craft, a small craft store in downtown Wilmington, soon discovered that Walmart was selling craft supplies to customers at a lower price than they could purchase them from their suppliers. Walmart's return policy was also problematic for Clinton Art Craft. Their suppliers would not take back returned items like suppliers did for Walmart. Customers would often get agitated when Clinton Art Craft wouldn't (because they couldn't afford to) have the same return policy as Walmart. Other downtown establishments experienced similar problems and, as a result, they shut down. Businesses moved to the western edge of town, away from the downtown area, to be closer to the Walmart traffic. Clinton Art Craft was able to stay in business in part because their service, with special attention to the customer, maintained a loyal customer base. However, some of those customers began going to Clinton Art Craft for advice and then heading to Walmart to buy the materials they needed. Clinton Art Craft was forced to add an additional focus to their business (framing and matting) in order to survive. They did survive and thrive but only because they were able to adapt to the environment Walmart created. It was difficult for a mom-and-pop store run by a husband and wife with an occasional part-time employee to make such adaptations. Resources were limited. Clinton Art Craft survived for over 35 years (until the couple's retirement). For a small business, that is quite a feat, especially in the wake of Walmart's impact on a small town.

The Nevada Small Business Association has claimed that Walmart practices "predatory pricing" to destroy smaller competitors (Reed, 2000). According to Ronna Bolante (2003), "Hawaii [small business] retailers have learned how to co-exist with big boxers: Don't compete with 'em" (p. 16). The plan is to find a niche of different products and services that will not be in competition with Walmart. However, "that's easier said than done, considering Wal-Mart and Sam's Club sell almost everything under the sun" (Bolante, 2003, p. 16). In a town in Colorado, the local government gives Walmart credit for turning the economy around:

> In Sterling, officials point to the local Wal-Mart, which opened a decade ago and expanded to Supercenter in 1995, as a key to turning around a once moribund economy. "They draw from a large geographic area," said City Manager Jim Thomas. "I see license plates from Kansas, Nebraska, and Wyoming." (Peterson, 2002, p. 20)

But while public officials feel the town has benefited from Walmart's presence, local business owners are not of the same opinion:

> To be sure, some of the benefits reaped from Sterling's Wal-Mart have come at the expense of local businesses. "When they come to town, if you're in competition with them, you're going to feel it," said Larry Hilty, proprietor of the Sterling Grocery Mart. "They just tear you up."
>
> When the Supercenter opened, Hilty's business suffered an immediate 50 percent drop in sales. "I'm surviving," he said, "but it'll never be back to what it was." (Peterson, 2002, p. 20)

Small towns all over the country have felt the impact of Walmart. This is not a new phenomenon. Walmart began having a tremendous impact on communities in the 1980s. For example, by the late 1980s, Iowa had felt the effects of the growing retail giant. According to an article by Edward O. Welles (1993), "Iowa towns within a 20-mile radius felt [Walmart's] pull. Their retail sales declined by 17.6% after five years"(para. 13).

But it wasn't just the retail stores that suffered. The specialty stores also felt the impact. The only hope for small merchants was to find a niche. Because of Walmart's size and strength with suppliers (which has grown tremendously since the late 1980s), the burden has been on the small business owner to change and adapt. Even if they had successful businesses, providing the same goods and products for as long as 50 years, small merchants have been forced to adapt to survive as Walmart enters their territory.

As Walmart prepared to enter Maine in the early 1990s, Ken Stone, a professor of economics at Iowa State University, traveled to the state to give them some advice:

> His advice was simple and direct: don't compete directly with Wal-Mart; specialize and carry harder-to-get and better-quality products; emphasize customer service; extend your hours; advertise more. (Welles, 1993, para. 25)

Merchants in small-town Maine had similar concerns to the Ohio and Iowa merchants—"that Wal-Mart would accelerate the drift of business out of downtown" (Welles, 1993, para. 48). In the minds of merchants, however, the impact goes beyond simply business. One Maine merchant put it this way:

> There's no argument that you can get a damn light bulb for 10 cents cheaper at Wal-Mart than you can at John Hichborns [sic] hardware store. But do people know that John Hichborn is a major contributor to Elmhurst [a local trade school for the handicapped]? He works at finding jobs for people from Elmhurst. If Hichborn goes out of business because people want a cheaper light bulb, then you lose more than just the tax revenues that business generated. (Welles, 1993, para. 69)

Walmart has been the topic of discussion at many Main Street associations across the nation. "'Wal-Mart has gone a long way to reduce opportunity for downtowns to be successful as far as traditional retailers,' said Bob Wilson, director of program services for the Mississippi Main Street Association" (Gillette, 2002, p. 16). Wilson went on to explain the following:

> It is a phenomenon a lot of downtowns are going through. A lot of areas have seen the short-term retail tax increases that happen when Wal-Mart comes to town, but it is not a long-term solution. Full-time jobs are replaced by part-time jobs with no benefits. And more employees come from surrounding areas so they don't really have that economic boost to the community. (Gillette, 2002, p. 16)

According to Wilson, Walmart does not have loyalty to the communities it enters and has no problem abandoning its original building in town to move to a larger facility with better traffic flow at the outskirts of town, with no concern as to whether or not it remains in the same taxing district (Gillette, 2002).

BEYOND THE SMALL-TOWN COMMUNITIES

But it is not just small towns and businesses that are affected. Walmart entered the grocery market with its "supercenters" around the Chicago area:

> The Jewel and Piggly Wiggly stores serving Antioch will be the first local grocers to feel the Wal-Mart effect. Eventually, the impact will spread to all Chicago-area grocery stores, including two other major combination discount/grocery chains, Meijer Inc., and Target Corp. (Murphy, 2004, para. 6)

The impact can be brutal for business owners. "In exurban Sycamore, Brown County Market lost 40% of its sales after a Wal-Mart Supercenter opened in nearby DeKalb in the late 1990s" (Murphy, 2004, para. 8). The store's owner laments one of the issues: "'I pay my grocery clerks $13 an hour plus benefits. Wal-Mart pays $7 an hour with no benefits,' says owner Daniel Brown. 'It's hard for me to compete against that'" (Murphy, 2004, para. 9). It is interesting to note, though, that 7 years later, Walmart's corporate fact sheet (Walmart Corporate, n.d.-a) states that the average, full-time hourly wage for Walmart stores is $11.75. The fact sheet indicates it is even higher in urban areas and that associates can receive performance-based bonuses.

It sounds like Walmart has made positive headway in the past decade. The corporate fact sheet found through the Walmart website (Walmart Corporate, n.d.-a) even states the following:

> Walmart is a diverse employer with more than 257,000 African-American associates; more than 41,000 Asian and 5,900 Pacific Islander associates; more than 171,000 Hispanic associates; more than 16,000 American Indian and Alaskan Native associates; more than 869,000 women; and more than 430,000 mature associates who are 50 and older.

However, on December 6, 2010, the Supreme Court agreed to hear Walmart Stores, Inc.'s bid to block a massive class-action lawsuit alleging that the retailing giant discriminated against as many as 1.5 million female employees (Bravin & Zimmerman, 2010). On June 20, 2011, the Supreme Court decided 5–4 in favor of Walmart. So the opinions seem mixed.[5]

Recently, an article in *Fast Company* discussed the impact of Walmart's low prices on its suppliers. A gallon-sized jar of Vlasic pickles sold for $2.97. What a deal! Fishman (2003) put it this way:

> Therein lies the basic conundrum of doing business with the world's largest retailer. By selling a gallon of kosher dills for less than most grocers sell a quart, Wal-Mart may have provided a service for its customers. But what did it do for Vlasic? The pickle maker had spent decades convincing customers that they should pay a premium for its brand. Now Wal-Mart was practically giving them away. And the fevered buying spree that resulted distorted every aspect of Vlasic's operations, from farm field to factory to financial statement. (p. 70)

Because Walmart has grown so big, it has developed the power to determine suppliers' prices. They put the pressure on suppliers to lower their prices, and because Walmart has such a big market share of retail sales, the suppliers concede to the Walmart way of doing things. Walmart offers to deliver low prices to consumers. The enticement to small towns is to make them feel as if they have some of the same amenities as a big city. After Walmart has descended on a town and local businesses (hardware stores, dime stores, clothing stores, etc.) have disappeared, Walmart offers to make things even better. Leslie "Buzz" Davis (2003) put it the following way:

> Later the Wal-Mart front man swoops into your little town, slaps you on your back and says, "Boys, have I got something you are going to love: a Supercenter!

---

[5] For reactions and points of view about the Supreme Court decision, see Biskupic (2011), Richey (2011), and Wal-Mart's Class Victory (2011).

This baby will be the size of four football fields and have everything you need to live except a birthing room and a funeral parlor. You won't ever have to shop anywhere else again. Aren't you lucky we chose your little city for all those great jobs the Supercenter will bring? And all that tax base we're just giving you free? Because you are such nice guys, I am going to throw in a large, late model used car lot at this Supercenter. This is a new business we are going into and you'll love it. Why, you'll be living just like those folks in the big city! Gee, aren't you lucky I came to town?" (para. 6)

Perhaps Davis's tone is a bit cynical, but there is an element that rings true. It all depends upon your perspective. Community members in Bristol, Tennessee, lost a battle to the retail giant on a rezoning issue. An online editorial titled "Bristol Wal-Mart Controversy" (n.d.) reported the following:

As accusations of "back room deals" and community anger fly in Bristol, city officials decide to sue citizens for opposing their despotic rule. All of this boils down to locating a Wal-Mart "super center" adjacent to two subdivisions and rezoning the property for business to accommodate them. Bristol goes even beyond "good old boy" politics to new lows. Citizens never had a chance.

ECONOMIC SPIN-OFF

Yet, Walmart has grown to be such a behemoth exactly because it has given customers what they wanted (or at least thought they wanted)—low prices and convenience. One can head to the local Walmart and do virtually all of one's shopping in one huge building. It is often possible to find a reasonable substitution for those specialty items that can't be found at Walmart. But if low prices are causing other local merchants to go out of business, are the conveniences that Walmart provides worthwhile in the long run? There is a whole other side to this community economic impact in terms of the economic spin-off of a dollar spent at Walmart versus a dollar spent at other local merchants. There have been myriad stories about low wages and minimal benefits provided to Walmart "associates," not to mention the hiring of illegal aliens or the fact that China has become a major supplier for the retail giant that used to tout that it only carried products that were made in America.

In 2004, Walmart's average employee worked a 30-hour week and earned about $11,700 a year, which was nearly $2,000 below the poverty line for a family of three (Miller, 2004; Wal-Mart Watch, n.d.). Only 38% of "associates" have company-provided health coverage—as compared to the national average of over 60% (Miller, 2004; United Food and Commercial Workers Union [UFCW] Local 227, n.d.; UFCW Local 770, n.d.; Wal-Mart Watch, n.d.). According to the United Food and Commercial Workers (UFCW) International Union Local 227 (n.d.), "Wal-Mart has increased the premium cost for workers by over 200% since 1993—medical care inflation only went up 50% in the same period."

Furthermore, the UFCW Local 227 (n.d.) indicated that "[t]he Walton family [owner of Wal-Mart] is worth about $102 billion—less than 1% of that could provide affordable health care for associates." There have also been a number of class action lawsuits against Walmart for underpaying associates by not paying them for overtime and making them work through daily scheduled 15-minute breaks. In addition, there is a suit alleging that Walmart "systematically deprived illegal workers of labor-law protections during at least the last three years" (Rasansky, 2003, p. 34). There is evidence that Walmart actually destroys more jobs than it creates and lowers community standards. "Research shows that for every two jobs created by a Wal-Mart store, the community loses three" (Flagstaff Activist Network, 2004; UFCW Local 227, n.d.; UFCW Local 770, n.d.; Wal-Mart Watch, n.d.).

However, as of 2010, the Walmart fact sheet (Walmart Corporate, n.d.-a) claims that "Walmart insures more than 1.2 million associates and family members making us among the nation's largest providers of private sector health insurance." Walmart also claims that in 2009 hourly associates received approximately $2 billion through financial incentives, including bonuses, profit sharing, and 401(k) contributions in addition to hundreds of millions of merchandise discounts and contributions to the associate stock purchase plan. And at the average of $11.75 an hour that Walmart employees earn, a 30-hour work week would net a little over $18,000 per year. This is still below the $22,000 poverty line for a family of three in a one-earner household, but a two-earner household would earn over $36,000 per year (over $40,000 if working 40-hour weeks).

Over the years, Walmart has touted their "buy America" program, yet over 80% of the clothing sold in their stores is produced overseas (Flagstaff Activist Network, 2004; UFCW Local 227, n.d.; UFCW Local 770, n.d.; Wal-Mart Watch, n.d.). In order to keep costs low enough to keep them in Walmart stores, suppliers are often forced to move their production overseas. This outsourcing has become more widespread in part because Walmart is big enough to demand the prices it desires from its suppliers. A Salt Lake City paper addresses this issue:

> The millions of people flocking to the Wal-Marts, etc., in order to save $0.11 per roll of toilet paper have exactly the same motivation as Corporate America has in seeking a lower price for what it wants to buy. This is not to say that outsourcing American jobs to China or India is OK. In fact, this newspaper has for many years been on record as not supporting that notion. It is, however, to say that if outsourcing is not OK because of the devastating impact on parts of our population, then the local government cooperation with the spread of the Wal-Mart virus is not OK either. ("Outsourcing American jobs," 2004)

COMMUNITY SATISFACTION

However one wants to criticize Walmart, though, one would be hard pressed to find some-one who has not purchased from a Walmart store. The other side of the argument is that Walmart does indeed help communities and give them exactly what they desire—low prices and convenience. It saves the customer time because he or she can consolidate shopping needs. Why go to four or five different stores when you can get everything you need at Walmart? Often, you will be able to purchase the same brand for less money as well. Some suggest that Walmart is good for consumers, business, and the economy. An article in *Advertising Age* ("Wal-Mart Creates Winners All 'Round," 2003) claimed, "Wal-Mart functions as the consumer's advocate and purchasing agent, badgering suppliers to get the best deal." The article further argued, "Economists say low Wal-Mart prices help keep inflation in check, and its efficiencies have been pushed down the supply chain, further improving productivity." Sheila Danzey (2002) opined that the St. Thomas (New Orleans) housing development would greatly benefit from a proposed Walmart in a "formerly troubled high crime-devalued neighborhood" through a proposed tax increment financing (TIF) plan that would help in the rebuilding of St. Thomas.

CUSTOMER CHOICE

Karen De Coster and Brad Edmonds (2003) dispelled some of the rumors often heard about Walmart, such as coming to town and selling below cost until the competition is gone and then jacking up the prices. De Coster and Edmonds argued that if community members want to discourage the acceptance of Walmart in their town, "they have scores of non-bullying options to pick from in order to try and persuade their fellow townsfolk that a new Wal-Mart is not the best option" (para. 16). The authors suggested that it is not easy to convince people to trade convenience for "the sake of undefined moral purposes" (para. 17). Certainly the growth of Walmart is evidence of what the American public as a whole value:

> To be sure, if Americans didn't love Wal-Mart so much it wouldn't be sitting at the top of the 2002 Fortune 500 with $219 billion in revenues. And we do love Wal-Mart. We love it because it gives us variety and abundance. We love it because it saves us time and wrangling. And we love it because no matter where we are, it's always there when we need it. (De Coster & Edmonds, 2003, para. 22)

BUSINESS SUCCESS

Walmart is big. Davis (2003) suggested that retailers of such size tend to monopolize markets:

> Wal-Mart is on its way to monopolizing the retail discount store and grocery trades. Over 1.4 million people now work for Wal-Mart. It's three times larger than General Motors. It's the largest private employer in the United States and the largest employer in over 20 states. It already has nearly 50 percent of the discount retail market. It already is the largest grocery store business in America. The company grosses over $250 billion a year, with profits over $8 billion per year. It is the largest corporation in the world. Wal-Mart is mean and hungry for more. Why stop at $500 billion in sales? Why not try for $1 trillion in sales and have 6 million employees? (para. 8)

Actually, according to their website, in the fiscal year ending in January 31, 2010, Walmart reported over $405 billion in sales through the operation of more than 4,300 facilities with more than 2.1 million associates worldwide. But isn't that the American way—to want more? In fact, accumulating more wealth is one of the things De Coster and Edmonds (2003) suggested Walmart helps enable its customers to do:

> Families who shop carefully at Wal-Mart can actually budget more for investing, children's college funds, or entertainment. And unlike other giant corporations, Wal-Mart stores around the country make an attempt to provide a friendly atmosphere by spending money to hire greeters, who are often people who would have difficulty finding any other job. This is a friendly, partial solution to shoplifting problems; the solution K-mart applied ("Hey, what's in that bag?") didn't work as well. (para. 19)

Edwin A. Locke (2004), dean's professor emeritus of leadership and motivation at the University of Maryland at College Park and a senior writer for the Ayn Rand Institute in Irvine, California, suggested, "Wal-Mart is one of the most impressive success stories in the history of business" (p. 32). He bemoaned the fact that Walmart is so often criticized for running its business effectively and attracting "hoards of customers." Locke (2004) admitted that Walmart has been successful in competing against other stores, but suggested it does this by "discovering new ways of using computer systems and other technology to manage its inventory and costs better and to reap the benefits of economy of scale" (p. 32). Walmart, according to Locke (2004), has earned its success:

> Wal-Mart is especially popular among low-income shoppers who cannot afford the prices of the more upscale stores. It has put other stores out of business, but that is the way capitalism works. The automobile replaced the horse and buggy. Sound motion picture replaced the silents. No one has a "right" to business success or a "right" to be protected from competitors through government intervention. One only has a right to try to compete through voluntary trade. In a free economy, companies that offer the best value for the dollar win and the losers invest their money elsewhere. (p. 32)

Locke believes Walmart should be admired rather than feared and that communities should thank Walmart for being so good at giving customers what they want.

A HELPING HAND

Walmart claims to contribute to the well-being of communities. Between January 1996, the year Walmart began posting pictures of missing children in the lobbies of Walmart facilities, and January 2010, 10,409 children have been featured, and 8,716 have been recovered.[6] It is clear that Walmart does much in the way of scholarships and philanthropy

---

[6] See the Walmart Missing Children's Network at http://www.walmartstores.com/AboutUs/212.aspx

in addition to offering convenience and low prices. Walmart's rhetoric centers on the three basic beliefs that Sam Walton established in 1962:

1. Respect for the Individual

2. Service to Our Customers

3. Strive for Excellence

If you are in a Walmart store at the right time, you can hear raucous sounds from the back of the store as the "associates" perform the Walmart cheer:

Give me a W!

Give me an A!

Give me an L!

Give me a Squiggly!

Give me an M!

Give me an A!

Give me an R!

Give me a T!

What's that spell?

Walmart!

Whose Walmart is it?

My Walmart!

Who's number one?

The Customer! Always!

A MATTER OF PERSPECTIVE

From the perspective of the Walmart executives and many patrons, it's all about the customer and the community. But often the community leaders have a different perspective. The *Economist* ("My Wal-Mart 'Tis of Thee," 1996) put it as follows:

Like America itself, Sam Walton's monument excites strong reactions. People are wary of this superpower. They mistrust its motives, fear its cultural clout, deride its brashness and scoff at its contradictions. Yet they also marvel at its convenience and admire its success. And, as with America, the people keep coming. (para. 15)

Refrigerated and Frozen Foods Retailer named Walmart their retailer of the year in 2009. Warren Thayer (2009) put it this way:

The Bentonville, Ark., chain executes well on nearly every level. It understands shoppers and meets their needs. And vendors give Wal-Mart high marks as a trading partner for its integrity and directness, making its money on the sale rather than on the buy. (p. 14)

Thayer (2009) went on to say the following:

We can't quibble with any of that. In fact, we'll go even further and say that Wal-Mart doesn't get enough credit for much of the good that it does. It has taken industry-leading positions on sustainability, diversity and charitable giving. When there's a national disaster, Wal-Mart is literally on the front lines. (p. 14)

It is a challenge to balance truth and loyalty to both customers and employees. It is not easy to determine the difference between duty (for employees, customers, and the community) and rights. Virtue may have a different meaning for the stockholder than it does to the competitor. Walmart now has a global reach and impact. This big-box retailer surely seems to be the store we "love to hate." Does Walmart communicate and act in an ethical manner? You make the call.

DISCUSSION QUESTIONS

1. Should Walmart be expected to protect small businesses in the communities within which it operates?

2. What does it mean for an organization to be ethical in its communication and practices?

3. Does Walmart truly harm the downtown areas of small communities, or does it just offer a challenge to change what is uncomfortable for the local merchants?

4. What kind of experience have you had with the local Walmart, and do you go there often?

5. Does Walmart's rhetoric communicate a different message than its actions?

6. Are Walmart's persuasive tactics concerning its value to communities ethical in approach and intention?

7. What other local organizations have had positive or negative impacts on communities?

8. How would you characterize the culture of Walmart?

REFERENCES

Biskupic, J. (2011, June 21). Supreme Court limits Walmart sex bias case. *USA Today*. Retrieved from EBSCOhost database.

Bolante, R. (2003, September). Friend or foe? How Wal-Mart will change urban Honolulu. *Hawaii Business*, 16–20.

Bravin, J., & Zimmerman, A. (2010, December 7). Wal-Mart case tests class rules. *Wall Street Journal*, p. B1.

Bristol Wal-Mart controversy. (n.d.). Retrieved from http://www.sullivan-county.com/id2/wal-mart/

Danzey, S. (2002, January 21). Why we win with Wal-Mart. *New Orleans CityBusiness*, p. 29.

Davis, L. B. (2003, September 1). Wal-Mart threatens our way of life, must be unionized [Editorial]. *Capital Times*. Retrieved from http://www.highbeam.com/doc/1G1-107145592.html

De Coster, K., & Edmonds, B. (2003, January 31). The case for Wal-Mart. *Ludwig von Mises Institute*. Retrieved from http://mises.org/daily/1151

Fishman, C. (2003, December). The Wal-Mart you don't know: Why low prices have a high cost. *Fast Company*, 67–80.

Flagstaff Activist Network. (2004). *Wal-Mart myths and reality*. Retrieved from http://www.flagstaffactivist.org/campaigns/walmyths.html

Gillette, B. (2002, June 10–16). Small town retailers finding ways to compete with big chains. *Mississippi Business Journal*, p. 16.

Locke, E. A. (2004, February 20). Thwarting Wal-Mart is simply un-American. *The Central New York Business Journal, 18*(8), 32.

Miller, G. (D-CA). (2004, February 16). *Everyday low wages: The hidden price we all pay for Wal-Mart*. A report by the democratic staff of the Committee on Education and the Workforce, U.S. House of Representatives. Retrieved from http://democrats.edworkforce.house.gov/publications/WALMARTREPORT.pdf

Murphy, H. L. (2004, March 15). Wal-Mart set to launch grocery invasion here. *Crain's Chicago Business 27*(11), 9. Retrieved from EBSCOhost database.

My Wal-Mart 'tis of thee. (1996, November 23). *The Economist, 341*(7993). Retrieved from EBSCOhost database.

Ortega, B. (1998). *In Sam we trust*. New York: Times Business/Random House.

Outsourcing American jobs: Wal-Marts and the quality of life. (2004, March 8–14). *The Enterprise,* 24.

Peterson, E. (2002, November). Wal-Mart's fans and foes. *ColoradoBiz*, pp. 18–20, 22.

Rasansky, J. (2003, December 5–11). Always lower prices? Wal-Mart could face epic battle over unpaid overtime claims. *Fort Worth Business Press,* 34.

Reed, V. (2000, January 10). Small business group decries chamber position on Wal-Mart. *Las Vegas Business Press,* 3.

Richey, W. (2011, June 20). Supreme Court rules in Wal-Mart's favor: How the sides are reacting. *Christian Science Monitor.* Retrieved from EBSCOhost database.

Thayer, W. (2009, June). Walmart our retailer of the year. *Refrigerated & Frozen Foods Retailer, 7*(5), 14–22.

United Food and Commercial Workers International Union Local 227. (n.d.). Retrieved from http://www.ufcw227.org/organizing/walmart.htm

United Food and Commercial Workers International Union Local 770. (n.d.). Retrieved from http://www.ufcw770.org/index.html

Wal-Mart creates winners all 'round. (2003, October 6). *Advertising Age, 74*(40), 20.

Wal-Mart Watch. (n.d.). *Bad neighbor fact sheet.* Retrieved from http://www.walmartwatch.com/bad/page.cfm?subsection_id = 108

Wal-Mart's Class Victory. (2011, June 21). *Wall Street Journal*, p. A14. Retrieved from EBSCOhost database.

Walmart Corporate. (n.d.-a). *Corporate fact sheet.* Retrieved from http://walmartstores.com/pressroom/factsheets/

Walmart Corporate. (n.d.-b). *Walmart Foundation fact sheet.* Retrieved from http://walmartstores.com/pressroom/factsheets/

Welles, E. O. (1993, July). When Wal-Mart comes to town. *Inc., 15*(7), 76–83. Retrieved from http://www.walmartstores.com/wmstore/wmstores/HomePage.jsp

Just Window Dressing?

The Gap (RED) Campaign

Michelle Amazeen

This case explores the extent to which a corporate social responsibility (CSR) campaign creates alignment between a company's mission and specific actions. It considers how tensions between the conflicting values of profits versus social ideals are common among many of today's organizations seeking to strengthen reputation and brand through CSR initiatives. The case also raises questions about CSR initiatives that increase consumerism and, in turn, produce negative impacts on society.

Sure, CSR talks the talk. But does it walk the walk? This case study takes a close look at how one CSR campaign does or does not align its words with its deeds. It is no surprise that many corporations today tout a virtuous line concerning how they care about society. It costs little to proclaim a policy of "caring for the world" and finding a fig leaf "cause" to cover the otherwise "heartless" perception of a profit-seeking company. Yet, after all, the corporation may truly be sincere. Some argue that morality resides in people, not inert corporations (Maynard, 2001), but it may just be the case that the corporate leadership earnestly believes in "doing good." To disentangle the lines of intent and to discover, if possible, the true motivation for launching a CSR campaign, this case study examines the Gap (RED) campaign.

CSR has become increasingly important as globalization becomes a central concern of nongovernmental organizations (NGOs) (Bronn & Vrioni, 2001; McGuire, Sundgren, & Schneeweis, 1988; Sen & Bhattacharya, 2001). While the social responsibility of a business was once arguably limited to increasing its profits (Friedman, 1970), today's environment suggests corporations must go beyond merely considering their profits by also accounting for the social costs and benefits of their presence around the world (Esrock & Leichty, 1998; McGuire et al., 1988; Perlmutter, 1991; Stiglitz, 2006). In Stiglitz's (2006) examination of the efficacy of globalization, he noted the vilification of the multinational corporation as "greedy, heartless entities that place profit above all else" (p. 187, also see Chua, 2004). To combat this notion, he argued that corporations must take into account how their actions impact employees, the environment, and the communities in which they operate.

Author's Note: An expanded version of this case first appeared as "Gap RED: Social Responsibility Campaign or Window Dressing?" in the *Journal of Business Ethics* (DOI:10.1007/s10551-010-0647-2).

Although CSR marketing has become increasingly popular, it is not a new concept. American Express began one of the first cause-related marketing campaigns in 1983. During this campaign, the Statue of Liberty restoration project received one penny for every purchase by a cardholder. American Express card usage increased 27%, card applications rose 45%, and $1.7 million was donated to the cause. However, the Product (RED) campaign has reportedly brought CSR marketing to a new level as one of the largest consumer-based, income-generating programs by the private sector for a global humanitarian cause (Nixon, 2008). This case study suggests that in the 21st century not only is CSR a necessary component of current business practice (see Bronn & Vrioni, 2001), but it must also be communicated as a genuine gesture of truthful social consciousness and not simply a disingenuous marketing ploy. Exemplifying a global CSR effort, the U.S.-based Gap clothing retailer was one of the original participants in the Product (RED) campaign. This case examines the extent to which the Gap's participation in the Product (RED) initiative positions the company as socially accountable. Alignment between the Product (RED) mission statement and the Gap's stated objectives is investigated along with whether or not the Gap adhered to the standards it attempted to project with this campaign. Tensions between the conflicting values of profits versus social ideals will become evident. Specifically, if the Gap's (RED) products are the "right" way to manufacture clothing, why isn't all Gap merchandise manufactured in the same way? How can a company strive to achieve socially responsible ideals without putting itself at a competitive disadvantage? Do CSR campaigns such as Product (RED) obscure the connection between consumerism and its negative impacts on society?

THE (RED) CAMPAIGN

Announced in January 2006, by cofounders Bono and Bobby Shriver, the Product (RED) website (n.d.) positioned its virtue as "When you buy (RED), you save lives." According to the campaign's website, "(RED) is a business model created to raise awareness and money for The Global Fund by teaming up with well-known brands to produce (PRODUCT) RED branded products." It was created to engage the private sector, primarily consumers, in the fight against AIDS in Africa. The website clearly stated that Product (RED) was neither a charity nor a cause. It was positioned as an idea to transform the collective power of consumers into a financial force to help others in need.

Participating companies, referred to on the website as "partners," licensed the use of the Product (RED) name and produced (RED)-branded merchandise or services. These (RED) products were promoted by Product (RED) using the licensing fees collected from partners. When consumers purchased these products, a portion of the profits from the merchandise, which varied by partner, was donated to The Global Fund by the partner company. A key tenet of the campaign was that consumers did not pay extra money to purchase a (RED) product. (RED) products were priced commensurately with the cost of materials and production expenditures involved. By sacrificing a portion of its profit margin, it was the partner company that paid for the contribution to The Global Fund. The (RED) website also specifically indicated that the licensing fee did not infringe upon the amount of money donated by the partner to The Global Fund.

Funds donated by partners from the sale of (RED) products supported Global Fund programs "that positively impact the lives of people affected by HIV and AIDS in Africa. (RED) money provides access to education, nutrition, counseling, medical services, and the two pills a day individuals need to stay alive" ([RED], n.d.). As an independent financing organization governed by an international board of directors, the mission of The Global Fund, established in 2002, is to attract, manage, and disburse resources through public/private partnerships to fight AIDS, tuberculosis, and malaria. According to its website, The Global Fund (n.d.) "does not implement programs directly, relying instead on a broad network of partnerships with other development organizations on the ground to supply local knowledge and technical assistance where required." As of March 31, 2009, The Global Fund had raised over $13 billion since its inception. Among the 44 countries listed as contributors to The Global Fund, the largest contributions were made by the United States (over $3.3 billion), France (over $1.7 billion), and Japan (over $1 billion). Funds raised by NGOs totaled just under $652 million. Within this category, itemized among 11 NGOs, the Bill & Melinda Gates Foundation was the largest contributor ($450 million) followed by Product (RED) (nearly $130 million) (The Global Fund, n.d.).

The Gap's (RED) Mission

As of April, 2009, the link to the Gap's (RED) website was not prominent on its retail website. Visitors in search of the Gap's participation in the (RED) campaign had to navigate to the bottom of the main website in order to find a link labeled "Gap (PRODUCT) RED." The link resided among others such as customer service, Gap credit cards, and terms of use. Despite being one of the initial partners in the (RED) campaign, the Gap's (RED) website made no mention of this distinction. Within the "community" link on the Gap (RED) website, visitors were offered specifics about Gap Product (RED). The following explanation was offered:

Gap (Product) RED is about helping you make a difference in Africa. As a (Product) RED partner, we're contributing half the profits from Gap (Product) RED products to The Global Fund, to help women and children affected by AIDS in Africa.

Further down this webpage, under the heading "Learn More About Us," visitors were informed that the Gap's participation in the (RED) campaign was but only one of the ways in which the Gap was committed to social responsibility. A link was provided to guide visitors to the "social responsibility" page of the Gap Inc.'s corporate website.

Gap Inc.'s Commitment to Social Responsibility

The Gap's corporate website positioned their commitment to social responsibility as follows:

At Gap Inc., we believe we should go beyond the basics of ethical business practices and embrace our responsibility to people and to the planet. We believe this brings sustained, collective value to our shareholders, our employees, our customers and society.

The Gap defined its purpose as "to make it easy for you to express your personal style throughout your life." Key values guiding their success were identified as "integrity, respect, open-mindedness, quality and balance." This Purpose & Values section of their corporate website closed with this statement: "Every day, we honor these values and exemplify our belief in doing business in a socially responsible way." Thus, on their website, the foundational ethics guiding the Gap seem to support their claims regarding CSR.

Gap (RED) Advertising

Two dedicated advertising campaigns were used to support the marketing of the Gap (RED) product line. In July 2007, the introduction of the GapKids and BabyGap (PRODUCT) RED collections were supported with a celebrity ad campaign, including an execution with Abigail Breslin and the headline "Can one kid change the world?" Other phrases in this campaign included "Every Generation Has a Voice," "Every Generation Has a Heart," and "Inspire The Next Generation To Change The World" (Gap Inc., 2007a).

The second dedicated ad campaign ran in November 2007, to support the 1-year anniversary of the global Gap (RED) product launch. The photography from both campaigns was provided by Annie Leibovitz, and as with the July campaign, this campaign also showcased "a diverse cast of socially conscious celebrities" (Gap Inc., 2007b). The November campaign explicitly encouraged consumers to "Do the (RED) thing," a play on the phrase "do the right thing," which was presumably purchasing Gap (RED) clothing. The implicit message was that by modeling the behavior of these famous individuals, the consumer would be more like these socially responsible celebrities. Conversely, if one purchased an article of clothing that was not a Gap (RED) product, then one was doing the wrong thing.

In the advertising campaigns supporting Gap (RED), an implicit trichotomy was established. In one category were the heroes, the virtuous consumers who help make a difference in Africa by trying to eliminate AIDS. According to the Gap (RED) website, the money raised by the consumer's purchase funded health and community support programs in Africa, which can help save a person's life. Accordingly, the implied victims in the narrative created by these ads were the Africans who suffered from the fate of AIDS. As a propaganda technique, often the struggle between good and bad is initiated by the introduction of victims (Conway, Grabe, & Grieves, 2007). Hence, if the Gap and other like-minded consumers were the heroes trying to help the African victims, then the "bad guys" were those competitive retailers who did not offer socially conscious products and those other consumers who chose not to purchase (RED) products.

Normative points of view were advanced by the use of the virtuous/villainous role-players (Conway et al., 2007) and the "Do the (RED) thing" tagline. The message advanced by the Gap (RED) advertising was normatively situational because its logic worked only in specific situations. When consumers wanted to purchase a T-shirt, they had the option of buying one from the Gap (RED) product line that aided Africans. However, moving past T-shirts, the consumers' choices to "do the right thing" became limited. What if the consumer wanted to purchase a pair of shorts? Defenders of this promotion used the operative word *when*. *When* the consumer had the choice between a Gap (RED) product and a non-(RED) product, the choice was easy (Nixon, 2008). Contemplating further the notion of "do the right thing," this line of argument also became problematic for the Gap's entire business model. If doing the right thing was purchasing a Gap (RED) product, then why wasn't all Gap merchandise following the (RED) business model? It is here where the Gap's seemingly duty-based ethics system is apparently situational rather than foundational.

HAS THE CAMPAIGN SUCCEEDED IN ITS GOALS?

For the partners, one of the purposes of the (RED) campaign was to distinguish them from their competitors, which was facilitated by the exclusivity of the licensing arrangement (High, 2007). To be sure, the ad campaign's attempt to implicitly classify the world into good versus bad offers confirmation of this goal. Participating in Product (RED) allowed the Gap to portray their products as the socially conscious choice in the retail clothing marketplace.

Aside from competitive distinction, another explicit goal of the Gap (RED) campaign, broadly defined on the Gap Product (RED) website (n.d.), was to "help eliminate AIDS in Africa." However, because no financial goal was publicly established, one cannot determine whether or not this goal was met. Furthermore, beyond indicating that 50% of the profit from product (RED) merchandise was donated to the campaign, no specific figures were provided about the profit margin of the Gap's products. Thus, it is impossible to calculate just how much money was donated from the sale of a $25 T-shirt. While a donation to The Global Fund of $2 million to $2.5 million was estimated by a Gap spokesperson in January 2007 (Spethmann, 2007), little in the way of financial specifics was otherwise offered. In fact, the only figures provided by the Gap corporate website came in the abstract form of the number of African women and children who *could be* treated with annual antiretroviral drugs for AIDS as a result of the funds raised from Gap (RED) products (Gap Inc., 2005–2006). While the aggregated amount of contributions from the (Product) RED campaign in general was provided, the individual contribution from the Gap's participation was not. Hence, to the degree that a single dollar raised by the Gap's participation in this effort constitutes a contribution to eliminating AIDS in Africa, then this loosely stated goal was met.

The Gap's most recently available CSR report provides additional details about the goals of the Gap's participation in the (RED) campaign. Recognizing that "donations alone are unlikely to resolve the major challenges faced by developing nations," the report cited the (RED) campaign as a means for their company to create a reliable stream of revenue "that will be complementary to, but far exceed the well-intended but insufficient contributions from corporate philanthropy budgets" in the fight against AIDS in Africa (Gap Inc., 2005–2006, p. 81). Thus, to the admittedly limited degree that it is helpful, the Gap was committed to Africa on an ongoing basis—on numerous levels that will be addressed in more depth later. Continuing participation in the (RED) campaign as of this writing, in March 2011, suggests the Gap is succeeding in meeting this goal.

Another reported goal of the campaign was to raise consumer awareness about AIDS in Africa. The Gap contends that they were "engaging consumers on a critical global issue and encouraging them to become part of the solution" (Gap Inc., 2005–2006, p. 81). Using generalities to cite the quantity of inventory that had been sold as well as the publicity generated by celebrities who had endorsed the effort, their *Social Responsibility Report* stated,

"We've been very pleased and inspired by the way our customers have embraced this movement" (Gap Inc., 2005–2006, p. 81). Definitively establishing that consumer awareness was raised as a result of the Gap's participation in the (RED) campaign necessitated quantitative research utilizing pre- and post-campaign measures. If the Gap had collected this sort of information, they did not make it available for scrutiny. Thus, it was not possible to determine success on this measure either.

Finally, and most interestingly, the Gap identified establishing "ethical trade" as a goal of the (RED) campaign. The Gap indicated that, while portions of their (RED) merchandise were manufactured in Africa, the current suppliers were unable to meet the demands of their entire product line. They stated the following:

> We are actively partnering with our approved manufacturers in Lesotho and other sub-Saharan countries to help them improve their production capabilities. It's a start —and our hope is that this work will help them attract more business and ultimately build vibrant, thriving economies. (Gap Inc., 2005–2006, p. 81)

Indeed, improving factory conditions was addressed on the Gap Inc. website with references to examining their business practices and how they impact labor standards.

To determine whether this goal of "ethical trade" is mere lip service or whether sincere efforts have been made, a look at reports from Labour Behind the Label was useful. This independent organization, based in the United Kingdom, has supplied research from a coalition of development agencies, labor rights groups, and trade unions revealing what efforts garment industry companies made to improve working conditions among their suppliers. Among more than 30 retailers surveyed in 2006, the Gap was one of two companies placed in Labour Behind the Label's top performing category: "Pulling ahead." The 2006 report stated, "While they still have a long way to go, they seem to be engaging more seriously with the issues we raised" (Hearson, 2006). The 2007 report concluded, "Gap remains one of the most progressive fashion brands when it comes to labour rights" (Hearson & Morser, 2007). However, the competition was regarded as not being particularly tough, and the Gap was noted for making seemingly little progress on its commitments in the previous 12 months. Nonetheless, the report praised the Gap for its collaborative approach with trade unions, NGOs, and other brands and retailers, indicating their tactic "is just what is needed if working conditions across the sector are to improve" (Hearson & Morser, 2007). Again in 2008, the Gap was noted as one of only two retailers in the report's top category that publicly committed to a project containing all four of Labour Behind the Label's pillars of a good living wages initiative: (1) a collaborative, multi-stakeholder approach; (2) worker organizing and participation; (3) examining commercial factors throughout the whole supply chain; and (4) a clear route-map to implementing the living wage for all workers (Hearson, 2008). The positive evaluation of the Gap continued in 2009, earning one of the highest report ratings for plans that "remain impressive in depth, with research completed and work now planned in seven countries. It is the one company to ensure that trade union rights are central to its plans" (McMullen & Maher, 2009). It was noted, however, that the implementation of their plans to improve wages needs to progress more quickly. These annual reports from Labour Behind the Label suggest the Gap was sincere and was making progress in its efforts to achieve "ethical trade."

Is Gap (RED) Window Dressing?

Because it was identified as a business model rather than a cause, the Product (RED) campaign was positioned to have staying power as a marketing strategy. Instead of being a one-time, short-term event, (RED) partners were committed for at least 5 years (Spethmann, 2007). The duration of the commitment to (RED) made partners, including the Gap, less open to accusations of being less than genuine in their commitment to social responsibility.

Attempting to create increased awareness of the AIDS epidemic facing Africa on an ongoing basis rather than through a one-shot promotion was a commendable and challenging endeavor. However, Nickel and Eickenberry (2009) raised concerns about the increasing conflation of consumption, media celebration, and philanthropy. They defined the notion of "consumption philanthropy" as occurring when one purchases a service or product because of a perceived association with a charitable aspect. Increasing awareness of, and dependence on, philanthropic giving to address communal problems has not allowed philanthropy to achieve its desired transformational potential, they argued. Instead, marketized philanthropy reframes the dominant discourse by reducing the ability to recognize the connection between the marketplace and the negative impacts it has on human well-being. They believe that "marketized philanthropy is an especially insidious case because it creates the appearance of giving back, disguising the fact that it is already based in taking away" (Nickel & Eickenberry, 2009, p. 975). In isolation, the Gap's participation in the (RED) campaign is suspect from this perspective.

From their *Social Responsibility Report*, the Gap was clearly aware that social responsibility is "a new theme in today's marketplace" (Gap Inc., 2005–2006). They also recognized the awakening of consumer consciousness on this issue as well as the power of the media in drawing attention to companies' both admirable and unworthy practices. In fact, noted Maynard (2001), it is often this media attention that is most effective in policing the ethical behavior of transnational conduct. He contended that it is public exposure and the mission-statement mentality that drives a corporation to create a distinct image favoring moral behavior. Furthermore, the Gap freely admits that they knew from past experiences "the power that celebrities can bring to marketing campaigns" (Gap Inc., 2005–2006). Thus, an argument can be made that the Gap was well aware of the scrutiny they were opening themselves up to by participating in the (RED) campaign. Not only was the international music celebrity Bono the spokesman, but the Gap actually elicited additional attention by supporting their (RED) efforts with celebrities in their own advertisements. To the degree that this attention was elicited to increase sales, it was, of course, a marketing strategy. It defies the marketing "gimmick" label in that it went beyond having little relevance or use. With the glare of the media spotlight came the scrutiny from those ready to expose illegitimate claims to social responsibility.

Another useful resource in considering the legitimacy of the Gap's claims to social responsibility was the ethical reputation reports offered by Covalence, a Geneva, Switzerland-based company. Using thousands of documents from the media, enterprise, NGOs, and other sources, Covalence provides a reputation index based upon criteria including labor standards, waste management, product social utility, and human rights policies (Covalence, 2008). Twenty multinational companies (MNCs) were analyzed in each of 10 major sectors totaling approximately 200 companies classified as the largest market capitalizations in the Dow Jones World Index. Covalence provides annual rankings of the top 10 performing companies in each of three categories across all analyzed sectors. That the Gap was even included in the Covalence analysis suggests the degree of international media attention was significant, lending credence to the argument that the Gap endured considerable public scrutiny.

Covalence's "Best EthicalQuote Score" established the amount of published positive minus negative news cumulated from 2002 through 2007. Among the 20 companies within the retail sector, the Gap was ranked fifth in 2005 (Covalence, 2006), third in 2006 (Covalence, 2007), and third in 2007 (Covalence, 2008). As an absolute measure of ethical popularity, these data suggest the Gap was a leading company on ethical reputation in the retail sector by the standards of Covalence.

While data were collected for the calendar year 2008, the methodology for calculating its EthicalQuote score and rankings was revised by Covalence (Covalence, 2009), making comparison to previous years' data not possible. This illustrates another challenge facing the assessment of social responsibility: how the concept of CSR is operationalized and measured (Esrock & Leichty, 1998; Maignan & Ralston, 2002; McGuire et al., 1988; Sen & Bhattacharya, 2001). Indeed, individual firms exist, such as Covalence, which measure particular aspects of social responsibility. Furthermore, shareholder activists as well as special interest groups, like Labour Behind the Label, have their own metrics for monitoring social responsibility. But for many in corporate industry, such as Gabriella Morris, president of the Prudential Foundation, "there continue to be no good metrics in the field. Major reason, it is difficult to nearly impossible to develop objective data on accountability measures" (personal communication, April 10, 2009). In 2009, researching all the metrics of CSR was a project in itself. Finding metrics that were internationally accepted was not possible.

For other critics, it was not the authenticity of socially responsible campaigns that was problematic but the aid generated in and of itself. For Dr. Dambisa Moyo, a Zambian economist, foreign aid was bad for Africa and bad for Africans because it "keeps Africa in a supplicant's role when its governments need to become self-sufficient" (Miller, 2009). Celebrity endorsements perpetuated the dependency relationship through negative stereotyping, argued Moyo. "Instead of aid, Moyo recommends other paths to financial and democratic independence: bond issues, trade, foreign investment" (Miller, 2009). Moyo's perspective lends a particularly credible argument against the legitimacy of the Gap's (RED) campaign.

Before writing off the campaign in its entirety as window dressing, however, one ought to examine its merits in a larger context. To Moyo's points of trade and foreign investment as means to self-sufficiency for Africa, one must keep in mind one of the three publicly stated goals of the Gap's (RED) campaign: the need for ethical trade. The Gap was committed to the long-term economic development of Lesotho, a sub-Saharan African kingdom of 2 million where manufacturing accounted for approximately 75% of its total exports (Gap Inc., 2005–2006). The following was explained in the Gap's *Social Responsibility Report*:

> We advocated for the U.S. Government to pass the African Growth and Opportunities Act (AGOA), which provides preferential trading arrangements for apparel products from Lesotho into the U.S. market. We also began working with Lesotho's government, business leaders and factory workers to enhance the apparel industry's technical capabilities and responsible labor practices. (Gap Inc., 2005–2006, p. 79)

These actions demonstrate efforts to promote ethical trade. Combined with (1) the Gap's long-term commitment to the (RED) campaign; (2) its goal of increasing awareness of the AIDS epidemic in Africa, which thereby increases scrutiny of its own practices; and (3) its comparatively high ethical reputation standings in the apparel industry, all of these considerations suggest that the Gap's participation in the (RED) campaign went beyond mere window dressing.

VERDICT

In isolation, the Gap (RED) campaign was about leveraging social responsibility for capitalistic enterprise. Yet, as its website pointed out, the (RED) campaign was but one of many components in the Gap's commitment to CSR. Because dismantling the U.S. capitalistic system is unrealistic, an alternative is to operate within the existing system in as socially responsible a manner as possible. Rhetoric in support of this agenda should be critically examined to determine its legitimacy. As a start, one must look to the companies that, under public scrutiny, are genuinely committed to social change.

DISCUSSION QUESTIONS

1. Why would some argue that the Gap exemplifies an ethical organization? Why would others disagree?

2. What do you think the Gap needs to do to dispel criticisms of its (RED) campaign participation?

3. Why does the author argue that Gap (RED) ads are problematic? What do you think?

4. What might be a better ad campaign?

5. How can companies like the Gap strive to achieve socially responsible ideals without putting themselves at a competitive disadvantage? Is there a way to follow a "moral universalist" approach (Maynard, 2001) without falling victim to moral relativism necessitated in a competitive marketplace?

6. Can you think of other examples of cause marketing? Which were successful and which were not? Why? How is "success" defined?

REFERENCES

Bronn, P., & Vrioni, A. (2001). Corporate social responsibility and cause-related marketing: An overview. *International Journal of Advertising, 20*, 207–222.

Chua, A. (2004). *World on fire: How exporting free market democracy breeds ethnic hatred and global instability* (pp. 229–258). New York: Anchor Books.

Conway, M., Grabe, M., & Grieves, K. (2007). Villains, victims and the virtuous in Bill O'Reilly's "No-Spin Zone": Revisiting world war propaganda techniques. *Journalism Studies, 8*(2), 197–223.

Covalence. (2006, February 1). *Covalence ethical ranking 2005*. Geneva, Switzerland: Author. Retrieved from http://www.covalence.ch

Covalence. (2007, January 2). *Covalence ethical ranking 2006*. Geneva, Switzerland: Author. Retrieved from http://www.covalence.ch

Covalence. (2008, January 2). *Covalence ethical ranking 2007*. Geneva, Switzerland: Author. Retrieved from http://www.covalence.ch

Covalence. (2009, January 20). *Covalence ethical ranking 2008*. Geneva, Switzerland: Author. Retrieved from http://www.covalence.ch

Esrock, S., & Leichty, G. (1998). Social responsibility and corporate web pages: Self-presentation or agenda-setting? *Public Relations Review, 24*(3), 305–319.

Friedman, M. (1970, September 13). The social responsibility of business is to increase profits. *New York Times Magazine.*

Gap Inc. (2005–2006). *Social responsibility report: What is a company's role in society?* Retrieved from http://www.gapinc.com/public/documents/CSR_Report_05_06.pdf

Gap Inc. (2007a, June 21). *GapKids and BabyGap introduce new (PRODUCT) RED collections*. Retrieved from http://www.gapinc.com/public/Media/Press_Releases/med_pr_kidsbabyRED062107.shtml

Gap Inc. (2007b, October 3). *Gap introduces inspirational marketing campaign to celebrate first anniversary of global launch of Gap (PRODUCT) RED*. Retrieved from http://www.gapinc.com/public/Media/Press_Releases/med_pr_REDmarketing100307.shtml

Gap Product (RED). (n.d.). *Products that help women and children affected by HIV/AIDS in Africa.* Retrieved from http://www.gap.com/browse/home.do?cid = 16591&mlink = 5058,1066504,9&clink = 1066504

The Global Fund. (n.d.). *The global fund to fight AIDS, tuberculosis and malaria.* Retrieved from http://www.theglobalfund.org/en/

Hearson, M. (2006). *Let's clean up fashion 2006: The state of pay behind the UK high street*. Bristol, UK: Labour Behind the Label. Retrieved from http://www.labourbehindthelabel.org/resources/itemlist/category/164-reports-guides

Hearson, M. (2008). *Let's clean up fashion 2008 update: The state of pay behind the UK high street*. Bristol, UK: Labour Behind the Label. Retrieved from http://www.labourbehindthelabel.org/resources/itemlist/category/164-reports-guides

Hearson, M., & Morser, A. (2007). *Let's clean up fashion 2007 update: The state of pay behind the UK high street*. Bristol, UK: Labour Behind the Label. Retrieved from http://www.labourbehindthelabel.org/resources/itemlist/category/164-reports-guides

High, K. (2007, September 24). Bobby Shriver sees (Product) Red. *Adweek.*

Maignan, I., & Ralston, D. (2002). Corporate social responsibility in Europe and the U.S.: Insights from businesses' self-presentations. *Journal of International Business Studies, 33*(3), 497–514.

Maynard, M. (2001). Policing transnational commerce: Global awareness in the margins of morality. *Journal of Business Ethics, 30*(1), 17–27.

McGuire, J., Sundgren, A., & Schneeweis, T. (1988). Corporate social responsibility and firm financial performance. *The Academy of Management Journal, 31*(4), 854–872.

McMullen, A., & Maher, S. (2009). *Let's clean up fashion 2009: The state of pay behind the UK high street*. Bristol, UK: Labour Behind the Label. Retrieved from http://www.labourbehindthelabel.org/resources/itemlist/category/164-reports-guides

Miller, L. (2009, March 30). Thanks, Bono, but no thanks. *Newsweek*, p. 16.

Nickel, P., & Eickenberry, A. (2009). A critique of the discourse of marketized philanthropy. *American Behavioral Scientist, 52*(7), 974–989.

Nixon, R. (2008, February 6). Bottom line for (RED). *New York Times*, p. C1.

Perlmutter, H. (1991). On the rocky road to the first global civilization. *Human Relations, 44*(9), 897–920.

(RED). (n.d.). Retrieved from www.joinred.com

Sen, S., & Bhattacharya, C. (2001). Does doing good always lead to doing better? Consumer reactions to corporate social responsibility. *Journal of Marketing Research, 38*(2), 225–243.

Stiglitz, J. (2006). The multinational corporation. In J. Stiglitz (Ed.), *Making globalization work* (pp. 187–210). New York: W. W. Norton.

Spethmann, B. (2007, January 1). The RED brigade. *Promo*, p. 18.

PART II

Dialogic Communication

Ethical Contradictions and E-Mail Communication at Enron Corporation

Anna Turnage and Joann Keyton

This case study examines the degree to which moral silence can negatively impact decision making in an organization, including its ultimate collapse. It addresses the difficulties of overidentification with an organization that may limit employees from raising concerns and confronting coworkers' behaviors. In addition, it also explores how the value of profit above all else created ethical dilemmas of truth versus loyalty and the individual versus the community.

Enron Corporation's epic failure in the waning months of 2001 has become a legendary representation of unethical corporate behavior. Numerous popular press and scholarly articles have been written about the company's failure in terms of its questionable accounting practices, pretentious corporate bragging, aggressive business tactics, and unethical internal culture. Many articles about Enron's failure have focused on *who* is to blame (e.g., its officers, board, accountants, and legal team). Other articles have focused on *what* is to blame (e.g., Enron's culture, accounting norms, or lack of government oversight). In between these two positions are articles that focus on ego and greed (Stein, 2007) as motivations for the unethical behavior. We take the position that it is also important to focus on *how* and *why* such a blatant disregard for ethical behavior was able to reach the level it did at Enron. We ultimately argue that employees' overidentification with the corporation and its values of profit and greed led them to look the other way until it was ultimately too late. Some people eventually began to question management ethics but not until it was clear to them that the company was about to collapse. The behavior of those inside the organization early on in the company's life, then, can best be characterized by Bird's (1996) concept of moral silence:

> Although they possess moral concerns, many businesspeople do not actively and forthrightly voice these convictions in relation to their work. They do not confront colleagues who are engaged in questionable activities. They fail to speak up forcefully for their ideals. They fail to bargain as hard as they might for their convictions. . . . People who are morally silent fail to voice and often thereby fail to act upon moral convictions that they in fact hold. (p. vii)

Moral silence, Bird (1996) said, is often reinforced by moral deafness and blindness—or the refusal of some in the organization (namely management) to acknowledge or even recognize patterns of unethical behavior in the organization.

We examine the case through Enron employee e-mails to CEO Ken Lay, which are available in the Enron E-mail Corpus. The analysis reveals the often insidious nature of strong organizational cultural indoctrination both in terms of praise for leadership and a failure to ask questions or challenge certain actions. An overidentification with the company's leaders and values of profit above all else created ethical dilemmas of truth versus loyalty and the individual versus the community. On the one hand, although employees may have at least sensed that management was being dishonest with internal and external stakeholders, the overidentification created a sense of loyalty so strong they were willing to ignore these suspicions. Enron's strong organizational culture of "Enronians," on the other hand, created a collective sense of being among employees so much so that for many their individual thoughts and beliefs became secondary to those pushed by the leaders and culture. Tourish and Vatcha (2005), in fact, argued that Enron was a company of employees who bought heart and soul into the company's leaders and their vision. In essence, the e-mails reveal that Enron employees engaged in moral silence, blindness, and deafness—ultimately setting the stage for the company's dramatic and catastrophic collapse. In addition, we argue that e-mail played a significant role in employees' ability to finally question management behavior and push back against certain value systems that led to unethical behavior.

THE ENRON SAGA

The Enron saga has been well preserved by journalists (Bryce, 2002; McLean & Elkind, 2003) and corporate insiders (Cruver, 2002; Swartz & Watkins, 2003), as well as documented on film (Gibney, 2006); we leave the broad story to those sources. The very brief version of the saga is this:

Enron Corporation was created in 1985 through a merger; Ken Lay was the CEO. Jeff Skilling joined a division of Enron in 1989 and became president and chief operating officer (COO) of Enron Corporation in 1996. During those years, Enron transformed itself from a pipeline company in which it developed, built, and operated electrical power plants and natural gas pipelines to a trading company in which Enron employees both speculated on and influenced the supply of energy commodities. During the Lay and Skilling reign, Enron

(1) articulated respect, integrity, communication, and excellence (RICE) as its corporate values; (2) was labeled as the one of the country's most innovative companies; and (3) grew from 7,500 to 20,000 employees. Also during that time, Andy Fastow was appointed chief financial officer (CFO); he developed off-balance sheet deals and partnerships (i.e., special purpose entities [SPEs]) to conceal Enron's poor cash position despite its rapid increase in stock value. The first negative press about Enron appeared in spring 2000 but was largely ignored; Enron stock continued to increase in value. By spring 2001, the press was asking, "How does Enron make its money?" In late spring, employees questioned why Lay and Skilling and other executives were selling their Enron stock; this event was followed by massive layoffs. Skilling resigned in August 2001 amid press skepticism. The next day, Sherron Watkins—the Enron executive who eventually blew the whistle on the scandal—sent a confidential memo to Lay describing the accounting problems. Lay took no action. But in the next 2 weeks, he sold $20 million in Enron stock while telling employees that the company was in strong financial shape and that the stock was a good buy. In October 2001, Fastow and his limited partnerships were exposed by the *Wall Street Journal*; he was replaced as CFO. In November 2001, Enron tried to merge with rival energy company Dynegy; Lay was poised to receive a $60 million parachute, but the merger failed. Enron was out of cash and declared bankruptcy on December 1, 2001; thousands of employees were fired and lost their retirement savings invested in Enron stock.

More important to this particular case is the organizational culture of Enron, which we argue was a powerful aspect in the company's rise and fall. The company's "cultish" culture is described next.

ENRON'S "CULTISH" INTERNAL CULTURE

Widely accepted as the set of artifacts, values, and assumptions that emerge from the interactions of organizational members (Keyton, 2005), Enron's organizational culture changed as the company's vision of itself changed. In terms of strategic vision, the change was staggering. First promoting itself as wanting to become the premier natural gas pipeline in North America, Enron later envisioned becoming the world's leading energy company and, finally, *the* world's leading company. RICE were the values Enron promoted and referred to as the organization's code of ethics (Cruver, 2002).

With those changes (the epic nature of these transformations to the *new economy* is well captured by Boje [2005]), guys who worked on the pipeline were replaced with traders and other deal-making executives. With those changes, values and assumptions about business practice changed as well. For example, CFO Andy Fastow is described as having "cleverly designed a scheme" (Wilson & Campbell, 2003, p. 7) based on manipulation of accounting practices, which then required manipulation of communication within the executive suite and to the board, outside investors, and employees. Enron's value of *integrity* was certainly at play. For the off-balance sheet deals, or SPEs, to work, the board was not given a full disclosure of information, subordinates were pressured to enact the questionable and speculative transactions, and auditors were paid to not reveal what they knew (Wilson & Campbell, 2003). On two occasions, Enron's board of directors voted to set aside its code of ethics to approve Fastow's deals, a prime example of the company's lack of transparency in decision making.

Although touted initially as an admirable value, Enron's value of *communication* eventually became suspect. Sherron Watkins (Swartz & Watkins, 2003) described how her questions about risk were not answered completely. The troubling conclusions she, as vice president of corporate development, presented in a memo to Ken Lay were met with silence from other executives and passed off by Lay with "Don't ask me, I thought Arthur Andersen [Enron's accounting firm] has signed off on this, I'm certain it's been blessed, they've scrubbed it, and you'll just have to ask someone other than me" (Swartz & Watkins, 2003, p. 9). Evidence later revealed that Arthur Andersen was simply a part of the larger scheme and went bankrupt along with Enron.

It is now obvious that Enron's top executives showed only a token commitment to the organization's RICE values (Prentice, 2003). The oft-promoted RICE values were overshadowed by a deal- and bonus-driven top management that looked the other way (Chandra, 2003; Cruver, 2002). It's not surprising then that Enron's culture was routinely labeled as arrogant (Chandra, 2003), aggressive, and morally flexible (Ghosh, 2008). For employees, *rank and yank* was a poignant reminder of this contested culture.

Enron's Rank and Yank Culture

One of the first things Skilling did when he was named president was to implement Enron's Performance Review Committee (PRC), otherwise known as "rank and yank," and "bag 'em and tag 'em" (Bryce, 2002, p. 127). In the PRC, associates were responsible for evaluating their peers, which caused a great amount of distrust and paranoia among employees. In contrast to the more traditional 360-degree performance review, the bottom 15% to 20% of evaluated employees were let go. Even more humiliating, the reviews were conducted in a public forum in which many employees were sent to the "redeployment" office or "office of shame" where they looked for work in other (often new) Enron divisions (Swartz & Watkins, 2003). According to Sims and Brinkmann (2003), Enron's reward system established a "win-at-all-costs" focus in which aggressiveness and greed were core values. The company's leadership promoted and retained only those employees that consistently helped boost the company's profits, with little regard to ethics. Beyond the push for high performance, dissent was discouraged, and employees did not dare question management's decisions (Bryce, 2002). This set up an atmosphere where employees lacked the ethical courage to step up and speak out against what they recognized as potentially unethical behavior.

Despite the level of apprehension or uncertainty employees felt in this aggressive, fear-laden culture, many still felt extreme pride and loyalty to the company and its leaders, especially Ken Lay (see Trinkaus & Giacalone, 2005). Enron was one of the largest companies in the United States, and to many employees, it seemed invincible. One employee told the *New York Times* the following:

> You either got with the system or you were out the door. You could feel the excitement at 6 a.m. You walked in the door and got energized, all those creative

juices flowing. You worked with the best, the most brilliant. It was a great, great company. (Bragg, 2002, pp. 15–16)

Simultaneously, Enron employees heavily invested in Enron stock (both as investors and in their retirement accounts) saw the increase in their accounts even when the tech stock bubble of 2000 burst. For some, employee loyalty may have been enhanced by their new wealth. As we discussed at the beginning of this case, this played a role in setting up the truth versus loyalty dilemma. Not only was loyalty strong because dissent was discouraged but also because of the handsome rewards for ignoring any kind of dishonesty.

Not surprisingly, many employees referred to the company's culture as nothing short of cultish. In particular, the charismatic leadership of Ken Lay and Jeff Skilling had many employees star struck and in awe. "There was a compelling and totalistic vision, and intellectual stimulation aimed at transforming employees' goals while subordinating their ethical sense to the needs of the corporation" (Tourish & Vatcha, 2005, p. 475). How did Enron do this? Its leaders promoted a common culture, which was maintained by punitive means (Tourish & Vatcha, 2005). Thus, a conundrum existed: Enron was an organization that was *supposed to be* integrated by its RICE values (see Seeger & Ulmer, 2003) but in reality was driven by aggression, competition, and greed.

E-MAIL MESSAGES FINALLY SHOW DISSENT

The compelling and totalistic vision is evident in e-mail messages from employees to Ken Lay earlier on in the company's life when the stock price was soaring. It is clear in these messages that employees either bought wholly into the culture of greed or were too afraid to question it given the oppressive culture. Most of the messages during this time—from the beginning of the database in 1997 until Jeff Skilling's departure on August 14, 2001—are mundane, business-related e-mails with little emotion or discussion about the company itself. The e-mails that do show emotion or discuss the company are in praise of it or Ken Lay. Here are some examples:

- "I am proud to be a part of this team and look forward to many years of prosperity and success."

- "Without your guidance and direction and the many employee based programs you have initiated, I would not be where I am financially today. I am looking forward to retirement without concern for me or my family's future."

- "Here in my group, and all over Enron, I see people working hard while some even go above and beyond. I am in my mid-thirties and will speak for so many in saying THANK YOU for your hard work, great planning and sacrifice made in the early years long before we came here to enjoy all the extra benefits provided. My family and I, along with so many others, appreciate the rewards you provide for hard work."

There is a stark contrast, however, in the language used in e-mails to Ken Lay after August 14, 2001—the day Skilling resigned. E-mails from that day until the company's demise reveal employee dissent and a great deal of emotion in the form of anger, sadness, and desperation. In many of these messages, employees talk *specifically* about ethics. Here are some examples:

- "The 'portfolio problem' is not loss of value, rather lack of values—*people need to get some personal values that are worth a damn!*"
- "I noticed how little confidence the top executives at Enron had in this company when they sold off hundreds of millions of dollars in stock between November and February. Many of us see that as the beginning of *the moral bankruptcy* at the top of Enron."
- "I believe ultimately justice will come to fruition. Reputations have been destroyed which in my opinion is more important to any amount of money or financial gain. Without integrity a person has nothing!"
- "For the first time in 22 years of service for Enron I'm ashamed to admit that I work for Enron! I have lost all respect for Enron Senior Management and agree with the Financial Analyst when they say that Enron Senior Management cannot be trusted. *Ethics and Morals are either something everyone else needs to have except Senior Management* or somewhere along the way Senior Management started believing the end justifies the means."

In other messages, employees show extreme anger and disrespect toward Lay. One e-mail, for example, signed as being sent by "Just another fucked over employee" said, "I particularly like your adherance [sic] to the core values—you 'respected' us, you 'communicated' brilliantly with us, your fucking us over was 'excellent', your 'integrity' was without question." Another message also taunted Lay over the company's values statement:

Every month in our team meetings we go over Enron's vision and values and describe what each one means to us. Little did we know that we were the only ones paying attention to what they stood for. Can you tell me what each one means to you right now. RESPECT? INTEGRITY? COMMUNICATION? EXCELLENCE? I am trying to keep my head up when people ask me what happened but it is getting harder all the time. I have stopped trying to defend you and the others that are involved.

VENTING OVER E-MAIL

Given Enron's internal culture—one that demanded an unemotional drive to succeed and an unquestioning loyalty and trust of the company's leaders—the content of some of the e-mails toward the end of the company's life cycle are remarkably emotional. E-mail as a communication medium provided an outlet for Enron employees to vent their frustrations and question the company's ethical shortcomings. In this sense, e-mail served as an actor in the Enron network, capable of changing the ongoing interaction within the network among employees and management. Actor-network theory (Latour, 2005;

Law, 1992) posits that objects, such as e-mail, when used in organizational life are all a part of what makes the organization and the communication what they are. Thus, e-mail has the power to both stabilize and change networks and relationships just as human actors do. In reviewing hundreds of e-mails in the Enron database, it is clear that employees did not express heightened emotion via e-mail during Enron's prosperous times. The medium, then, was in many ways responsible for the actions of the human users as they attempted to cope with the company's problems. The Enron database gives us a glimpse of the effect that technology has on human users. Thus, employee e-mails to Lay were depositories for emotions but also acted in combination with employees, who first accepted and enhanced the culture then later challenged it. Yet, as the data from the Enron Corpus show, while e-mail had previously not been used for such purposes, employees eventually used e-mail as a tool enabling them to buck these cultural tenets and finally begin to publicly discuss the unethical behavior that had thus far been ignored. The irony is this: If the employees had felt empowered to use e-mail to Enron's top management to express their opinions and emotions from the beginning, the company might very well have survived. In the sense of social networking and commenting on Enron's culture, e-mail serves as an enabling agent for employees not only to express themselves but also to share important ideas and concepts that could improve operations and make things more ethical. Diesner, Frantz, and Carley's (2005) research on the corpus demonstrates that e-mail exchanges peaked during the August 2001 (the same month Jeff Skilling resigned) period of the company's crisis and that the number of people involved in these exchanges also increased. They concluded that the patterns suggested that subcultures had formed and that "previously disconnected people began to engage in mutual communication, thus strengthening the cohesion of the system" (Diesner et al., 2005, p. 214).

ORGANIZATIONAL OVERIDENTIFICATION

Cheney and Tompkins (1987) argued the following: "Many an organization has been 'shipwrecked' because of an unshakable commitment to an otherwise unwise course. Overidentification with a course prevents the navigator from seeing other courses, other options" (p. 11). Cheney (1983) said organizational identification occurs when employees make decisions with the organization as the primary concern—above their own individual interests. It could be argued that an overidentification among employees with the organization and its course is, in part, what led to the "shipwrecking" of one of the world's largest companies. This identification came about as a result of certain discourses in the organization that prevented both leaders and employees of the company from seeing other courses or options.

The e-mails in the Enron database provide a unique opportunity to see the identification process at work *in situ,* or as it occurred, while at the same time providing insight as to how communication technologies contribute to the process. It also provides insight as to how employees' organizational identification may change over time. Employees' e-mails to Ken Lay clearly demonstrate a change in how they referred to the company once they realized the company and its values were not only unethical but were contributing to the company's demise. The messages from this time period praising Ken Lay, for instance, could indicate overidentification—messages containing phrases such as "Thanks to you my financial position far exceeds what I had ever thought would be the case," "Without your guidance and direction . . . I would not be where I am financially today," and "THANK YOU for your hard work, great planning and sacrifice in the early years." In this sense, they are identifying with Lay on the level of messianic leader in a manner that Tourish and Vatcha (2005) argued is indicative of cults. By contrast, the e-mails toward the end of the company's life reveal a *dis*identification with the organization and its leaders. Messages with phrases like "trust was misplaced and worth nothing," indicate a move toward identification with ethical values over monetary values. This move becomes even stronger in the messages dealing almost solely with metaphors of ethical values, such as "People need to get some values that are worth a damn!" "Reputations have been destroyed," "Without integrity a person has nothing," "Morals are either something everyone else needs to have except senior management" and "moral bankruptcy." These messages indicate a disidentification with the company's profit-driven goals, but also with the company's leadership.

MORAL SILENCE, DEAFNESS, AND BLINDNESS

We argue that an overidentification with the company's values of profit and greed is what led to moral silence, deafness, and blindness among Enron management and employees. This overidentification set up the tensions discussed earlier of truth versus loyalty and individuality versus collectivity. Employees in many ways did not want to see the truth as a result of their extreme loyalty to Enron, its management, and value system. Can an employee tell or ask for the truth at the same time he or she acts loyally toward the company? At what point does the organizational collective negatively influence individual morality and courage? These tensions set up the recipe for moral silence, deafness, and blindness as Bird (1996) defines it. There are several contributing factors, according to Bird (1996), for moral silence, deafness, and blindness. Moral silence involves avoiding any kind of action against unethical behavior. Moral deafness involves an unwillingness to listen or an inattentiveness when approached about unethical issues. And moral blindness includes failing to see problems and the ensuing consequences of unethical behavior. It is clear that Enron employees engaged in moral silence on a number of levels by not speaking up earlier about obvious unethical behavior. We could also argue, however, that employees also engaged in moral deafness and blindness given the lavish rewards they received for engaging in questionable behavior in the name of profit. Certainly, Ken Lay engaged in moral deafness when he ignored warnings from Sherron Watkins. There are also signs that he engaged in moral blindness, by failing to see or acknowledge Andy Fastow's questionable SPEs. Conditions for moral silence, deafness, and blindness involve three main factors (Bird, 1996): (1) cultural, (2) individual, and (3) organizational. Cultural factors include "a dominant economic philosophy of rational self-interest" (Johannesen, 2002). That philosophy was one of greed at Enron. Indeed, many have argued that Enron's management and employees engaged in ethically suspect behavior because of that culture of greed at Enron. Individual factors include fear or feelings of vulnerability or lack of control over situations. It is possible that employees took no action earlier on, because of the performance review committee, and Enron's ability to squash and penalize dissent. And finally, organizational factors do include the penalizing of dissent as a reason for not coming forward or questioning unethical behavior.

SUMMARY

As artifacts of the day-to-day communication in Enron, e-mails from employees to Ken Lay illustrate how an organizational culture can perpetuate and sustain unethical and even illegal practices. The oppressive culture is evident in that there are few e-mails questioning management's practices until the unethical behavior was publicly revealed. And, despite the e-mails shown here, and reports of other e-mails that were apparently deleted from the Enron Corpus (see Boje, 2005), warnings about improprieties in accounting and concerns about the degradation of Enron's values were largely ignored in favor of profits and power. Beyond this, the e-mails reveal the often insidious nature of strong organizational cultural indoctrination. Even as the company was collapsing around them, many employees continued to praise both Ken Lay and the espoused corporate values, which were no longer being enacted. Other e-mails to Ken Lay, however, reveal a rising subculture of employees that not only questioned the company's leadership and lack of values but expressed an unusual display of vitriolic emotion.

Employees in both subcultures could arguably be characterized as delusional. E-mails from the loyalists revealed their continuing commitment to and belief in Lay as a leader. Even if Enron employees were not aware of the few negative press stories, their vested interest in Enron stock, which was rapidly plummeting, should have suggested that something was wrong. In essence, the e-mails reveal that Enron employees also violated the RICE values. They portrayed unfailing respect for leaders, lacked the integrity to address the violation of moral and ethical principles, failed to communicate by not asking questions, and allowed themselves to be subordinated to the excellence of others. They were "distracted from truth seeking" by allowing themselves to be economically manipulated and swayed by information asymmetry (Boje, Adler, & Black, 2005, p. 52). The e-mails provide a rare look at upward communication during times of crises and, in particular, help explain how a company's culture can become so dominant as to blind employees to larger issues that could challenge their own personal ethos.

DISCUSSION QUESTIONS

1. What are employees' obligations in dealing with unethical issues in the workplace?

2. What is management's obligation to employees when they are confronted with potential unethical behavior in the workplace?

3. What systematic issues need to change in order to stop unethical behavior as a result of corporate greed and corruption?

4. What role do communication technologies play in Enron employees' ability to communicate with management about unethical issues?

5. Can employee action against unethical behaviors such as those at Enron make a difference in a culture so entrenched in greed as it was at Enron?

6. If employees had been willing to question management earlier on, could it have made a difference? If you were an employee, how would you expect the values of respect, integrity, communication, and excellence to be enacted? Would your expectations be different if you were a member of management?

7. Thinking of your current and past work experiences, how willing would you be to write an e-mail to the CEO, president, or founder of the organization about some problem you observed in the company?

REFERENCES

Bird, F. B. (1996). *The muted conscience: Moral silence and the practice of ethics in business.* Westport, CT: Quorum Books.

Boje, D. (2005). Enron, postmodern capitalism, and answerability: Introduction to the Enron special issue. *Tamara: Journal of Critical Postmodern Organization Science, 3*(2), iv–vi.

Boje, D. M., Adler, T. R., & Black, J. A. (2005). Theatrical facades and agents in a synthesized analysis from Enron theatre: Implications to transaction cost and agency theories. *Tamara: Journal of Critical Postmodern Organization Science, 3*(2), 39–56.

Bragg, R. (2002, January 20). Enron's collapse: Workers feel pain of layoffs and added sting of betrayal. *New York Times.* Retrieved from http://query.nytimes.com/gst/fullpage.html?res = 990 6E5DB143BF933A15752C0A9649C8B63&scp = 1&sq = bragg%20enron&st = cse

Bryce, R. (2002). *Pipe dreams: Greed, ego, and the death of Enron.* New York: PublicAffairs.

Chandra, G. (2003). The Enron implosion and its lessons. *Journal of Management Research, 3,* 98–111.

Cheney, G. (1983). On the various and changing meanings of organizational membership: A field study of organizational communication. *Communication Monographs, 50,* 342–362.

Cheney, G., & Tompkins, P. K. (1987). Coming to terms with organizational identification and commitment. *Central States Speech Journal, 38,* 1–15.

Cruver, B. (2002). *Anatomy of greed: The unshredded truth from an Enron insider.* New York: Basic Books.

Diesner, J., Frantz, T. L., & Carley, K. M. (2005). Communication networks from the Enron email corpus: "It's always about the people. Enron is no different." *Mathematical and Computational Organization Theory, 11,* 201–228.

Ghosh, D. (2008). Corporate values, workplace decisions and ethical standards of employees. *Journal of Managerial Issues, 20*(1), 68–87.

Gibney, A. (Writer/Director/Producer). (2006). Enron: The smartest guys in the room [Motion picture]. (Available from Magnolia Pictures, 49 West 27th Street, New York, NY 10001)

Johannesen, R. L. (2002). *Ethics in human communication.* Long Grove, IL: Waveland Press.

Keyton, J. (2005). *Communication & organizational culture: A key to understanding work experiences.* Thousand Oaks, CA: Sage.

Latour, B. (2005). *Reassembling the social.* Oxford, UK: Oxford University Press.

Law, J. (1992). Notes on the theory of the actor-network: Ordering, strategy, and heterogeneity. *Systems Practice, 5,* 379–393.

McLean, B., & Elkind, P. (2003). *The smartest guys in the room: The amazing rise and scandalous fall of Enron.* New York: Portfolio.

Prentice, R. (2003). Enron: A brief behavioral autopsy. *American Business Law Journal, 40,* 417–444.

Seeger, M. W., & Ulmer, R. R. (2003). Explaining Enron: Communication and responsible leadership. *Management Communication Quarterly, 17,* 58–84.

Sims, R. R., & Brinkmann, J. (2003). Enron ethics (Or: Culture matters more than codes). *Journal of Business Ethics, 45,* 243–256.

Stein, M. (2007). Oedipus Rex at Enron: Leadership, Oedipal struggles, and organizational collapse. *Human Relations, 60,* 1387–1410.

Swartz, M., & Watkins, S. (2003). *Power failure: The inside story of the collapse of Enron.* New York: Doubleday.

Tourish, D., & Vatcha, N. (2005). Charismatic leadership and corporate cultism at Enron: The elimination of dissent, the promotion of conformity and organizational collapse. *Leadership, 1,* 455–480.

Trinkaus, J., & Giacalone, J. (2005). The silence of the stakeholders: Zero decibel level at Enron. *Journal of Business Ethics, 58,* 237–248.

Wilson, A. C., & Campbell, W. M. (2003). Enron exposed: Why it took so long. *Business & Economic Review, 49*(2), 6–10.

Toyota—Oh, What a Feeling, or Oh, What a Mess?

Ethics at the Intersection of Industry, Government, and Publics

Rebecca J. Meisenbach and Sarah B. Feldner

This case considers the role of communication prior to, during, and after a product recall. More specifically, it explores the importance of dialogue and transparency to create public trust and maintain a company's reputation. It also addresses potential conflicts of interest between corporate lobbying and government regulation, as well as the challenges of balancing individual and community concerns.

The Toyota Corporation has a long-standing reputation of quality and safety in the United States regarding its automobiles. However, this reputation was called into question in 2010 when Toyota made three separate significant recalls that affected nearly 8 million vehicles. Beyond problems with the vehicles themselves, Toyota faced challenges about how it communicated the issue of safety concerns with various publics. Despite these challenges, Toyota as a corporation is emerging relatively successfully from this crisis. This case study examines the communication efforts of the Toyota Corporation within the framework of issue life cycle theory (Crable & Vibbert, 1985). In particular, this chapter examines some of the ethical dilemmas of the Toyota case by considering the potential for dialogic transparency, conflicts of interest between corporate lobbying and government regulation, and balancing individual and community concerns. The case suggests how the current organizational environment challenges ethical conceptions and expectations of corporate communication practice.

UNINTENTIONAL ACCELERATION? AN OVERVIEW OF THE CASE

The Toyota recall issue reached a turning point on August 28, 2009, when an off duty highway patrolman called 911 from his Lexus as it sped out of control down a San Diego highway. The call ended with the Lexus crashing into another vehicle and careening over a cliff. All four passengers were killed (Vlasic, 2010). The accident brought the issue into mainstream public conversation because the 911 tape was released publicly and the credibility and driver training of a highway patrol officer highlighted the seriousness of the problem. In fall 2009, Toyota announced that the unintended acceleration problem was solely due to a floor mat design issue that could cause the gas pedal to get stuck on the floor mat. Unfortunately, in December 2009, another acceleration incident occurred that took the lives of another four individuals. The floor mats were found tucked safely inside the trunk as Toyota press releases had instructed customers to do. Thus, 2010 ushered in a series of recalls and congressional inquiries into the actions of the Toyota Corporation.

TABLE 6.1 Toyota Recall Timeline: Some Key Dates	
September 2007	Toyota issued a Lexus part recall to fasten floor mats to car floors to avoid acceleration problems.
August 28, 2009	Uncontrolled acceleration crash of a Lexus killed four people, including an off duty highway patrol officer.
September 29, 2009	Toyota issued a safety advisory on floor mats of approximately 4 million cars.
November 25, 2009	Toyota announced a redesign to address floor mats and brakes.
December 26, 2009	A Toyota Avalon crashed into a lake in Texas after accelerating out of control. All four occupants died. Floor mats were found in the trunk of the car.
January 21, 2010	Toyota recalled 2.3 million vehicles for "sticky" gas pedals.
January 26, 2010	Toyota halted sales and production of certain Toyota vehicles.
February 1, 2010	Toyota announced a part to fix sticky gas pedals, and the part was shipped to dealers.
February 5, 2010	The Toyota president apologized at a news conference.
February 23, 2010	Congressional investigative hearings of Toyota began.
May 18, 2010	Toyota paid a $16.4 million fine to settle regulatory charges that Toyota was too slow to issue a recall for the acceleration problem.
July 2010	Toyota recalled 280,000 cars for engine problems.
December 2010	The Motor Vehicle Safety Act stalled on the House floor.

EXAMINING THE LIFE CYCLE OF AN ISSUE

In this case study, we use Crable and Vibbert's (1985) five issue management stages to organize the details of the case. An issue exists "when one or more human agents [attach] significance to a situation or perceived 'problem'" (Crable & Vibbert, 1985, p. 5). The first stage, the potential stage, of issue management occurs when very few people are interested in the issue but at least one person or human agent perceives a situation as significant. During the imminent phase, the issue begins being accepted and endorsed as an issue by multiple groups. During the current phase, the issue is an accepted and widely disseminated topic; this includes significant media involvement. In the critical phase, key stakeholders take sides and make decisions for managing the issue. Finally, an issue enters the dormant phase once a decision is made. Whether the issue remains dormant for any length of time or begins moving through the life cycle again depends on the significance that publics attach to the new situation.

An examination of the Toyota recall crisis within the context of the issue life cycle is revealing and raises a number of key questions about the ways in which corporations make decisions about how issues might best be defined and effectively managed. In what follows, we examine key ethical tensions related to transparency and dialogue that were present in the communication choices of various stakeholders in the life cycle of the "sticky pedal" issue.

Silent or Quiet? Communication During the Potential and Imminent Phases

An initial review of this case might suggest that Toyota remained silent during the potential and imminent phases of this issue. However, taking a broader view of Toyota's long-standing relationships with individuals connected to regulating bodies and lobbyists leads to a different conclusion. The reality for the automobile industry is that manufacturing, technical, and safety problems with vehicles are always a possibility. For example, consider the Ford Motor Company safety problems in the late 1990s involving rollovers in the Explorer and even back in the 1970s involving the infamous exploding gas tanks in the Pinto. As a result of such possibilities, corporations like Toyota invest both time and money in developing relationships with those who create policy about and oversee the industry. In this way, Toyota has actively but quietly managed potential vehicle problem issues through the establishment and maintenance of relationships with key government officials. In recent years, Toyota has had over 31 lobbyists in Washington. According to a *New York Times* report (Lichtblau, 2010), the $25 million that Toyota spent on U.S. lobbying in the 5 years prior to this incident was the most spent by any foreign automaker. Further, Toyota routinely hires former employees of the National Highway Traffic Safety Administration (NHTSA) and maintains personal and professional relationships with legislators who chair key committees related to automobile industry oversight. Thus, it can be argued that despite any appearance of inactivity, Toyota did, in fact, actively manage this issue (and others) during the potential phase—but in a manner that is rarely seen or understood by the general public.

It is difficult to pinpoint an exact time at which safety concerns over the accelerator pedals moved from the potential to imminent stage. It is possible that Toyota engineers and other officials were the first to be aware of the potential problem with sudden acceleration, but there is no public record of them attaching any significance to it. Thus, the origin of this issue resided in isolated unintended acceleration incidents of particular drivers' experiences, some of which were reported to the NHTSA. A later study found that 20% of a random sample of Toyota complaints from 2002 to 2005 involved acceleration problems in Toyota cars (Vlasic, 2010). During the congressional hearings about the sticky pedals, the NHTSA received documents from the Toyota Corporation that indicated company employees had been aware of some of the design flaws that could cause the unintended acceleration as early as February 2006 (Reuters, 2010).

Further evidence helping identify when Toyota began to recognize the accelerator issue comes from an internal July 2009 PowerPoint presentation that became public in February 2010.[1] The presentation provided an update to Yoshi Inaba, the chief operating officer (COO) and president for Toyota, North America. The presentation, developed by Toyota's extensive government relations office, sketched Toyota's overall stance toward managing vehicle safety issues. Among the points highlighted was the role of the government relations office to "protect our [Toyota's] interests," "maintain a receptive environment to grow our business," and "shape policies & regulations for One voice decisions." The "one voice" reference repeats throughout the presentation, pointing to a particular culture that promotes a unified front on corporate issues. The presentation also identified legislation that was delayed or abandoned altogether and "favorable recall outcomes" as "wins" for Toyota and the industry.

While evidence suggests that Toyota was aware of the acceleration issue, as is typical in these early phases, the company attempted to manage the issue out of the public eye. Toyota statements suggest that company representatives believed that they were acting correctly in remaining silent or very quiet regarding the sticky gas pedal issue.

Investigation, Defense, and Apology: Current and Critical Phases of the Toyota Recall

Once the September 2009 crash thrust the issue into the current phase, publics called for government investigations and interventions. However, Toyota continued to engage in minimal public communication until February 2010 when the company announced it had come up with a solution to the sticky gas pedal problem. It seems plausible that remaining silent was in keeping with the "one voice" policy. However, the "one voice" stance was challenged on January 16. Five days before it announced a recall of 2.3 million vehicles, a U.S. spokesperson for Toyota e-mailed a Japanese colleague urging Toyota to go public with the issue saying, "The time to hide on this one is over. We need to come clean" (as cited in Maynard, 2010). Such comments from inside the corporation are rare and make it difficult to draw conclusions, but they do suggest that well into the current phase of this issue Toyota continued to rely on its strategy of communicating directly with governing agencies rather than engaging in full, transparent communication with broader publics.

---

[1] See http://hosted.ap.org/specials/interactives/_documents/toyota_presentation.pdf

Although certainly Toyota is accountable for its quiet management of the issue at this stage, others have also noted the role of the NHTSA in how the issue was managed. Some have challenged that the agency did not push Toyota hard enough to fully address these early incidents. The *New York Times* reported "Six separate investigations were conducted by the agency into consumer complaints of unintended acceleration, and none of them found defects in Toyotas other than unsecured floor mats" (Vlasic, 2010). Of course, responsibility for the lack of pressure exerted by NHTSA might be due to the powerful influence automobile companies like Toyota have over regulatory agencies. *The Guardian* quoted U.S. Department of Transportation spokesperson Olivia Alair as saying, "It's not just the federal government's job to catch safety defects. It's the responsibility of automakers to come forward when there is a problem" (as cited in McCurry, 2010).

When Toyota did begin publicly to address the issue of the sudden acceleration, its communication strategy focused on public statements that explained the actions the company was taking to address potential problems with the accelerator. An analysis of Toyota's press statements during this time reveals that up until the U.S. president of Toyota Motor Corporation, Jim Lentz, spoke with Congress on February 23, Toyota was apologizing for the inconvenience caused by the recalls but stopped short of apologizing for the company's actions to date.[2]

Toyota's public response to this current phase of this issue focused on two main areas: (1) responding directly to allegations and requests for information from the NHTSA and other government entities and (2) refuting media reports about the nature of the problem—seeking to define the issue based on scientific evidence. Direct apologies for how the issue and relevant information had been managed and communicated only came much later, when the sheer amount of media coverage seems to have forced the company's hand. Apologies still comprised a minor focus of the company's strategy. The president of Toyota even initially refused to appear before one of the investigative committees (Sanchanta & Takahashi, 2010).

During the most public phase of the sudden acceleration issue, a great deal of the comments coming from Toyota were issued via press releases and formal statements posted to the company website—eventually leading to a specific page devoted to the recall information.[3] Some of the communication from Toyota was devoted to the specifics of the recall (e.g., identifying how the fixes were to be made and how Toyota owners could handle the situation). Toyota also outlined steps that it would make in the production of future Toyota models. At the same time that Toyota was suggesting the modifications that it would make to both recalled and future vehicles, it stated that a number of fixes (e.g., the inclusion of a brake override in all new models) were not directly related to the problems but rather that they were about making consumers feel comfortable and confident.

Although Toyota did speak to the concerns of Toyota owners, a great deal more attention was given to responding to Congress, the NHTSA, and media accounts of the events. These responses were most often in the form of press releases that specifically refuted individual claims about the causes leading to problems with the vehicles, particularly

---

[2] See http://pressroom.toyota.com/pr/tms/toyota/toyota-update-regarding-recalls-153243.aspx and http://www.toyota.com/recall/videos/jim-lentz-important-message.html

[3] See http://www.toyota.com/recall/

suggestions that the problem was connected to the electrical systems in the cars. Toyota was quick to point out what it felt were inaccurate or misrepresented statements. In this, Toyota emphasized the need to focus on "science not suggestion"[4] when evaluating the situation. Throughout the statements, Toyota outlined the significant testing conducted and focused on the evidence that could be verified—implying that that which could not be supported with scientific evidence (or replicated scientifically) should be ignored. But these defenses were unsuccessful in avoiding fines.

The issue moved toward the dormant stage when investigating committees issued the maximum fine to the company. In the end, Toyota did not contest and paid $16.4 million for waiting 4 months to tell federal authorities about the faulty gas pedals. Six months later, it agreed to pay another $34 million in fines for similar wrongdoing on earlier recalls (CNN Wire Staff, 2010). The assessment and payment of the fines represents the critical decision making involved in this issue's life cycle. Toyota moved on, offering car buying incentives to potential customers, and sales seem to be recovering. Although Toyota's U.S. sales dropped in 2010, the company is still the world's leading automaker in total vehicles sold (Kageyama, 2011). Some of the decline may have been tied to lingering concerns that the problem was still lurking in the electrical system of the cars. However, in February, 2011, yet another federal study found no evidence of any problems in Toyota's electrical systems (Wald, 2011). In short, Toyota's sales indicate that the automaker will likely recover.

Beyond direct repercussions to Toyota, a closely related decision involved legislators pulling together to write the Motor Vehicle Safety Act as a result of the Toyota recall issue. It was originally written to abolish the $16 million limit on fines for wrongdoing such as those present in the Toyota case. However, by July 2010, the initially radical auto safety bill that was going to change current corporate practices dramatically was scaled back into something much more familiar. What was going to be a potentially unlimited fine on offending companies was to be capped at $200 million (still much more than Toyota was required to pay). An attempt to set safety standards on vehicle electronics was no longer required but was listed as something that the transportation secretary could "consider," and there was no mandated deadline for automakers to meet such standards should they be developed. The *Los Angeles Times* quoted a former head of the NHTSA as saying, "The auto industry has had undue influence on this legislation" (Vartabedian & Bensinger, 2010). In the end, Congress adjourned in December 2010 without passing the bill, effectively killing all versions of the Motor Vehicle Safety Act.

Clarence Ditlow, executive director of the Center for Auto Safety, reacted to the nonvote by releasing a statement that lamented this outcome: "In a year that began with runaway Toyotas & ended with Windstar rear axle fractures, one thing is clear—[NHTSA] does not have the authority or resources to stand up to an auto industry that always has and always will place profits above safety" (Ditlow & Center for Auto Safety, n.d.). Thus, the question of equitable public dialogue regarding automobile safety remains an imminent issue in the United States.

---

[4] See http://pressroom.toyota.com/pr/tms/2010-toyota-electronic-throttle-154266.aspx

BALANCING GOVERNMENT, INDUSTRY, AND COMMUNITY INTERESTS: ETHICAL CHALLENGES AND QUESTIONS

Toyota's troubles continue in 2011 as new recalls continue to be issued on these same vehicle lines, and questions remain about what led Toyota to choose its course of action, one that largely occurred behind the scenes and avoided dialogic communication with many publics. In this context, the case not only leaves us considering the ethical choices made by the Toyota Corporation but also poses challenges to conventional understandings of ethical frameworks.

First, the ways in which the case unfolded, particularly in the potential and imminent phases, suggest a need to consider ethical tensions present in relationships among corporations, governments, and broader publics. Toyota's relationship-building strategies overwhelmingly focused on inner circles of government. Automobile manufacturers spend a combined $40 to $60 million each year to lobby their interests in Washington, D.C., suggesting a potential ethical tension between individual and community, in this case the individual financial interests of the Toyota Corporation versus the less financially supported automobile safety interests of the general public.

If corporations are representing their own interests, then one might look to nonprofit organizations (NPOs) to represent more general public interests. Yet, finding organizations that lobby for the public's interest in automobile safety is much more difficult. Consider AAA, the nonprofit auto club that has over 50 million members. Although it is the largest organization representing the community of U.S. drivers, critics suggest AAA as an organization advocates for traffic safety rather than automobile safety in its public documents. That the organization even takes a stance on public policy issues surprises many AAA members. The closest option to a pro-community automobile safety organization is the Center for Auto Safety, founded by the Consumers Union and Ralph Nader in 1970. It is a 501c3 organization, however, and as such is subject to careful restrictions on its lobbying activities.

Typically, 501c3 organizations are automatically governed by a standard judgment that lobbying must be less than "a substantial portion" of the organization's work. Alternately, the organization may elect to be governed by the 1976 lobby law under which the organization is subject to more explicit lobbying expenditure regulations. Specifically, this law allows an NPO to spend 20% of its first $500,000 of operating expenses on lobbying and 15% of its next $500,000. Many 501c3 organizations do not elect or even know about the 1976 law, yet it is a much safer position for NPOs, setting clear and objective financial guidelines for their lobbying activities.

Thus, these restrictions mean that even the Center for Auto Safety is not primarily a lobbying organization. It is one organization with a $700,000 yearly operating budget for all of its work, and it is allowed to spend up to $130,000 of that annually on lobbying. In comparison, the Toyota corporation spends $5 million annually directly on lobbying, not counting any campaign donations or charitable activities. One might consider whether this kind of difference in financial resources impacts issue management and legislative outcomes. What challenges to ethical public dialogue might be posed by this disparity in financial resources?

As the sticky pedal issue moved into the current and critical phases, publicly involving Congress, other individual versus community tensions were raised about the biases toward Toyota that many of these representatives might have. For example, the chair of the Senate Committee that investigated the recalls was Jay Rockefeller, who had known Toyota's founding family for 50 years and who lobbied heavily for Toyota to build a factory in his home state of West Virginia. Other members of the investigating committees had similar financial and personal ties to the Toyota Corporation, including Toyota factories existing in many of the committee members' home states and large personal Toyota stock portfolios. Furthermore, Rockefeller's committee also was charged with investigating how well NHTSA had regulated Toyota. Media outlets raised concerns that the NHTSA chief had worked on Rockefeller's staff for 8 years prior to his post as chief (Theimer, 2010). Would Rockefeller and other committee members be unfairly swayed by their relationships and personal and states' interests in the longevity of the Toyota Corporation? Although not all committee members were reported on by the media, assumedly some members of these committees did not have personal and state interests in perpetuating the Toyota Corporation. But if those in key positions favored Toyota, media outlets and politicians raised concerns about whether a fair dialogue could occur in the hearings (Lichtblau, 2010; Theimer, 2010).

The case also highlights dialogic and transparency dilemmas. Toyota's decision to focus on political lobbying efforts represents a strategy that focused on stakeholder groups with the most (perceived) power (i.e., government bodies). The company's close relationships with key legislators raises critical questions about corporate/government relationships. In particular, the imbalance between corporate and organized public interest access to interaction with government bodies creates a situation in which the public's voice in managing these issues is limited. Habermas's (1984, 1987) theory of communicative action provides one means by which the openness of communication processes might be judged. To allow for open and balanced communication, all stakeholder groups should have the ability to accept or reject claims made in the public sphere. In this case, because many discussions occurred outside the public eye, it is questionable (though it might be argued that the congressional officials represented the consumer public) whether the consumer public had a genuine opportunity to hear and reject Toyota's claims that its vehicles were safe.

The case also serves as a cautionary tale against what at best might be called over-confidence and at worst might be characterized as hubris. During the recall crisis, Toyota presented itself as a corporation that was supremely confident in the superiority of its technology. It also seems plausible that company officials were not intentionally withholding information but rather fully believed that they were correct in promoting the vehicles as safe. Along with its emphasis on the science behind the vehicle operations, Toyota continually included references to the strong past reputation of the company. An oft-repeated sentiment was that Toyota officials were confident in the directions that they were taking to address the problem.[5] When read against the backdrop of the "one voice" philosophy, the reliance on science and confidence in the company could have functioned as a particular form of discursive closure. Discursive closure functions to limit options for participation in dialogue and suppresses conflict (Deetz, 1992). In considering Toyota's communication,

[5] See http://pressroom.toyota.com/pr/tms/document/Lentz_Testimony_to_House_Committee_on_Energy_and_Commerce.pdf and http://pressroom.toyota.com/pr/tms/toyota/toyota-announces-comprehensive-153311.aspx

one must wonder to what extent questioning the science or superiority of Toyota was even imaginable within the company.

Many may argue that in this case Toyota's management of this issue was entirely flawed and wholly unethical; others may argue that Toyota was just doing business as it needs to be done. But both stances would belie many of the nuances of the case. In part, the complexity lies in determining what represents the individual and what represents the community in this case. For some, the organization represents collective interests (see Boyd & Waymer, 2011); yet, the corporation has been granted the rights of an individual in the United States. Given this, when we speak of individual interests, whose interests are we referencing? Is it the company, its executives, all its employees, Toyota dealers, Toyota owners, those who share the road with Toyotas, and/or communities whose economies are supported by Toyota? Deetz (1995) suggested considering corporate responsibility through a lens of pro-profit versus pro-people. Yet, in this case study the lines between profit and people, individual and community are blurred.

By way of a final coda, we offer the example of the many Toyota dealers who came to lobby Congress during the Toyota hearings. In short, they argued that their livelihood depended on the ability of Toyota to continue operating. Extending this logic, then, one can begin to see Toyota's dilemma in a different light. Certainly, Toyota was acting in self-interested ways, and clearly the company had many missteps, but if it had decided to engage in full transparency from the beginning of the issue and the company had experienced significant financial setbacks, the negative impacts might have been far reaching in this country and touched the lives of any number of individuals and communities. Finding the tipping point seems to be the issue.

In the end, what at first seemed such a clear-cut case raises more questions than it answers. Despite the many ways in which Toyota failed to engage publics and act transparently, the company has emerged relatively unscathed. This outcome begs the question of what type of event would compel an organization to act more responsibly earlier than Toyota did. In this framing of the issue, the NHTSA, legislators, and the general public also may have needed to play a larger role earlier in the issue. Thus, the Toyota case can be viewed as a call to rethink the role of both external and internal organizational stakeholders in maintaining ethical standards of corporate practice—that is, corporations, employees, consumers, government bodies, advocacy groups, and communities all may need to take more ownership of ethical challenges.

DISCUSSION QUESTIONS

1. Is it reasonable to expect corporations to serve community interests above their own corporate interests? What ethical standards that you have studied suggest corporations should serve community interests above their own? In what ways, if any, did Toyota serve community interests above its own?

2. What limitations, if any, should be placed on the ability of corporations to influence government through lobbying and related efforts? How might nonprofit voices be allowed to gain equal influence in policy making and regulatory processes?

3. To what extent were the views of the general public present and/or silenced in the Toyota congressional hearings?

4. How and why do you think Toyota employees may have convinced themselves that their company's technology could not be responsible for the acceleration problems?

5. If you were working for Toyota, would you have recommended a more transparent and dialogic communication stance earlier in the life cycle of the issue? Why or why not?

6. What were the ethical obligations of Toyota, the NHTSA, and the general public in this case? How did each of these stakeholders fulfill those obligations?

REFERENCES

Boyd, J., & Waymer, D. (2011). Organizational rhetoric: A subject of interest(s). *Management Communication Quarterly, 25,* 474-493.

CNN Wire Staff. (2010, December 21). Toyota to pay U.S. $32.4 million over recalls. Retrieved from http://edition.cnn.com/2010/BUSINESS/12/20/toyota.recall.penalties/index.html

Crable, R., & Vibbert, S. (1985). Managing issues and influencing public policy. *Public Relations Review, 11*(2), 3–15.

Deetz, S. (1992). *Democracy in an age of corporate colonization: Developments in communication and the politics of everyday life.* Albany: State University of New York Press.

Deetz, S. (1995). *Transforming communication, transforming business: Building responsive and responsible workplaces.* Cresskill, NJ: Hampton Press.

Ditlow, C., & Center for Auto Safety. (n.d.). *Statement on failure to pass Motor Vehicle Safety Act of 2010.* Retrieved from http://www.autosafety.org/statement-failure-pass-motor-vehicle-safety-act-2010

Habermas, J. (1984). *Theory of communication action, volume 1: Reason and the rationalization of society* (Thomas McCarthy, Trans.). Boston: Beacon Press.

Habermas, J. (1987). *Theory of communicative action, volume 2: Lifeworld and systems* (Thomas McCarthy, Trans.). Boston: Beacon Press.

Kageyama, Y. (2011, January 24). Toyota sold 8.4M vehicles in 2010 to hold top spot. *Associated Press Newswire.* Retrieved from http://hosted.ap.org/dynamic/stories/A/AS_JAPAN_TOYOTA?SITE = DCS AS&SECTION = HOME&TEMPLATE = DEFAULT

Lichtblau, E. (2010, February 23). Lawmakers' ties to Toyota questioned at start of inquiries. *New York Times,* p. B1.

Maynard, M. (2010, April 12). Toyota delayed a U.S. recall, documents show. *New York Times,* p. A1.

McCurry, J. (2010, February 23). Leaked memo about safety savings increases pressure on Toyota boss. *The Guardian,* p. 23.

Reuters. (2010, April 9). Toyota knew of flaws in 2006. *The Gazette,* p. B6.

Sanchanta, M., & Takahashi, Y. (2010, February, 18). U.S. panel won't hear Toyota. *Wall Street Journal,* p. 1.

Theimer, S. (2010, February 8). The influence game: Toyota's powerful DC friends. *The Associated Press.* Retrieved from http://abcnews.go.com/Business/wireStory?id = 9774391

Vartabedian, R., & Bensinger, K. (2010, July 12). Auto safety bill is scaled back in face of industry opposition. *Los Angeles Times*. Retrieved from http://articles.latimes.com/2010/jul/12/business/la-fi-0712-toyota-legislation-20100712

Vlasic, B. (2010, February 1). Toyota's slow awakening to a deadly problem. *New York Times*. p. 1A.

Wald, M. W. (2011, February 8). Electronic flaws did not cause Toyota problems, U.S. says. *New York Times*. Retrieved from http://www.nytimes.com/2011/02/09/business/09auto.html

Sanlu's Milk Contamination Crisis

Organizational Communication in Conflicting Cultural, Economic, and Ethical Context

Shari R. Veil and Aimei Yang

This case study examines how organizations can manage issues by effectively communicating with a range of stakeholders, both internally and externally. It also explores how cultural factors and media context may impact organizational decision making. More specifically, it considers how organizational commitment, face maintenance, and personal networks can impede ethical decision making.

Issue management is essential for organizations to effectively communicate with the public and establish and maintain relationships with stakeholders (Taylor, Vasquez, & Doorley, 2003). Most issues do not evolve into crises; however, some may be exacerbated by inappropriate issue management strategies and eventually threaten the existence of an organization (Heath, 1997). This case study analyzes how cultural factors and media context may have influenced the ethical decision-making process of a Chinese dairy company in the midst of a product quality issue that ultimately sickened almost 300,000 infants, killing at least 6, and spurring the demise of the Chinese dairy industry in 2008 (Vause, 2009). The case is followed by a discussion of Confucian organizational culture and the lack of media transparency in China to demonstrate how context may influence the issue management strategies of an organization.

SANLU'S MILK CONTAMINATION CRISIS

In 2008, Sanlu Group was a state-owned dairy product company based in Shijiazhuang in the Hebei Province of China with annual sales of about $1.5 billion (Seng, 2009). Fonterra, a New Zealand company, owned 43% of Sanlu stock as part of a collective ownership enterprise. According to Customs of China records, Chinese milk exports had increased 50.4% from 2007 to 2008. Sanlu had steadily been increasing sales of milk, but the productivity of milk from its own farms could not meet the increasing demands. To accommodate the demand, Sanlu had to buy large quantities of milk from brokers, who collected milk from multiple smaller farms. Sanlu had set quality standards for the collected milk and measured protein content through a hydrogen test.

In October 2007, two brokers began producing and selling "protein powder." The "protein powder" contained melamine, an industrial chemical used as a fire retardant and pesticide, which when mixed with water increases hydrogen levels. The brokers were able to dilute the collected milk with water and thereby sell more milk, without failing the hydrogen test. As the strategy proved to be profitable, 19 other milk brokers imitated the actions, and a substantial amount of milk was contaminated with melamine (*ChinaDaily*, 2009; Seng, 2009).

Internal Issue Management

In December 2007, Sanlu started to receive complaints from consumers who found red solid matter in their babies' urine, all of whom had been fed with Sanlu milk formula (Seng, 2009). In March 2008, Sanlu Vice President Yuliang Wang was informed. Sanlu internally confirmed the milk formula had a quality problem in April. In May, CEO Tian Wenhua was informed, and Sanlu confidentially paid a total of $130 million for the medical bills of sick infants (Bian, 2009).

In July, there was a spike in the number of babies with reported kidney problems. News coverage started to link the sick children to milk formula without identifying the responsible company (Bian, 2009). On August 1, 2008, in an administration meeting held at Sanlu headquarters, Vice President Yuliang Wang reported they confirmed Sanlu milk formula had been contaminated with melamine. CEO Tian Wenhua asked to keep the information to a handful of high-level administrators. Even in documents distributed inside of Sanlu, names such as "A material" or "B material" were used to denote melamine (Bian, 2009). On August 2, Sanlu notified the board members from its venture partner Fonterra, who encouraged Sanlu to announce a full recall. After almost 2 weeks went by without action, on August 14, Fonterra reported the contamination to the Ministry of Foreign Affairs (O'Sullivan, 2008).

External Issue Management

Sanlu formed three special groups to address the issue externally. The first one was a technology research group, the second was a consumer affairs group, and the last one was a media relations group. During court testimony, the head of the media relations group stated that, especially in Hunan Province and Hubei Province where consumers' complaints were most frequent, Sanlu used its advertising contracts to influence media coverage, and asked the local media to keep silent (Long, 2008).

Sanlu also attempted to collaborate with Baidu, the leading search engine website in China. A public relations agency working for Sanlu (the name of the agency was not reported by any news source) suggested Sanlu should pay Baidu 3 million Yuan (about $500,000) as an advertisement fee to get "special protection" (Lin, 2009). The "special protection" meant that Baidu would block out negative news about Sanlu from small websites and personal blogs (Wen, 2008).

In addition, Sanlu sent a letter to the Shijiazhuang Government on August 2 to report the problem and ask the government to strengthen regulations over dairy producers (Seng, 2009). The vice mayor of Shijiazhuang told Sanlu administrators not to make the contamination public "for fear of social unrest and so as not to embarrass the country so soon before the Olympics" (Spencer, 2009, para. 12). China hosted the 2008 Olympic Games August 18 through 24. Sanlu sent another letter to the Shijiazhuang Government on August 29 asking for assistance in quieting the potential story. The letter stated the following:

> The government should stop the media coverage of this quality problem of Sanlu formula milk for babies. This regulation over media coverage can avoid leading to panic on the side of consumers; could reduce the possibility of an earthquake on the Chinese dairy industry, and could avoid a series of negative influence on the development of dairy industry. (Seng, 2009)

On September 2, China Central Television (CCTV) aired *The Story Behind 1100 Times of Quality Examination* (Lin, 2009), a documentary showing how the Sanlu milk formula was produced and how much Sanlu cares about the quality of its products.

Public Response

On September 9, New Zealand foreign affairs officials contacted Beijing food safety authorities (O'Sullivan, 2008). Two days later, the first coverage that identified Sanlu as responsible for the sick infants was published by the *Oriental Morning Post,* one of the leading market-oriented media of Shanghai (Jian, 2008a). Hundreds of websites posted the news within a few hours. According to the blog of the journalist who wrote the story, Sanlu called several times on September 11 to ask him to withdraw the story and even threatened to sue him (Jian, 2008b). On the morning of September 11, Sanlu denied there was a quality problem with Sanlu milk formula. The head of media relations told the media they had heard rumors about the quality issue but were confused how that could happen when they have such a high sense of social responsibility and have been specially preparing the formula for 60 years. He stated, "We do not wish to hide any problem from our consumers. And, I surely can tell you with one hundred percent certainty that there is no quality problem with our formula milk for babies" (Song, 2008). By that evening, Sanlu changed its position and stated that about 700 tons of the Sanlu milk formula had been contaminated by melamine, and it was possible that competitors may have poisoned Sanlu milk formula (Sun & Jing, 2009).

On September 12, the chief manager of the marketing department told the media that farmers illegally added the chemical to their milk. That evening, CEO Tian Wenhua told the media the following: "This issue is caused by some illegal activities in the purchase process of original milk. Sanlu is innocent in the entire case, and is also a victim" (Xiang, 2008). On September 15, Sanlu Vice President Zhenglin Zhang signed and aired the following apology letter:

> The severe quality problem of Sanlu formula milk for babies has considerably damaged the health of many babies and deeply concerned their parents. We feel extremely sorry and wish we can express our sincere apology. . . . Our company

now states that we will recall all products produced before August 6, 2008. . . . Our company will also help to cure the sick babies and be responsible for the medical expenses. Again, please accept our sincere apology for all the sick babies and their parents. (Sanlu Group, 2008)

Aftermath

On September 17, CEO Tian Wenhua was arrested and sentenced to life in prison 4 months later. Vice President Wang was sentenced to 15 years in prison after attempting suicide; two other administrators of Sanlu were sentenced to 5 to 8 years. Three milk brokers were sentenced to death, and two brokers were sentenced to life in prison. Six farmers were sentenced to terms varying between 5 and 15 years (*ChinaDaily*, 2009; Vause, 2009). Including the mayor of Shijiazhuang, several top officials of the local government were removed from their offices (Liu, 2008). On December 25, Sanlu announced bankruptcy. The assets worth $3 billion were sold to pay for the medical bills of the sick children (Long, 2008).

Across China, more than 20 milk producers were eventually linked to the contamination. Almost 300,000 babies were reported to have suffered kidney damage, and at least 6 died (Vause, 2009). According to Customs of China records, dairy product exports in October 2008 declined by 99.2%. By the end of December 2008, hundreds of dairy farms and companies announced bankruptcy. Analysts estimate the Chinese dairy industry may need 5 to 10 years to recover (The Beijing News, 2008). The following discussion examines how cultural factors and media context may have influenced Sanlu's ethical decision-making process.

CONFUCIAN ORGANIZATIONAL CULTURE

In Chinese organizational settings, three core Confucian values have been reported as commonly existing in interpersonal and interorganizational relationships: (1) organizational commitment, (2) face maintenance, and (3) network and relationship—*guanxi* in Chinese (Chen & Chung, 1994; Cheng, Jiang, & Riley, 2003; Sriramesh, Kim, & Takasaki, 1999).

Organizational Commitment

Organizational commitment is an individual's level of identification with a particular organization (Cheng et al., 2003). The in-group bond can be very strong, and individuals are often expected to sacrifice personal or out-group interests for in-group interests (Chen, 1991). In a Confucian culture, one of the most important functions of leadership is to cultivate a united in-group identity and encourage members to show their respect and loyalty to their group (Cheng et al., 2003). Subordinates are expected to obey their supervisor as sons and daughters obey their parents.

Following the traditional Confucian family model, CEO Tian Wenhua was the householder and highest authority in the family. She stated in an earlier interview that "I always think that Sanlu is my family, and my family is Sanlu" ("Tian Wenhua Attempted to Commit

Suicide," 2008). In managing the milk contamination issue, the in-group interests of the Sanlu family were prioritized in the corporation's strategy. Sanlu sacrificed quality control for faster expansion in market share, which is at the root of the issue. Sanlu also failed to identify, analyze, and monitor the early signs of the issue, therefore missing the opportunity to take a proactive response.

Tian Wenhua's and the other administrators' narrowly defined loyalty toward Sanlu as the in-group may have misled ethical judgment. When the administrators of Sanlu confirmed the quality problem in May 2008, they chose to cover up the issue instead of informing parents who were still feeding their babies Sanlu milk formula. This decision led to further illnesses and even deaths. Sanlu's strategy was blinded by its in-group interests and failed to fulfill Sanlu's obligation as a member of a society.

Face Maintenance

Face refers to an individual's or organization's socially approved self-image. To save face is to protect one's image (Lim & Bowers, 1991). Although the need to save face is universal, in Chinese society, it is highly valued and can strongly influence individual or organizational decision making (Chen & Chung, 1994). Confucianism encourages pursuit of face for moral reasons (Chang & Holt, 1991). However, face is also valued for instrumental reasons. Good face can increase a businessperson's influence over relationships and his or her accomplishment level. Members of a group are expected to protect the face of their group. To cause one's own group to lose face is considered unacceptable and unfaithful (Yu & Wen, 2003).

Although Sanlu formed three special groups to address the quality issue, the overall guideline was to cover up the contamination instead of warning consumers and taking responsibility. In other words, the major concern was placed on saving the face of the company. Thus, loyalty to Sanlu was prioritized over telling the truth. With the Olympic Games approaching, government officials also sought to save face and not "embarrass the country" (Spencer, 2009, para. 12). After the issue escalated, multiple administrators of Sanlu attempted to commit suicide, demonstrating how difficult it is for individuals to deal with losing face in a Confucian culture.

Guanxi

Guanxi is a network of personal relationships. The maintenance of relationship harmony requires individuals to respect social roles and authority. Having guanxi with an important leader in the government can help a businessperson gain social approval, respect, and other favorable conditions (Park & Luo, 2001). In China, many business leaders, especially administrators of state-owned enterprises, develop deep relationships with local governments. Such relationships allow these companies to enjoy less supervision and more protection from the government (Vanhonacker, 2004).

When Sanlu realized the serious nature of the quality issue, it informed the local government and asked the local government to help manage the crisis and limit news coverage. Before the mayor and top officials in Shijiazhuang were removed from office, little negative news coverage could be found. Sanlu also used its guanxi with the media to influence media content by leveraging its advertising contracts both off and on-line (Long, 2008; Wen, 2008). The use of guanxi with the media demonstrates the further concern of media nontransparency.

MEDIA TRANSPARENCY IN CHINA

Media transparency refers to the ideal condition that reporters and the media are subject to limited influence from the state or corporations, and, as a result, they can provide objective coverage on social issues. Media nontransparency, on the contrary, describes "any form of payment for media coverage or any influence on editorial decisions that is not clearly indicated in the finished product or the media" (Tsetsura & Zou, 2009, p. 3). Although Chinese media are still categorized as government departments, other than important party mouthpieces such as the *People's Daily*, governmental subsidies for media outlets have been gradually reduced since the 1990s (Shi, 2008). As the government has reduced the financial support for media, severe competition has pushed some media to value profit-making over journalistic integrity. An international index of media bribery ranked China, among 66 countries, the country in which media nontransparency is most likely to occur (Kruckeberg, Tsetsura, & Ovaitt, 2005).

Sanlu took advantage of the lack of media transparency in China. While Sanlu gained a short-term advantage, this practice caused greater risk to thousands of babies. The existence of a nontransparent media system complicated the situation because such a system allows greater leeway for unethical practice in issue management. Although Chinese consumers have the same right to know as their counterparts in any other country, such rights cannot be fully guaranteed in a nontransparent media system. As shown in this case, media were purposefully influenced by Sanlu. The media nontransparent problem was especially evident in local media, which were subject to both local government influence and the relationship with Sanlu.

The Sanlu case reveals that cultural factors impact issue management strategies. In addition, organizations operating in a media environment with limited transparency can manipulate relationships with local government and media in an attempt to reduce traditional and new media coverage of an issue. Thus, the cultural context in which Sanlu operated and the lack of transparency in Chinese media may have profoundly influenced Sanlu's ethical decision-making process.

DISCUSSION QUESTIONS

1. To what extent do the economic pressures of supply and demand influence an organization's ethical boundaries?

2. Do you believe Sanlu leadership received fair punishment in light of the case findings and contextual background?

3. What lessons does this case provide for international organizations considering collaboration with Chinese organizations?

4. What examples of media nontransparency can be seen in the U.S. media?

5. How can the penetration of the Internet and free flow of information online contribute to resolving media nontransparency problems?

REFERENCES

The Beijing News. (2008, December). *Affected by the Sanlu crisis, the export of milk declined by 90%*. Retrieved from http://news2.eastmoney.com/080916,923232.html

Bian, C. Y. (2009, January). "How does the A material" be covered and exposed: Three meetings in Sanlu. *Financial Daily*. Retrieved from http://www.china-cbn.com (In Chinese).

Chang, H. C., & Holt, G. R. (1991). More than a relationship: Chinese interaction and the principle of kuanhsi. *Communication Quarterly, 39*, 251–271.

Chen, M. C. (1991). Family culture and management. In G. S. Yang & C. S. Tseng (Eds.), *A Chinese perspective of management* (pp. 189–212). Taipei: Kwei Kwan.

Chen, G. M., & Chung, J. (1994). The impact of Confucianism on organizational communication. *Communication Quarterly, 42*, 93–105.

Cheng, B. S., Jiang, D. Y., & Riley, J. H. (2003). Organizational commitment, supervisory commitment, and employee outcomes in the Chinese context: Proximal hypothesis or global hypothesis? *Journal of Organizational Behavior, 24*, 313–334.

ChinaDaily. (2009, March 26). Court upholds death penalty in milk scandal. Retrieved from http://www.chinadaily.com.cn/china/2009-03/26/content_7620098.htm

Heath, R. L. (1997). *Strategic issues management*. Thousand Oaks, CA: Sage.

Jian, G. Z. (2008a). After drinking Sanlu Milk, 14 babies from Gansu Province got Kidney Diseases. *Oriental Morning Post*, p. A20 (In Chinese).

Jian, G. Z. (2008b). Why I have to point out "Sanlu." Retrieved from http://news.163.com/08/1218/11/4TEN8LLI00012QEA.html

Kruckeberg, D., Tsetsura, K., & Ovaitt, F. (2005). International index of media bribery. In *The Global corruption report 2005: Transparency International* (pp. 258–261). London: Pluto Press.

Lim, T., & Bowers, J. W. (1991). Facework, solidarity, approbation, and tact. *Human Communication Research, 17*, 415–450.

Lin, H. B. (2009, February 5). "Song of praise" for CCTV and Baidu Search Engine. *Nanfang Weekend*, p. D21 (In Chinese).

Liu, J. (2008, September 18). China milk scandal shows ties between companies, city officials. *Bloomberg*. Retrieved from http://www.bloomberg.com/apps/news?pid = newsarchive&sid = aph p1fx8M0Mw&refer = india

Long, L. (2008, November 21). The biography of Sanlu. *21 Century Business News*. Retrieved from http://www.21cbh.com (In Chinese).

O'Sullivan, F. (2008, September 21). Embassy officials slow to call toxic alert. *New Zealand Herald*. Retrieved from http://www.nzherald.co.nz/nz/news/article.cfm?c_id = 1&objectid = 10533363

Park, S. H., & Luo, Y. (2001). Guanxi and organizational dynamics: Organizational networking in Chinese firms. *Strategic Management Journal, 22*, 455–477.

Sanlu Group. (2008). Apology letter to the sick babies and their parents. Retrieved from http://www.cmda.gov.cn/News/redianhuati/redianhuatizhuanti/sanlunaifenshijian/xinwenbaodao/2008-12-03/1195.html

Seng, Y. (2009, May). The ten months before the exposure of Sanlu quality problem. *Nanfang Weekend*. Retrieved from http://www.infzm.com/content/22472 (In Chinese).

Shi, Y. (2008). The rise of China's media supermarket: An appraisal of cultural imperialism's relevance to the Chinese TV industry. *International Journal of Communication, 2*, 1199–1225.

Song, W. G. (2008, September). *Sanlu claimed it has stopped produce 18 Yuan formula milk for babies*. Retrieved from http://news.21cn.com/domestic/difang/2008/09/11/5186343.shtml

Spencer, R. (2009, January 22). Two sentenced to death over China melamine milk scandal. *The Telegraph*. Retrieved from http://www.telegraph.co.uk/news/worldnews/asia/china/4315627/Two-sentenced-to-death-over-China-melamine-milk-scandal.html

Sriramesh, K., Kim, Y., & Takasaki, M. (1999). Public relations in three Asian cultures: An analysis. *Journal of Public Relations Research, 11*, 271–293.

Sun, S., & Jing, Q. (2009). Crisis communication and food safety: What Sanlu crisis showed to us. *Modern Business Trade Industry, 6*, 31–32 (In Chinese).

Taylor, M., Vasquez, G. M., & Doorley, J. (2003). Extending issues management: A case study of engagement between Merck and AIDS activists. *Public Relations Review, 29*, 257–270.

"Tian Wenhua attempted to commit suicide." (2008, December 26). *Takungpao*. Retrieved from http://www.takungpao.com.hk/news/08/12/26/images_0706-1009812.htm

Tsetsura, K., & Zuo, L. (2009). *Guanxi, gift-giving, or bribery? Ethical considerations of paid news in China*. Paper presented at the 2009 AEJMC conference, Boston.

Vanhonacker, W. R. (2004). *Guanxi* networks in China. *China Business Review, 31*(3), 48–53.

Vause, J. (2009, January 22). Death sentences in China tainted milk case. *CNN*. Retrieved from http://articles.cnn.com/2009-01-22/world/china.tainted.milk_1_sanlu-group-tian-wenhua-chinese-dairy?_s=PM:WORLD

Wen, M. (2008). Sanlu crisis communication: What are their problems? *Foreign Business, 10*, 36–37. (In Chinese).

Xiang, Y. L. (2008). *Whose fault, if Sanlu is "innocent"?* Retrieved from http://admin.sinoth.com/Doc/article/2008/9/13/server/1000024256.htm

Yu, T., & Wen, W. (2003). Crisis communication in Chinese culture: A case study in Taiwan. *Asian Journal of Communication, 13*, 50–64.

What About the People in the "People's Car"?

Tata Motors Limited and the Nano Controversy

Rahul Mitra

This case examines the economic, social, and political responsibilities of multinational companies (MNCs) in developing countries. In particular, it considers the extent to which companies should play an explicit role in strengthening political governance in emerging economies throughout the world. In addition, it explores whether a company can be considered virtuous if its corporate social responsibility (CSR) initiatives are opposed to citizens in the country where it operates.

The increasing global relevance of MNCs from emerging economies, such as China and India, makes it imperative to consider organizational ethics and practices in these contexts. This case study examines Tata Motors Limited (TML), one of India's most prominent and well-respected companies. TML is a good candidate for study both because of its recent global expansion (in 2008, it acquired Jaguar and Land Rover from Ford Motors) and its relationship with the political establishment in India. While traditional frameworks of business ethics tend to downplay the political role of corporations, emphasizing behavior that is *voluntarily* virtuous, this case study shows how emerging economy contexts might involve an explicitly political role for corporations. Here, I examine a particular episode involving TML: Its breakthrough launch in 2008 of the world's cheapest car (costing only $2,500), billed as the "people's car" (Faro, 2008), which ran into a fair amount of controversy.

This case highlights four key ethical dilemmas. Briefly, these are (1) How may stakeholders be meaningfully engaged with, rather than engaged merely as an exercise in public relations? (2) Are a firm's CSR efforts on the ground (perhaps with the best intentions) meaningful if there is strident opposition to the company's overall policies? (3) Are companies really "above and beyond" politics, or how might they be connected to politics in emerging economy contexts? (4) Finally, how does the emerging economy context reframe ethical organizational action?

This case begins by providing a brief background and arguing its relevance to organizational communication. I then describe TML's discursive strategy during the events described and conclude with the ethical issues—and their implications—that arise here.

CASE BACKGROUND AND RELEVANCE

TML is India's largest automobile company, with revenues upwards of $8.8 billion, the world's fourth largest truck manufacturer and second largest bus manufacturer (OICA, 2007). The firm has consistently been voted one of India's most trusted, socially responsible, and responsive to national needs (Kumar, Murphy, & Balsari, 2001; Tata Motors, 2007, 2008). Its Chairman Ratan Tata conceived the world's cheapest car, christened the Nano, in 2004 "to provide safe, all-weather personal and family transport at an affordable price of Rs 1 lakh" (Tata Motors, 2008, p. 5), or around $2,500. In a country with very low car penetration (only 7 cars per 1,000 people) and a large gap between prices of two-wheelers and small cars, the company concluded there was "a huge opportunity" for a cheap, reliable entry-level car and that "the TATA Nano would address this huge potential in demand" (Tata Motors, 2008, p. 30). The Nano was also explicitly connected to the emerging economy aspirations among (urban) middle-class Indians, identified by TML (Faro, 2008) as their main customers: "We are happy to present the People's Car to India and we hope it brings the joy, pride and utility of owning a car to many families who need personal mobility." From 2004 to 2006, while the company's engineering team worked on the Nano's design, top management scouted possible locations for its new factory. On May 11, 2006, TML announced that the Nano factory would be built at Singur, in the state of West Bengal,[1] for which 997 acres of land would be acquired from local farmers by the government.

The announcement was greeted by contrasting reactions. On the one hand, the urban media was largely amenable to the decision (Mitra, 2010). West Bengal had enjoyed a fair degree of industrial prominence prior to the 1970s but had seen a severe outflow of business since then. Bagging the prestigious TML project was widely heralded as a reversal of fortunes; for instance, a TML release said, "This investment is a reflection of the confidence that the Tata Group has in the investment climate and the Government of West Bengal. We look forward to the opportunity of revitalizing the automotive industry in the state" (Ray, 2006).

In Singur itself, the reaction was mixed. The owners of the land to be acquired were monetarily compensated by the State, and few of them had any objections. The opposition stemmed from the landless agricultural laborers or sharecroppers, whose source of livelihood was about to be taken from them for a relatively small sum of money. Because of the prominence of the Nano project, political parties soon got involved. The main opposition

---

[1] For the sake of readers unfamiliar with the Indian Constitution, India is a federal but unitary nation-state in that although there is a central government at New Delhi, the country is composed of separate states, each with their own government. West Bengal and Gujarat, mentioned in this case study, are two such states. I distinguish between "state" and "State" here: while the former (small "s") signifies geographical territory (for instance, "the state of West Bengal"), the latter (big "S") indicates governmental authority exercised by its agencies and representatives (so that the State becomes a stakeholder for corporations operating in a territory).

party in the national Parliament disrupted legislative proceedings, calling on the West Bengal government to halt land acquisition (PTI, 2006), and the leader of the main state-level opposition party (the Trinamool Congress), Mamata Banerjee, rushed to organize protests and rallies at Singur. The discord came to a head on March 14, 2007, resulting in the deaths of 50 protestors at Nandigram, another site earmarked for land acquisition. Nevertheless, the state government remained firm on Singur, blaming the opposition party for the violence (Sen, 2007).

Through most of the fracas, TML maintained silence, delegating voice to the State. The protests hurt both the company's reputation and stock price, as analysts worried about the impact of further costs/delays to its bottom line (for instance, see Equitymaster, 2008). While there had been media speculation as early as 2006 that the company would relocate from Singur if the situation did not calm down, senior company executives quelled these rumors (TOI, 2006). It was only in September 2008—8 months after the unveiling of the Nano—that a press release issued by TML (Ray, 2008b) acknowledged the ongoing protests and announced a suspension of construction work at the site. Soon after, the company moved from the state.

This case study is relevant for organizational communication, at large, and the discussion of business ethics, in particular, for at least four reasons. First, existing theories and research on business ethics focus on American and European contexts, despite the increasing clout of emerging economy MNCs. This case study thus answers the call to consider organizational communication and ethical practices in other geographical regions, examining non-Western cultural subjectivities and sociohistorical contexts, particularly the unique discourses at play in emerging economies. Second, this case considers organizational ethics from a social perspective, as mediated through linkages among the firm, State agencies, and mainstream media. Through the examination of media releases on the Nano, this case examines how the organization and State are embroiled together. Following from this is its third contribution: Namely, the demonstration of how political discourses may allow corporations in emerging economy contexts to close off dissidence via the "beyond politics" economic objective and "delivering emerging economy aspirations" frame. Finally, this case affords an examination of CSR in conjunction with regular firm operations, not divorced from these. Thus, we must consider TML's CSR work at Singur *with* its goals of establishing the Nano plant there.

While reading the following case analysis, you are encouraged to think about the "right-right" dilemmas at stake: For instance, is TML correct in emphasizing jobs for individual people through the Nano project, or should it have focused on collective benefits for the entire community? Also, consider the framing of ethical practices: Was the company acting in line with its declared mission statement and code of conduct? Should companies be required to engage in participative decision making all the time, above and beyond these codes? What might be the benefits and downsides of these different approaches—*are* they, in fact, all that different? It might also be useful to think about the guiding ethical principles for both TML and the protesters: Is the issue here that of citizens' *rights,* the *duty* of corporations to make money, an organic *relationship* between community and company, or perhaps all of these? Can the controversy be traced to a fundamental disconnect here?

CASE ANALYSIS: TATA MOTOR LIMITED'S DISCURSIVE STRATEGY

TML's discursive strategy was composed of four main "stages"[2]: (1) ignore and divert, (2) engagement (?), (3) all-out offensive, and (4) finally, ignore again. These stages are not discrete phases in time, however, but frequently overlap; for instance, the second stage of engagement (?) may be construed as a type of diversion (the first stage), and so on.

Ignore and Divert

For most of the period examined, TML was silent on the protests at Singur; it was only as late as September 2, 2008, that the firm directly acknowledged them and suspended work at the site. Prior to that, the strategy seems to have been threefold: (1) ignore the protests entirely, (2) reify a social reality where the project enjoyed "enthusiastic support" (Ray, 2007a) from locals, and (3) divert attention away from the protests using alternative subjects.

Reification of the organization-preferred view occurred by using key words to manufacture the illusion of consent, giving prominence to relatively minor events or visits, and taking approval to be implicit where it is not voiced. TML (Tata, 2007a) went beyond "whole-hearted welcome" to posit an "ineradicable emotional bond between the company and the community," using evocative wordplay to amplify affirmation. The visit by a small delegation of Singur villagers to the company's prized Jamshedpur facility was showcased as evidence of "whole-hearted support" by the Singur community (Ray, 2007a). TML waxed eloquent about the "enthusiastic participation of Singur villagers in various unskilled jobs" (Ray, 2007b) and their response to its training program (Ray, 2007a, 2008a; Tata, 2007b). In none of the releases that dealt with the training, testing, or employment schedules for locals was there feedback from the villagers or trainees. There was *no* grappling with the issue that some community members may *not* seek employment at the Nano factory—these people and their rural narratives were completely erased and disqualified from consideration.

The diversionary strategy focused on several alternative themes: corporate development being elevated to national progress, the benefits of employment generation in the region, and CSR programs at Singur. Consider this representative excerpt: "Tata Motors is confident that the plant will become a catalyst for both greater well-being of Singur families and growth of the region" (Tata, 2007a). There are several abstractions here that do not provide concrete detail on corporate policy: "catalyst," "greater well-being," and "growth in the region." Instead of addressing the protests, the release showcased the Nano factory as a growth "catalyst," without explaining exactly what kind of growth it sought and how it might eventually work. The same holds true when the release mentions "well-being" of the local families: How does the firm understand well-being? How will it measure its increments? How will the car project contribute to it? These remain unanswered. These themes

---

[2] These stages were identified through a thematic analysis (Lee, 1999) of all TML media releases pertaining to the Nano project, starting with the announcement of the factory site (dated May 18, 2006) and ending with the car's commercial launch from its relocated plant (dated February 26, 2009). A total of 23 releases were analyzed, with TML Chairman Ratan Tata's speech at the unveiling ceremony. There were 33 pages of text in all.

and their central words (e.g., "growth," "development," "employment," and "future" for the corporate development theme) were found throughout the other releases.

Engagement (?)

The question mark here signifies the ambiguous nature of the firm's engagement with protesters: Engagement might even be an offensive strategy. When TML first acknowledged the Singur protests, they were referred to as "continued confrontation and agitation at the site," "environment of obstruction, intimidation and confrontation," and "intimidation and fear" (*One India News,* 2008)—hardly conducive for genuine engagement with alternative views. The use of terms like "continued" and similar descriptions (e.g., "five continuous days," "no change") imply the firm had addressed the situation earlier, though this is untrue. TML never explicitly entered into dialogue with the protesters, stressing that it was the role of the State to do so (Ray, 2008b, 2008c; *One India News,* 2008). When negotiations between the State and "the agitators" were underway, it remained merely "distressed at the limited clarity on the outcome of the discussions" (Ray, 2008b). In its limited role, TML (*One India News,* 2008) declared "there is no way this plant could operate efficiently unless the environment became congenial and supportive of the project," underlining that if things did *not* turn out conducive, it had the option of moving lock, stock, and barrel. Though TML (Ray, 2008c) signaled engagement by stressing the need to "evoke a positive response from the residents of Singur . . . [and] create a congenial environment . . . [for] all stakeholders," it is questionable if it recognized the protesters as legitimate stakeholders, given the "hostile and intimidating" (*One India News,* 2008) rhetoric.

Offensive

On October 3, 2008, TML announced its decision to relocate from Singur. The company referred to its long history to stress its noble intentions regarding economic growth and argued that the Nano had been "an expression of faith in the investor friendly atmosphere created by the State Government" (Tata, 2008a):

> The project was to be a showcase plant that would have considerably enhanced the visibility of the State, created jobs for the younger citizens of the State, and through the company's community programs would have enhanced the quality of life of the urban and rural population.

The Nano project's benefits to the local community were naturalized both by universalizing urban industrial concerns to larger societal needs of economic growth and invoking the legitimacy of the State. While earlier discursive attempts to avoid the Singur protests, pacify the protesters with talk of concern (but little engagement), or use abstractions to produce ambiguity had failed, the releases now framed the land acquisition protesters as violent, volatile, illegal, repressive, and antinational/community. The dissidents are posited to be everything the company is *not*. As opposed to TML's (Tata, 2008a) "immense patience," the protesters were a "volatile" mob (*One India News,* 2008), whose goal was not so much wanting to hold on to their way of life as it was refusing national growth/development. While the organization was a paragon of legal virtue, the dissidents were violently indulging in illegal modes of protest. They created a "heightened level of agitation and hostility," an atmosphere of "intimidation and fear" that made it impossible for law-abiding company representatives to operate: "Threats, intimidation and instances of assault and general obstruction in one form or the other have been the order of the day" (Tata, 2008a). While TML was the *facilitative* growth-driver for the community and nation as a whole, the dissidents were *repressive,* preventing people from going about their normal work activities. The firm's decision to relocate the Nano project stemmed out of its "concern for the physical security of their staff, contractors and vendors," even as it expressed "extreme anguish."

Finally, the protesters were politically motivated, in contrast to TML's agenda of apolitical growth. The dominance of the Trinamool Congress in the protests by this time strengthened the firm's case, as it declared "categorically that the NANO project having to be moved from West Bengal is entirely due to the continued agitative actions by the opposition party led by Ms. Mamata Banerjee with total disregard for the rule of law" (Tata, 2008a). Political interests were linked with the protests, which then constituted an obstacle to national growth: "In light of *the opposition's continued agitation* [italics added], there was no option but to move the project out of the State of West Bengal" (Tata, 2008a).

Ignore Again

Direct references to the Singur protests vanished after the October 3, 2008, release announcing TML's decision to relocate. In the last two releases studied, the focus shifted once more to the Nano's launch and expected economic benefits to its new home of Gujarat state. TML stressed the "overwhelming support from several states for relocating the plant" (Tata, 2008b) and the "unprecedented interest" (Tata, 2009) in the Nano. Ratan Tata was portrayed as the fearless leader, leading his company and the citizens of Gujarat to newer opportunities and better economic prospects. Abstractions (like "strong industrial progress" and "cascading impact," among others), with little concrete details, reinforced the organization's perspective. Importantly, TML defined "progress" as urban- and industry-oriented, rather than agriculture-based; its espoused economic growth relied on a top-down or trickle-down mechanism, rather than direct engagement with those on lower income levels. The release thus blended capitalist concerns and (urban) middle-class emerging economy aspirations to define the Indian nation-state. As far as the Singur protests were concerned, it is as if the company had washed its hands of the entire incident and decided not to address the topic again. While one of the earlier releases (*One India News,* 2008) mentioned the company was "exploring the possibility of absorbing" the locally trained employees at its other factories, this was both tentative and abstract ("exploring" and "possibility") and not mentioned again in later releases. Singur was a closed chapter.

THE ETHICAL ISSUES AT STAKE

This case study concludes with a discussion of the ethical issues at stake with TML—Nano. Four broad concerns have been identified here.

First, the case study highlights a *lack of meaningful stakeholder engagement* and participation. While choosing the Singur site, TML did not consider the wishes of the local community, especially the sharecroppers, though their land would be acquired and livelihood disrupted. While the company promises factory jobs to some locals, it was taken for granted that the community would welcome this overall turn of events. This highlights a "right-right" ethical dilemma in which the same bloc of stakeholders may be split: While some locals did in fact welcome the factory, a larger group opposed it. In such a situation, we must question the ethical practice adopted—that is, was there was any other way TML and the State could have obtained wider, more participative deliberation involving the local community, without it being purely a public relations exercise? Could and/or should TML have attempted to link its project to the local community more effectively, rather than emphasizing its role as a profit-making corporation? Or does its engagement with potential customers and vendors trump its relationship with the local community, since corporations need to make profits to survive?

Second, and related to this, is the ethical question of the *relevance of CSR* if, in fact, companies are strongly opposed by locals for their regular business practices/policies. In this case study, TML was reportedly committed to its CSR and goals of social uplift (evidenced both by its prior good record *and* its excellent activities at Singur, involving education, health care, women's organizing, etc.) but failed to consider the vehement opposition on account of the land acquisition. It became futile to argue that the State (and not TML directly) was the acquiring agency, because the company was then receiving the land from the State at a highly subsidized price. This is thus a double bind for CSR practitioners and organizational managers to consider: Given that the firm's very presence may be resisted actively by local communities, should the firm persist and try to assuage feelings by engaging in CSR, or should it leave? Perhaps the fault lies in a fundamental disconnect on the ethical base of CSR: Should CSR be based on the company's duty and role to make profits and be sustainable in the long run or on "virtuous" relationships with impacted stakeholders? Are these approaches mutually exclusive? In any case, how can companies make CSR more meaningful to communities opposed to them—and at what point does it become untenable for them to remain? What does this mean for their reputation, and how can companies safeguard it? For instance, TML suffered a grievous blow to its otherwise strong reputation in this case study.

Third, this case study highlights the *political entanglements* companies often negotiate, despite traditional theories of the firm that treat it as apolitical. While TML repeatedly stressed that it was "above and beyond" politics and accused the Singur protestors to be politically motivated (i.e., arguing that they were led by the Trinamool Congress opposition party), it showed itself to be profoundly political in turn. It enjoyed close links with the ruling party in the state, and State officials were actively involved in both land acquisition and TML's CSR activities (e.g., industrial training for locals offered at State facilities). Moreover, it can be argued that, in vehemently blaming the opposition Trinamool Congress, TML did in fact take a political stand in favor of the ruling party. This case then raises questions about the political ties, ideologies, and commitments avowed by corporations: Is it ethical for companies to take such political stands? Is this even avoidable, or are companies inevitably politically implicated in their decisions and practices? What are the different ways that companies may be involved with the dominant political machinery of the context? In the United States, for instance, corporate lobbying is a strategy that comes to mind, but are there other subtler mechanisms whereby companies may influence—and be influenced by—politics? How and why is this ethical, or not? Is this a "right-right" or a "right-wrong" dilemma, in the first place?

Finally, the case provokes questions on how the *emerging economy context may reframe organizational ethics*. TML justified the Singur land acquisitions through three routes: (1) enhanced mobility for several million Indians (hence, the "people's car"), (2) industrial growth for the West Bengal state ("revitalization"), and (3) employment in the industrial sector for people whose land was acquired (which was the main thrust of CSR at Singur). Ethical problems arise in (first) defining these aspirations and (second) effectively removing a community's livelihood and way of living, while attempting to deliver them. That is, these aspirations are centered on the urban middle-class, rather than poor rural communities, who are marginalized as antigrowth and antinationalist. Other discourses situated in emerging economy nations may be similarly used to reify corporate actions and marginalize dissidents, for instance, discourses of Confucian leadership in China (Mitra, 2011). Thus, managers located in emerging economy contexts must grapple with the ethics of organizational practice, keeping in mind their unique tensions.

This case, then, has focused on one of India's most prominent and well-respected companies to highlight how unique ethical challenges may arise in emerging economies. Managers and students of organizational communication should be aware of these and not be completely blindsided by traditional theories of the firm largely based in the West.

DISCUSSION QUESTIONS

1. What were the "right-right" and "right-wrong" dilemmas highlighted in this case study?

2. How can companies meaningfully engage stakeholders when there may be clear differences between them or when representative authority is debated (for instance, while the State is presumed to represent citizenry, what happens if stakeholder communities take a stand apart from that of the State)?

3. Does participation always lead to meaningful stakeholder engagement for ethical organizational practice? When can this be problematic?

4. Should companies base their CSR on duty, rights, utility, virtue, or relationships? Who should these be targeted to?

5. When corporate presence is strongly opposed by local communities but there are strong profit motives to stay, should companies try to win communities over or should they leave? How effective is CSR in this situation?

6. How may companies safeguard their reputation when their actions are strongly opposed by stakeholders? Is such safeguarding ethical?

7. Should companies be involved in political decisions of a region, community, or nation? Is such political involvement inevitable or not? What interests or ethical frameworks should guide companies' political involvement?

8. How may organizational ethics be affected by historical events and cultural discourses?

9. How may emerging economy aspirations in countries such as China, India, and Brazil affect organizational actions? Should companies be especially attuned to national and social interests in such contexts, where so many people are in poverty? If so, how?

REFERENCES

Equitymaster. (2008, October 17). Tata Motors Ltd. (TELCO). Research reports: Research on Indian large cap and mid cap stocks from Equitymaster.

Faro. (2008, January 10). *Tata Motors unveils the people's car: A comfortable, safe, all-weather car, high on fuel efficiency & low on emissions*. Retrieved from http://www.faro.com/contentv2.aspx?ct = mx&content = misc&item = 1473

Kumar, R., Murphy, D. F., & Balsari, V. (2001). *Altered images: The 2001 state of corporate responsibility in India poll*. London: Tata Energy Research Institute-Europe.

Lee, T. W. (1999). *Using qualitative methods in organizational research*. Thousand Oaks, CA: Sage.

Mitra, R. (2010). Organizational colonization and silencing strategies in the Indian media with the launch of the world's cheapest car. *Communication, Culture, & Critique, 3*, 572–606.

Mitra, R. (2011). Discursively grounding leadership in corporate social responsibility (and vice versa): The case of top 3 public Chinese banks. Presented at the annual conference of the International Communication Association at Boston.

OICA. (2007, July). World motor vehicle production by manufacturer. *Organisation Internationale des Constructeurs d'Automobiles (International Organization of Motor Vehicle Manufacturers)* Retrieved from http://www.oica.net/

One India News. (2008, September 3). Tata Motors suspends work on Nano plant in Singur. Retrieved from http://news.oneindia.in/2008/09/03/tata-motors-suspend-work-at-singur-nano-plant.html

PTI. (2006, December 4). Singur issue paralyses Parliament. *The Times of India*.

Ray, D. (2006, May 18). Tata Motors' first plant for small car to come up in West Bengal. *Tata Motors Limited*. Retrieved from http://www.tatamotors.com/media/press-releases.php?id = 224

Ray, D. (2007a, January 24). *Singur community comes forward for Tata Motors Small Car plant: About 250 villagers at work on a daily basis*. Tata Motors Limited. Retrieved from http://www.tatamotors.com/media/press-releases.php?id = 279

Ray, D. (2007b, February 8). *First self-help group of Singur women start food supply for Tata Motors project*. Tata Motors Limited. Retrieved from http://www.tatamotors.com/media/press-releases.php?id = 282

Ray, D. (2008a, January 16). *Tata Motors inducts batch of 80 youth as apprentices at Singur plant: 311 others under training*. Tata Motors Limited. Retrieved from http://www.tatamotors.com/media/press-releases.php?id = 341

Ray, D. (2008b, September 8). *Official press statement*. Tata Motors Limited. Retrieved from http://www.tatamotors.com/media/press-releases.php?id = 386

Ray, D. (2008c, September 14). *Official Tata Motors statement*. Tata Motors Limited. Retrieved from http://www.tatamotors.com/media/press-releases.php?id = 387

Sen, S. (2007, January 20). Singur an exception, Nandigram a blunder, says Buddhadeb. *The Times of India*. Retrieved from http://timesofindia.indiatimes.com/articleshow/msid-1323813,flstry-1.cms

Tata. (2007a, January 21). *Tata Motors begins initial steps for construction of Small Car plant in West Bengal*. Retrieved from http://www.tata.com/company/releases/inside.aspx?artid = fZjykGPaN3M =

Tata. (2007b, February 12). *Second batch of ITI-educated Singur youth take tests for Tata Motors training*. Retrieved from http://www.tata.com/company/releases/inside.aspx?artid = dC + clyCIklg =

Tata. (2008a, October 3). *Tata Motors to relocate Nano project from Singur*. Retrieved from http://www.tata.com/media/releases/inside.aspx?artid = wbGZ6WJ/Yko =

Tata. (2008b, October 7). *Tata Motors' new plant to come up in Gujarat: Chosen site is at Sanand, near Ahmedabad*. Retrieved from http://www.tata.com/article.aspx?artid = 5qUlIGBzAdY =

Tata. (2009, February 26). *Tata Motors announces the launch of Tata Nano*. Retrieved from http://www.tata.com/media/releases/inside.aspx?artid = + IVLhfLaNYA =

Tata Motors. (2007). *Sustainability*. Retrieved from http://www.tatamotors.com/sustainability/sustainability.php

Tata Motors. (2008). *Global compact—Communication on progress, 2007–2008*. Retrieved from http://www.tatamotors.com/sustainability/pdf/COP-2007-2008.pdf

TOI. (2006, November 26). Satisfied, Tatas stick to Singur. *The Times of India*.

PART III

Participation

Resistance and Belonging

The Chicago Blackhawks and the 2010 Chicago Annual Pride Parade

Dean E. Mundy

This case explores how an advocacy organization decides which voices within a diverse set of interest groups will be heard. In addition, it considers how members of such organizations can negotiate the relationship between their values and those of others participating in community events, with particular emphasis on addressing the tension between communicating an original message of resistance and communicating a message of mainstream inclusion.

Each summer, typically during the last weekend in June, LGBT (lesbian, gay, bisexual, and transgender) communities in major cities across the United States celebrate "Pride," multiday events highlighted by massive parades that bring together LGBT citizens and their supporters in order to raise crucial awareness of the LGBT experience. The roots of these celebrations can be traced to the June 1969 Stonewall Riots in New York City, when New York's gay community for the first time physically retaliated against police discrimination. What began as a protest to a police raid of the Stonewall Inn (a bar in Greenwich Village) coalesced into a 5-day, 500-person, community-wide, organized resistance. While the riots certainly were not the beginning of the gay movement, they precipitated a more vocal era in the movement that reflected a community willing to stand up to discrimination. The parades that have developed in the years since Stonewall have become perhaps the most visible markers of community activism and protest.

Today's Pride celebrations have become lavish, high-profile celebrations during which individuals reveal their LGBT identity and politicians take a stand in support of (or in opposition to) the LGBT community; many businesses now clamor to associate their name and products with the all-important LGBT market niche. The parades at the center of the celebrations always make good copy for media outlets. As in the days following the Stonewall Riots, these celebrations are important because they provide crucial markers of visibility for the LGBT community externally, and they reinforce to LGBT individuals the support network that is available to them locally. Today's support networks, though, increasingly include mainstream sources of power and influence and as such, raise interesting questions regarding what is communicated through 21st-century Pride celebrations. It creates a tension between communicating Stonewall's original messages of resistance and communicating 21st-century messages of mainstream inclusion.

The case of the 2010 Chicago Annual Pride Parade and the National Hockey League's (NHL's) Chicago Blackhawks reflects this tension and the corresponding ethical dilemmas facing Pride organizers and potential participants. Pride organizers must craft an event that celebrates the LGBT citizen and vocalizes the needs of the LGBT community while strengthening the relationship between LGBT citizens and the broader community. In so doing, they must determine which voices within the LGBT community are heard, the extent to which their events will reflect Pride's original messages of resistance, and the external organizations they seek to engage. Similarly, potential Pride participants must decide if they will join in the celebration and determine the appropriate manner of participation. These potential participants also must balance their own stakeholder expectations and make very clear determinations regarding short- and long-term goals regarding support for the LGBT community specifically and community outreach generally.

Ethical decision making therefore requires organizers and participants to answer two fundamental questions: (1) What are their duties as organizers and participants? (2) With whom do their loyalties lay? The answers are related, and they reveal the tensions between potentially competing duties and competing loyalties. Twentieth-century philosopher William D. Ross (1930) argued, for example, there exists a core set of competing duties from which individuals must choose in determining ethical action.[1] Different contexts, however, influence which duties become more or less salient, and the decision maker must determine which of the competing duties is most important in a specific situation.[2] In the process, decision makers also must determine to whom they are most loyal. Questions of loyalty are inherently social; they reveal the relationships in society that a decision maker values. Similar to questions of duty, though, these loyalties often compete and indeed conflict. It is up to the decision makers to determine which loyalties are most important, decisions that have important social implications.

As the case of the 2010 Chicago Annual Pride Parade will highlight, ethical decision making—in this case, determinations of duty and loyalty—does not occur in a vacuum. In many ways, the organizers and potential participants depend on each other to convey important public messages, and the actions of one have direct implications for the ethical choices available to the other. For example, participation in Pride celebrations by local businesses benefits Pride organizers financially while helping to provide crucial legitimacy for the broader community and the LGBT voice and reinforcing the importance of acknowledging the LGBT experience. Similarly, participation benefits local businesses because it provides an opportunity to demonstrate their involvement in the local community and their commitment to local citizens. Doing so legitimizes their own place in the local community.

It is important to ask, however, if the message of LGBT Pride changes as more "mainstream" organizations participate. Is there a point at which community involvement detracts from the celebration's goal of bringing awareness to the LGBT community and community-specific

---

[1] Ross's duties are fidelity (faithfulness), reparation (making amends), gratitude, justice (being fair), beneficence (doing good), self-improvement, and not injuring others. He argued that these duties are one's prima facie duties.

[2] In different ethical dilemmas, Ross argued that the specific context determines which prima facie duty becomes one's duty proper.

issues? Similarly, to what extent must organizers be mindful of sponsors' past relationship with the LGBT community? Does sponsorship by a business that previously has not demonstrated extensive support for the LGBT community create a perception of the LGBT community "selling out" for the sake of mainstream inclusion? In other words, should the mission of Pride celebrations change based on 40 years of progress since the Stonewall Riots? Can performances of resistance and belonging occur simultaneously? The case of the 2010 Chicago Annual Pride Parade provides an opportunity to explore potential answers to these questions.

THE 2010 CHICAGO ANNUAL PRIDE PARADE

Two first-time entries highlighted the 2010 Chicago Annual Pride Parade: Major League Baseball's Chicago Cubs and the NHL's 2010 Stanley Cup World Champion Chicago Blackhawks. The Cubs entered a float for the parade. The Blackhawks, on the heels of their championship, returned the Stanley Cup early to Chicago in order to walk in the parade. These entries were a milestone; "Gay Pride" and professional sports do not always mix.

Specifically the Blackhawks' case, however, elucidates important ethical questions regarding the intersection of corporate interest and social advocacy. In the midst of the NHL's Stanley Cup playoffs, the Chicago Gay Hockey Association (CGHA) invited the Blackhawks to participate in the Pride parade.[3] The Blackhawks beat the Philadelphia Flyers for the Stanley Cup on June 9, 2010; the Chicago Annual Pride Parade occurred shortly thereafter, on June 27. The Blackhawks agreed to participate approximately 1 week before the parade, but the circumstances and timing of their decision raised some eyebrows in the community. The day before the Blackhawks clinched the Stanley Cup, the *Chicago Tribune* distributed posters in support of the team that mockingly showed Flyers' player, Chris Pronger, dressed in a skirt. The picture was labeled "Chrissy Pronger" with the headline, "Looks like Tarzan, skates like Jane" (Obernauer, 2010). Subsequently, when media reported the Blackhawks celebrating with the Stanley Cup in their locker room, they also captured a whiteboard listing that same opposing player, Chris Pronger, followed by "is gay" (Wyshynski, 2010a).

Certainly, both instances reflected a heated competition—"trash-talking" in the midst of a world championship run. But they also certainly reflected derogatory statements regarding gender and sexuality. The case is not presented, however, to criticize the Blackhawks (or *Chicago Tribune*) or detract from the symbolic importance of the Blackhawks' decision to participate. The CGHA, the Pride organizers, and Chicago's LGBT community welcomed the Blackhawks with open arms. In addition, the Blackhawks' parade messaging demonstrated amazing support for the LGBT community. The example, however, illustrates the issues raised earlier regarding the line between using such a public, high-profile event as good public relations and participating in the true spirit of the event. Again, the decisions are as important for parade organizers as they are for the parade's participants; this specific case illuminates the tensions between messages of resistance to mainstream oppression and messages of inclusion in mainstream society. To that end, it is important to isolate and examine the two perspectives: the Pride organizers and the Chicago Blackhawks.

---

[3] The Stanley Cup is awarded to the NHL's world champions each year.

The Organizers' Perspectives

The comments made by parade organizers and the CGHA provide important insight regarding their decision to seek participation by the Blackhawks. Moreover, reviewing these comments in chronological order demonstrates the original rationale to invite the Blackhawks, the organizers' subsequent reaction to the controversial images, and their response to the Blackhawks' ultimate decision to participate. For example, the *Windy City Times*—an LGBT-focused publication—first reported on June 16 the CGHA's motivation to invite the Blackhawks. CGHA President Andrew Sobotka explained in the article, "The CGHA realized that there are plenty of opportunities for the Hawks to increase their presence in the gay community by being more inclusive" (Forman, 2010). The article also quoted CGHA member, Tony Tiet, who explained, "The Pride Parade is nothing close to the championship parade, but it is a parade to celebrate diversity and acceptance of the LGBT community. We would be honored to have the Hawks organization show their support by being there." The article concluded with "The Pride Parade is not simply an LGBT event, many CGHA players stressed. Consider all of the politicians and members of the media, radio and TV personalities, who march in the event, they said" (Forman, 2010).

Of course, the Blackhawks' decision to participate in the parade made headlines. Media were interested in addressing the derogatory *Chicago Tribune* and Blackhawk locker room images that emerged in the final week of the playoffs. For example, in one article, CGHA President Sobotka acknowledged, "For the 'Hawks, there might have been a little bit of motivation (for image rehab). We actually invited them before that story broke" (Wyshynski, 2010b). The article also juxtaposed the timing of the Blackhawks' decision with the earlier decision by Major League Baseball's Chicago Cubs to participate. In response to the journalist question, "Peer pressure?" Sobotka replied, "It definitely helped. . . . Having the Cubs there may have opened the 'Hawks' eyes a little bit" (Wyshynski, 2010b). That said, while the CGHA was hopeful that the Blackhawks would participate—perhaps with the Stanley Cup trophy in tow—Sobotka admitted, in this same article, that the organization, was "humble enough to take what we can get."

Despite the context of the Blackhawks' decision, Chicago Annual Pride Parade coordinator Richard Pfeiffer emphasized 3 days before the event the symbolic importance of the Blackhawks' and Cubs' participation. One reporter explained, for example, "Pfeiffer believes the prominent representation of two of Chicago's major sports teams reflects a major step forward in breaking down stereotypes and fostering positive attitudes" (Modrowski, 2010). Pfeiffer added, "It's a major breakthrough. Everybody is thrilled. I think it says something about the changing of our culture. So much has changed as far as attitudes" (Modrowski, 2010).

The Participants' Perspective

The Blackhawks did not comment on the derogatory images that emerged during the last week of the playoffs.[4] Regardless, the *Chicago Sun Times* broke the story that the

---

[4]One media outlet commented that given the postgame, championship atmosphere in the Blackhawks' locker room, someone who was not associated with the team easily could have added "is gay" to the whiteboard.

Blackhawks would participate in the Pride parade, explaining that the organization's president, John McDonough, planned to return the Stanley Cup to Chicago early (from the NHL draft in Los Angeles) in order to make an appearance. In commenting on the decision, the *Chicago Sun Times* quoted McDonough: "The power of the Cup is incomprehensible, and we recognize the importance of doing this. . . . It's important for the city and important for the franchise" (Sneed, 2010).

At the parade, the trophy was carried by Blackhawk defenseman Brent Sopel, who participated with his wife and four children. Sopel commented at his decision, "I'm honored to do it" (Sneed, 2010). In fact, several media outlets explained that Sopel and the Blackhawks dedicated their participation to Brendan Burke, the son of the NHL Toronto Maple Leafs general manager Brian Burke, who was killed in a car accident in February 2010, 3 months after coming out to his friends, family, and University of Miami hockey teammates. Sopel explained the following:

> Anybody who has had to bury a child has suffered a heartbreak and this was the first thing that came to mind. . . . Everything that happened last year with Brendan coming out last year and dying three months later, it was a tragedy. (Yerdon 2010)

In response to the Blackhawks' dedication, the Maple Leafs' Brian Burke commented as follows:

> Our entire family is touched by the kindness of Brent and Kelly Sopel, and that of the Blackhawks. . . . This is not a small step—it's a bold and important one. We are grateful that a statement of this magnitude is being made by the Sopels, the Blackhawks and the National Hockey League. (Yerdon, 2010)

THE COMMUNICATION CHALLENGE

Certainly, the context and timing of the Chicago Blackhawks championship and Chicago Annual Pride Parade celebration play a part in influencing public perception. Yes, in the days leading up to the Pride celebration, the *Tribune*'s derogatory poster and the image captured during the team celebration indicated a lack of sensitivity regarding representations of gender and sexuality. Similarly, the Cubs' earlier decision to participate in the parade may have added a degree of peer pressure. That said, the comments made during the parade by the Blackhawks and the dedication of their participation to a fellow NHL hockey family reflect a sincere interest to participate in the true spirit of Pride. These circumstances did not go unnoticed by the parade organizers and CGHA, yet they reinforced the importance of participation by such a mainstream, symbolic organization—an organization emblematic of Chicago in the midst of celebrating a world championship. Their comments indicated that participation by the Blackhawks was perhaps a teaching moment for the organization and certainly represented a teaching moment for the Chicago area and the broader hockey community.

Evaluating the individual perspectives in the case returns us to the original questions. To what extent must organizers be mindful of sponsors' past relationship with the LGBT community? Is there a risk that sponsorship by a business that previously has not demonstrated extensive support for the LGBT community may create a perception of the LGBT community "selling out" for the sake of mainstream inclusion? In other words, what is the balance between resistance and belonging? It seems, at least from this example, that the purpose of Pride has shifted from the protests and activism witnessed in the days following Stonewall. Yet, to what extent has this shift occurred, and to what extent is that shift beneficial? On one hand, Pride is about promoting acceptance of the LGBT community and raising awareness regarding community needs and the LGBT identity. On the other hand, as the CGHA argued, the Chicago Annual Pride Parade is no longer simply an LGBT event.

Embedded in these questions are the ethical dilemmas facing the organizers and participants: What are their respective duties in this context, and with whom do their loyalties lay? When choices between duties and loyalties compete or conflict, it is important to evaluate how organizers and participants determine which duties and loyalties are most important. For example, as newly crowned world champions, did the duties of the Chicago Blackhawks perhaps change—from individual hockey competitor to international league spokesmen? How did the *Chicago Tribune* and locker room images, as well as Pride participation by the Cubs, influence those perceived duties? Along the way, to what extent did the Blackhawks' actions indicate a loyalty to themselves, the NHL, the Burke family, or the LGBT community? Similar questions should be asked from the organizers' perspective. Did the decisions made by the Chicago Annual Pride Parade organizers reflect a duty to communicating messages of resistance or inclusion, and are these duties necessarily opposed? In the process, did their decisions reflect differing degrees of loyalty to different internal and external stakeholders?

The parade organizers in particular faced three key challenges that help explicate this decision-making process. First, parade organizers must represent an infinitely diverse community. As such, they must make important decisions regarding how (and the extent to which) the community is represented. Second, organizers must determine the optimal balance in forging effective organization-to-public relationships. Not only must parade organizers develop productive relationships with constituents and supporters in the LGBT community but they also must forge productive relationships with businesses, politicians, and opinion leaders who potentially could influence the extent to which the LGBT movement succeeds. Finally, and perhaps most importantly, organizers must be prepared to critically evaluate their own effectiveness by studying its communication practices. Doing so helps ensure its accountability to the LGBT community and contribution to broader movement objectives and reinforces the public choices made in terms of duty and loyalty.

Movement organizations must address these three challenges in multiple contexts. Along the way, they must acknowledge how diverse LGBT communities intersect with a culture's power structure. Foucault (1994) explained the following:

> In a given society, there is no general type of equilibrium between goal-directed activities, systems of communication, and power relations; rather there are diverse forms, diverse places, diverse circumstances or occasions in which these interrelationships establish themselves according to a specific model. (p. 338)

To that end, important communication theory helps guide the discussion. In terms of the first challenge—representing an infinitely diverse community—the theory of communicative action posits how effective communication can (and should) result from processes that value participation by all voices equally. Relationship management theory responds to the second challenge of forging important organization-to-public relationships by offering important guidance regarding the characteristics of effective, long-term relationships. Third, Ganesh, Zoller, and Cheney (2005) reinforced how, by explicating the discursive processes of organizing, it is possible to evaluate the transformational potential and effectiveness of social movement organizations. Accordingly, Ganesh (2003) provided additional guidance regarding the delicate balance movement organizations must maintain in justifying their actions on behalf of and contributions to the broader movement. In order to tease out the challenges facing the 2010 Chicago Annual Pride Parade organizers and participants, these theoretical perspectives are outlined next, followed by a short discussion regarding the pervasive role of power embedded within the process of communication.

Raising Voices

In the process of organizing Pride celebrations and reaching out to mainstream organizations such as the Blackhawks, organizers are making very important decisions regarding whose voice in the movement is heard and whose voice is silenced. In an infinitely diverse community, this task proves challenging. Epstein (1994) explained the following:

> Recent studies of social movements . . . have emphasized the critical importance of collective identity as something whose existence cannot simply be assumed by the analyst of the social movement. Yet queer politics raises perplexing questions about the relations between identity and action. (pp. 198–199)

One way of addressing this challenge is by applying Jurgen Habermas's (1979, 1987) theory of communicative action, which emphasizes that truly legitimate communication and decision making in the movement results from all perspectives being included in the process equally. Ethical communication forges collective understanding, the creation of meaning between individuals, and the interaction between the private and public realms. Collective understanding, in turn, results from rational discourse as reflected through an "ideal speech situation," a context that requires "freedom of access, equal rights to participate, truthfulness on the part of participants, absence of coercion in taking positions, and so forth" (Habermas, 1993, p. 56).

This perspective is important for a mobilized gay community. The focus on equality, truthfulness, and freedom of access are central to the gay movement's mission and served as the impetus for the gay pride celebrations. For Habermas, the goal of communication is to pursue the ideal, egalitarian forum through which all voices can be heard. His theory goes beyond the actual substance of ideal conversation and focuses on the process of its pursuit. The ideal speech situation therefore is critical for culturally driven, broad-based public relations campaigns such as that of the gay movement, but it also illustrates the key challenge of mobilizing a diverse constituency and achieving consensus regarding movement goals and actions. In the case of the 2010 Chicago Annual Pride Parade—given the theory of communicative action's premise—it is worth examining which voices are being heard and the extent to which those voices reflect equal access to the decision-making process.

Forging Relationships

While the theory of communicative action helps ensure all voices within the LGBT community can be heard, relationship management theory—developed and used primarily by public relations scholars—focuses on the ideal organization-to-public connection. Ledingham and Bruning (1998) explained an organization-public relationship is "the state which exists between an organization and its key publics in which the actions of either entity impact the economic, social, political and/or cultural well-being of the other entity" (p. 62). In essence, relationship management focuses on maintaining the quality of an organization-public relationship as the core goal of communication (Ledingham, 2003, p. 195). Simply put, quality relationships result from a focus on communication that pursues long-term outcomes, not short-term outputs. This approach also acknowledges that an organization and its publics have set expectations of each other—expectations that if not fulfilled, or if incongruent altogether, could jeopardize a critical relationship (Coombs, 2000). To maximize *positive* social exchange, parties must communicate trust, openness, involvement, investment, and commitment; communication must seek mutual benefit while achieving mutual interests (Ledingham, 2003; Ledingham & Bruning, 1998).

The relationship management perspective offers perhaps the most appropriate way to explore the intersection of Pride organizers and potential participants. Pride organizers, as representatives of LGBT communities, must communicate clear expectations, establish internal and external stakeholder trust, and demonstrate both openness and sincerity in the process. More importantly, the prerequisite of quality relationships underlies many (if not all) movement objectives. The organized gay public must first establish productive relationships with those stakeholders it is trying to influence before it can achieve specific goals. What is potentially key for the gay movement is relationship management's assertion that communication strategies should focus first on relationship quality rather than the output of that relationship. As their comments indicated, the Chicago Annual Pride Parade organizers and Blackhawks emphasized the symbolic importance of their partnership for the celebration. The question remains, however, the extent to which the Chicago Annual Pride Parade and Blackhawks' relationship reflects the goals of relationship management theory: trust, openness, involvement, investment, commitment, and the pursuit of mutual benefit and mutual interests.

Being Effective; Being Accountable

The theory of communicative action emphasizes the need for an ideal speech situation in which all voices can be heard equally. Relationship management theory adds to this focus the importance of forging long-term, quality relationships that can help contribute to movement goals. The final challenge, then, is how to evaluate the effectiveness of social movement organizations. Here, Ganesh et al. (2005), provide important guidance.

They emphasize the importance of teasing out the internal decision-making processes of social movement organizations and the potential power disparity among movement participants—teasing out the discursive processes of protest and the organizing process of collective resistance. Studying collective resistance is informative in four ways. First, protests are important. They are a form of rhetoric and help instruct movement members in a collective message. Second, protests encourage others to have the courage to stand up, and they create networks and connections between otherwise disparate groups fighting for similar causes. Third, the study of protests is interdisciplinary—bridging multiple areas of academic inquiry such as communication, media, politics, social movements, and culture. Finally, studying protests reveals dynamics of power, and the power disparity evident between protest stakeholders.

Studying today's many gay pride parades in the context of their Stonewall protest-based roots also reinforces, however, the importance of examining if Stonewall's messages of resistance have transitioned in recent decades to messages of belonging. Such an examination, in turn, asks if messages of resistance and belonging are necessarily opposed. To that end, Ganesh et al. (2005) offer an effective way to evaluate the case of the 2010 Chicago Annual Pride Parade. In short, determining the effectiveness of movement organizations requires an investigation of a movement's goals, potential for change, communication in the public sphere, and degree of inclusiveness throughout the process. Ganesh et al. (2005) provide four specific questions to guide this investigation:

Goals: "What norms, practices, structures, and power relations are targeted by resistance efforts?" (p. 179)

Potential: "To what degree does resistance provide the potential for disrupting the hegemonic forces and systems?" (p. 180)

Communication in the public sphere: "What is the relationship between process and outcome of resistance efforts and democracy?" (p. 181)

Inclusiveness: "To what degree do resistance efforts address multiple forms of inequality, gender, race, nationality, sexuality?" (p. 181)

These questions help isolate ways of investigating the present case. It is important to consider the goals of the Pride organizers, the potential for influencing existing power structures, the types of public communication observed and its relationship to the democratic process, and the extent to which the Parade reflects the diverse voices within the community.

In the process, movement organizations—such as the organizers for the 2010 Chicago Annual Pride Parade—must be accountable for their decisions regarding the types of representation integrated in the celebration and the types of relationships forged with community stakeholders. Here, Ganesh (2003) offered additional guidance, cautioning that these organizations must balance messages of legitimacy with accountability. Ganesh defines legitimacy as, "the extent to which an organization searches for justification for its existence from its environment" and accountability as "the extent to which a organization is publicly required to justify its actions to its environment" (p. 565). He cautions, however, "A narcissistic organizational identity privileges legitimacy over accountability. . . . The organization is more concerned with justifying its own existence than in serving the public good" (Ganesh, 2003, p. 568). An effective movement organization therefore must accommodate stakeholder expectations while achieving community buy-in for movement objectives—certainly a balance pursued by the 2010 Chicago Annual Pride Parade organizers.

Acknowledging Power

Of course, relationships within the LGBT community and between the community and influential stakeholders bring with them specific power dynamics. These parades are much more than annual events. They are markers of the broader movement for LGBT equality. As such, they engage the democratic process, which requires movement members and participants to acknowledge—and negotiate—various power dynamics. For example, Clegg, Courpasson, and Philips (2006) argued, "What is the peculiar interconnection between democracy, power and morality? Power without morality is despotism, while morality without power is sterile" (p. 364). In other words, is it possible for organizers to play the familiar game of assimilation—a game played by the rules of the powerful—while sincerely reflecting the diversity of the LGBT community? Movement leaders must address power disparities between members within the LGBT community as well as the power disparities between the LGBT community and the institutions and leaders the movement seeks to influence. That said, in the spirit of today's lavish Pride celebrations, "The emergence of the mass spectacular . . . may be the only means capable of mobilizing sufficient energy and social vibrations to foster collective social dynamics" (Clegg et al., 2006, p. 365).

As Pride's message has shifted from Stonewall's focus on resistance to Chicago's focus on belonging, it is important to remember that power is a process, not an object. Moreover, power cannot exist without the potential for resistance or revolt (Foucault, 1994, p. 324). In the days immediately following Stonewall, the movement relied on vocal, combative protests, standing up against discrimination by the powerful. As bastions of traditional ideology—such as an NHL team—join in the Pride celebration, however, the power differential lessens, and—per Foucault—so do the messages of resistance communicated by the LGBT community.

DISCERNING DUTIES, DISCERNING LOYALTIES: QUESTIONS OF RESISTANCE AND BELONGING

So what is the balance between messages of resistance and belonging? This is the fundamental question facing Pride parade organizers and potential participants. The answers require decision makers to make important ethical choices that communicate an organization's values regarding duty and loyalty. Indeed, the ways in which a diversity of voices within the LGBT community are (or are not) represented, the types of long-term relationships forged with key stakeholders, the accountability to the LGBT community demonstrated by movement organizations, and the navigation of pervasive power disparities along the way reveal which duties and loyalties an organization deems most important. As Deetz (1992) challenged, "Processes of determination of the social good, decisions as to who should participate, and the nature of meaningful participation require a deeper look at democracy and communication" (p. 4). Certainly, there is no easy resolution. But discussing the communication challenges helps tease out important ethical considerations facing stakeholders in the gay movement and how today's movement compares to the original message of Stonewall.

DISCUSSION QUESTIONS

1. What is the fundamental duty of a Pride parade? Are there potentially competing duties?

    a. What does a Pride parade communicate through those individuals and organizations that participate? Does it say something different with "Dykes on Bikes" (a regular parade entry in many cities) than it says with the Chicago Blackhawks?

    b. Is it possible to represent *all* voices in the LGBT community? If so, how? If not, which voices are left out? Why do you think that? And is that OK?

2. What is the duty of "mainstream" organizations as they decide if and how they will participate in community Pride celebrations? Do these organizations have potentially competing duties?

    a. What does an organization communicate by choosing to support certain events at certain times? Compare the Chicago Cubs' decision to participate with the Blackhawks' decision. Does the way in which they participate, their eagerness, and their history influence our assessment of the organization?

    b. With which types of organizations—potential participants—is it most important to develop long-term relationships? Why? How does this affect the overall message of Pride?

3. To what extent should today's Pride celebrations reflect Stonewall's original message of resistance?

4. How do social advocates and corporate interests negotiate messages of resistance with messages of belonging? Is it possible?

5. Based on your discussions concerning questions 1 through 4, please answer the following questions:

    a. To whom were the 2010 Chicago Annual Pride Parade organizers most loyal (both internal and external to the Chicago LGBT community) in their decision-making process?

    b. To whom were the Chicago Blackhawks most loyal?

    c. Are there potentially competing, conflicting, or misplaced loyalties at play?

REFERENCES

Clegg, S., Courpasson, D., & Philips, N. (2006). *Power and organizations*. Thousand Oaks, CA: Sage.

Coombs, T. (2000). Crisis management: Advantages of a relational perspective. In J. A. Ledingham, & S. D. Bruning (Eds.), *Public relations as relationship management: A relational approach to public relations* (pp. 73–93). Mahwah, NJ: Lawrence Erlbaum.

Deetz, S. A. (1992). Democracy in an age of corporate colonization: Developments in communication and the politics of everyday life. Albany: State University of New York.

Epstein, S. (1994). A queer encounter: Sociology and the study of sexuality. *Sociological Theory, 12,* 188–202.

Forman, R. (2010, June 16). Blackhawks invited to Pride Parade. *Windy City Times.* Retrieved from http://www.windycitymediagroup.com/gay/lesbian/news/ARTICLE.php?AID=26946

Foucault, M. (1994). *Power: Essential works of Foucault 1954–1984* (Vol. 3). (J. D. Faubion, Ed.). New York: The New Press.

Ganesh, S. (2003). Organizational narcissism: Technology, legitimacy, and identity in an Indian NGO. *Management Communication Quarterly, 16,* 558–594.

Ganesh, S., Zoller, H., & Cheney, G. (2005). Transforming resistance, broadening our boundaries: Critical organizational communication meets globalization from below. *Communication Monographs, 72*(2), 169–191.

Habermas, J. (1979). *Communication and the evolution of society* (T. McCarthy, Trans.). Boston: Beacon Press.

Habermas, J. (1987). *The theory of communicative action, Vol. 2: Lifeworld and system* (T. McCarthy, Trans.). Boston: Beacon Press.

Habermas, J. (1993). *Justification and application: Remarks on discourse ethics* (Ciaran Cronin, Trans.). Cambridge, MA: MIT Press.

Ledingham, J. A. (2003). Explicating relationship management as a general theory of public relations. *Journal of Public Relations Research, 15*(2), 181–198.

Ledingham, J. A., & Bruning, S.D. (1998). Relationship management and public relations: Dimensions of an organization-public relationship. *Public Relations Review, 24,* 55–65.

Modrowski, R. (2010, June 24). Cubs have float in Chicago Pride Parade. *ESPN.* Retrieved from http://sports.espn.go.com/chicago/nhl/news/story?id=5316909

Obernauer, M. (2010, June 9). Chris Pronger brushes off Chicago Tribune ad showing him in skirt before Game 6 of Stanley Cup Final. *NY Daily News.* Retrieved from http://www.nydailynews.com/sports/hockey/2010/06/09/2010-06-09_chris_not_cross.html

Ross, W. D. (1930). *The right and the good*. Oxford: Clarendon Press.

Sneed, M. (2010, June 22). Hawks pride. *Chicago Sun Times,* p. 4.

Wyshynski, G. (2010a, June 11). Pronger mocked during Blackhawks' locker room celebration. *Yahoo Sports.* Retrieved from http://sports.yahoo.com/nhl/blog/puck_daddy/post/Pronger-mocked-during-Blackhawks-locker-room-ce?urn=nhl-247420

Wyshynski, G. (2010b, June 22). Stanley Cup, Blackhawks will march in Chicago's gay Pride Parade. *Yahoo Sports.* Retrieved from http://sports.yahoo.com/nhl/blog/puck_daddy/post/Stanley-Cup-Blackhawks-will-march-in-Chicago-s-?urn=nhl-250390

Yerdon, J. (2010, June 27). Brent Sopel takes Stanley Cup to Chicago's Pride Parade. *NBC Sports.* Retrieved from http://prohockeytalk.nbcsports.com/2010/06/27/brent-sopel-takes-stanley-cup-to-chicagos-pride-parade

Is Agriculture Spinning Out of Control?

A Case Study of Factory Farms in Ohio: Environmental Communication, News Frames, and Social Justice

Jeanette Wenig Drake

This case discusses the emergence of factory farms and their impact on food safety, animal care ethics, and neighboring communities. Focusing specifically on news coverage of Buckeye Egg Farm, the case asks what groups should participate in decision making regarding the location and legislation of factory farms. It considers what, if any, obligations such facilities have to broader communities and how their relationships with neighbors and legislators should be managed. This case represents the enormous challenges that still face the industrialized production of meat and dairy foods. It provides historical context via a longitudinal view of a yet unfolding situation. A recent development in several states to sharply restrict the close confinement of hens, hogs, and veal calves is the latest sign that factory farming, a staple of modern agriculture, is on the verge of significant change.

In Mercer County, Ohio, one of the top two egg-producing counties in the United States, citizens were warned in July 2010 not to take boats out onto the 13,000-acre Grand Lake St. Marys, not to touch the water, and not to eat any fish caught there due to manure and runoff that turned the lake toxic. Later that same year, a 4-week investigation by Mercy For Animals documented horrific animal abuse by workers at a megafarm in central Ohio. Worried about the divisive issue of confinement farm practices going to the polls, Ohio Governor Ted Strickland urged industry leaders to negotiate with opponents, led by the Humane Society of the United States. Both sides agreed to bar new construction of egg farms that pack birds in cages and to phase out the tight caging of pregnant sows within 15 years and of veal calves by 2017. Still, a new plant that will hold 6 million chickens is being proposed in southwestern Ohio and is being met by stiff protest from citizens and officials—an all-too-familiar setting for Ohioans and others.

The names and places have changed, but problems in the agricultural industry remain the same as those epitomized more than a decade ago by the now infamous icon of factory farming, Buckeye Egg Farm, which is the subject of this case study. Ohio ranks second in the nation in egg production, boasting 7.1 billion eggs in 2008 with an annual estimated value of $585 million. That same year, poultry operations purchase 33 million bushels of corn and 16.2 million bushels of soybeans from Ohio farmers (Ohio Poultry Association, n.d.). Clearly, the state's economy benefits from megafarms, but not so clear is whether the benefits outweigh the costs to the environment, public health, animal welfare, and the quality of life for many Ohioans.

WHEN THE S*** HIT THE FAN

In August 1997, a beetle infestation of farmhouses in central Ohio swiftly mounted to the intensity of an Alfred Hitchcock film. That is how J. P. Miller (1997) of the *Wall Street Journal* described it. A nearby factory farm had imported beetles to help combat "fly populations of biblical proportions" by eating fly larvae in the mountains of chicken manure. Armies of beetles invaded up to 20 nearby homes when the manure was spread on fields. "One resident went upstairs and discovered 'the floor was just black with them.' She swept them away again and again, and each time hundreds more materialized" (Miller, 1997). This factory farm wreaked so much havoc that people across the country would come to know it by name—Buckeye Egg Farm.

Although they have been banned in some European countries and significantly restricted in others, factory farms have mushroomed in the United States since the 1980s. By and large, Americans remain unfamiliar with this relatively new phenomenon, also known as *confined animal feeding operations* (CAFOs), or megafarms, that jam thousands and hundreds of thousands of animals in close confinement. More familiar are the corporate brands behind the trend: Eggland's Best, Smithfield Foods, and Tyson Foods to name a few. Unlike traditional family farms, factory farms are usually owned, managed, and operated by different entities. Using vertical integration, they create monopolistic conditions with the same corporation often controlling all aspects of production. The industrialized practices produce unprecedented high volume and profit with little regard for public health and the environment.

During a tumultuous 8-year history, Buckeye Egg Farm accrued more than $1 million in fines for egregious violations, including infestations, fish kills, and the selling of old eggs. The organization rarely followed ethical practices of dialogic communication, transparency, participation in decision making, accountability, and alignment of company values and practice. Ohio was cited as having the worst environmental record with factory farms, a designation brought about by this single operation, which, at its peak, had more than 14 million hens producing 2.6 billion or 4% of the nation's eggs. Ultimately, the intensity of citizen protest, media coverage, and the company's continual wrongdoing produced some changes in regulations and a state order to shut down. However, the facilities never closed; they merely changed name (now called Ohio Fresh Eggs) and ownership—leaving behind the same root problems.

Studies have shown that CAFOs negatively impact public health, property values, and the quality of life for neighbors along with detrimental long-term effects on the environment.

In the United States, these facilities produce 2.7 trillion pounds of animal waste each year that often leaks into rivers—killing fish and contaminating drinking water. A single operation produces as much waste as a large city. The unprecedented concentrations of animals pollute the air and water and spread disease.

Proponents say industrialization is the only way to keep food prices down and to feed the world's growing population. Opponents favor sustainable agriculture. Moreover, the United Nations in 2010 reported that a shift toward a vegan diet is vital to save the world from hunger, fuel poverty, and the worst impacts of climate change as the world's population surges toward 9.1 billion people by 2050.

Factory farms precipitate myriad ethical questions, including those about animal treatment, environment, public health, and powerful government-industry alliances. Just as difficult as the physical realities of factory farms are the challenges of the socially constructed realities that are played out in the media, where the way an issue is *framed* or presented is as important as the issue itself.

HATCHING BUCKEYE EGG

In March 1995, a local newspaper announced that Anton Pohlmann, a poultry farmer from Germany, intended to build a large egg-laying plant in its small rural Ohio community. Over the next 5 years, the company (originally called AgriGeneral and later renamed Buckeye Egg Farm) would expand to the size of 90 "barns," each the length of two football fields. When neighbors learned that the operation would put millions of chickens at several plants within a 7-mile radius in their community, they organized to form Concerned Citizens of Central Ohio. Throughout, citizens faced many obstacles, including the operation's strategic plan to cross three county lines—Marion, Hardin, and Wyandot. For residents, this meant difficulty in communicating and organizing because there were multiple governing bodies, media, and publics involved. Although activism was foreign to these residents, up to 400 citizens gathered in protest.

At the time, no regulations in Ohio governed CAFOs even though problems from factory farms had transpired for years in other states. To set up one of the country's largest egg-laying operations, Pohlmann needed only to obtain a permit from the Ohio Environmental Protection Agency (OEPA) upon showing a satisfactory waste management plan. The OEPA ignored the owner's criminal record and his environmental degradation in Croton, Ohio, where he'd had a facility since the 1980s. Regulations specific to CAFOs were not instituted in Ohio until 2002—after all the Buckeye Egg facilities were up and running. Until then, the state played a jurisdictional game of hot potato with CAFOs that set up roadblocks for citizens and paved the way for permits.

PROBLEM? WHAT PROBLEM?

From 1995 to 2004, proponents and opponents employed various frames to make their case because how an issue is framed plays a key role in whether it will be perceived as a problem. To frame is to "select some aspects of a perceived reality and make them salient in a communicating text in such a way so as to promote a particular problem definition, causal interpretation, moral evaluation, and/or treatment recommendation" (Entman, 1993, p. 52). In other words, how something is portrayed will determine if there is a problem, what it is, who is to blame, and how it should be remedied.

As an issue plays out in the media, *master frames*—or major themes—will develop and evolve. News coverage is replete with frames and though framing is not always intentional it is not neutral. The influence of any given frame rests, in large part, with the power of the framing agent or the extent of that agent's resources such as money and access to information, the political process, and the media. Since the most effective power prevents conflict from arising in the first place (Reese, 2003), the agricultural industry is highly motivated to keep factory farms out of the news.

An asymmetrical relationship in this debate may be seen by comparing finances. The Ohio Department of Agriculture (ODA) in 2003 had a budget of $52.5 million, with some $335,000 being earmarked for communication. Its communication budget nearly tripled since 1995, when the controversy began. By contrast, Concerned Citizens raised and spent less than $25,000 during the entire 8-year controversy.

Though opponents were successful in making headlines and raising awareness, they were less able to influence content or policy. Ultimately, government and industry agents were most successful at framing the issue to create the perception that all sides were appeased. During the debate, four master frames evolved in the news as a result of unfolding events or influence from various parties: (1) progress is good, (2) regulation is necessary, (3) Buckeye is a bad egg, and (4) the ODA will take care of everything.

GREED IS GOOD

For the first 4 years while Buckeye Egg was seeking and obtaining permits, the governor and ODA stayed out of the debate, which made it difficult for the issue to gain legitimacy. News coverage focused on the fight between the residents and company but did not delve into the issues behind the controversy. Reporting followed a *progress frame* by highlighting economic benefits. Through an overreliance on official sources, coverage granted assumed legitimacy to the CAFO while it questioned the legitimacy of the protestors each time quotations appeared around the group's name, for example, or when a reporter used the qualifier *so-called* in regard to statements from citizens.

While the company awaited its first permit, citizens contacted officials and protested at the State House and public forums. In February 1996, the newspaper reported Pohlmann had been charged in Germany with animal cruelty and other crimes. So the timing was conspicuous when, in March, the OEPA granted Pohlmann a permit to build the first facility. One news article reported the permit was granted and that the facility would be "safe" while an adjacent story reported that the "the public's knowledge of the chicken and egg business is a little scrambled." Both claims would be disproved by subsequent events but only after it was too late. Both articles used government and industry sources, who lent automatic legitimacy to factory farms. Just 3 months later, Pohlmann was convicted in Germany and banned from raising chickens there.

VICTIMS: REGULATIONS ARE NECESSARY

Shortly after the first facility was constructed, neighbors began suffering from fly and beetle infestations, as well as a horrible stench, as a result of the massive amounts of untreated waste. It was so bad that families couldn't go outside or even sit down to eat inside without a flyswatter. In an ongoing saga, the company accrued one fine after another from state and federal agencies for mismanagement, waste runoff, and spills that polluted waterways and killed fish. Citizens began to take legal action. The organization came under attack from the EPA, the Occupational Safety and Health Administration, labor unions, immigration services, the Sierra Club, religious groups, family farmers, local and national media and others, but the governor remained silent. A coalition of 10,000 citizens asked the state to place a moratorium on factory farms until the new form of agriculture could be studied and public health assured. The request was ignored.

To overcome opposition while the remaining facilities went through the permit process, the organization used lawsuits, cash incentives to local governing bodies, public relations ploys, and denial. In 1997, the company bought a township trustee vote in their favor, hired a new CEO, changed its name from the now much-maligned AgriGeneral to Buckeye Egg Farm, and staged an open house for the media. Sending mixed messages, the company's actions did not line up with their stated values. AgriGeneral threatened to sue neighbors for complaining about the conditions yet promised "to be a good neighbor" while at the same time denying accountability and claiming, "they're not our flies."

News coverage focused on isolated events, or *episodic framing,* rather than *thematic framing,* which would provide context and in-depth coverage. Given the magnitude and frequency of violations, news coverage of Buckeye Egg fueled the master frame: Proper regulation is necessary—a theme that still allowed the company to expand.

March of 1998 marked a turning point when a local health official declared the perennial fly infestations a "clear threat" to health. The company promptly slapped him with a lawsuit, just one of many examples of stifling dialogue about both the company and the industry practice of factory farming. Nevertheless, the health director's decree, along with approaching elections, forced Governor George Voinovich and state officials to call for increased oversight. Although opponents and proponents disagreed on the legitimacy of CAFOs, they agreed regulations were needed. Concerned Citizens gained instant credibility. Still, while state officials were talking the talk, the OEPA continued to issue permits. It was 4 years before regulations were instituted—only after Buckeye's entire operation was up and running.

VILLAIN! BUCKEYE IS A BAD EGG

By 1999, the issue had gotten out of control—everyone except the organization agreed that there was a problem and that the factory farm was the cause. Mounting pressure from federal agencies motivated state officials to take action. With Voinovich now safely elected to a seat in the U.S. Senate, newly elected Governor Bob Taft was forced to speak out on the issue. The coalescence of opinions resulted in a master frame with more resonance than any other throughout the debate. Newspaper editors said it plainly: Buckeye is a bad egg.

This master frame, fueled by state and industry officials, diverted attention away from the larger issue of factory farms.

Yet this period was full of contradictions. As it expanded, the company continued to cause more of the same problems. Buckeye Egg was fined the largest amount in the state's history, and the newspaper called for the governor to shut it down, but the OEPA continued to grant the final permits for the additional planned facilities amidst a convenient catch-22 of jurisdictional ambiguities.

The state and industry were eager to calm public opinion; they also were motivated to get the entire operation up and running since it would set precedence. Once all the facilities had received permits, the state's activity level intensified. Clearly, citizens had become the victims, but who was to be held accountable for the problems? Using classic framing strategy, industry propaganda began painting this single factory farm as the villain and the ODA as the emerging vindicator. The industry regained control of the issue by turning Buckeye Egg into a scapegoat, dominating media coverage, and establishing industry-friendly regulations pushed through by Republican Senator Larry Mumper, a member of the Farm Bureau, which is a staunch supporter of CAFOs. It appeared the state was rectifying the problem, but new legislation merely took oversight away from the OEPA and gave it to the ODA—in essence, allowing the industry to regulate itself.

VINDICATOR: ODA WILL TAKE CARE OF EVERYTHING

Under fire from all sides now, Pohlmann changed top management five times in as many years. Throughout, Buckeye Egg continued to pledge to be a good neighbor but continued to violate health and environmental regulations. In 2001, 2002 and 2004, Mercy for Animals broke in and documented inhumane conditions at two Ohio factory farms; one was Buckeye Egg. Their videotapes (available at http://www.mercyforanimals.org/investigations.aspx) reveal chickens with their heads trapped between the cages unable to reach food or water; dead chickens decaying next to live hens; and sick, featherless birds with large ulcers. Public exposure of factory farm conditions was the last thing the industry wanted, so following the break-in, the legislature enacted strict laws against trespassing on agricultural property. The result was one more roadblock for citizens and the media who act as watchdogs.

After being fined hundreds of thousands of dollars and sued millions, Pohlmann threatened bankruptcy. The governor, attorney general, and other state officials now dominated the news coverage, which helped them to maintain control over the issue. Finally, in a grandiose gesture after repeated attempts at correction and compliance failed, the state threatened to send Pohlmann to jail. Citizens were quiet as they watched the heroics and waited for resolution, but neither bankruptcy nor jail time ever came to fruition. By November 2001, the state attorney general called for the shutdown of the CAFO. In August 2002, the ODA (whose mission is to "promote agriculture") took over from the OEPA the permitting and regulating functions of megafarms. In July 2003, ODA also ordered Buckeye Egg to close. By this time, Pohlmann had left the country.

The process of closing the facilities began but never materialized. By February 2004, ODA promptly issued permits to a new owner for the same old facilities. The facility is now known as Ohio Fresh Eggs, which is jointly owned by Don Hershey and Orland Bethel. The state was able to frame Buckeye Egg Farm as the problem so it could get rid of "the problem" that was tarnishing the industry but still keep the facilities. In this case, the perception of the problem was gone, but the realities of the problem remained. The transfer of ownership of the egg production facility did not put an end to the repeated, environmental pollution from this facility. Likewise, CAFOs creating similar problems across the country remained. The number of factory farms in Ohio has tripled and continues to grow since the ODA has streamlined the permit process. Each new CAFO causes heated protests where they locate, but the ODA has successfully contained them to local issues.

THE STATE OF AGRICULTURE

This is not a case of one bad egg; factory farms remain largely unchecked across the country, and problems have become a part of doing business. The phenomenon of factory farms diffused quickly across the country because they were kept out of public view during their emergence (Drake & McCoy, 2009). *Food, Inc.*, a 2009 documentary, attempted to lift the veil on this lack of transparency within the industry and raise consumer awareness about modern food production practices. CAFOs now dominate the beef, dairy, pork, poultry, and egg-laying industries with just 3% of U.S. farms producing more than 60% of America's agricultural goods. Industry experts continue to tout efficiency even though increased efficiencies do not account for *externalities* or costs of production, such as environmental costs borne by someone other than the producer. In other words, when industry officials claim that industrialized practices are more cost-efficient, they fail to factor in related costs such as those involved in air and water pollution or the increased cost of government regulation.

While farming has become further removed from the daily lives of most citizens, the food-agro industry has grown to be the second most profitable industry in the country—second only to pharmaceuticals (Magdoff, Foster, & Buttel, 2000). At the same time, reporting of agricultural issues has significantly decreased in quantity and quality (Pawlick, 2001). This means decreased citizen participation and increased politicization. The Bush administration actually reduced federal regulations on CAFOs, exempting them from air pollution standards. A lack of federal regulation has precipitated state-to-state competition to attract agribusiness, and, as a result, the industry has targeted environmentally lax states, such as Ohio, that allow factory farms to operate unhindered.

PUBLIC HEALTH AND THE ENVIRONMENT

One of the most dangerous practices of factory farming is the storage and use of liquefied animal waste. The massive quantities of manure generated by CAFOs are stored in holes dug in the earth (referred to as "lagoons") and then spread onto cropland. These manure pits often leak or overflow, releasing toxic bacteria and excess nutrients into groundwater. Decomposing manure emits hazardous gases that degrade air quality. Spreading waste on the ground leads to odor problems and water pollution when more manure is applied than the surrounding land can absorb. The USDA estimates that animals in the U.S. meat industry produced 1.4 billion tons of waste in 1997—130 times the nation's volume of human waste and five tons of animal waste for every U.S. citizen.

In 1995, 25 million gallons of manure spilled from an eight-acre "lagoon" into North Carolina's New River, killing 10 million fish and closing 364,000 acres of coastal wetlands to shell fishing. Manure at cattle feedlots can produce substantial amounts of methane and nitrous oxide, both greenhouse gases that add to global warming.

According to a 2002 Iowa State University study, exposure to airborne factory farm emissions can lead to tension, depression, reduced vigor, fatigue, confusion, nausea, dizziness, weakness, fainting, headaches, plugged ears, runny nose, scratchy throat, and burning eyes. The American Public Health Association in 2004 asked for a moratorium on factory farms, but no such stopgap has been considered.

The Food and Drug Administration is concerned about the use and misuse of animal antibiotics, reporting 29 million pounds of antibiotics were used in food animals in 2009. Multidrug resistance is more than three times greater near CAFOs than in agricultural streams not impacted by CAFOs, according to a 2010 study.

ETHICAL RESPONSIBILITIES TO FARM ANIMALS?

Atrocities at factory farms by way of both sadistic individual behaviors and standard industry practices have been well documented (Coats, 1989; Global Resource Action Center for the Environment [GRACE] Factory Farm Project, n.d.). Undercover videos documenting abuse to chickens, cattle, and pigs are available at www.mercyforanimals.org/. Americans care how farm animals are treated; a 1999 survey found that 44% of consumers would pay 5% more for food labeled humanely raised.

Only after activists bring conditions to light have small changes come about. McDonald's announced in 2002 it would not buy eggs from producers who give hens less than 72 square inches of cage space each or use starvation to induce molting. The United Egg Producers have since adopted guidelines that will increase each bird's living space to about the area covered by a Kleenex. After employees at a Pilgrim's Pride slaughterhouse were shown in a 2004 videotape throwing live chickens against concrete walls and stomping on them, KFC threatened to stop purchasing from this supplier.

ENVIRONMENTAL INJUSTICE?

Since nonmetropolitan areas do not have zoning that separates industrial from residential properties, these factory facilities are built next door to people who have lived in a community for generations. As a result, many end up leaving their homes. Others stay and suffer the consequences, which the industry says is "just the way it is."

Just as reality is socially constructed, so, too, is risk. Goshorn and Gandy (1995) argued that "the determination of acceptable levels of risk is explicitly political" (p. 136). This was evident when Ohio's Governor Voinovich characterized citizens as NIMBYs (a disparaging term that stands for "not in my backyard"). His successor, Governor Taft, inaccurately portrayed protestors as city folk unaccustomed to country life. Both tactics were part of a larger framing strategy to delegitimize protestors and characterize the industrialized practices as normal. Goshorn and Gandy (1995) challenged, "Why do we regard some uncertainties as constituting risk, yet see other classes of harms, to which different classes of persons have different chances of being exposed, as descriptions of 'the way it is,' however unjust that status may appear to be?" (p. 138).

For instance, little was done about North Carolina's hog farm problems until two events touched more people and, specifically, people in power. In 1997, after a proposal surfaced for a factory farm near golf courses in a powerful legislator's home district, the legislator pushed through a moratorium on new facilities. Then, only after Hurricane Floyd swirled hog waste into waters throughout the eastern part of the state did pressure mount to solve the problems that had been plaguing other parts of the state for years.

CIRCUMVENTING DEMOCRATIC PARTICIPATION

Understandably, a state will promote the growth of agriculture within its borders, which is why federal standards are needed. A good student of capitalism might argue that the free market will provide necessary checks and balances; however, Mattera (2004) argued that "policies on issues such as food safety and fair market competition have been shaped to serve the interests of the giant corporations that now dominate food production, processing, and distribution" (p. 4). He contended the USDA has promoted factory farms "with little or no regard to their public health consequences" (p. 6).

Indeed, during the Buckeye Egg debate, citizen participation was curtailed through government-industry manipulation of bureaucratic, legislative, and media processes. Although the state held public hearings, it did not listen to the public. The OEPA staunchly rebutted criticism and defended the legitimacy of factory farms. The governor refused to involve himself in the issue until forced by elections. Backroom talks were going on long before the public was apprised of the coming factory farm.

Buckeye Egg fired, denied, sued, threatened, and paid off critics. In one instance, the company paid $100,000 to win a township trustee vote in favor of its facilities. On another occasion, industry-sponsored research (that was later disproved) denied culpability on the part of Buckeye Egg. Finally, large settlements for class-action suits quelled opposition but did not solve the problem.

Proposed legislation attempted to turn citizens who complained into criminals. When Mercy for Animals (n.d.) videotaped the conditions inside two Ohio factory farms, the state legislature promptly passed new legislation to penalize and prevent future attempts of "vandalism or violence on farms" by the citizenry. As more and more neighbors of factory farms began using the courts as the only recourse left them, the state legislature went to work on a bill to limit punitive measures against corporations. When the Buckeye Egg problem grew too big, citizens were appeased through a pseudo shutdown. Citizens were left impotent when a new owner took control within 5 months.

Government-industry agents attempted to curtail the media as well. The Farm Bureau did not like what the *Dayton Daily News* printed about CAFOs, so its public relations employee visited the editor and "picked a fight." At the height of the controversy, *The Columbus Dispatch* dropped the agriculture beat altogether. After 8 years of substantial coverage of Buckeye Egg, the local newspaper, *The Marion Star,* suddenly experienced a remarkable drop in coverage in 2003 after being called to the carpet by the state for being too critical. These incidents represent a *web of impediments* (Drake, 2004), or activities of political actors to obstruct nonconforming actors. They serve to curtail public dialogue and cloud public view of the food production industry.

SUMMARY

The most heated environmental debates of the new millennium are over the ancient vocation of farming. Even the name is contentious since industrialized practices more closely resemble factories with tens of thousands of animals produced in factory settings.

Opposition to factory farms is taking place at the local and national levels. Political rhetoric, along with dramatic and simplistic reporting, has polarized the extremely complicated issue. Rural Americans have been caught up in a losing battle with an industry that searches for regions where local control is weak, creating pockets of environmental injustice in poor communities with little political clout. Others, who are concerned with humane treatment for animals, the environment, and public health, continue to wage their own, usually separate, campaigns against CAFOs.

A 2005 investigation revealed the change in management from Anton Pohlmann to Ohio Fresh Eggs had done nothing to stop the "horrific cruelty these chickens are forced to endure on a daily basis" (Farm Sanctuary, n.d.). Mercy for Animals is challenging the "Animal Care Certified" label that United Egg Producers started as a marketing tool to capture the interest of consumers concerned about animal welfare.

Since public opinion is shaped by the power to name and frame an issue, industry agents seek to control the debate by spending millions not to involve but to influence—still relying on the "bad egg" frame and scapegoat tactic as a defense every time abusive practices at a factory farm come to light. Clearly, Buckeye Egg Farm violated legal and ethical boundaries; however, much larger ethical questions face the agricultural industry as similar crises surface again and again at factory farms around the world.

Déjà Vu: Ohio Fresh Eggs

In 2004 Buckeye Egg was sold and renamed Ohio Fresh Eggs. It and other factory farms throughout the U.S. and around the world continue to generate problems.

2004

Defendants Buckeye Egg Farm and Anton Pohlmann agree to a $50 million consent judgment to citizen claimants in Marion, Wyandot and Hardin counties and promise to never return to agricultural operations there.

Buckeye Egg is sold to Don Hershey and Orland Bethel and renamed Ohio Fresh Eggs. New owners fail to disclose ties to Jack DeCoster, a well-known environmental offender.

2005

Mercy for Animals reveals inhumane conditions continue at Ohio Fresh Eggs.

Ohio Fresh Eggs is cited for federal safety violations, exposing employees to dangers from construction, hazardous energy sources and other unsafe environments.

The Ohio Department of Agriculture revokes permits for Ohio Fresh Eggs when the state learns of the company's anonymous investor, Jack DeCoster, a chronic and habitual violator of environmental laws in Iowa. An appeals panel will overturn the revocation.

2006

Ohio Fresh Eggs is barred from selling over 4 million eggs deemed unfit for human consumption. A company spokesman says the eggs were not intended for retail sale.

2009

Ohio Fresh Eggs pleads guilty to environmental violations—illegally discharging egg wash water into a tributary of Tymochtee Creek.

Agribusiness interests work with the Ohio legislature at lightning speed to block regulations requiring more-humane treatment of animals proposed by U.S. Humane Society. Led by the powerful Farm Bureau lobby, industry proponents spend $4 million to get Issue 2 passed. Issue 2 passes, changing the Ohio state constitution to establish a "Livestock Care Standards Board" with power to dictate standards for livestock and poultry. The board gives a dozen appointees broad power to decide animal welfare rules thus effectively limiting citizen participation in decision-making.

2010

A quarter of a million hens are euthanized after Ohio Fresh Eggs is hit by fire. Some ten years ago when building permits were granted, state officials ignored warnings from firefighters about the safety hazards created by the behemoth structures.

Ohio Fresh Eggs recalls 288,000 eggs because salmonella is found at the factory farm.

Source: Farm Sanctuary (n.d.)

DISCUSSION QUESTIONS

1. As world citizens, what ethical responsibilities do we have regarding the food we eat?

2. Is balance possible between short-term food supply and long-term care of the environment? Between the state's economic health and environmental or public health?

3. What positive or negative social impact have factory farms had on our culture?

4. What, if any, ethical responsibilities do we have to farm animals?

5. What should be done to protect our air and water? Can we rely on business to protect them, or is regulation the only way to ensure safety? Can we rely on the state and industry to practice responsible stewardship? Who should pay the cost of externalities?

6. Should citizens have the right to decide whether factory farms move in next to them or into the community? Do CAFOs precipitate environmental injustice by locating in poorer communities? If a CAFO moves in, should residents be compensated for losses to property values, quality of life, or other factors? Should new technologies be allowed until proven harmful, or should corporations have the burden to prove the safety of new technologies?

7. What ethical responsibilities regarding food production do corporations have? The agricultural industry? Government? Individuals?

8. Is the traditional American farm worth preserving, or are CAFOs inevitable? What social costs are involved in the loss of the family farm?

9. Should the agricultural industry be exempt from pollution standards required of other industries?

10. Should Americans' First Amendment rights be restricted in what they can say about food and the agricultural industry?

REFERENCES

Coats, C. D. (1989). *Old MacDonald's factory farm: The myth of the traditional farm and the shocking truth about animal suffering in today's agribusiness.* New York: Continuum.

Drake, J. L. (2004). *Would a farm by any other frame smell as sweet? News frames, factory farms, and social protest.* Unpublished doctoral dissertation, Bowling Green State University, Ohio.

Drake, J. L., & McCoy, J. R. (2009, October). Subterfusion of innovations: PR methods used to diffuse and defuse a controversial new process in food production. *Ohio Communication Journal, 47,* 1–25.

Entman, R. M. (1993). Framing: Toward clarification of a fractured paradigm. *Journal of Communication, 43*(4), 51–58.

Farm Sanctuary. (n.d.). *Factory farm offender.* Retrieved from http://www.farmsanctuary.org/mediacenter/reports.html

Goshorn, K., & Gandy, O. H., Jr. (1995). Race, risk and responsibility: Editorial constraint in the framing of inequality. *Journal of Communication, 45*(2), 133–151.

Global Resource Action Center for the Environment Factory Farm Project. (n.d.). *Facts and data.* Retrieved from http://www.factoryfarm.org/

Magdoff, F., Foster, J. B., & Buttel, F. H. (Eds.). (2000). *Hungry for profit: The agribusiness threat to farmers, food, and the environment.* New York: Monthly Review Press.

Mattera, P. (2004, July 23). *USDA Inc: How agribusiness has hijacked regulatory policy at the U.S. Department of Agriculture.* (Available from Corporate Research Project of Good Jobs First, 1311 L Street, NW, 4th floor, Washington DC, 20005)

Mercy for Animals. (n.d.). *Undercover investigations: Exposing animal abuse.* Retrieved from http://www.mercyforanimals.org/investigations.aspx

Miller, J. P. (1997, November 3). That crunchy stuff in your cereal bowl may not be granola: Beetles invade an Ohio town when chicken farm's plan for fly control goes awry. *Wall Street Journal,* pp. A1, A13.

Ohio Poultry Association. (n.d.). *Ohio egg facts.* Retrieved from http://www.ohpoultry.org/fastfacts/index.cfm

Pawlick, T. F. (2001). *The invisible farm: The worldwide decline of farm news and agricultural journalism training.* Chicago: Burnham.

Reese, S. D. (2003). Prologue—Framing public life: A bridging model for media research. In S. D. Reese, O. H. Gandy Jr., & A. E. Grant (Eds.), *Framing public life: Perspectives on media and our understanding of the social world* (pp. 7–31). Mahwah, NJ: Lawrence Erlbaum.

Ethical Storm
or Model Workplace?

Joann Keyton, Paula Cano, Teresa L. Clounch, Carl E. Fischer,
Catherine Howard, and Sarah S. Topp

This case addresses a class action sexual discrimination lawsuit by several female employees at Mitsubishi and explores their claims, as well as the company and union responses to them. It considers how an organization that espouses commonly held virtues such as honesty, fairness, and respect undercuts these values when it denies some workers' voices to be heard. It also addresses the degree to which organizations meet their ethical duty by developing and implementing sexual harassment policies, complaint procedures, and training.

Honesty, fairness, and respect are desirable ethical characteristics and are often touted as core values of organizations. Beyond mission and value statements, these foundational values have been institutionalized into organizations through labor laws, such as state and federal discrimination and harassment laws. Because employees expect that employers will treat them honestly, fairly, and with respect, they complain when these values are espoused in policy but not embodied in practice. These characteristics are central to the story[1] of Mitsubishi Motors Manufacturing America, Inc. (MMMA), a medium-sized automobile manufacturing plant in Normal, Illinois. MMMA was the site of a landmark sexual harassment case brought by the U.S. Equal Employment Opportunity Commission (EEOC) and settled for $34 million. Beyond the monetary relief, court-imposed remedies included the development and implementation of sexual harassment policies, procedures, and training and helped the organization evolve into a model team-based workplace.

In 1994, 29 female employees filed suit claiming sexual harassment—the first public notice of ethical problems at MMMA. From 1994 until the May 23, 2001, filing of the consent decree court monitor's final report, MMMA was at the center of an ethical storm in which the values of honesty, fairness, and respect were violated. Why would male

---

[1] The case was compiled from publicly available news stories, press releases, and legal documents.

employees sexually taunt, harass, and humiliate their female colleagues who were also their neighbors? Why did MMMA managers or union leaders to whom the women brought their complaints do nothing? Why did so few women initially complain about their sexual harassment when ultimately more than 300 would be certified as claimants in the class action lawsuit brought by the EEOC? What did MMMA hope to achieve in sponsoring a protest against the EEOC? Is it possible that the procedural and policy changes that the court monitors oversaw at the plant could create a welcoming environment for women? Can a zero tolerance policy ever really be successful in eliminating sexual mistreatment at work? These questions, and the ethical dilemmas they raise, can be explored in the case of *EEOC v. Mitsubishi Motor Manufacturing of America, Inc.,* and by exploring the cultural, political, and legal milieu in which this case is situated.

SEXUAL HARASSMENT IN AMERICAN SOCIETY

The Working Women United Institute and the Alliance Against Sexual Coercion have been credited with the first use of the phrase *sexual harassment.* But it was journalist Lynn Farley (1978) and law professor Catherine MacKinnon (1979) who brought sexual harassment from obscurity into the legal, organizational, and public domains by conceptualizing it as a feminist issue. Farley described sexual harassment as unsolicited and nonreciprocal behavior of men toward women in which female sex roles overshadow female work roles; and she blamed capitalism and patriarchy as its foundations. MacKinnon defined sexual harassment as "the unwanted imposition of sexual requirements in the context of a relationship of unequal power" (p. 1) and argued that since workplace sexual harassment is primarily a problem for women it should be regarded as sex discrimination and that victims of sexual harassment should be provided the same legal protection as other forms of discrimination. Soon after, the EEOC—the federal government's agency to protect American workers against discrimination and harassment—developed this country's definition of sexual harassment.

The U.S. Equal Employment Opportunity Commission

Created when Congress enacted Title VII of the Civil Rights Act of 1964 (Title VII), the EEOC began operations in July 1965. The EEOC enforces federal statutes prohibiting employment discrimination in the private, public, and federal sectors; interprets employment discrimination laws; is responsible for the federal sector employment discrimination program; provides funding and support to state and local Fair Employment Practices Agencies (FEPAs); and sponsors outreach and technical assistance programs. EEOC headquarters in Washington, D.C., and its 50 nationwide offices are primarily responsible for conducting EEOC enforcement litigation under Title VII, the Equal Pay Act (EPA), the Age Discrimination in Employment Act (ADEA), and the Americans with Disabilities Act (ADA).

Adopting many of MacKinnon's positions, the EEOC published guidelines to define sexual harassment and ruled that sexual harassment would be considered an unlawful employment practice under Title VII of the 1964 Civil Rights Act. Prior to issue of the EEOC guidelines in 1980, circuit courts had not been receptive to claims of sexual harassment, viewing them as characteristic of ineffective relationships or the result of natural or romantic attraction. Thus, the EEOC's administrative guidelines defining sexual harassment became a powerful force in directing attention toward the intersection of the societal imbalance of power between men and women and male–female relationships in American workplaces.

The EEOC guidelines defined sexual harassment as follows:

> unwelcome sexual advances, requests for sexual favors, and other verbal or physical conduct of a sexual nature when (1) submission to such conduct is made either explicitly or implicitly a term or condition of an individual's employment, (2) submission to or rejection of such conduct by an individual is used as the basis for employment decisions affecting such individual, or (3) such conduct has the purpose or effect of unreasonably interfering with an individual's work performance or creating an intimidating, hostile, or offensive work environment. (U.S. Equal Opportunity Commission [EEOC], n.d.b)

Ultimately, this statement and the subsequent judiciary findings testing or reaffirming it have proven to be a powerful cultural force in advancing victim's rights and social awareness (Wood, 1994).

Although intended to provide direction, the guidelines are admittedly vague. "To be sure, the EEOC very intentionally wrote a broad, general definition so all possible forms of sexual harassment would be covered" (Linenberger, 1983, p. 243). As a result, the definition leaves executives, managers, and individual employees with the responsibility of recognizing sexual harassment on a day-to-day basis as it occurs, as circuit courts lack agreement about the behaviors that meet the test of the EEOC guidelines (Woerner & Oswald, 1990). Despite the problems presented by a case-by-case determination of sexual harassment (McCaslin, 1994), the EEOC guideline became the basis by which individuals could allege sexually harassing treatment at work and pursue civil lawsuits against their employers. In those cases where there are many plaintiffs with comparable claims, the EEOC files a class action suit on their behalf—many of which end in some type of settlement before the case is heard at jury trial.

In addition to providing a definition of sexual harassment, the EEOC guidelines distinguished between two types of sexual harassment: (1) quid pro quo and (2) hostile work environment. Quid pro quo was characterized as intentional harassment in which the victim is required by the harasser to provide sexual favors to avoid threatened loss of economic opportunity. The U.S. Supreme Court upheld this characteristic ruling that this type of unwelcomed behavior is a form of illegal sex discrimination (*Meritor Savings Bank v. Vinson*, 1986). A sexually hostile work environment was characterized as that which interferes with an employee's work performance or creates an intimidating, hostile, or offensive work environment and has been upheld by the Court of Appeals for the Eleventh Circuit (1982; *Henson v. City of Dundee*) who put the responsibility for a harassment-free workplace on the employer.

ORGANIZATIONAL HISTORY OF MITSUBISHI

MMMA began its American organizational life in October 1985 when a joint venture between Chrysler and Mitsubishi Motors Corporation (MMC) created Diamond-Star Motors.

This agreement put Japanese executives in charge of design and construction of the plant, as well as production of the vehicles at the plant—half of which would bear the Chrysler logo. Placing Mitsubishi in a central role in both production and management reflected U.S. automakers' deference to Japan for manufacturing small cars. In 1991, MMC purchased Chrysler's 50% share and took over operations in the Normal, Illinois, plant, which became a wholly owned American subsidiary of MMC. On July 1, 1995, Diamond-Star Motors was renamed MMMA. The 2.5 million square foot plant covering 6.36 acres can produce nearly a quarter-million vehicles each year and has produced 10 different Mitsubishi, Chrysler, Dodge, and Eagle models for domestic use and exportation to 14 countries.

The communities of Normal (Illinois) and Bloomington (Illinois) are home to about 100,000, surrounded by farmland and situated halfway between Chicago and St. Louis along key interstates (I-39, I-54, and I-74) and rail lines. The twin city community is a predominantly white population center situated in a productive agriculture area enhanced with insurance, manufacturing, health care, and educational employment opportunities. In the 1980s, Japanese companies sought out isolated, homogeneous communities in the United States for overseas expansion of its manufacturing plants. Towns, like Normal, jockeyed for position and granted tax abatements and other enticements to attract the huge multinational interests that brought economic growth. Although most of the 4,000 employees were hired from the twin cities area, about 70 Japanese managers were transferred to the plant, most in senior management.

MMMA is one of Normal's largest employers, employing 4,600 in 1996. Although not the largest, MMMA became the highest-paying employer, paying an average of $19 per hour with average annual salaries ranging from $35,000 to $40,000 in addition to generous benefits. The town's largest employer, State Farm Insurance, and two universities offered employment opportunities but no other employer offered the salary or benefits provided by MMMA. Securing employment at the plant was perceived as a good opportunity, and landing a job there was cause for celebration. Despite the economic benefits, employment at the MMMA Normal plant soon became associated with a different set of characteristics.

THE UNION

The 1935 enactment of the National Labor Relations Act gave skilled and unskilled employees in the United States the right to form together as unions, in order to protect the interests of the workers and bargain collectively on their behalf. Founded the same year, The International Union, United Automobile, Aerospace, and Agricultural Implement Workers of America, or the United Auto Workers (UAW) has become one of the largest and most diverse unions in North America, with 710,000 members employed in 3,200 organizations ranging from multinational corporations, small manufacturers, and state and local governments to colleges and universities, hospitals, and private nonprofit organizations. The UAW has been credited for a number of collective bargaining breakthroughs, including employer-paid health insurance for industrial workers, cost-of-living allowances, job and income security provisions, and comprehensive training and education. According to the UAW website, the UAW has had a voice in every piece of civil rights legislation including the Civil Rights Act of 1964, the Voting Rights Act, the ADA, and legislation fighting discrimination against women.

FIGURE 11.1   Mitsubishi Timeline

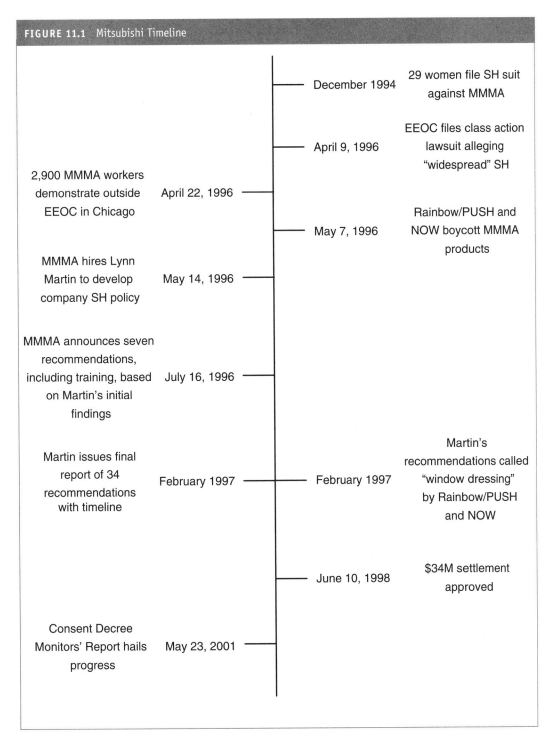

Note: EEOC = Equal Employment Opportunity Commission; MMMA = Mitsubishi Motors Manufacturing America,
Inc.; PUSH= People United to Save Humanity; SH = sexual harassment.

The *local,* or UAW Local 2488, began representing workers at MMMA in 1989. Unlike UAW contracts with other auto manufacturers, Local 2488's contract with MMMA lacked an equal-application clause—a clause that would have required joint union-company investigation of sexual harassment complaints. As a result, the union contract did not contain specific provisions for handling sexual harassment claims. Although Local 2488's civil rights committee initially presented the clause to MMMA, company officials rejected it.

ACCUSATIONS OF SEXUAL HARASSMENT

Although the sexual harassment suit against MMMA was not filed until 1994, female plant employees begin compiling public complaints in November 1992. A variety of sources reported that sexually harassing behavior was part of the plant's culture as early as the late 1980s—implying that women perceived that sexually inappropriate behavior was directed toward them but took no formal actions. Maintaining a division of the sexes common to Japanese culture, Japanese managers acted in ways that reinforced the inequality of women and men. Although hired, female employees were told that they should not be working in factories. According to one woman, they were treated as second-class citizens from the time that they were hired.

In making their complaints, women alleged they were repeatedly told they did not "belong in the plant, they were not welcome, and they were considered second class employees"; another reported that she was told to shut up because she was "just a woman." Women claimed men taunted them routinely, calling them "bitch," "whore," and "slut." Crude drawings depicting sexual acts and sexual graffiti were drawn on the cars being manufactured; graffiti also appeared in the bathrooms, often including the names of female employees. Models of male and female genitalia were created from scrap material and displayed publicly. Male employees were reported as exposing or fondling themselves and simulating masturbation in front of women. Large pneumatic air guns were placed between women's legs and fired. In one particularly graphic and violent example, a male employee was reported as speaking frequently of wanting to kill women by forcing a woman to perform oral sex on him and then blowing (shooting her with a gun) her away as he ejaculated. As if suffering through these types of sexually abusive behaviors were not enough, the women who made the complaints and followed through by filing a lawsuit also faced ridicule, ostracism, physical threats, disciplinary action, and retaliation after filing reports with MMMA about the harassment. Many found their workstations sabotaged.

More Women Come Forward

Twenty-nine women filed the initial private lawsuit against MMMA alleging sexual harassment, as well as sexual and racial discrimination after receiving a right-to-sue letter from the EEOC, which had investigated the credibility of the charges brought against shop floor workers, supervisors, and managers. This filing, one of the 14,420 filed nationwide in 1996 with the EEOC (n.d.-a), was so severe that the federal agency launched its own

15-month investigation and uncovered additional cases. During the EEOC investigation, the original 29 complainants faced additional harassment and retaliation.

The final EEOC sexual harassment suit filed April 9, 1996, represented between 350 and 400 female employees. In all, estimates suggest 50% of the female employees in MMMA's plant were sexually harassed. According to one woman, a 4-year employee at the plant, women at all levels were harassed. "It's not just down on the [plant] floor," she said (Grimsley, 1998, p. A9). Another female employee described widely varying conditions from one part of the plant to another. In her work area, she was exposed to sexually harassing behavior within her first 2 weeks of work but initially endured the sexist treatment because it was a good job with generous salaries and benefits—and plenty of overtime. Eventually her work environment improved when a female supervisor was transferred in and put an end to the overt sexual harassment. But still, she sought to leave her work area; she requested a transfer to a different section where the work conditions were better.

Although women have long worked in automobile manufacturing facilities, these operations—and the automotive industry in general—are dominated by men. Consider the way in which women are often positioned in the auto industry—glamorously dressed pointing to new models or as scantily clad celebrants at the finish line. Moreover, there are few car salespeople who are women; even fewer women are auto mechanics. These stereotypical views of women relative to cars combined with the MMMA's subordination of women dictated by the cultural norms of its management made MMMA a difficult place for many women to gain acceptance and respect.

MMMA's Response to the Allegations

MMMA's first response to the charges of sexual harassment was an unmitigated denial. Going on the offensive, MMMA mounted an aggressive campaign to discredit its accusers and to portray itself as a victim of corporate slander. In a dramatic step on April 22, 1996, just 13 days after the EEOC filed its sexual harassment suit against MMMA, 59 buses with approximately 3,000 workers were driven to Chicago to protest and picket in front of the EEOC regional headquarters in Chicago. Although initially claiming that the employees arranged the bus trip and protest, it was later revealed that MMMA provided the transportation and lunch *and* paid a day's pay to those who participated. Those who stayed behind? Ironically, they were mandated to attend sexual harassment training.

Despite MMMA's denial, the EEOC submitted a formal memorandum on September 15, 1997, describing, in graphic detail, specifics of the sexual harassment the female employees endured. The EEOC memorandum described the sexually harassing behavior as constituting a hostile work environment in the following ways:

1. Female employees were characterized as inferior during orientation, a time at which men were given hosted trips to sex bars.

2. Women were told they were unwelcome in the plant and treated less favorably.

3. The work environment included sexual graffiti, comments, objects, and gestures—male employees exposed themselves to female employees.

4. Pornography was on display, including images of MMMA employees and members of management engaged in sexual acts at company sex parties.

5. Women were victims of verbal and physical assaults.

The harassment was widespread with reports indicating that 400 male employees were involved—one out of every eight employees—in the sexual harassment of between 300 and 500 women.

Within a month, MMMA hired former U.S. Secretary of Labor Lynn Martin to evaluate its workplace policies and procedures and to provide recommendations for future policies and practices. Martin, who had served as the U.S. Secretary of Labor under President George H. W. Bush, was promoted by MMMA as a noted authority on sexual harassment training. Concluding a 9-month investigation in February 1997, Martin presented a 34-point model workplace initiative with an accompanying road map for implementation. According to an MMMA press release, Martin developed recommendations addressing management incentives, salary structures, promotion opportunities for women and minorities, quality of life issues, streamlining of rules and procedures, and sexual harassment prevention and policy enforcement—including a zero tolerance task force and mandatory sexual harassment training for all MMMA employees by February 20, 1997. Upon formal release of the plan, MMMA asked Martin to remain and coordinate the implementation and monitoring phase. Both her hiring and the report she generated were met with great skepticism because neither focused directly on the alleged sexual harassment. Indeed, many critics characterized the report and even Martin's role as an independent consultant as window dressing and a public relations device. For her efforts, Martin earned $2.2 million.

The Union Response

The local union did try to defend some of the women in their initial complaints but were themselves the target of hostile gestures. Union members were warned about sexual harassment, and the EEOC's phone number was printed twice in the union newspaper. In practice, however, the union took a middle ground position defending itself by saying that disputes between members were hard to mediate, without knowing who was telling the truth. Without the equal-application clause in the MMMA/UAW contract, the union could not file a grievance with MMMA until employees first talked with their direct supervisor. If dissatisfied, they could speak with their union coordinator, who then had to meet with MMMA officials. After that lengthy process, a grievance could then be filed.

Despite 20 women bringing complaints to the local union, union leadership refused to investigate or intervene. One woman complained to the union for years about a male coworker's disgusting behavior. She tried to file a grievance with the union against the MMMA. Eventually, MMMA fired him—but then the union filed a formal grievance to reinstate him. Although dozens of complaints were presented to its leaders, the union filed only six sexual harassment complaints with MMMA—this compared to the hundreds of grievances filed on other issues in the same 8-year period. One woman, a union leader and ex-MMMA employee, said that the Local 2488 raised sexual harassment complaints with MMMA every week, "but the company wouldn't acknowledge that any claim had merit.

Neither the company nor the union knew how to deal with sexual harassment. They didn't know the complexity of it. They probably didn't believe a lot of it" (Sharpe, 1996, para. 9).

The Public Response

Reactions from equal rights organizations to the claims of harassment at MMMA were swift and critical. In May 1996, National Organization for Women (NOW) president Patricia Ireland led a national campaign to improve working conditions at the MMMA plant, alleging "rampant" harassment. Rev. Jesse Jackson, founder and president of the National Rainbow Coalition and PUSH (People United to Save Humanity)—a multiracial, multi-issue, organization working for social, racial, and economic justice—called for a boycott of Mitsubishi cars, and Jackson personally led a protest at a Mitsubishi dealership in suburban Chicago. But by January 1997 when changes at MMMA were made public, Ireland and Jackson implored their supporters to suspend boycotting and protests announcing a breakthrough in negotiations between the organizations.

THE SETTLEMENTS

On August 29, 1997, MMMA settled the private lawsuit out of court with 27 of the original 29 women for a reported $9.5 million. Walter Connolly, attorney for MMMA, indicated that the company was not admitting wrongdoing by settling the case. Rather, the settlement was in response to an obligation the company had for dealing with the women. John Hendrickson, regional attorney with the Chicago Regional EEOC office, saw it differently. "The agreement represented an assumption of responsibility by the company for many of the employee practices" ("MMMA, Accusers Settle," 1997).

Then nearly a year later on June 10, 1998, MMMA agreed to a consent decree to settle the out of court lawsuit filed by the EEOC. Not only did MMMA put $34 million in a settlement fund to provide monetary relief to eligible claimants covered by the EEOC's class action but MMMA also agreed to revise its sexual harassment policy and complaint procedures, implement policies designed to promote supervisor accountability with respect to sexual harassment, and provide mandatory annual sexual harassment training to all employees as efforts to effectively support MMMA's zero tolerance policy and equality objectives. The consent decree, agreed to by all parties, also required that both MMMA and the EEOC appoint consent decree monitors who would for 3 years oversee the implementation of these requirements. Finally, the consent decree admonished all parties to not disclose the names of the claimants or the amounts they were awarded from the settlement fund and required that MMMA bear all costs associated with the consent decree monitors' 3-year review.

Although the consent decree's legal language indicates that the decree was not a finding on the merits of the case or to be used as evidence of liability, the settlement was viewed as an indication that the MMMA discriminated against women at the plant. John Hendrickson, EEOC attorney said, "It suggests that those charges had merit, and it also suggests that the company recognized that and is now prepared to do something about it" (Wills, 1997, para. 3). Patricia Benassi, attorney for 27 of the original 29 plaintiffs, was also optimistic, "It's a real credit to MMMA that they chose to try to resolve this. There are lots of companies out there that wouldn't try to resolve this. In fact, they drag women constantly through the mud" (Wills, 1997, para. 7).

CHANGES AT MITSUBISHI MOTOR MANUFACTURING OF AMERICA

Even before the settlement of the lawsuits, MMMA began implementing corrective actions. MMMA made changes to its internal organizational structures and procedures based extensively on recommendations contained in an initial report from Lynn Martin, an independent reviewer hired to evaluate its workplace policies, procedures, and practices. MMMA's Chairman and CEO Tsuneo Ohinouye announced these changes in a July 16, 1996, press conference.

Organizationally, two new positions were created: (1) a director of opportunity programs to strengthen equal economic opportunities for women and minorities, and (2) a director of corporate and community communications to be responsible for internal and external communications. Six months later, MMMA created a manager of diversity operations position at its national office to interface with NOW and other advocacy groups and promised to promote women and minorities to top management positions—a move announced in January 1997 in a NOW press release.

Procedurally, MMMA began comprehensive restructuring of its sexual harassment training and education programs. The initial training plan called for separate and thorough programs for all employees from senior executives to the lowest level employees under an aggressive timeline (e.g., all managers were to have received training within 45 days of this announcement). Upon receipt of the formal report in February 1997, MMMA initiated its zero tolerance policy and the formation of a corporate Zero Tolerance Task Force charged with oversight of sexual harassment and equal employment opportunity complaints as well as the authority to hold management accountable for their performance in these areas.

The Monitors' Report

But the settlement called for more than an internal consultant to recommend changes. The consent decree required that MMMA cooperate with court appointed monitors who over a 3-year period documented that the company did comply with all aspects of the settlement. According to the final report of the monitors, the following was found:

> MMMA has complied with its obligations under the Consent Decree and deserves credit for its efforts. There has been a significant change in "culture" on the plant floor. . . . MMMA's procedures for investigating and disciplining sexual and sex-based harassment generally work as intended.

The report points out that the increased role of first line supervisors in "detecting, discouraging and disciplining violators . . . is one of MMMA's most notable achievements under the Decree."

As a result of changes at MMMA, serious incidents of sexual harassment are "rare." A "great majority" of employees believe that the atmosphere has greatly improved. Although complaints are not gone, they have decreased over the 3-year decree period.

Over the monitoring period, employees filed 140 complaints, and MMMA determined that 52 violated the zero tolerance policy leading to the termination of 8 employees, suspension of 14, and less severe discipline for the remaining 30. The monitors reviewed these cases and determined that MMMA's zero tolerance policy "is much stricter than the requirements of federal and state anti-discrimination statutes."

In the end, John Hendrickson, regional attorney of EEOC's Chicago District Office said, "The report of the monitors confirms that, although our litigation and the consent decree did not create a perfect world at Mitsubishi, they did make a huge and positive difference in the daily work life of many women."

POSTSCRIPT

After a downturn in sales, North American operations were restructured and consolidated; this plant is the only remaining passenger car plant in North America, which was renamed in 2002 as Mitsubishi Motors North America, Inc., or MMNA. In 2009, the 3,000,000th vehicle rolled out of MMNA. Early in 2011, the company announced that it would stay in the twin cities of Normal and Bloomington, Illinois, ensuring jobs for 1,300 workers (Denham & Hansen, 2011) while manufacturing the Outlander Sport, Galant, Endeavor, and Eclipse. As in the 1990s, the company's mission statement still promotes honesty, fairness, and respect as its values ("Mission Statement," n.d.).

Despite the praise that MMNA has received for cleaning up its tarnished reputation, this case is often mentioned as one of the biggest and most influential sexual harassment cases (Kaminsky, 2006). The significance of the case is underscored as most accounts of Mitsubishi's business history mentions the sexual harassment case at the Normal, Illinois, plant as one of the company's challenges. Additionally, the Mitsubishi sexual harassment case is often used as an example in describing what companies should do (or not do) when sexual harassment claims are brought to management's attention. As a result, the name *Mitsubishi* continues to be negatively anchored.

DISCUSSION QUESTIONS

1. What ethical obligations do managers and union leaders have to their employees or members?

2. Why is sexual harassment an ethical issue in the workplace?

3. After sexual harassment has occurred in a workplace, what is an appropriate organizational response? Union response? Interpersonal response? What is the role of communication in facilitating these responses?

4. Can a monetary settlement ever be a sufficient remedy for ethical misconduct in the workplace? Why or why not?

5. What is the moral imperative of the federal government for bringing class action lawsuits on behalf of harassment victims?

6. In what way do societal and organizational norms influence what is perceived as sexually inappropriate or unethical workplace behavior?

7. In what ways or to what degree do supervisors, managers, and executives have a moral responsibility to create a harassment-free workplace?

8. In what ways do organizations satisfy their ethical responsibilities by developing and implementing sexual harassment policies, complaint procedures, and training?

9. Do organizations develop sexual harassment policies, procedures, and training to protect employees? Or to reduce liability for the organization? Which of these has a stronger moral imperative?

10. Do organizations have a moral obligation to treat their employees honestly, fairly, and with respect?

REFERENCES

Denham, R., & Hansen, K. (2011, February 4). MMNA plant in Normal to build Outlander Sport. *Pantagraph.com*. Retrieved from http://www.pantagraph.com/news/local/article_520b0946-3073-11e0-8d04-001cc4c03286.html

Farley, L. (1978). *Sexual shakedown: The sexual harassment of women on the job*. New York: McGraw-Hill.

Grimsley, K. D. (1998, July 12). Slings and arrows on the job: Incivility at work can hurt profits as well as feelings. *Washington Post*, p. A9.

Jackson, D. (2004, February 4). *Mitsubishi stays in Normal*. Retrieved from http://www.centralillinois-newscenter.com/news/local/115325214.html

Kaminsky, M. (2006). *Five biggest sexual harassment cases*. Retrieved from http://www.legalzoom.com/legal-headlines/corporate-lawsuits/five-biggest-sexual-harassment-cases

Linenberger, P. (1983). What behavior constitutes sexual harassment? *Labor Law Journal, 34*, 238–247.

MacKinnon, C. (1979). *Sexual harassment of working women*. New Haven, CT: Yale University Press.

McCaslin, L. R. (1994). *Harris v. Forklift Systems, Inc.*: Defining the plaintiff's burden in hostile environment sexual harassment claims. *Tulsa Law Journal, 29*, 761–779.

Mission statement: Mitsubishi Motors North America, Inc. (n.d.). Retrieved from http://www.mitsubishimanufacturing.com/about/mission/index.asp

MMMA, accusers settle. (1997, August 29). *The Pantagraph*, p. A1.

Sharpe, R. (1996, July 10). Women at Mitsubishi say union fell short on sexual harassment. *The Wall Street Journal* Online. Retrieved March 30, 2004, from http://online.wsj.com

U.S. Equal Employment Opportunity Commission. (n.d.a). Retrieved from http://edocket.access.gpo.gov/cfr_2009/julqtr/pdf/29cfr1604.11.pdf

U.S. Equal Employment Opportunity Commission. (n.d.b). *Sexual harassment charges: EEOC & FEPAs Combined: FY 1992–FY 1996*. Retrieved from http://www.eeoc.gov/eeoc/statistics/enforcement/sexual_harassment-a.cfm

Wills, C. (1997, August 29). Federal case still in the works. Associated Press. Retrieved February 26, 2004, from http:// www.ardmoreite.com/stories/082997/news/news04.html

Woerner, W. L., & Oswald, S. L. (1990, November). Sexual harassment in the workplace: A view through the eyes of the courts. *Labor Law Journal, 41*, 786–793.

Wood, J. T. (1994). Saying it makes it so: The discursive construction of sexual harassment. In S. G. Bingham (Ed.), *Conceptualizing sexual harassment as discursive practice* (pp. 17–30). Westport, CT: Praeger.

Gaming the System

Ethical Challenges in Innovative Organizations

Natalie Nelson-Marsh

This case raises questions about the complexity of organizational processes such as innovation and decision making in a decentralized structure. It also explores how volunteers contributing to organizations should negotiate their participation when they differ in their deeply held assumptions about what constitutes ethical behavior. As such, the case seeks to account for the struggle over what kinds of organizational practices should be deemed acceptable or unacceptable and what forms of resistance are considered appropriate or inappropriate.

If you use the Internet for e-mail, social media, shopping, surfing, or any other purpose, then you are taking advantage of the Internet infrastructure[1] built by the largely invisible group of volunteers at the Internet Engineering Task Force (IETF). The IETF is the organization responsible for the development and maintenance of the Internet infrastructure. The IETF is not a typical organization, however. There is no CEO, no board of directors, no official members, no salaries, or other monetary gain from their work. Rather, the IETF is a flat, decentralized organization where the work of Internet maintenance and development is managed and controlled by voluntary participants. For decades, the work of these volunteers has produced the largest, most used communications network in the world. The IETF case that will be presented illustrates the complexity of organizational processes such as innovation and decision making in a decentralized structure. Not only are these processes complex due to the large number of volunteers participating but they are also complex because of the diverse cultural assumptions that guide volunteers to participate in particular ways. Specifically, this case examines the ethical dilemma that emerges when two organizational cultures differ in their deeply held assumptions about what is the right

---

[1] If you think of the Internet infrastructure or architecture like the foundation of a house, applications and services would be like the furnishings of a house. The Internet Engineering Task Force (IETF) aims to develop an open architecture that enables any corporation or organization to furnish the Internet. Interestingly the foundation is a set of documents or standard protocols that instruct computer engineers on the steps and norms involved in building a technology that will interoperate with the current Internet infrastructure or improve the existing infrastructure.

and ethical way to develop the Internet. Some participants deeply believe that *control* of Internet technology should be limited to a large corporation in order to develop a disciplined product. These participants believe in *loyalty* and *faithfulness* to the large corporations that sponsor their participation at the IETF. Others deeply believe in *liberation* of technology from closed corporate control and *commitment* to fostering Internet development that is open to any *capable, responsible* individual who has the desire to work hard, as messy as that process may be. This case examines how participants from both cultures purposefully "game the system" by violating established IETF rules in order to ensure that the "right" kind of Internet technology will be built. How participants negotiate this ethical dilemma results in innovations and decisions that are then built into the Internet infrastructure, impacting users like you.

The originators' philosophy behind the development of the Internet infrastructure challenged—and continues to challenge—many traditional or classical management assumptions about the right way to organize, the right kinds of goals for an organization, and the right kind of technology an organization should produce. Not only is the organization decentralized, enabling anyone who wishes to participate to do so, so too, is the goal of the IETF *not* to make money, but to produce their work for free for the public in order to continue to "make the Internet work better." The underlying belief is *openness*. Openness at the IETF means two things. First, organizationally it means an *open* process or the ability for anyone to participate in the collective work of developing Internet Standards that benefit all Internet end users (like you or me). The idea is based on the notion that the more participants involved in the development process, the greater the possibility that engineers will build standards into technologies that enable seamless interoperable communication across the globe. Second, participants produce open Internet Standards meaning that anyone who wishes to use or improve the standard has access to this standard for free. In essence, the IETF operates under an assumption of openness believing that the best communication technology is not owned by one corporation but is open to continued improvement and change by anyone with the know-how and desire to improve it. IETFers believe that if technology is open to improvement by the many experts out in the world, then the consequence will be a technology that is always improving for the benefit of a global base of users. Given the success of the Internet as a communication technology, this method of organizing, this goal, and this principle of openness must be working.

In order to ensure the openness of the organization and the openness of an Internet Standard, the IETF requires participants to adhere to two practical rules. First, participants must shed their corporate identity and affiliation once they start participating. This means that participants work to produce standards that benefit the Internet infrastructure and do not benefit one company. Second, all work produced at the IETF belongs to the IETF Trust so that Internet Standards remain freely accessible to the public and corporations cannot claim control of the Internet. This second rule requires that all participants disclose any patents that might be built into the Internet infrastructure.

However, these rules are not always adhered to by participants. Failure to practice these guidelines presents challenging ethical problems during innovation and decision-making processes. For example, IETFers are often challenged with choosing to participate openly and honestly when this openness does not fit with their ethical assumptions or choosing to defy the rules and misrepresent participation as open and honest when it is not. Potential ethical problems like this emerge due to two overarching subcultures within the IETF: (1) the "Inner Circle" and (2) the "Suits." These subcultures embody different ideological assumptions that guide what ethical participation at the IETF looks like. While the Inner Circle subculture deeply believes in the IETF's original decentralized philosophy, the Suits deeply believe in a more traditional, centralized philosophy that assumes one corporation should own the rights to a technology in order to both control technology development and benefit monetarily through this ownership. For example, some of the Suits might represent large corporations like MCI, Sprint, AT&T, Apple, or Microsoft. This is not to say that participants from these large organizations automatically become members of the Suits. There are those participants from large corporations like those previously listed who buy into the decentralized philosophy of the Inner Circle. What makes a Suit a Suit is the assumption that it is one's ethical responsibility to protect the interests of one large corporation rather than develop standards that benefit the collective good.

These two contradictory perspectives manifest in various questionable, if not unethical, practices by both groups during innovation and decision-making efforts associated with infrastructure development and design. Despite the IETF requiring participants to disclose patents held by corporations, there have been cases in which a small faction of the Suits work to covertly game the system with the goal of secretly building a patent into an Internet Standard in order for one corporation to gain a competitive edge in the market and profit from the Internet infrastructure. If successful, building in a patent that benefits only one organization breaks the decentralized Internet infrastructure. However, due to the limited top-down oversight, Inner Circle participants also game the system by engaging in informal strategic practices that work to limit the participation of the Suits in an attempt to defend the original decentralized and open views of organizing and technology. Yet these practices do not align with their deeply held beliefs about open organizing. As this case will demonstrate, cultural beliefs about what is "right" and "wrong" guide how participants make decisions, decisions that have global impacts.

CULTURE CLASH

The IETF conducts most of its innovation, negotiation, and decision making online or virtually through e-mail Listservs. This enables global participants to get involved at any time of day to conduct the large amount of standards development work needed to maintain and further develop the infrastructure. However, the IETF also holds three annual conferences, dubbed "dweeb fests" by participants, to "hash out" complicated or controversial technical problems face-to-face. These dweeb fests take place three times a year in hotels across the globe.

With the majority of participants committed to a vision of organizational and technological decentralization, the original mission and values of the IETF continues today. Their mission states that the IETF is open to anyone with an interest in "making the Internet work better by producing high quality, relevant technical documents that influence the way people design, use, and manage the Internet" (Internet Engineering Task Force, n.d.).

Those who fully embrace the values of decentralization and openness volunteer countless hours of design and development work in addition to their "day job." As one participant highlighted, volunteers who believe in decentralization include the following:

> [People] who [are] looking out for the Internet's best interest . . . it takes a lot of time and you put up with a lot of annoyance. And, I mean ultimately I think it's interesting. I must kind of like it, like arguing with people, [but I participate because] I have an opinion about what's right for the Internet.

This participant and others in the Inner Circle believe in participating in order to better the Internet and characterize themselves as "Protagonists" who see it as their ethical responsibility to protect the original decentralized model of the Internet infrastructure. Protection refers to the ethical practices that are expected from participants. In addition to shedding a corporate identity when innovating and disclosing any applicable patents, ethical participation also includes "doing your homework" in order to participate "with merit" in the innovation and decision-making processes. Doing your homework involves reading through many documents that are hundreds of pages, looking into archives, and talking with other participants in order to ensure that you have the necessary information to contribute "quality" ideas that will better the Internet as it grows.

Although an unspoken Inner Circle rule, ethical participation also includes doing what is necessary strategically and potentially behind the scenes in order to protect the Internet infrastructure from participants who threaten it. As Inner Circle participants explained, a participant who threatens the Internet includes one who does not buy into the decentralized architecture. For example, one Inner Circle participant stated the following:

> There is a great deal of changing the notions of *who* owns the infrastructure. . . . The [centralized corporate perspective] operated very much with the mindset that the communication medium was theirs and theirs alone. And the users were things that the infrastructure needed to be protected *from* at all costs. There were only a limited set of things [the users could do or control]. . . . That the things at the ends . . . were as *dumb* as possible and the things in the middle [i.e. the corporation and corporate technology] were where all the smarts were. This doesn't resonate with the Internet model where you know the entire idea . . . was you wanted smart things at the edges and dumb things in the middle.

Like many Protagonists, this participant highlighted the idea that those who believe communication technology must be centrally controlled by the corporation act as antagonists in the ongoing story of Internet development. In both engineering and human interaction, the Inner Circle subculture identifies with the idea that the ends are intelligent and should be enabled to add value for all Internet users. The infrastructure should not "unduly favor one type of interest" but should be a transparent, neutral, and open foundation empowering current and future users to continue constructing the communication infrastructure through the ongoing discussion and debate involved in decentralized innovation and decision making expected at the IETF.

While the IETF and the Internet were founded on the Inner Circle's cultural assumptions, other participants, known broadly as the Suits, told a different story—claiming that as the Internet grows Inner Circle volunteers are just "kids in a sandbox" who need to "grow up." In particular, Suits believe that the open process at the IETF and open standards are immature if not problematic for satisfying the needs of a global economy. One Suit (from a confidential interview) explained as follows:

> Back in the early days, [the open process was fine]. . . where they were just growing, but now [Internet Standards are] becoming *mainstream* protocol(s), right? . . . When you become a mainstream protocol, as a standards organization, you have to *grow up*. . . . You *have* to respond to business needs.

As this participant claimed, corporations have a stake in the development of new Internet Standards at the IETF that will affect their business models on a global scale. As such, Suits described their role as "protectors" of their corporation's interests. Another Suit noted this about his corporate employer:

> "Decides what their boundaries are, what will be ok to develop at the IETF and what won't, what fits into the business model and what doesn't. I am there [at the IETF] to listen and learn about what is going on. I only stand up and protest a development of a standard that is not within the parameters that [the corporation] has defined."

Despite the fact that this method of participation breaks the first practical rule of participation in the IETF process by not shedding his corporate identity—and while this may annoy the Inner Circle participants—it is the right of this volunteer to participate in this way. In fact, these protests might highlight areas for improvement in a protocol. However, other Suits take their vision of ethical protection of the corporation further and argue the need to end the "religion" of the Inner Circle. Another Suit adamantly noted this:

> "God damn fucking [Inner Circle participants] who come to the IETF and promise that the product can do things that it can't. They promise that [Internet Standards] can do these things, can be interoperable. [They] can't! . . . This (uses fingers to quote) "organization" believes that they can create "open" standards from . . . their "computers." . . . People like to think that the Internet is free, nothing's for free.

Many Suits, like this participant, believe that it is the ethical responsibility of the IETF as an organization to change into a centralized organizational model and produce a more centralized technological infrastructure. And if the organization won't change, then breaking the second practical rule at the IETF by not disclosing corporate patents is justified and ethical.

What emerges here are two different, deeply held ideologies that influence the ethics behind organizing and developing communication technologies. For instance, the Inner Circle subculture believes in a utility perspective of ethics where individual actions have global consequences. These participants believe in a decentralized or "end-to-end" organizational and technological infrastructure. In this model, the "ends," both human ends and technological ends, are intelligent actors in an organizational or technological infrastructure. For example, volunteers are considered the organizational ends whose actions have consequences that impact how the IETF organization operates and how the Internet infrastructure develops. Thus, the IETF expects the human ends or participants to "do their homework" and "invest" time into researching and developing Internet Standards that will benefit global users of the Internet. The underlying ethical principle here is that the utility of the volunteers lends to faster-paced innovation benefiting the larger, global collective. The Inner Circle participants believe all IETF participants are accountable for large-scale consequences and thus should be concerned with the long-term effects and sustainability of an Internet infrastructure. Every individual action or decision has global consequences.

This principle of utility is also built into the technology in that all the Inner Circle innovations and decisions aim to develop technological ends that are the "smarts" of the infrastructure. The Inner Circle develops Internet Standards specifying how engineers should build the capabilities for communication into the technological ends so that if I make an Internet call from my computer the computer knows how to call another computer. Building communication control into the ends of the technology enables people to use and change the technology based on the utility and usefulness of the ends. If something does not work or if there is the potential to add to the communicative capabilities of a technology, then it is possible for individuals to change the technology without permission from a corporation. This belief in the utility of the ends lends to fast-paced growth and change of the technology because it is driven by the desire to improve the technology, not the desire to improve the bottom line for one organization. If the Inner Circle perceives any threat to the end-to-end infrastructure (organizationally or technologically), they interpret it as a threat to their ethical responsibilities to the global collective and therefore they feel justified in adopting practices that will counteract such threats, even if these practices go against their open philosophy.

In contrast, the Suits ideologically believe in a duty perspective of ethics. They oppose the belief that the ends are intelligent and believe instead that the ends should be "dumb." In other words, it is the duty of those at the top of an organization to control what is of interest and importance in technological development and it is the duty of the human end to act as a representative of the corporate interest. The belief here is that it is the duty of the organizational member to act in the best interest of the corporation in order to further the bottom line. So, too, do the Suits believe that the technological ends are representative of, and controlled by, the corporation. Thus, while many of the Suits participate simply to observe Internet Standards development and protest if a standard appears to threaten their corporate sponsor's interest, a small faction of the Suits believe in more extreme measures. This group of the Suits believes it is their duty *not* to disclose patent(s) held by the corporation they represent, despite the overt and transparent intellectual property rights (IPR) rules at the IETF, if doing so will benefit their corporation's monetary goals. Their goal is simple: If an Internet Standard includes a patent held by their company, their company will have built in control of Internet communications on a global scale, requiring users of the Internet to work with this company by purchasing their products and services over the long term. The corporation then controls the changes to the technology enabling them to charge more for innovations. For example, changes like Facebook or Internet telephony would, if developed at all, be available to users for an increased charge. Obviously this creates problems for the IETF, whose aim it is to keep the architecture open and nonproprietary so that any individual or company can innovate new communication capabilities for Internet technologies.

Both the Inner Circle and the Suit subcultures work to game the system in an effort to fulfill their ethical perspectives of responsible organizing. Specifically, the Suits game the system due to their obligation to their corporate benefactors. These efforts, however, violate the principle of openness of standards. Alternatively, the Inner Circle participants game the system by developing covert strategies to silence the voices of the Suits in an attempt to prevent them from building an architecture that contains patents that would threaten the utility of the infrastructure built for *all* Internet users, not just certain customers. Both these efforts to game the system violate the principle of openness in different ways, but each relies on the ideological assumptions of the "right" way to influence organizational and technological development. Next, these efforts emerge in one example of innovation and decision making at the IETF.

THE ETHICAL DILEMMA: GAMING THE SYSTEM

Innovation and decision-making practices, as organizing processes, reveal the deeply held cultural assumptions by the Inner Circle and the Suits subcultures that violate the principles of openness and contribute to questionable, if not unethical, practices. While the Suits believe that nondisclosure is justified if it protects the corporations' best interest, the Inner Circle believes that engaging in certain strategies to protect against building in limited corporate interests is justified and ethical if it protects the decentralized model of the Internet infrastructure. The case developed next illustrates how subcultural ideological perspectives influence innovation and decision-making practices that impact the development of the Internet.

Most work on Internet Standards takes place in teams, called Working Groups that collectively decide to focus on a particular area of Internet development. Working Group debates are facilitated by Working Group Chairs, two individuals (nominated by volunteers) who facilitate online discussions and meetings and organize which document drafts are contentious or problematic enough to discuss during dweeb fests.

As with all dweeb fests, this Working Group meeting occurred in a typical hotel conference room. The chairs were positioned behind a long table at the front of the room facing approximately 50 to 100 volunteers sitting in rows. Nearly all participants had laptop computers open on their laps. A large presentation screen faced the audience, and two microphones stood in the aisle running down the middle of the rows of chairs, one near the front of the room and the other near the back. As the meeting began, the room was full of murmuring chitchat. The Working Group Chairs called to the floor the author of the controversial standard under development that was the main subject of the discussion. The author, a Suit from one of the largest computer technology firms in the world, stepped to the front of the room, turned toward the audience, and began to describe the key issues and changes that the group needed to understand in order to move forward in developing this standard. Several participants were recognizable as the Suits due to their "business" attire as they sat reading e-mail, looking up when items of interest emerged. Other participants, more casually dressed in T-shirts and jeans, congregated near the microphone in the aisle ready to respond to items presented that interested them or needed discussion, and the cycle of debate began.

Standing at the front of the room in freshly pressed olive green slacks and a button-up shirt, the Suit looked ready for a business presentation. As the Suit pressed through the main points of concern, rumblings of a private conversation began between the Inner Circle participants who lined up behind the microphone in the audience. At first the tone of the questions from the Inner Circle was neutral. But the response by the presenter changed the tone from one of neutrality to one of contempt. The Inner Circle participant nearly spat into the microphone as he asked, "OK, so you'll have in there the available media [and] you'll also show which streams are currently being used?" The Suit interrupted before he could finish the question and stated emphatically, "NO! You have to . . . guys please, please read. . . ." The Suit proceeded to explain the answer to the question. A second and third Inner Circle participant jumped up to the microphone, their facial expressions tense, frustrated. The second Inner Circle participant laughed into the microphone, scoffed, and shook his head. He seemed at a loss for what to say and dropped back into his chair. The Suit launched into the presentation again but was immediately interrupted by an Inner Circle participant at the mic. Both the Suit and the Inner Circle participant interrupted each other, talking over one another, voices raised to a near yell. Finally, the Suit yelled, "I resubmitted this version three times in *the last two months*. And *each* time in the last second there are new comments." Nearly panting and staring at the Inner Circle participants at the mic, the Suit mumbled, "All these comments that come in just before last call. . . ." The Chair stated, "That's usually what happens when something isn't really to the point where we all understand it." The Suit retorted, red faced and jaw clenched, "Or don't want to understand it."

Due to the contentious nature of the document, it was not surprising to observe participants engaged in a heated debate or what participants call "dog piling" an idea to "see where the edges of an idea break." IETFers believe there is value in challenging an idea in order to ensure that the recommendations published for the larger public indeed work and enable seamless interoperable communication across time and space. Heated debate then, is the rigor and reputation of the IETF. As such, silencing becomes a tactic to game the system when the Inner Circle notices an idea that threatens the Internet infrastructure or suspects the nondisclosure of a patent that threatens the Internet infrastructure. In this case—and in other cases like this—the Inner Circle engaged in three strategic practices that aimed to silence the author and reject the idea. These silencing strategies include: attack, "send it to the list," and reauthor.

For example, when the Suit stated, "I resubmitted this version three times in *the last two months*. And *each* time in the last second there are new comments," the Suit highlighted the silencing tactic of attack, which often begins online when the Working Group Chairs suggest a contentious document be discussed face-to-face at a dweeb fest meeting. A few weeks prior to the actual meeting, the Working Group Chairs will make a "last call for comments" on the draft. Inner Circle participants will say nothing online in the Listserv making it seem that the draft is ready for discussion at the dweeb fest. However, just before the meeting, the Inner Circle will overwhelm the list with comments regarding potential problems in the draft arguing the draft is "too broken" to implement. With so many comments about problems so close to the meeting, the author of the idea cannot make all the changes before the presentation, which opens up the document to an attack in the face-to-face meeting. This attack method that began online continued in the Suit's face-to-face presentation when it appeared that the idea was moving through the process despite the clear threat it posed to the end-to-end model. Thus, the Inner Circle also engaged in an attack on the presenter to silence the proposal and effectively "kill" the idea.

At this point in the face-to-face debate, the Working Group Chair stated, "Let's just say we're not going to close this issue today, and there are other issues in the pipeline," which is code for another silencing strategy: Send it to the list. Send it to the list is a mechanism to start the process over. The author revised the document and presented it to the Listserv participants who ignored it until "last call for comments" and again overwhelmed the author with changes that were needed.

The Suit, recognizing this strategy, interrupted stating, "I just want to present. I just want to present." During an awkward pause, those behind the mic continued to hover near the mic, waiting. The Suit paused, turned, and approached the Working Group Chairs' table arguing with them, stating, " . . . this always happens . . . I cannot work on this any harder than I have the last few months." All eyes in the room watched the commotion at the Working Group Chairs' table. Slowly, the Suit's shoulders slumped forward while stating, "It's all right, I'm OK. I have one more slide. Turn back please. No, it's fine." The tone changed from one of angry defiance and frustration to one of defeat. After this, it was difficult to hear the presentation as the Suit spoke so softly that people in the room strained to hear. The quiet audience, no longer engrossed in their computers, watched the front of the room intently.

In the cycle of innovation and debate that was previously described, the Suit presenting the idea not only experienced the silence and then barrage of comments on the e-mail Listserv just prior to this meeting (and other meetings) but also experienced attack and another call to send it to the list when the Working Group Chair stated that the issue would not be solved today. Dejected, the Suit nearly pleaded to have the idea heard but was defeated. It is important to note that this was the fourth time this document had been presented at a dweeb fest because the silencing tactics online and face-to-face contact allowed the Inner Circle participants time to engage in the last silencing strategy: reauthoring the proposal by developing a document with an alternative solution that countered the ideas presented by the Suit.

Silence is a tactic to game the system when the Inner Circle notices an idea that threatens the Internet infrastructure or suspects the nondisclosure of a patent that threatens the Internet infrastructure. In cases like this, the Inner Circle engaged in three strategic practices that aimed to silence the author and reject the idea. These silencing strategies include: (1) attack, (2) send it to the list, and (3) reauthor. Despite the fact that these strategies do not align with the ideological assumptions of open participation and decentralized organizing, the Inner Circle believes that without these kinds of practices, Internet users will become enslaved to one corporate interest and the lack of ability to shape and grow the Internet. As such, efforts to game the system align with their ethical perspectives of utility for all. In contrast, the Suits believe that protecting the monetary business interests is a universal ethic that trumps the IETF rules for disclosure of patents. They believe that it is their duty to protect their corporation's ability to make money in the field of technological communication.

SUMMARY

While one might assume that participants at the IETF believe standards development is an objective, rational process, this is not the case. One IETFer stated the following:

> Making standards is an *extremely* human process. It's people. People who do the thinking and people who do the arguing and people who do the decision making and people who have fun . . . And what the world sees is not the IETF, it's the Internet and *that's* the thing that we are proud of. The Internet is an idea of connectedness, the idea that communication is good. It's the network that *realizes* the idea, and it's a society of the people who use it. The IETF *exists* to make the internet work well. And we *do* it together because individually we cannot do it . . . we're still working, we're still doing good work. . . . The Internet has changed . . . from being a *new and powerful* addition to society to being an *integrated* part of it.

As highlighted in this quote, innovation and decision-making processes at the IETF are human communicative processes in the control of the individual participants. The decentralized structure promotes the voices of many in order to create a space for creativity and innovation. However, the decentralized structure also creates a space for a diversity of deeply held cultural beliefs that influence what participants interpret as the "right" way to develop technology and the "right" kind of technology to develop. Some participants engage in questionable if not unethical practices in order to "game" this process and benefit the corporate organization they represent despite the stated rules at the IETF. Other participants engage in strategies that aim to protect the end-to-end Internet infrastructure from commercial control. However, all participants assume that what they are doing is "right" and necessary. This case illustrates the cultural and ethical complexity of innovation and decision making at the IETF, which has global impacts for the future of Internet infrastructure.

DISCUSSION QUESTIONS

1. What complexities arise in innovation and decision-making processes in a decentralized organizational system?

2. What insights does an organizational cultural perspective provide for this case? What insights would a critical perspective provide?

3. Describe the sociotechnological issue at stake in this case. What would you propose as a potential solution to the ethical tension at the IETF?

4. How would you describe the ethical (or unethical) practices at the IETF? How does this explanation demonstrate your ethical and cultural assumptions about organizing?

5. How might alternative ethical perspectives change the practices at the IETF?

REFERENCE

Internet Engineering Task Force. (n.d). *Mission statement.* Retrieved from http://www.ietf.org/about/mission.html

PART IV

Transparency

Reward, Identity, and Autonomy

Ethical Issues in College Athletics

John Llewellyn

This case examines scandals and fraud in several university athletic departments. It explores the ethical tension in college athletics to pursue success while fostering integrity. It also addresses important issues regarding the responsibilities of coaches, athletic directors (ADs), and university presidents for compliance to NCAA regulations, as well as the transparency by which decisions are made regarding student–athletes.

Sports do not build character. They reveal it.

—Attributed to both Heywood Hale Broun and John Wooden

As I sit down to write this case study, in comes an e-mail from my doctoral alma mater, the University of Texas. University president Bill Powers told the alumni that the campus has cut a deal with ESPN (Entertainment and Sports Programming Network) and IMG College, a multimedia rights marketer; $300 million will flow to the university and IMG over the next 20 years. He observed, "I'm delighted to announce the creation of a 24-hour television network dedicated to covering intercollegiate athletics, music, cultural arts, and academics" (personal communication, January 19, 2011). My alma mater, one of the great public universities in America, has effectively become a channel, a de facto entertainment outlet.

What will be done with the proceeds of this deal? For the first 5 years, the annual payout of $10 million will be split evenly: $5 million apiece for academics/faculty support and athletics. After that period, the allocations will be reexamined. Will there be some respite for undergraduate students from the huge lecture classes that are the staple of this campus? What are the responsibilities of the administration to the rank-and-file student? Will there be a chance to take more classes taught by faculty as opposed to graduate students? Time will tell. Immediately, however, there will be a pair of million-dollar endowed faculty chairs funded in physics and philosophy to bring glory and prestige to the campus. While the Longhorn Network would showcase campus features including the performing arts,

183

humanities, and sciences, can there be any doubt that its reason for existence is to televise sports? If the University of Texas has made this choice, how many other universities will eagerly follow suit?

This case study describes the myriad ways that college athletics have become big business and inventories the ethical challenges that accompany this development. This emerging reality brings with it vexing questions: What are the rights and duties of student–athletes and, for that matter, coaches, in this "big business"? Who gets paid in this system, and who does not? How are athletic identities created and with whose symbols? Who enjoys autonomy within this system, and who does not? All of these questions reside at the intersection of organizational communication and ethics.

It is a business concept that is behind the central term of the discussion. Legal scholars examine the National Collegiate Athletic Association's (NCAA) behavior in light of the basic tenets of American labor law. They point out that the NCAA adopted the term *student-athlete* in 1953 and, from that day forward, has insisted on that label. Why? A 1953 Colorado decision, *University of Denver v. Nemeth*, allowed football players injured or killed in the sport to apply for workers' compensation. In other words, the athlete in this case was also recognized as an employee of the university and could pursue benefits under the law. The phrase *student-athlete* highlights the education-gaining part of the process (regardless of actual graduation rates) while distracting from the entertainment-providing and profit-generating side of the equation.

This case study examines several high-profile issues regarding collegiate athletic programs. The purpose, however, is not to assign blame. In the aggregate, these instances summarize the challenge of ethical leadership at the highest level of universities. Coaches, ADs, and university presidents pursue multiple objectives: build a better university, field winning teams, educate and graduate athletes, deal with misbehavior of student-athletes, placate alumni, and satisfy the rules of the NCAA. Can this system produce both ethical decisions and a winning tradition? How can those two goals be harmonized? Ethics provides a framework for working through these competing interests.

If these tensions are so common and so widely recognized, why do they persist? The question highlights the ethical dimensions of leadership and the countervailing forces within the academy: the athletic/academic tension, the exorbitant salaries paid to revenue-sport coaches, and the thinly veiled demand that a new coach produce an immediate winner.

The late Charles Redding of Purdue University, father of organizational communication, saw its inevitable and necessary linkage to the study of ethics. In a 1992 lecture at the Center for the Study of Ethics in Society, he highlighted the issue through his subtitle: "When will we wake up?" Redding gives a call to arms: "We have remained oblivious to an area that has enormous potential for serious research: namely, the ethical dimension of organizational communication" (Redding, 1996, p. 17). He identified six categories of unethical communication that deserve scholarly attention: (1) coercive (intimidating, threatening), (2) destructive (being aggressive, abusing), (3) deceptive (being dishonest, lying), (4) intrusive (using surveillance), (5) secretive (not responding), and (6) manipulative-exploitative (hiding intentions, patronizing). Organizations take shape one conversation at a time. What policies, decisions, and actions can universities promote to see that the organization takes shape through ethical processes? These problematic communication behaviors are illustrated in this case study.

REWARD IN COLLEGE REVENUE SPORTS: WHO GETS TO BE A MILLIONAIRE?

As the University of Texas Longhorn Network deal confirms, college sports have become big business in the first decades of the 21st century. The Atlantic Coast Conference (ACC) has a deal with ESPN to broadcast football, men's basketball, and some Olympic sports. Its term covers 12 years at a reported total cost of $1.86 billion; this figure amounts to $155 million per school per year. This arrangement more than doubles the ACC's previous broadcast payout of $67 million per school per year (Berman, 2010).

The ACC's deal pales in comparison to the ESPN/CBS deal with the Southeastern Conference (SEC). The 15-year contract struck in 2008 nets each conference school $205 million per year. Coaches' salaries have also risen geometrically. For example, Mike Krzyzewski, men's basketball coach at Duke University, received $4.2 million for fiscal years 2008 and 2009, according to IRS forms. For the 2007 to 2008 season, Wake Forest University's football coach Jim Grobe was also paid $4.2 million, although the AD explained that the more accurate salary figure was $2.172 million; the difference was deferred compensation. In contrast, for the 2010 to 2011 school year, the state of North Carolina pays a public school teacher with a master's degree and 10 years' experience $42,010, which is 1% of either coach's salary. Does this ratio say anything about the values and priorities in American society? Of the 120 head coaches in the football bowl subdivision, 62 are paid more than $1 million per year including 28 who receive more than $2 million. Six coaches are paid more than $3 million; Alabama and Texas top the list with salaries of $5.996 million and $5.1 million, respectively.

Athletic equipment manufacturers are adding to universities' and coaches' wealth, as well. For example, Nike has an 8-year deal with the University of North Carolina at Chapel Hill (UNC–Chapel Hill) that calls for $28.3 million in payments, including $18 million in free products. The Chancellor's Academic Enhancement Fund received $800,000. Every year, $200,000 is given to the athletic department, $100,000 of which is designated for coaches' bonuses. In addition, $175,000 is provided to enable five teams to make foreign exhibition tours. Florida State's deal with Nike totals $34 million for 10 years, including $50,000 per year (1.5%) expressly for women's sports. The Adidas deal with the University of Tennessee covers 5 years and totals $19.3 million; one half is in cash, and the balance in equipment. Some contracts include performance bonuses: $15,000 for the team making the Sweet 16; making the Final Four is worth $25,000 for the men's team and $10,000 for the women's team.

These ostensible gifts are actually marketing and publicity arrangements. Most require a set number of appearances by football and basketball coaches as well as others, if requested. The arrangements are exclusive, and no other sort of apparel may be worn. The Virginia Tech contract specifies that the Nike logo on shoes may not be taped or polished over; the first violation results in a 10% payment reduction for that year; the second, a 15% penalty; and the third cuts the payment by 25%. The Nike contract establishes the market value of its deal with Virginia Tech: $2 billion.

Against this lucrative backdrop, the issue of paying student-athletes, many of whom come from modest circumstances, emerges once again. The standard rebuttal is that students are amateurs and are properly and completely compensated with tuition, room, board, and books. As the world of college sports climbs higher and higher up a mountain of money, those arguments come under greater strain.

Recent events underscore the economic tensions in what one noted sociologist has labeled the "Athletic Industrial Complex" (Smith, 2009). A litany of high-profile cases illustrates issues of rewards and ethics in college sport: charges of improper payments of Reggie Bush while a student-athlete at the University of Southern California (USC) along with the returning of the 2005 Heisman Trophy and the departure of coach Pete Carroll for the NFL's Seattle Seahawks; the disqualification of several football players at UNC–Chapel Hill for accepting improper gifts from a sports agent and the resignation of an assistant coach who had a sports agent on speed dial; the deferred suspension, to be served after the 2011 Allstate Sugar Bowl, of several stars of the Ohio State University (OSU) football team who were found to have sold athletic memorabilia and to have received improper discounts on services with local businesses; the repeated hiring of basketball coach John Calipari, famous for bringing to universities (Massachusetts and Memphis) NCAA championships and investigations that vacate them; and, finally, the issue of graduation rates for revenue-sport athletes, in general, and African Americans, in particular.

THE SUM OF ALL ETHICS: ORGANIZATIONAL LEGITIMACY

These examples illustrate how individual incidents can add up to serious problems for coaches, schools, leagues, and even the enterprise of college athletics. Organizations can survive in a society because they are deemed to be legitimate: They use their power in ways that meet with public approval. The concern for ethics is not an abstract exercise. An organization's legitimacy lives or dies through the public's response to its behavior. Classic illustrations of legitimacy are the enduring public respect (and sales) that have followed Johnson & Johnson since its handling of the criminal poisoning of Tylenol capsules that resulted in seven deaths in 1982. The downside is exemplified by negative feelings toward oil giant British Petroleum (BP) for its blown-out well and massive oil leak into the Gulf of Mexico that began in April 2010 and was capped in July. In total, 11 lives were lost, and 205 million gallons of oil spilled.

Legitimacy is more than complying with law; it is satisfying social norms as they evolve, even on questions such as compensating student-athletes. As college sports emerge as a multibillion dollar industry and universities morph into entertainment networks, the argument that those who fuel this money machine are completely compensated for their contributions by "books and tuition" begins to sag. How these tensions will play out is unclear, but as folk artist Bob Dylan once famously sang, "The Times They Are a-Changin'."

Reggie Bush took cash and gifts from sports agents during his time at USC, the NCAA concluded in June 2010. It found the school failed to monitor athletes closely enough and administered a 2-year ban on postseason play by USC football and reduced scholarships by 30 over 3 years. The school also forfeited all football wins in the 2004 to 2005 season and two from the previous season. The coach and the athlete were beyond the NCAA's jurisdiction long before the verdict. In January 2010, 6 months before the NCAA's ruling, head coach Pete Carroll left his $4.4 million university position to lead the NFL's Seattle

Seahawks for $33 million over 5 years. Bush became the first athlete in 75 years to forfeit the Heisman Trophy, though without an admission of guilt.

He led the Trojans to the 2005 Bowl Championship Series (BCS) championship game only to lose to the University of Texas quarterbacked by Vince Young. A lawsuit by a pair of sports agents asserted that they had given Bush $290,000 in gifts, including paying for the limousine ride to the Heisman Awards. They sued when he signed with another agent; the case settled for between $200,000 and $300,000. Bush pledges his continuing affection for USC: "I'm here to lend a helping hand to USC and anytime they need me . . . I'm just a phone call away." That call will not be coming; the NCAA ordered USC to permanently dissociate from Bush.

Bush offered an analysis of the current revenue-sport environment:

> Obviously something has to be changed. You've got universities making millions of dollars off these kids and they don't get paid. The majority of college athletes who come in on scholarship come in [with] nothing. That's where you have a problem. You're making all this money off these kids and you're giving them crumbs and then you're surrounding these kids with money and telling them not to touch it. (Associated Press, 2010)

At UNC–Chapel Hill, they know the perils of athlete-agent contact. During the 2010 to 2011 season, two football players were ruled permanently ineligible and a third dismissed when gifts of jewelry and trips from sports agents were uncovered. An assistant coach with close ties to a sports agent resigned mid-season. The NCAA investigation trumped the football season itself. On December 30, 2010, the remaining players won a dramatic double-overtime victory in the Music City Bowl over the University of Tennessee to end a season that tarnished the school's exemplary athletic program. Professor Robert Malekoff, a sports studies scholar, summarized the impact of such scandals: "When there's huge publicity about something like this, that's one more chink in the educational non-profit status" (Sander, 2010).

The Allstate Sugar Bowl played in January 2011 was a cutting-edge example of the crosscurrents of economics and ethics in college athletics. The game was to pit perennial powerhouse OSU against the University of Arkansas. Then came reports that five OSU players had sold merchandise and/or received improper benefits. Of the players involved, four were starters, including the quarterback and a leading receiver. The upshot was that the five were to be suspended for the first five games of the 2011 to 2012 season but would be eligible for the Bowl game. All are juniors who can declare for the NFL draft, so the ultimate effect of the sanctions is a matter of conjecture.

How did they remain eligible despite these violations? Sugar Bowl CEO Paul Hoolahan defended his product: "I made the point that anything that could be done to protect the integrity of this year's game, we would greatly appreciate that." He added his perspective on the violations and the sanctions: "I appreciate and fully understand the Midwestern values and ethics behind that. But I'm probably thinking of this from a selfish perspective" (Gordon, 2010). OSU officials sought to explain the players' actions by noting that the sale of the Big Ten Championship rings and a sportsmanship award was intended to help the players' families. The OSU AD noted: "The time this occurred with these young men was a very tough time in our history" (Lesmerises, 2010). One player's mother observed that there was no involvement with agents and no stolen property; what the players sold belonged to them. The NCAA and OSU held that the athletes remained Bowl-eligible because they had not been adequately educated about NCAA rules during the period of the violations and thus were not aware that they were committing violations. OSU won a hard fought game, beating Arkansas 31 to 26 as 73,879 watched in the Louisiana Superdome; quarterback Terrelle Pryor was MVP. Tickets for the 2012 Allstate Sugar Bowl went on sale on the website immediately after the game.

In March 2011, it came to light that Coach Tressel had been alerted to the players' actions 9 months before the story broke. Despite a specific clause in his contract requiring immediate action on potential NCAA problems, he had told no one in the athletic department and went through the entire "discovery" process in December without admitting what he knew. OSU suspended him for the first two games of the 2011 season and fined him $250,000 (6.6% of his $3,777,000 salary). Tressel later requested the same suspension that the NCAA meted out to the players—five games: "so that the players and I can handle this adversity together." The AD granted his wish. The players' mistakes were attributed to immaturity, an impoverished background, and lack of familiarity with NCAA rules. Which of these reasons apply to Tressel? In May 2011, Tressel resigned as the head football coach at Ohio State; in September, he was hired as instant replay consultant for the Indianapolis Colts of the NFL.

The legitimacy of the entire BCS was put under the spotlight in April 2011 due to an audit of the Fiesta Bowl. The longtime director of the Bowl, John Junker, was fired when it came to light that he had used the organization's funds to improperly reimburse Bowl employees for contributions to politicians, including two U.S. senators. The actions are under review as possible violations of campaign finance laws. A 2009 investigation into these donations by an attorney, formerly Arizona's attorney general, turned up nothing; a host of Fiesta Bowl employees had been prescreened and coached on their testimony by a hired lobbyist. Only a whistle-blower brought out the truth. At the organization's expense, Junker had hosted a $33,000 birthday party for himself and a $1,200 trip to a strip club as well as memberships in four private golf clubs. His annual salary was in excess of $680,000. The BCS is considering severing its relationship with the Fiesta Bowl, which has contritely promised "sweeping reforms."

The saga of Coach John Calipari is a morality tale about the compromises that come with a university's ambition to win a men's national basketball crown. His championships won at the University of Massachusetts and the University of Memphis were both vacated for serious rules violations. Nevertheless, in 2009, Calipari was selected to lead the storied program at the University of Kentucky and given a contract for 8 years and $31.65 million *plus incentives*. Kentucky was attracted by his career record of 445 wins, 140 losses, at the time. Former coach Bobby Knight commented on the hire and the state of college basketball: "We've gotten into a situation over the years where integrity is really lacking and in a way I'm glad I'm not coaching" (Associated Press, 2009).

GRADUATION FOR STUDENT-ATHLETES: REALISTIC GOAL OR LONG SHOT

As many of the preceding cases illustrate, the financial rewards for revenue-sport coaches and student-athletes present significant ethical challenges. Most student-athletes in football fully expend their eligibility, often including a fifth, or "redshirt," year. Yet the saddest truth is that for all that time spent on campus the graduation rates of athletes are often disgracefully low, and this is especially so for African American males.

There are many ways to compute graduation rates; the NCAA compares student-athletes' performance against all students. In this process, the performance of revenue-sport athletes is mixed in with cross country runners and swimmers to dilute problems and elevate the aggregate graduation rate. In fact, revenue-sport athletes have relatively little success with graduation. The NCAA's numbers say that 79% of all athletes graduate within 6 years of enrollment, based on the performance of 2000 through 2004 enrollees. According to a 2010 NCAA report, in football, 18 of 25 schools in the BCS standings graduate at least 60% of their football players; Miami, Iowa, and Virginia Tech had success in the 79% to 81% range, and Oklahoma and Arizona's rates were below 50%. In basketball, the NCAA's reported overall graduation rate is 66% with African Americans moving up from 57% to 60%; 12 of the past year's top 25 football teams had rates at 50% or lower with California at 30% and Connecticut at 31%, though Villanova and Illinois graduated everyone and Duke and Butler hit 83% (Schilken, 2010).

Other studies show that, among basketball players, African Americans graduate at a 58% rate compared to 81% for whites. In the 2010 NCAA men's tourney, programs such as Marquette University, Brigham Young University, Wofford College, Wake Forest University, Utah State University, and the University of Notre Dame graduated 100%; powerhouses like the University of Pittsburgh, Duke University, Villanova University, the University of Kansas (KU), and Georgetown University were in the 67% to 100% range. Schools like the University of Maryland; the University of Texas; University of Nevada, Las Vegas (UNLV); and the University of Kentucky represent real problems. The University of Maryland's overall rate is 8%, and it has graduated no African American player in the past 3 years; over the past decade the rate has never exceeded 25% and has been 11% four times. Graduation rates for African American basketball players at the University of Texas over the past 3 years are poor: 29%, 14%, and 22%. Over the past 4 years, the graduation rate at UNLV has ranged from 10% to 14% for African American basketball players. The University of Kentucky's 6-year graduation performance rates for African American basketball players range from 0% to 18%. The University of California, Berkeley has a campus graduation rate of 85% for all students and 62% for African American students: "The graduation success rate for both its black and white players is zero" (Jackson, 2010). This claim is based on the single year of men's basketball in question; to take a longer view, the NCAA reports that, for the 1999 through 2002 cohort of student-athletes, male basketball players graduated at a 20% rate. Would we accept these percentages as case closure rates for a local police department or success rates for surgeons or even as a class-wide graduation rate from a university? If not, what makes these figures acceptable in this context?

Student-athletes' graduation rates matter for many reasons; only 1.3% of senior players will be drafted by the NBA. William C. Friday, chairman of the Knight Commission on Intercollegiate Athletics, described the problem: "When you see poor graduation rates, recruiting violations and instances of academic fraud, any thoughtful sports fan can see that we've created an entertainment industry and, in the process, it has eroded the integrity of the university" (Drape, 2004). Friday is clearly inventorying the markers of a shift and then condemning that shift in the organizational culture of contemporary universities. Countervailing pressure comes from those with an appetite for glory and the $750,000 that each round of the men's tournament brings. U.S. Secretary of Education Arne Duncan, who played basketball at Harvard, decried this exploitation and has informally proposed that schools with less than a 40% graduation rate should be barred from postseason play. That standard would have barred 15 of the teams in the 2010 NCAA tournament field.

IDENTITY: SWOOSHES, SEMINOLES, AND STADIUMS

While graduation is the long-range goal for student-athletes and universities, on the path to graduation there are persistent ethical questions regarding athletics and identity that both groups must confront. There is no more fundamental notion for people and organizations than identity. "Who are you?" may be the first question; "I am _____" might be the first answer. Identification choices are a big part of the world of college sports. At UNC–Chapel Hill, fans will sing, "And when I die, I'm a Tar Heel dead." At the University of Tennessee, "Rocky Top" will bring a chorus of 10,000 voices. Loyalty to an institution means lifelong identification. But what are the implications of commercial encroachments on those identifications? Can you even buy a T-shirt for State U that does not bear the mark of its athletic sponsor?

Issues of organizational ethics and identity appear in many forms: the requirement to wear in contractually specified ways the gear of the official supplier; the use of players' likenesses and numbers in athletic video games, thus appropriating their likeness and behavior with no compensation to the athlete; the sale of jerseys displaying the athlete's name and number again without compensation; the use of Native American tribes' names and symbols for logos and mascots without permission; and the realignment of conference memberships in service of television ratings without concern for tradition, geography, or safety.

As Nike's contract with Virginia Tech made clear, the coaches and players are to be mannequins for specific brands. There can be no obstruction of the corporate image. James Keady, an assistant soccer coach at St. John's, claimed that he was fired for refusing to wear Nike gear; he objected to their treatment of overseas workers. His lawsuit was dismissed.

Adidas and Nike were at loggerheads over Jordan—not *that* Jordan but his son, Marcus. When he was being recruited in 2009, Marcus, a 6'3" 200 lb. guard, told officials at the University of Central Florida (UCF) that, for reasons of family sentiment, he wanted to play in Air Jordans although Adidas had the $1.9 million sponsorship deal with UCF. Officials, after checking, told him that would not be a problem and he enrolled. As the season neared, it came out that Adidas did not approve of this arrangement even though all of Jordan's other gear would be Adidas. The sports blogosphere was abuzz with myriad opinions of who was at fault and what should be done. An associate AD chirped the hope that things could be "worked out amicably." That was not to be. Ultimately, Adidas asserted, "The University of Central Florida has chosen not to deliver on their contractual commitment" and ended the relationship that was estimated to be worth $3 million at its next renewal (Penner, 2009).

In July 2009, former UCLA basketball star Ed O'Bannon filed suit against the NCAA and licensing and video game firms seeking damages for the use of his image and likeness from his playing days. In January 2011, hall-of-fame basketball star Oscar Robertson joined the suit as have other former college basketball and football players. The suit against the NCAA and the others argues that student-athletes' images and likenesses were being licensed for commercial use without their permission. The stakes are high; collegiate licensing and merchandizing is a $4 billion per year business. For their contributions to these products, NCAA student-athletes are paid nothing. The former players have argued that the NCAA requires all athletes to sign away their licensing rights without benefit of counsel; the NCAA insulates itself against such claims by declining to license athletes' names for use with video games. The virtual players are not named but have the same number, physical characteristics, and home state as the actual player. In addition, game players can download rosters from online services and upload the players' names into the game. The plaintiffs have argued that the NCAA is violating antitrust laws and the players' rights of publicity and have looked to force the NCAA to compensate players' for the use of their images and likenesses. In May 2011, the suit was dismissed against the video game maker on the grounds that it had not been part of any alleged conspiracy against the players' interests; the NCAA and its licensing agent remain targets of the suit (Associated Press, 2011).

Logos and mascots are central elements of universities' identities, but their meaning and origins are matters of serious ethical deliberation. The issue centers on appropriation of Native American tribes' names and symbols to represent an institution or its sports teams without the approval of the relevant group. Proponents of the practice assert that this usage represents a tribute to the indigenous peoples and should cause no offense. Can this framework be understood as virtuous or ethical? What sort of assumptions must one make to normalize these practices? Opponents of the practice, including representatives of the groups in question, argue that it reflects unwarranted dominance and insensitivity. Take, for instance, the North Dakota "Fighting Sioux." The controversy has raged for three decades even as most Sioux tribes do not support the university's use of the name and logo. The argument that appropriating Native American tribes' names and logos is inconsequential is belied by the strong and persistent opinions on the topic.

AUTONOMY: FREEDOM TO CHOOSE AND THE REVENUE-SPORT STUDENT-ATHLETE

For many students, college is the time of transition between dependence on family and adult independence. It is a time for trying out behaviors and learning from the consequences. Attending classes (or not), building relationships, living in an apartment, managing time, and doing a host of other life skills are worked out through these experiments in daily autonomy. For college students who are athletes, this process can be very different, often in ways that delay their adult learning and invite them to remain dependent on others, at least until their eligibility runs out. Then they are often turned out on their own but without the growth experiences their peers have had. There are a number of specific issues related to autonomy: scheduling of free time, "voluntary" athletic activities and mandatory events; surveillance and control by authorities; and discipline, conformance, and intimidation.

The first ethical issue relating to autonomy is the issue of time itself. NCAA rules limit in-season time demands on student-athletes to a maximum of 20 hours per week and 4 hours per day; the actual time burden seems to be much greater. NCAA athletes responding to a survey noted long hours in-season; for football it is 43 hours per week and only slightly less for baseball and men's basketball (Wieberg, 2011). How is it that the actual hours spent double those allowed by rule? Professor Murray Sperber, of Indiana University, has studied college athletics and taught student-athletes for 30 years. He said, "I've encountered very few dumb jocks. I think that's a media myth. But I've met many, many young men and women who are physically and mentally exhausted from working this tremendously hard job. And as a result, academically underachieved" (Merz, 2004).

Incidentally, trust between athlete and coach is in remarkably short supply. Can that development be good for any of the parties? Has this relationship been corrupted by the high-stakes, big money atmosphere of college sports? The survey of NCAA athletes revealed that only 39% of women basketball players say that their head coach "defines success by not only winning, but winning fairly" (Wieberg, 2011). Male athletes are only slightly more positive about their coaches; to the proposition that their coach is as interested in fairness as in winning, there is agreement by 43% of baseball players, 50% of basketball players, and 57% of football players. What sort of ethical compromises might these players have seen their coaches make in order to reach these judgments?

The time and trust issues blend easily into the topic of "voluntary" versus mandatory training activities for student-athletes. In the past season, football programs at the University of Michigan and East Carolina University were both found to have conducted off-season activities that were improper because athletic officials were observing. What is a student-athlete to do if a coach directs him/her to do something improper? Do conventional organizations really reward whistle-blowers? Does the coercive authoritarianism in athletics encourage athletes to confront abuse? In announcing "voluntary" activities, coaches are prone to observe that playing time is also "voluntary," thus making it clear to the player the consequences of skipping them. What are the ethical implications of this sort of communication?

Surveillance and control are persistent features of the student-athlete's life. Study halls, grade and attendance monitoring, and course selection by an advisor are all constraints that apply to athletes but not to other students. These activities might be described as helpful but also serve the primary purpose of maintaining the athlete's eligibility. In any case, they preclude the individual's developing those skills on their own. A related question of control deals with discipline, including its functions and limits. In college athletics, even extreme instances of discipline are virtually unchallenged.

At KU, the athletic department employs class checkers to be certain that athletes attend classes. They stand in the hallway with notebooks full of photos that identify their targets; when athletes arrive, they sign in on a clipboard before entering the classroom. Such surveillance is hardly unique in the life of college athletes. KU has added a twist, however; in place of student class checkers, they use senior citizens who are less likely to let athletes "slide" if they offer up a good excuse. But signing in is not enough; the checkers hang around to be sure that no one leaves early. From the hallway, the checkers even "peer through windows to make sure that the athletes are still in their seats and aren't sleeping, shopping, Googling, or Facebooking on their laptops—offences that can be reported to academic counselors as well" (Karp, 2011). One grandmother among the checkers refers to the basketball players as "her babies." While nominally chagrined by these practices, the associate AD in charge defends them: "19-year olds don't always make the best decisions" (Karp, 2011).

Consider the case of Julia Finlay, a member of the UNC Wilmington women's basket- ball team. For an unspecified violation of team rules, she was to run as punishment. Since she suffered from plantar fasciitis, an assistant coach devised an alternative punishment: Julia was ordered to log roll from end to end of the gymnasium for 30 minutes, making 12 trips along the floor. In the course of this punishment, she vomited three times; no trainer was present for the first half of this time. The men's basketball team was prac- ticing in the gym while the punishment was being carried out; no one intervened. The women's head coach, Cynthia Cooper-Dyke, a Naismith Hall of Fame inductee, was out of town when the punishment happened. She apologized for it: "It was never meant to demean or degrade or in any way hurt anyone" (Mull, 2010). The assistant coach was given an undisclosed punishment; the coaching staff remains intact. The AD, whose fund-raising skills had been criticized, resigned within a week of this incident. Julia Finlay has left the team though she remains in school. How does unchecked authority influ- ence judgment so that this kind of "punishment" could ever be seen as appropriate? Why did no one intervene after Finlay's first, second, or third attack of nausea? What are the ethical dimensions of this story? Who, if anyone, was held accountable for this debacle? Who should have been?

SUMMARY

University leaders face ethical challenges in managing successful athletic programs and maintaining the institution's integrity. The issues appear to be perennial because the tensions between ethical means and success-driven ends are perennial. In the realms of reward, identity, and autonomy, we can find notable failures and some successes as uni- versities promote ethical behavior on the part of the organization and its members. In a greater or lesser way, you have probably seen these very tensions at work on your campus.

DISCUSSION QUESTIONS

1. What clear examples of ethical lapses do you find in these cases?

2. Does a president need a different perspective on the institution from that of an AD or coach? If so, why? How would one be established? Enforced?

3. What is the best action to be taken for the preservation of the institution's reputa- tion in the cases recounted here?

4. How can ethical standards be maintained and defended in an environment where there is a strong sense that other competitors are bending/breaking the rules?

5. Do you know students who cheer for the team on game days but roll their eyes if a student-athlete struggles with issues in the classroom? What are the ethical dimensions of behavior such as that?

REFERENCES

Associated Press. (2009, December 18). Bob Knight calls out John Calipari over integrity. *USA TODAY.* Retrieved from http://www.usatoday.com/sports/college/mensbasketball/2009-12-18-knight-calipari_N.htm

Associated Press. (2010, September 16). Reggie Bush: Giving up Heisman not an admission of guilt. *USA TODAY.* Retrieved from http://www.usatoday.com/sports/football/nfl/saints/2010-09-16-reggie-bush_N.htm

Associated Press. (2011, May 5). EA dismissed from antitrust lawsuit. *ESPN.* Retrieved from http://m.espn.go.com/ncb/story?storyId = 6487782&wjb

Berman, Z. (2010, July 9). Under new TV deal with ESPN, ACC schools to see increased payout. *Washington Post.* Retrieved from http://www.washingtonpost.com/wp-dyn/content/article/2010/07/08/AR2010070803383.html

Drape, J. (2004, March 24). N.C.A.A.: Men's Round of 16; Graduation is secondary for many in Final 16. *New York Times.* Retrieved from http://www.nytimes.com/2004/03/24/sports/ncaa-men-s-round-of-16-graduation-is-secondary-for-many-in-final-16.html

Gordon, K. (2010, December 29). OSU football: Players sorry; Sugar Bowl isn't. *Columbus Dispatch.* Retrieved from http://www.dispatch.com/content/stories/sports/2010/12/29/players-sorry-sugar-bowl-isnt.html

Jackson, D. Z. (2010, March 17). Poor graduation rates show NCAA still shortchanging athletes. *Boston Globe.*

Karp, H. (2011, February 8). Making some athletes go to class. *Wall Street Journal.*

Lesmerises, D. (2010, December 23). Terrelle Pryor among five Ohio State players suspended for first five games of 2011. Retrieved from http://www.cleveland.com/osu/index.ssf/2010/12/terrelle_pryor_among_five_ohio.html

Merz, S. (2004, February 16). NCAA news archive: Seminar debate opens perspective on academic reform. *National Collegiate Athletic Association.* Retrieved from http://fs.ncaa.org/Docs/NCAANewsArchive/2004/Association-wide/seminar % 2Bdebate % 2Bopens % 2Bperspective % 2B on % 2Bacademic % 2Breform % 2B- % 2B2-16-04.html

Mull, B. (2010, September 21). UNCW women's basketball coach apologizes after player punishment goes too far. *StarNews Online.* Retrieved from http://www.starnewsonline.com/article/20100921/ARTICLES/100929919

Penner, M. (2009, November 8). Marcus Jordan's school gets no reward for brand loyalty. *Los Angeles Times.* Retrieved from http://articles.latimes.com/2009/nov/08/sports/sp-random8

Redding, W. C. (1996). Ethics and the study of organizational communication: When will we wake up? In J. A. Jaksa & M. S. Pritchard (Eds.), *Responsible communication: Ethical issues in business, industry and the professions* (pp. 17–24). Cresskill, NJ: Hampton.

Sander, L. (2010, October, 1). Game over for 3 UNC football players who accepted agents' gifts. *The Chronicle of Higher Education*. Retrieved from http://chronicle.com/blogs/players/game-over-for-3-unc-football-players-who-accepted-agents-gifts/27557

Schilken, C. (2010, October 27). NCAA reports record graduation rates for athletes. *Los Angeles Times*.

Smith, E. (2009). *Race, sport and the American dream* (2nd ed.). Durham, NC: Carolina Academic Press.

Wieberg, S. (2011, January 14). NCAA survey delves into practice time, coaches' trust. *USA TODAY*. Retrieved from http://www.usatoday.com/sports/college/2011-01-14-ncaa-survey_N.htm

The Case of Wyeth, DesignWrite, and Premarin

The Ethics of Ghostwriting Medical Journal Articles

Alexander Lyon and Mark Ricci

This case explores the role of ghostwriters in the marketing of drugs, as pharmaceutical companies seek greater profits through the medicalization of normal parts of life. As the authors note, the practice of ghostwriting raises serious questions about the transparency and trustworthiness of the information in medical journals and, in turn, the decision making of physicians and their patients. The case considers the challenges of pharmaceutical companies to address the tension between profits and patients.

Medicine has become big business. "Big pharma" companies like Eli Lilly, Bristol-Myers Squibb, Merck, and others earn over $20 billion a year, more than the Coca-Cola Company earns selling soda in the United States. Companies like Pfizer and Johnson & Johnson earn even more at $50 and $60 billion, respectively (Fortune 500, 2010). This financial success, however, is not without its costs. Company leaders feel compelled to continue this upward trend in revenue and growth. It has become clear, however, that leaders' and investors' expectation for continued growth is unrealistic. People do not truly *need* medicine all of the time.

As such, these companies have turned to a variety of strategies to sell more drugs and keep growing. For example, part of the rise in pharmaceutical sales over the past 15 + years can be attributed to the direct-to-consumer advertising in the mass media that pushes viewers to "ask your doctor." Patients have become conditioned to proactively request particular medicines from their doctors for illnesses they may or may not have. In addition, most pharmaceutical companies have turned their research and development investments to optional "lifestyle drugs." Medications that treat erectile dysfunction, baldness, cosmetic/skin concerns, and various age-related issues now dominate the pharmaceutical landscape as companies try to create the latest "blockbuster drug."

Further, some experts now claim that these companies "brand" diseases (Elliott, 2010) or "medicalize" (Mirivel, 2008) normal parts of everyday life that may lead to overdiagnosis of "conditions [restless leg syndrome, overactive bladder, premenstrual dysphoric disorder, etc.] that were once regarded as rare until a marketing campaign transformed the brand" (Elliott, 2010, para. 5). Other studies (Lyon, 2007; Lyon & Mirivel, 2010, 2011) conclude that some pharmaceutical companies now clearly favor the pursuit of profit at the expense of patients' health and are driven by "business" rather than medical concerns. From a purely business perspective, the desire for continuously increasing profit is somewhat understandable. Collectively, pharmaceutical companies employ hundreds of thousands of people who depend on these organizations' financial success. Company leaders also feel great pressure from their investors and stockholders to provide a good return on their investment. The line between right and wrong, thus, may look rather blurry to leaders when they simply *must* produce positive financial results to compete with other pharmaceutical companies. Still, at what point does the aggressive pursuit of financial goals put patients' health at risk? Regardless of the money at stake, what ethical and moral duty do pharmaceutical companies have toward patients?

These "business" pressures have caused some pharmaceutical companies to go beyond the strategies previously mentioned and use more questionable, and often illegal, practices. For instance, several companies have hidden or downplayed the sometimes-deadly risks of drugs, manipulated research data to make their drugs appear safer or more effective, and marketed their drugs "off label" for purposes the Food and Drug Administration (FDA) has never approved (e.g., Cronin Fisk, Lopatto, & Feeley, 2009). Practices like these have made physicians so suspicious of drug companies that they now refuse to meet with drug representatives and do not consider marketing materials to be a trustworthy source of information. To respond to physicians' resistance, some pharmaceutical companies created more covert marketing methods. This case study examines a recently exposed practice by a large pharmaceutical company, Wyeth. More specifically, we consider the ethicality of Wyeth's use of hired ghostwriters to produce medical journal articles that promoted one of the company's most profitable drugs. Instead of listing the ghostwriters' names and crediting Wyeth for paying for the research, however, expert physicians who did not actually write the articles were deceptively given credit for doing so.

Normally, ghostwriting is not secretive but is an accepted practice in many industries. Professional ghostwriters are paid to write various types of speeches, books, articles, and other texts credited to the prominent people that hire them. Often the listed author or speaker works with the ghostwriter to conceptualize and create a finished work that satisfies both parties, especially the person who gets authorship credit. Presidents Reagan, Clinton, and Obama, for instance, all had/have open and collaborative working relationships with well-known professional speechwriters. In cases like these, the process is transparent. In contrast, ghostwriting in medical journals was, until recently, one of the pharmaceutical industry's best-kept secrets. In the past few years, drug companies such as Forest Laboratories, American Home Products, Merck, and Pfizer have all been caught using ghostwriters to promote numerous brand-name drugs (Fugh-Berman, 2010).

This practice raises serious questions about the transparency and trustworthiness of the information in medical journals because ghostwriting hides the commercial, for-profit interests behind a supposedly objective, expert author's name.

THE CASE OF WYETH, DESIGNWRITE, AND PREMARIN

Wyeth was one of the nation's largest pharmaceutical companies.[1] The company made many well-known over-the-counter products such as Advil and Robitussin. Wyeth's most popular prescription medication was a hormone replacement therapy drug, Premarin. Hormone therapy (HT) began in 1942 when the FDA approved Premarin as a treatment for symptoms of menopause (Fugh-Berman, 2010). For decades, doctors prescribed HT to millions of female patients. In 1975, however, researchers noticed an increase in several types of cancer that affect the lining of the uterus for patients who used HT drugs. In response, hormone replacement therapy (HRT) became popular in the 1980s after another pill was added that was supposed to counteract the risk of cancer. Although HRT enthusiasts promoted a reduced risk of cardiovascular disease, colon cancer, and Alzheimer's disease, a 15-year study in 2002 conducted by the Women's Health Initiative (Writing Group, 2002) found that HRT not only failed to limit cardiovascular disease but also amplified the risk of breast cancer, stroke, and blood clots. The risk was significant enough to justify stopping the study prematurely because of these increased risks for participants taking the hormone treatment (Dooren, 2010).

Nevertheless, for over a decade starting in the mid-1990s, Wyeth pursued an aggressive "publication plan" as a key part of its overall marketing campaign to promote Premarin. In short, Wyeth paid ghostwriters to produce articles about Premarin but kept this practice a secret. Instead, they listed respected outside physician–experts as the articles' authors (referred to here as "listed authors," "signing authors," or "signing experts"). To do so, Wyeth worked mainly with DesignWrite (www.dwrite.com), a medical writing firm, to produce favorable publications about Premarin that not only emphasized the drug's benefits but also downplayed its risks, especially the "misconception" about Premarin's link to cancer. DesignWrite employed highly educated writers (which we refer to here as the "ghostwriter," "hired writer," or "writer") to cocreate journal articles with Wyeth. DesignWrite and Wyeth then used the allegedly unbiased findings in those journal articles to further market the drug. While long-term scientific research done outside of Wyeth points to potentially deadly risks, many physicians still maintain positive perceptions about Premarin. Some experts (e.g., Fugh-Berman, 2010) believe that Wyeth's use of ghostwriters helps explain why some physicians still prescribe a potentially harmful drug merely to lower the symptoms of menopause, a natural stage of women's lives. The details to come explain how Wyeth and DesignWrite (1) developed an article publication plan, (2) conceptualized and wrote the articles, and (3) recruited physicians to be the listed authors.

Article Publication Plan

Wyeth's goal was to sell more Premarin through covert marketing in medical journals. Its publication plan was a crucial part of a larger, ongoing marketing effort (including advertising, sales representatives, etc.) to promote Premarin. An internal document[2] explains why this company chose to use medical journal articles as a way to market its

---

[1] Wyeth was purchased by Pfizer in 2009.

[2] This case study was constructed, in part, with Wyeth's internal documents released to the public after being disclosed in a 2010 lawsuit against the company.

drug: "Research show[s] high clinician reliance on journal articles for credible product information" ("Premarin Publication Plan," 1997, p. 3). That is, physicians read medical journals to weigh their patients' treatment options. Wyeth and DesignWrite wanted these peer-reviewed publications to "have an impact on physicians' decisions to prescribe [more Premarin]" ("Premarin Family," 1999, p. 9). To do so, the publication plan was meant "to establish a greater need" for Premarin "while allaying unrealistic fears that physicians may have" ("Medical Educational and Communications Plan," 1996, p. 7). The fear that Wyeth was most concerned about was "the negative perceptions associated with estrogens and cancer" ("Premarin Publication Plan," 1997, p. 3). Wyeth's articles systematically downplayed the connection of HRT and cancer. As its documents explained, "Articles will be published that support [Premarin's] clinical efficacy and safety" ("Publication Plan," 2002, p. 10). Wyeth's articles, thus, only shared good news.

Wyeth and DesignWrite also agreed on particular journals in which their various key messages should be communicated based upon the journals' circulation and the types of physicians who read them. The company's goal was to communicate its message in the "most influential publication sources" ("Premarin Publication Plan," 1997, p. 4). Tier 1 journals had high circulation and were read by many primary care physicians. Journals such as *JAMA* (i.e., *Journal of the American Medical Association*) with a circulation of 372,000 per week, the *New England Journal of Medicine* with a circulation of 228,000 per week, and *The Lancet* with a circulation of 50,000 per week were some of the top-rated journals they targeted. Tier 2 journals generally had less circulation and/or were read by more specialized physicians ("Premarin Family," 1999).

DesignWrite's proposals also included various prices. Articles that published data that had not been used before cost the most, and articles that analyzed or reviewed already-published data cost less. On a regular basis, DesignWrite submitted business proposals that outlined the number and types of articles it was prepared to write for Wyeth. The ghostwriters offered discounts when Wyeth purchased articles in bulk and offered other promotional ways to use Wyeth's data once that date had been published in a journal. Table 14.1 re-creates the details from a 2001 price list at the end of an actual proposal.

TABLE 14.1 Publication Program Budget	
Chart 1:	
Publication program budget	
Five review articles/clinical trial manuscripts (10% discount for five or more)	$125,000 (– $12,500)
Six posters (including production)	$54,000
Slide development	$15,000
Editorial assistance/special projects	$21,000
Total	$202,500

Source: "Low-dose HRT" (2001, p. 3).

A proposal ("Publication Plan," 2002) to Wyeth explained that the potential for market growth for HRT drugs like Premarin would grow from $3.1 billion in 2000 to "$5 billion in 2005, [and] + $10 billion in 2015" (p. 3) in the U.S. market alone. One document ("Medical Educational and Communications Plan," 1996) summarized the goal of these publications plainly: "maximiz[e] the sales potential of the Premarin family of products"[3] (p. 2). The use of ghostwriters was a business strategy, and Wyeth's leaders saw their publication plan as a way to sell more Premarin. The company's goal was to invest in a robust and continuous stream of articles promoting the use of Premarin each year.

Writing the Article

While the general public may find it hard to believe, physicians who did not actually write these journal articles were listed as authors. Wyeth's process explains how this deception was accomplished. The design of each essay was carefully planned and began with the specific messages about Premarin that Wyeth wanted prescribing physicians to accept. As a proposal from DesignWrite explained, "Central to the success of any publication plan is the development of appropriate key communication messages . . . [that] serve as the basis for a strategic dissemination of relevant data" ("Publication Plan," 2002, p. 11). Wyeth and DesignWrite agreed upon a master list of almost two dozen "key communication messages" before the articles were written. In other words, these messages were marketing statements that stressed the need for HRT and the "documented benefits" of Premarin (DesignWrite, 2003, p. 1). The following are sample messages from the master list ("Publication Plan," 2002):

- "Premarin [is] the 'gold standard' in estrogen replacement" (p. 9).
- "[E]xtensive clinical experience with Premarin has confirmed its efficacy and safety, and physicians and patients are comfortable with its use" (p. 10).
- "Premarin . . . is associated with favorable effects on lipid metabolism with an increase in HDL and an improved LDL/HDL ratio" (p. 14).

Each article was conceptualized to include six to eight messages from the master list that promoted Premarin's effectiveness and safety. Further, the specific message that Premarin resulted in "an increase in HDL and an improved LDL/HDL ratio" is a key statement about cholesterol levels and was used to promote the unsubstantiated idea that Premarin was "cardioprotective" or had cardiovascular benefits.

Wyeth provided DesignWrite with data on Premarin that supported those key messages. A proposal from DesignWrite sketches out the writing stages: "Client [Wyeth] provides data report [to DesignWrite] . . . DesignWrite prepares outline/manuscript . . . client [Wyeth] does an] internal review . . . DesignWrite consolidates [Wyeth's] comments—[into the] next draft" ("Premarin/TMG 300," 2003, p. 5). It is important to note, thus, that Wyeth did

---

[3] Premarin had different dosages and was sometimes combined with other drugs. Wyeth referred to these combinations of drugs specifically and at other times generally as the "Premarin family of products." For the sake of consistency and readability, we substitute technical or confusing terms simply with "Premarin" at various points in the essay.

not simply turn over all available data on Premarin, both good and bad, to the ghostwriting company. Wyeth handpicked data to promote Premarin. One of Wyeth's "business strategies" was to "Identify key data for publication content" ("Premarin Publication Plan," 1997, p. 4). Wyeth's research on Premarin, thus, conflicts with traditional principles of objective, scientific research. That is, researchers develop a hypothesis and collect data to test it. As much as humanly possible, their conclusions are formed in an unbiased fashion to develop trustworthy medical knowledge. In contrast, Wyeth's leaders decided what they wanted their conclusions to be ahead of time (i.e., key message) and then supplied data to DesignWrite that supported their message. An internal e-mail exchange states plainly that the publication plan "is a marketing initiative," and its desired outcomes are "not necessarily related to [other] internal research" (Conti, 2002, para. 1).

The following quotation shows how both Wyeth and DesignWrite were in control of the manuscript and its content rather than the listed author:

> After Wyeth has reviewed and released the manuscript for journal submission, DesignWrite will see it through the necessary production stages . . . any revisions requested by the journal will be handled by DesignWrite, in conjunction with the client [Wyeth] and the [listed] author. Should the journal reject the manuscript, DesignWrite will restyle it for submission to another journal within 10 working days. ("Premarin/TMG 300," 2003, p. 5)

In other words, DesignWrite handled the writing and the management of manuscripts while Wyeth made decisions and ultimately approved the ghostwriters' changes. The "author," in contrast, is mentioned only in passing.

Wyeth and DesignWrite sent complete drafts of the articles back and forth for fine-tuning until the manuscript was complete. As one internal memo read, "Enclosed is the SERMs paper, incorporating the changes you [Wyeth executive] suggested" (Mittleman, 2005, p. 1). The memo then lists seven minor changes about adding words and fine-tuning sentences. Minor changes like these indicate that the writing and revision process was essentially finished before recruiting listed authors. Importantly, the listed authors never saw the original data. They only saw the handpicked data in an essentially completed manuscript.

Recruiting Physicians to "Author" Articles

Wyeth then approached reputable physician-researchers to be listed authors. They wanted "key opinion leaders and investigators as authors" ("Publication Plan," 2002, p. 10). An early Wyeth e-mail described them in blunt terms as "signing expert[s]" who would be "identified at a later date" (Bissett, 1992, p. 3) when the writing was complete. Wyeth and DesignWrite used their professional relationships to network with and recruit potential authors. In the following e-mail, Mark, an employee at Wyeth, asked Tony, a fellow employee, to put him in touch with a potential author:

> Tony, I have got a favor to ask. We would like to approach Dr. Karas to write an article . . . focused toward a cardiology journal such as "Journal of the American

College of Cardiology." DesignWrite would assist in the preparation of this article for Dr. Karas. As always, we cannot pay him to write the article but could offer DesignWrite's assistance. (Barbee, 2000, para. 1)

When contacted, some of the physicians were naturally hesitant to work with ghostwriters. The following internal e-mail shows DesignWrite and Wyeth employees making sense of an interaction with a potential expert signer.

Matt, . . . I know you had contact with [Dr.] Paul Ridker a few times. We asked Pam to contact him about authoring a review article on CV markers. He was somewhat hesitant and would not commit. . . . [I] [w]as not sure if he just didn't know Pam well enough or was uncomfortable with us ghostwriting for him. (Conti, 2000, para. 1)

When physicians didn't initially agree, Wyeth and DesignWrite pushed a little harder to persuade them, as the following e-mail exchange illustrates:

Alice: When I spoke to [Dr. Ridker] I suggested that he come to Wyeth and present to the group. This might be a good way to get him in and explain to him the significance of the issue. . . . You might just discuss with Ridker the importance of having the reviews in a journal read by women's health physicians. Matt. (Rhoa, 2000, para. 1)

As the e-mail mentions, the listed authors were not paid any money. If the physicians accepted money, they would be required by most journals to disclose their funding source and would likely have exposed Wyeth's use of ghostwriters. Wyeth, thus, attempted to convince expert signers to join their effort in other ways. "[H]aving reviews in a journal read by women's health physicians," for instance, might tempt an expert author to put his or her name on the publication. Additionally, one could speculate that physicians wanted more publications listed on their academic resumes to boost their visibility and help establish their expertise.

Naturally, some physicians refused and others sought to clarify exactly what was expected of them. One physician responded in an e-mail to a Wyeth executive, "I would be more of an 'editor' rather than the major writer—that is, you guys would be writing the versions—with me 'altering, editing, etc.?' Is that correct?" (Leiblum, 2001, para. 2). The physician's questions reveal that the title of "author" misrepresents the type of contributions made. When sent to the medical journals, however, the letters clearly claimed that the physicians were the authors of the articles. No ghostwriters or pharmaceutical companies were ever mentioned. The following e-mail to a signing expert shows how this was accomplished:

Dear Dr. . . . I received word from Wyeth to go ahead and submit the manuscript for publication. . . . I will be sending you the appropriate number of copies on bond paper required for submission. I am also drafting a submission letter for you, which I will email to you when complete so that you can print it out on your letterhead, sign it and include it with the submission packet. . . . Best Regards, Kathy. (Ohleth, 1999, para. 1–2)

The date on these letters was left blank (e.g., "June ____, 1999"). The physician needed only to fill in the date and send it to the journal editor. As far as the journal editors were concerned, the articles were written and submitted by the listed authors. Most listed authors merely proofread and/or made minor editing suggestions. Once involved, of course, some signing authors felt at liberty to suggest more substantial changes to the essays. As Adriane Fugh-Berman (2010), an expert witness in a legal case against Wyeth's ghostwriting, noted, "In general, authors' revisions were permitted if marketing messages were not compromised" (p. 4).[4]

Outcomes

In many ways, Wyeth and DesignWrite's publication plan worked. Over two dozen ghostwritten articles appeared in first- and second-tier journals that backed "the use of hormone replacement therapy in women" (Singer, 2009, para. 1). DesignWrite claimed ("Premarin Publication Plan," 1997) an impressive 80% success rate in publishing articles in first-choice journals. An additional 15% of the articles were placed in second-choice journals. The articles were published under expert physicians' names and listed with the added credibility of their employing medical institutions (e.g., "Department of Obstetrics and Gynecology, New York University School of Medicine"). Once in print, the articles and results were used as the basis for more traditional marketing strategies. For example, Wyeth "mailed or delivered [the articles] via drug reps to doctors" (Fugh-Berman, 2010, p. 9). Physicians who received these articles, of course, had no idea the listed authors did not write the articles, and the research was not conducted with the cooperation of the listed authors' medical schools.

Once the research was published, there was no way to distinguish authentic articles from ghostwritten articles. In fact, though many documented reasons exist not to prescribe Premarin, some physicians continue to do so. Fugh-Berman (2010) explained it this way:

> Today, despite definitive scientific data to the contrary, many gynecologists still believe that the benefits of [hormone replacement therapy] outweigh the risks in asymptomatic women. . . . This non-evidence-based perception may be the result of decades of carefully orchestrated corporate influence on medical literature. (p. 1)

Further, in at least one sense, DesignWrite and Wyeth were correct; physicians rely on medical journals for their information. Until recently, most patients and many physicians assumed that medical journal articles contained—to the extent that it is possible—the latest unbiased medical knowledge. Now, however, the use of ghostwriters threatens the transparency and trustworthiness of medical journal articles generally.

This case study highlighted the ethical dilemmas some companies face when their business interest in making the company money clashes with their ethical obligations to customers. The exact percentage of ghostwritten articles in all medical journals is not known. We do know, however, that Wyeth's use of secret ghostwriters is not an isolated

---

[4] It is unclear what, if any, professional consequences physicians will face because of their participation in these ghostwritten articles.

arrangement. DesignWrite worked for other pharmaceutical companies before being hired by Wyeth in the mid-1990s, other medical marketing firms like DesignWrite currently exist, and industry insiders (e.g., Fugh-Berman, 2010) claim that numerous large pharmaceutical companies employ ghostwriters. This is clearly a cause for concern. If the journals themselves have been compromised to this extent, where can physicians find the best, most up-to-date medical knowledge? In turn, how can patients be sure their physicians' advice has not been tainted by a ghostwriter? On a broader level, what moral and ethical responsibilities do pharmaceutical companies have toward patients?

DISCUSSION QUESTIONS

1. To what extent is it ethical for Wyeth or other companies to use covert marketing tactics like ghostwritten medical journal articles? What marketing strategies would be ethical?

2. How ethical is it to publish research with handpicked favorable data? What ethical responsibilities do Wyeth and other pharmaceutical companies have to disclose unfavorable data about their drugs?

3. Are medical journal articles an appropriate channel though which to communicate marketing messages about medications? What are the likely long-term consequences for physicians and patients?

4. What ethical obligations do medical ghostwriting firms like DesignWrite have to the physicians who read their work? To patients who take the medicine they promote?

5. Is it ethical for DesignWrite's employees not to list their names on their writings? In what ways does hiding the fact that Wyeth paid them for the articles—and listed expert physicians instead—make the articles appear objective and unbiased?

6. What ethical responsibilities do physicians who signed on as authors have to journal editors, the scientific community, and Premarin patients generally?

7. To what extent is it ethical for physicians to frame themselves as authors of research in which they had no meaningful or genuine role?

8. What procedures or boundaries between doctors and pharmaceutical companies should be established to ensure more ethical working relationships and, by extension, patients' well-being and safety?

REFERENCES

Barbee, M. (2000, December 6). [E-mail]. Retrieved from http://dida.library.ucsf.edu/pdf/eub37b10
Bissett, D. (1992, May 4). [E-mail]. Retrieved from http://dida.library.ucsf.edu/tid/vvb37b10
Conti, A. (2002, June 8). [E-mail]. Retrieved from http://dida.library.ucsf.edu/pdf/bec37b10
Conti, P. (2000, November 7). [E-mail]. Retrieved from http://dida.library.ucsf.edu/pdf/etc37b10

Cronin Fisk, M., Lopatto, E., & Feeley, J. (2009, June 12). Lilly sold drug for dementia knowing it didn't help, files show. *Bloomberg.* Retrieved from http://www.bloomberg.com/apps/news?pid = newsa rchive&sid = aTLcF3zT1Pdo

DesignWrite. (2003). Low dose Prempro publication plan [Proposal]. Retrieved from http://dida .library.ucsf.edu/tid/eic37b10

Dooren, J. (2010). Research finds hormone therapy speeds up breast-tumor growth. *Wall Street Journal Online.* Retrieved from http://online.wsj.com/article/SB10001424405270230355090457556251137 4951120.html

Elliott, C. (2010). How to brand a disease—to sell a cure. *CNN Opinion.* Retrieved from http://articles.cnn. com/2010-10-11/opinion/elliott.branding.disease_1_reflux-disease-overactive-bladder-bladder-control?_s = PM:OPINION

Fortune 500: Our annual ranking of America's largest corporations. (2010, May 3). *CNN Money.* Retrieved from http://money.cnn.com/magazines/fortune/fortune500/2010/industries/21/index .html

Fugh-Berman, A. J. (2010). The haunting of medical journals: How ghostwriting sold "HRT." *PLOS Medicine, 7*(9), 1–11.

Leiblum, S. (2001, December 1). [E-mail]. Retrieved from http://dida.library.ucsf.edu/pdf/exb37b10

Low-dose HRT 2001 publication plan proposal. (2001, May 16). [Proposal]. Retrieved from http://dida .library.ucsf.edu/tid/cpc37b10

Lyon, A. (2007). "Putting patients first": Systematically distorted communication and Merck's market-ing of Vioxx. *Journal of Applied Communication Research, 35,* 376–398.

Lyon, A., & Mirivel, J. C. (2010). The imperative of ethical communication standards in an era of com-mercialized medicine. *Management Communication Quarterly, 24,* 474–481.

Lyon, A., & Mirivel, J. C. (2011). Reconstructing Merck's practical theory of communication: The eth-ics of pharmaceutical sales representative-physician encounters. *Communication Monographs, 78,* 53–72.

Medical educational and communications plan for the Premarin product line. (1996, August 12). [Proposal]. Retrieved from http://dida.library.ucsf.edu/tid/jrb37b10

Mirivel, J. C. (2008). The physician examination in cosmetic surgery: Communication strategies to promote the desirability of surgery. *Health Communication, 23,* 53–70.

Mittleman, K. (2005, January 11). *Premarin publication plan* [Memo]. Retrieved from http://dida .library.ucsf.edu/tid/iqb37b10

Ohleth, K. (1999). [E-mail]. Retrieved from http://dida.library.ucsf.edu/tid/ewc37b10

Premarin family of products medical and scientific communications plan. (1999, September). [Proposal]. Retrieved from http://dida.library.ucsf.edu/tid/sub37b10

Premarin publication plan. (1997, May 15). [Proposal]. Retrieved from http://dida.library.ucsf.edu/ tid/juc37b10

Premarin/TMG 300—US publication plan proposal. (2003, June 3). [Proposal]. Retrieved from http:// dida.library.ucsf.edu/tid/wqc37b10

Publication Plan 2002: Premarin/Trimegestone working draft. (2002). [Proposal from OCC North America to Wyeth]. Retrieved from http://dida.library.ucsf.edu/tid/awb37b10

Rhoa, M. (2000, November 7). [E-mail]. Retrieved from http://dida.library.ucsf.edu/tid/etc37b10

Singer, N. (2009, August 4). Medical papers by ghostwriters pushed therapy. *New York Times.* Retrieved from http://www.nytimes.com/2009/08/05/health/research/05ghost.html

Writing group for the Women's Health Initiative investigators. (2002). Risks and benefits of estrogen plus progestin in healthy postmenopausal women: Principal results from the Women's Health Initiative randomized controlled trial. *JAMA, 288,* 321–333. Retrieved from http://jama.ama-assn .org/cgi/reprint/288/3/321.

Fired Over Facebook

*Issues of Employee Monitoring and Personal Privacy
on Social Media Websites*

Loril M. Gossett

*This case explores the ways in which employers monitor employees' behavior inside
and outside of the workplace as we increasingly use social media to communicate
with others. The surveillance of social media use raises interesting questions
related to the desire for organizations to retain their reputation and image and the
need for employees to maintain some degree of privacy. As such, the case considers
the ways in which organizational duties may conflict with personal rights.*

This case examines organizational surveillance practices and their impact on employee
communication (e.g., ability to engage in dissent, opportunities for collective resistance). The
increased popularity of social media sites on the Internet (e.g., Facebook, Twitter) has added
a new dimension to the struggle between managers and their employees regarding workplace monitoring tactics. Managers want to ensure employees are not compromising organizational interests by criticizing their company on public websites. However, workers often
object to the idea that employers have the right to review or restrict their communication
choices outside the formal boundaries of the office, particularly when they are *off the clock*.
In order to examine this issue in more detail, this chapter examines the public controversy
that erupted when a waitress in a North Carolina restaurant was fired over a comment she
made on her personal Facebook page. Examining this case enables communication scholars
to consider a growing topic of debate in the contemporary work environment: the degree
to which organizations have the right to monitor their employees' behavior on the Internet.

Recent technological innovations and changing legal landscapes have converged to create new questions about the nature of workplace privacy. From an ethical theory perspective, this might be seen as a debate between those who support a *duty* perspective toward
organizational ethics versus those who favor an individual *rights* perspective. When the
interests of corporate leaders and their employees are in conflict (e.g., managers want to
keep track of their employees' online activities but employees do not want their Internet
behavior monitored), which side should prevail?

Drawing from a duty perspective, one might argue that workers have an obligation to support the interests and rules of their organization if they want to remain employed. Using this logic, employees should willingly participate in online surveillance practices that management believes to be in the best interests of the organization (e.g., to deter theft, to maintain a safe workplace). In order to ensure that all members of the company behave in an ethical fashion, some loss of individual privacy may be warranted. In contrast, a rights perspective might argue that collective systems have a responsibility to protect the individual interests of their members. Organizational leaders typically have more resources and power than any single employee. When the interests of management and workers are in conflict, it is not a fair fight. New workplace surveillance practices, such as the monitoring of employee behavior on social media websites, simply increases this power imbalance. As such, an ethical organization might consider protecting the online privacy of individual members rather than enhancing the supervisory power of its managerial staff.

Workplace privacy is a complex issue that requires an interdisciplinary discussion of how technological innovations, new social networks, and mediated forms of connectivity have shifted the presumed boundaries of self and others within both the public and private sphere. The interconnections presented through emerging technologies create a shifting landscape upon which individual privacy is based. These new boundaries change our sense of identity, as well as our relationships with other individuals and organizations.

THE CHANGING NATURE OF ORGANIZATIONAL SURVEILLANCE

The organizational use of technology to monitor employee behavior has a long history, from the 1879 "Incorruptible Cashier" that printed receipts (Campbell-Kelly & Aspray, 1996) to contemporary video and data monitoring systems that can track every movement of an employee for later analysis and managerial critique. The affordability and sophistication of information and communication technologies (ICTs) as surveillance devices has led to workplace monitoring becoming increasingly prevalent. If employees use computers, phones, or GPS-enabled company cars, they can be monitored in real time for specific information or patterns of behavior (Alder & Tompkins, 1997; Attewell, 1987; Botan & McCreadie, 1993). The "common quality is that these devices [ICTs] are more sensitive than ever before and overcome previous limits of time, space, and distance in gathering information about individuals" (Gandy, 1989, p. 62).

A survey conducted in 2007 by the American Management Association found that corporations engage in a number of different methods of technological surveillance, with 45% of firms reporting that they track the specific content employees produce on their workstations, their individual keystrokes, and actual time spent at the keyboard. This survey also revealed that 28% of firms have fired employees for e-mail-related offenses and 66% monitor the websites their workers access when at work (American Management Association, 2008b). Similarly, a commercial 2009 survey of U.S. companies with more than 1000 employees found that 38% of these firms have hired staff specifically to read or otherwise analyze outbound e-mail (Proofpoint, Inc., 2009).

Companies are increasingly concerned that their employees' use of social media may enable corporate espionage efforts, foster negative PR, or undermine the managerial control of important organizational information (Crawford, 2005). Any employee with a website or Twitter account can instantly alert their friends, family, and members of the general public to issues that their supervisors may want to keep private or "spin" in a particular fashion. Even if workers do not use their own names or identify their employer, the information they disclose may undermine their firm's business strategy or public image. For example, in 2005, Nadine Haobsh lost her job as a beauty editor at *Ladies' Home Journal* when her employer discovered that she was the author of "an anonymous blog that revealed shocking truths about the fashion and beauty industries . . . swag, editor gifts, and workplace hierarchy, things known in the industry, but often not divulged to the general public" (Dhami, 2010, para. 2). Even though Haobsh did not provide specific names or identify any organizations, her employer determined that her blog "scandalized" the industry, and she was fired as a result. It is not enough to simply avoid "naming names"; anything said online can become grounds for termination.

To emphasize this fact, firms have increasingly added "social media" clauses to employment contracts (Bahney, 2006; Foley, 2005; Gossett & Kilker, 2006). Recent survey results indicate that at least 12% of U.S. firms "monitor the blogosphere to see what is being written about the company, and another 10% monitor social networking sites" (American Management Association, 2008a, para. 5). This practice has become so common that an entire industry has emerged to help managers more effectively track their employees' online activities. For example, companies can subscribe to services such as "Social Sentry," which does the following:

> for $2 to $8 per employee . . . [it] will track their every move on Facebook and Twitter, whether it's from their desktop computer or their own smartphone or anywhere else. It will also provide charts tracking exactly how much time employees are spending (wasting?) on social media. (Rubin, 2010b)

In 2009, 8% of U.S. firms reporting firing workers specifically for violating their company's social media policy, compared to only 4% citing this as a reason for termination in 2008 (Proofpoint, Inc., 2009). These new surveillance techniques raise this question: Where do the boundaries and authority of an employer end and an individual's personal space and right to privacy begin?

As we consider when and where employers have the right to monitor the communicative behavior of their workers, we should also reflect upon the implications these policies might have on society as a whole. As individuals share their workplace experiences online, they essentially provide a separate and independent method of organizational surveillance. It is through online tools like Facebook and Twitter that workplace boundaries become fluid and control over organizational information shifts, at least slightly, toward the employees. This phenomenon has been observed in other marginalized groups interacting online: "On the internet, the marginalized can call out to the dominant and put the dominant in the difficult position of either having to acknowledge the marginalized, or further distance the dispossessed by ignoring the call" (Mitra, 2001, p. 31). The famous organizational whistle-blowers of our past (e.g., Karen Silkwood, Jeffrey Wigand) turned to more traditional media outlets in order to share their stories; however, the next generation of whistle-blowers may more likely arise out of the pages of Facebook. If employers are able to effectively silence the voices of their workers on social media sites, they may also reduce the ability of these employees (and the public in general) to hold them accountable for inappropriate or illegal behavior. While there may be compelling managerial reasons to limit the degree to which employees are allowed to share organizational information, we must also consider the consequences for society if we create a system in which workers are forced into online silence simply to keep their jobs.

THE WAITRESS, THE RESTAURANT, AND THE "PIECE OF **** CAMPER"

In May 2010, the BRIXX restaurant in Charlotte, North Carolina, fired a 22-year-old waitress (Ashley Johnson) after learning that she had used her personal Facebook page to complain about a customer who left a $5 tip after occupying a table for 3 hours. Ms. Johnson was upset by the amount of her tip and posted the following comment on her personal page: "Thanks for eating at BRIXX, you cheap piece of ****[1] camper."

The restaurant justified firing Ms. Johnson because it claimed she had violated company policy with her Facebook posting. Like many organizations, this restaurant had a clause in its employment contract that strictly forbade workers from making negative statements about the company on social media websites. BRIXX management explained the policy on their own corporate Facebook page: "We respect everyone's right to free speech, and our employees can engage in social media. As employees, they are ambassadors for Brixx Wood Fired Pizza. Our company social media policy clearly states that employees are not to disparage our customers, and there are consequences for those who do." According to the local newspaper, the *Charlotte Observer*, Ashley publically apologized for the comments she made on her Facebook page and did not fight the termination of her employment at BRIXX.

At first glance, this case may not seem all that unique or even of enormous social importance. Ms. Johnson was not trying to alert the public to some great danger or illegal activity. She was simply complaining about a bad tip. However, what makes the BRIXX case worthy of discussion is the fact that Ms. Johnson *did not* make her comments available to the general public. While she did post her message to Facebook, the privacy settings on her account limited this message to her immediate friends (which did not include members of BRIXX management or the poor-tipping customer). As such, it is not clear how Ashley Johnson's employer was made aware of her online gripe. Officials from the restaurant indicated that the waitress's comments were sent to her manager by a third party; however, they have not identified the person who forwarded this information.

> Johnson can't pinpoint the leak. She has about 100 Facebook friends (mostly high school and college friends), but her page is private and she says she doesn't add

---

[1] Ms. Johnson's actual quote was censored by the press and has since been removed from Facebook. As such, we can only guess at the actual wording she used to describe her customer.

people she doesn't know to her network. Brixx partner Jeff Van Dyke said he wasn't sure how the company learned of Johnson's indiscretions. "It's just like high school students posting stuff on their social networking sites and thinking it's not going to get back to their parents," he said. "But somehow, it does." (Rubin, 2010a)

Ms. Johnson admitted to posting the offending comment but seemed surprised that it was something that could get her fired. "It was my own fault . . . I did write the message. But I had no idea that something that, to me is very small, could result in my losing my job" (Frazier, 2010).

THE RIGHTS OF THE ORGANIZATION VERSUS THE RIGHTS OF THE WORKER

The BRIXX/Facebook incident not only received attention in the Charlotte media. It was also picked up by several national and international news organizations (e.g., MSNBC, *Huffington Post, INC Magazine, Metro UK*). The story generated thousands of comments on various online forums and prompted a public debate about the rights of workers to speak their mind versus the rights of employers to protect the public image of their organizations. While there were a number of issues brought up in these comment sections, six central themes emerged. Next, these themes are summarized and examples are provided to help illustrate the complicated nature of this case.

If You Don't Like the Rules, Find Another Job

Some people argued that companies have the right to set any rules they want for their employees. As long as workers are made aware of the rules and agree to abide by them, they have no reason to complain if they are fired for breaking company policy.

Hey, the girl violated company policy. Her fault, not the company's, that she can't act professionally and adhere to policy, especially on a very public forum like the Internet. If she didn't like it, she could have gone elsewhere. (Deidre, BRIXX Facebook Page)

Has this society gone so far astray to not realize an employer has all the rights to set work rules and standards, so long as they don't require an employee to be unethical or do anything illegal? This reminds me of the lawsuits about requiring head coverings, uniforms, and hand washing I have read about. She knew about the rules, she broke them, end of story. (Krock65, *Charlotte Observer* Forum)

Brixx has a policy stating you can't write bad things about the company on social networking sites. She broke the rule and got fired. They didn't just fire her because of what she said—she broke the policy which she was aware of when she was hired. (Jef, Charlotte City Blog)

Talking About Your Job Online Is Okay as Long as You Cover Your Tracks

Another common response was that workers have the right to complain about their jobs online as long as they do not identify anyone (client, company, themselves, etc.) by name. If workers keep their online activity relatively anonymous, their employers should not interfere.

That's a dumb reason to fire someone . . . but you shouldn't be venting on public sites like Facebook anyway—that is what Muttr.com is for: venting anonymously is definitely the way to go! (Nate, *Metro UK* "You Say" Section)

Had Ashley not mentioned Brixx then it would be just another person complaining about her job. By revealing the company name her comment becomes a reflection on the company. (Scott, Charlotte City Blog)

The only thing she did wrong was mention her employer's name on a social networking site. She should be able to say anything about cheap customers that she wants to say. It's her page. (Guest, *Inc. Magazine* Forum)

The Employee Was Wrong But Should Have Been Given a Second Chance

Some people argued that the waitress was wrong to make comments about her job online but that her punishment (e.g., being fired) did not fit the crime (e.g., griping about a bad tip).

I think a written warning would have been enough for the comment. I mean really Brixx, was firing her necessary? What about her frustration?? At least she didn't say it to the customer! (Teach72, *Charlotte Observer* Forum)

They could have given her a warning and asked her to remove the complaint on her Facebook page. While yes she violated policy, waitresses and waiters depend on tips as part of their income (they are paid less than minimum wage) and customers who stiff them or don't give at least 15 percent are very frustrating. (Pennsylvanianne, *Huffington Post* Forum)

It seems a bit harsh to have fired a waitress over a Facebook status in which all she really does is vent to her friends. According to the news story, she did not talk bad about BRIXX, just vented. Could you not have got your point across by giving her a warning and suggesting she take a look at her privacy settings? (Joe, BRIXX Facebook Page)

The Managers Had an Obligation to Preserve the Image of the Restaurant

Another theme in the public comments was that negative online comments can do a lot of damage to an organization's image and corporate culture. As such, these people argued that organizations not only have a *right* but they actually have a *duty* to monitor the Internet behavior of their employees.

> Firing Ashley was very severe but everyone knows that you shouldn't publicly speak ill of your employer or your employer's customers. Employers know that the words spoken on social network sites can be far reaching and very damaging. (Carmay3600, *Inc. Magazine* Forum)

> It doesn't matter that she did it on her own time, it doesn't matter that the people were inconsiderate, what matters is that she ranted about a customer in a public forum and mentioned the name of the company, this puts the company in a bad light and many companies have policies in place stating that you cannot have negative comments about the company, the employees or the customers. The company was completely within their legal boundaries in firing this person, if those customers had somehow seen the comment, they could have known it was about them and been upset with the company. In the end, the company has to watch out for themselves. (natedom, MSNBC Website)

> Do not make negative comments about the customers or the company on a public stage and expect no consequences. It is your job to represent the company you work for in the best light possible. Otherwise why does the company want you around? (Kcohne, *Inc. Magazine* Forum)

The Worker Didn't Violate the Rules Because the Message Was to Her Friends and Not the General Public

Some people argued that the waitress should not have been fired because she did not actually violate the restaurant's social media policy. Ms. Johnson limited her Facebook comments to her immediate friends and family. As a result, these people claimed that she did not engage in *public* speech against her employer.

> The waitress did not speak bad about the customers publicly, she did it on private. She did it to her 100 Facebook friends and this is the same of doing it by e-mail or by phone once at a time. (FOM, *Charlotte Observer* Forum)

> If Johnson were to verbally complain to a few friends, she would clearly be within her rights to do so. If she were to take out an ad in Creative Loafing saying the

same thing, the company's policy against dissing customers would probably prevail. Now take it to Facebook. If she has the usual 100 friends or so, upon which side of the line does it fall? 200? 20? (Dan, Creative Loafing Website)

I think it's perfectly fine for her to vent. Facebook is meant for friends and being able to talk about your day and how it went. Brixx is stupid for firing her for doing something on her OWN time. Now, if she was doing this while on the clock and venting on her iphone or blackberry THEN maybe they'd have reasons for termination. (Audrey, BRIXX Facebook Page)

It's Okay to Complain About Your Job; Just Don't Do It Online

A final set of comments focused on the specific communication channel the waitress used to complain about her tips. These people argued that it is reasonable for employees to talk about their work experiences with others; they should just not use the Internet to do it.

Facebook is like shouting on the street corner. Whether a tip is bad or there is some other problem with your job, if your employer sees it they can fire you. The same can happen if you are sitting at another restaurant complaining to a friend. If your boss is at a nearby table and overhears you using the company name in a bad light, then they can fire you. It may not seem fair, but that is the way it is. If you are going to complain, get on the phone and call a friend. Gripe to your spouse or roommate. Call your mom. You have the right to complain to your heart's content. Just don't post it on the web if it can be traced back to you. (Bike Commuter, *Huffington Post* Forum)

Once you post something on Facebook, it ceases to be a private matter. It doesn't matter what your settings are. It's like having a private conversation in public and getting pissed when someone butts in. (Robyn, BRIXX Facebook Page)

When you accept employment you also accept to abide by company policy. Most employers make you sign off on the handbook at hiring. If you want to complain about work call your girlfriend or your mom and talk on the phone. Don't do it on facebook or twitter. (Schwarzfalke, MSNBC Website)

EVOLUTION OF THE ISSUE

In the months following the BRIXX incident, other Facebook-related terminations received attention by the press. In most situations, the courts upheld the rights of organizations to set the terms of employment (e.g., restrict worker comments on social media sites, monitor employee internet activities both on and off the clock). However, one notable exception to this trend was a recent case against the American Medical Response (AMR) Company. In 2009, AMR fired an employee after discovering that she had posted what the company considered disparaging remarks about her supervisor on her Facebook page. More specifically, this employee described her supervisor as "a dick" in one posting and "a scumbag" in another. On February 7, 2011, the National Labor Relations Board ruled that firing an employee for this reason "violated the National Labor Relations Act, which allows employees to discuss the terms and conditions of their employment with co-workers and others" (Musil, 2011, para. 4). One issue that made the AMR case different from the BRIXX case was the fact that the AMR employee was a member of the Teamsters Union. The union argued AMR denied the employee access to her union representatives during the termination proceedings, which was a violation of her rights as an employee.

In the end, AMR reached a financial settlement with their former employee and agreed to "revise 'overly broad rules' in the employee handbook regarding how employees can communicate on the Internet and with co-workers regarding their work conditions" (Musil, 2011, para. 6). It is important to note that this case differs from the BRIXX case in that the AMR employee's relationship with a union gave her additional rights with respect to her company's termination practices. As a result, it is not clear that nonunionized employees (e.g., the majority of the private U.S. workforce—such as the employees at BRIXX) would have the same protections.

ISSUES TO CONSIDER

The previous discussion helps to illustrate the range of issues organizational communication scholars must consider when evaluating employee privacy rights and corporate social media policies. To what extent is forwarding a private website posting to a third party (who would not have access to this post on their own) significantly different from sharing an e-mail in which a person says something negative about his/her work situation? In an era when most people carry phones that can record personal conversations, nearly all interactions can be preserved on a digital file and sent to people who are not the intended recipient of this information. What limits (if any) should there be on an employer's ability to use a worker's private statements as justification for termination? Companies certainly have an interest in getting rid of disgruntled or disruptive employees. However, when and where does an organization no longer have the right to monitor an employee's behavior? Companies need to protect their public image, and managers should defend their employees against harassment from coworkers. However, to what extent should an employment contract (or a manager's desire to keep employees civil toward each other) be used to restrict an individual's right to free speech?

Does it matter *when* an employee communicates (i.e., *on* versus *off* the clock)? Does it matter *where* an employee communicates (e.g., in their own home, in the company break room, in a shopping mall)? Does it matter *how* the employee communicates (e.g., a public website, over e-mail, on the phone, in person)? Does it matter *who* the employee communicates with (e.g., their friends, their family, other employees, current customers, the general public)? Does it matter *what* the employee says (Can they use the organization's name? Are *positive* comments okay but *negative* comments forbidden)?

DISCUSSION QUESTIONS

1. If you were Ashley Johnson's manager, what would you do in this situation? How would you interpret BRIXX's "social media" policy? What standards would you use to justify your interpretation of this policy and the action (or lack of action) you decided to take?

2. What limits (if any) should organizations be allowed to place on the communication choices of their members when they *are* at work? What about when employees are *not* at work?

3. If employees share embarrassing information or criticize their employer to people outside the organization, should this be grounds for termination? Does it matter where/how the information was shared (e.g., on a public website, to friends in a restaurant where others might overhear the conversation, in a private e-mail to a family member)?

4. Should employees have *any* expectations of privacy and job protection when it comes to sharing their opinions (positive or negative) about their organization with others? Why or why not?

5. Companies have an economic incentive to manage their public image and ensure that employees are not disrupting the corporate culture. As such, when should managers (if ever) have the right to fire people who make negative comments about their job, their coworkers, or their employer? When (if ever) might online free speech cross the line and become cyberbullying or other forms of workplace harassment?

6. Given the restrictions some firms want to place on their employees' use of social media, is it appropriate or inappropriate for these organizations to also encourage workers to "Friend" or "Like" their own company Facebook pages?

7. Many people, particularly the younger members of the workforce, interact with their peers through digital media (e.g., social media sites, texts, e-mail). How might the fact that managers monitor these channels impact these workers' ability or willingness to share employment information with each other or engage in workplace dissent?

REFERENCES

Alder, S. G., & Tompkins, P. K. (1997). Electronic performance monitoring: An organizational justice and concertive control perspective. *Management Communication Quarterly, 10*(3), 259–288.

American Management Association. (2008a, February 28). *2007 electronic monitoring & surveillance survey: Over half of all employers combined fire workers for e-mail & internet abuse.* Retrieved from http://press.amanet.org/press-releases/177/2007-electronic-monitoring-surveillance-survey

American Management Association. (2008b, March 13). *The latest on workplace monitoring and surveillance.* Retrieved from http://www.amanet.org /training/articles/The-Latest-onWorkplace-Monitoring = and-Surveillance.aspx

Attewell, P. (1987). Big brother and the sweatshop: Computer surveillance in the automated office. *Sociological Theory, 5,* 87–100.

Bahney, A. (2006, May 25). Interns? No bloggers need apply. *New York Times,* pp. E1–E2.

Botan, C., & McCreadie, M. (1993). Communication, information, and surveillance: Separation and control in organizations. In J. R. Schement & B. D. Ruben (Eds.), *Between communication and information* (Vol. 4, pp. 385–397). Piscataway, NJ: Transaction Publishers.

Campbell-Kelly, M., & Aspray, W. (1996). *Computer: A history of the information machine.* New York: Basic Books.

Crawford, K. (2005, February 14). Have a blog, lose your job? *CNN/Money.* Retrieved from http://money .cnn.com/2005/02/14/news/economy/blogging/index.htm

Dhami, A. (2010, September). The beauty blogosphere. *ANOKHI Magazine: Fashion, lifestyle & entertainment.* Retrieved from http://www.anokhimagazine.com/beauty/beauty-blogosphere

Foley, J. (2005, January 31). The weblog question. *InformationWeek.* Retrieved from http://www .informationweek.com/story/showArticle.jhtml?articleID = 59100462

Frazier, E. (2010, May 17). Facebook post costs waitress her job: Online gripe is like standing on a corner with a sign, lawyer says. *CharlotteObserver.com.* Retrieved from http://www.charlotteobserver .com/2010/05/17/1440447/facebook-post-costs-waitress-her.html

Gandy, O. H., Jr. (1989). The surveillance society: Information technology and bureaucratic social control. *Journal of Communication, 39*(3), 61–76.

Gossett, L., & Kilker, J. (2006). My job sucks: Examining counter-institutional websites as locations for organizational member voice, dissent, and resistance. *Management Communication Quarterly, 20*(1), 63–90.

Mitra, A. (2001). Marginal voices in cyberspace. *New Media & Society, 3*(1), 29–48.

Musil, S. (2011, February 7). Company settles Facebook firing case. *CNET News.* Retrieved from http:// news.cnet.com/8301-1023_3-20030955-93.html

Proofpoint, Inc. (2009, August 10). *Proofpoint survey says: State of economy leads to increased data loss risk for large companies.* Retrieved from http://www.marketwire.com /press-release/Proofpoint-Survey-Says-State-Economy-Leads-Increased-Data-Loss-Risk-Large-Companies-1027877.htm

Rubin, C. (2010a, May 25). Would you fire an employee over a negative Facebook post? *Inc.com.* Retrieved from http://www.inc.com/news/articles/2010/05/waitress-fired-for-facebook-post.html

Rubin, C. (2010b, May 30). Keeping tabs on your employees' Facebook activity. *Inc.com.* Retrieved from http://www.inc.com/news/articles/2010/03/tracking-employees-on-social-media.html

Daimler's Bribery Case

Roxana Maiorescu

This case study explores the practice of bribery, which is common in some business environments. In addition, it examines how companies should negotiate their business roles in different countries and the responsibilities they bear in bringing about positive changes in developing countries through their commitment to ethical business practices. Finally, this case raises questions regarding the communication strategies that a company should employ in order to inform its stakeholders about a crisis and the extent to which they should engage them in a democratic process of dialogue that would allow for various opinions and voices.

This case study raises two major ethical questions regarding (1) whether multinational corporations should bear the responsibility of changing the social and political milieus in which they operate by setting standards of transparent business practices and (2) the crisis communication strategies employed by corporations whose brand is too strong to be affected by a crisis.

The global business environment has been recently shaken by scandals such as the ones faced by Daimler, Siemens, and HP, corporations that were accused and found guilty of bribery under the Foreign Corrupt Practices Act (FCPA). The aforementioned companies paid hundreds of millions of dollars in civil and criminal fines for corrupt business practices in developing countries such as Russia, China, and Turkmenistan (Gatti, 2010, para. 3).

Bribery crises that strike corporations raise tensions about what constitutes ethical behavior. On one hand, corporations should have a set of core values and principles to enact regardless of the environment in which they operate. On the other hand, organizational behavior needs to be context-specific and focused on the culture in which a company conducts its business. In this respect, corporations can make use of cost-benefit analysis to determine the business practices they should enact at an international level. This utility perspective, which revolves around short-term benefits, allows companies to focus on their future profit without bringing about any changes in a specific environment in which they operate. Conversely, by focusing on their possible role as agents of change, corporations can contribute to the transitional process to democracy and economic prosperity in developing countries. This, in turn, may boost the reputation of corporations by adding to their reservoir of goodwill and their positive performance history.

Additionally, the ways in which corporations address their stakeholders during times of crisis can affect the impact the crisis has on their reputation, brand, and their future performance. In this respect, transparency and dialogic communication are keys to a successful crisis management process. Yet, out of legal concerns, corporations may feel compelled not to reveal much information about their crises. In addition to the legal concerns, powerful brands with an excellent reputation and no history of crises may prefer not to give away much information since scandals have little impact on their performance.

On April 1, 2010, the U.S. Department of Justice (DOJ) found Daimler guilty of bribing government officials in 22 countries around the world from 1998 to 2008. The Stuttgart automobile manufacturer was found guilty of making a profit of hundreds of millions of dollars from the contracts the company obtained after transferring large sums of money to government officials, paying for their luxurious vacations, and giving away expensive gifts. Daimler settled the matter in court for $185 million and agreed to the monitoring of its subsidiaries in China and Russia for 2 years.

It is important to note that corporations like Daimler, Siemens, and HP faced legal consequences for their business practices based on the FCPA. This legislation was enacted in the United States in 1977 to forbid American corporations as well as foreign companies that operate in America from engaging in any bribery practices around the world. Regarded by the Congress as a law whose purpose is to promote democratic values and ease the transition to democracy in developing countries, the FCPA has also been criticized for failing to take into consideration the cultural aspects imposed by international business environments: In other milieus, bribery is a common business practice and a way to express gratitude. Additionally, critics of the FCPA predicted that the law would significantly reduce foreign investments (Hines, 1995; Murphy, 2005; Wayne, 2000).

Another ethical dimension of Daimler's bribery case relates to the way in which companies with a powerful brand should engage their stakeholders in dialogue in times of crisis. During the bribery crisis, Daimler's communication with its stakeholders lacked transparency, and the company provided no response to the bribery accusations until the matter was settled in court on April 1, 2010. Although ethical crisis communication should address all parties that are affected by the situation and should display regret and remorse (Anthonissen, 2008; Benoit, 1995; Coombs, 2007; Hearit, 2006; Jonsen & Toulmin, 1988; Ulmer, Sellnow, & Seeger, 2007), Daimler focused its response on corrective action and, hence, the company provided information only with regard to the measures it planned to take to prevent future cases of bribery.

Despite Daimler's crisis and the way in which the company communicated about it, its reputation has not necessarily been tarnished. For example, Daimler was declared one of the most powerful brands in the world a few months after the crisis was resolved. An example of how consumers perceived the German corporation a few days after Daimler pleaded guilty for bribery were the enthusiastic comments the company got on a well-known social media website. None of the comments posted made any reference to the crisis but, rather, denoted loyalty to the Mercedes-Benz brand:

> Mercedes-Benz Cars are cars designed by Gods for human use only. The car that does what the human wants . . . [I] can only say Gods should continue to be Gods.

Mercedes-Benz, I don't know how you guys do it but your cars are so beautiful! Every time I see the new C-class I almost faint! Thank you Mercedes-Benz for allowing us to even look at your genius.

Additionally, some of the comments revealed that Mercedes was still a dream for potential consumers:

Mercedes is one of my favorite cars. Every day at school during gym I walk out the weight room to get a drink and I stand there for five minutes staring at a pretty black Mercedes. One day when I get my job I will stare at it on my driveway.

In sum, the tensions that play out in Daimler's case concern the way in which companies should negotiate their roles in different international environments and the responsibilities they bear in bringing about positive changes in developing countries through their commitment to ethical business practices. Additionally, Daimler's crisis raises questions regarding the communication strategies that a company should employ in order to inform its stakeholders on the developments of the crisis as well as to engage them in a democratic process of dialogue that would allow for various opinions and voices.

In order to better understand the context in which Daimler's crisis developed, I will first provide a brief overview of the company's history, values, and culture.

DAIMLER

Daimler is the second largest luxury automobile manufacturer in the world after BMW with a history that goes back 125 years. What is nowadays one of the strongest brands worldwide started when its founding fathers Carl Benz and Gottlieb Daimler, the inventors of the first automobiles, joined forces to create vehicles that would become "the best or nothing."

The name of Daimler's most known core brand, Mercedes-Benz, is related to a successful Austrian diplomat and businessman, Emil Jellinek, the son of a well-known rabbi in Vienna. Jellinek developed an interest for automobiles and racing and regarded the invention of the vehicle as one of great importance for the future. In 1897, he ordered his first Daimler car, a belt-driven vehicle with a six-horsepower two-cylinder engine, and a top speed of 15 mph that he planned to use for racing. Because he strongly believed that his 10-year-old daughter's endearment name would bring him good luck in the races, he named the car after her: Mercedes, a Hispanic word that means "grace" and "mercy." Emil Jellinek later became a member of the executive board, and Mercedes was a registered trademark in 1902.

The symbol of the three-pointed star enclosed in a circle started to be used in 1923 and stands for Gottlieb Daimler's ambition for universal motorization "on land, on water and in the air" as well as for Carl Benz's aspiration for innovation, made famous by his remark: "The love of inventing never dies."

Since its establishment in 1886, Daimler has set the standards in areas of innovation and safety for the automobile industry worldwide. With its own research institute that today comprises 17,000 researchers and developers around the world, the company introduced pioneering safety systems that were later adopted by other car manufacturers. For example, in 1933 Mercedes-Benz introduced the wheel suspension, a technology that is being used even today. In the years that followed, Daimler focused on safety and innovation and became the first car manufacturer that tested its vehicles by reproducing real-life collisions, nowadays a requirement for the entire car industry. Some of Daimler's most recent innovations include the Attention Assist drowsiness detection system that allows for automatic braking in risk of collisions as well as the Active Blind Spot Assist, whose purpose is to make the driver aware of a possible collision when changing lanes on a highway. Daimler's innovative concepts transformed its vehicles into cars capable of thinking, seeing, and feeling with the ultimate purpose of alerting the driver and the passengers of possible risks.

Apart from its famous and successful Mercedes-Benz brand, Daimler is known for other upscale products such as Maybach as well as for the Freightliner and the Daimler trucks, all of which have gained an impeccable reputation for safety, quality, and comfort.

The 2008 economic crisis affected the company most profusely in America, where its sales waned by 33%. While other manufacturers like Honda, Hyundai, Ford, and General Motors advertised that their products were designed for everyone, Daimler decided to stick to its image of the provider of the car of the future. Consequently, in 2009 Daimler spent $57 million for an advertising campaign meant to promote the Mercedes E-Class, an ad campaign known to be the biggest that Daimler engaged in over a period of 2 years. In this respect, in an interview with the *New York Times,* Alex Gellert, a partner for the company that created the advertising campaign, made the following assertions:

> I'd rather tell our brand story, our innovative story, our value story, than join the chorus of everyone else that's screaming "sale"—that's about the only message that's out there now. . . . I don't have to go out saying "value," "value"—that's not appropriate for our brand.

As of 2010, international studies published on Daimler's website classified its core brand Mercedes-Benz as one of the world's leading brands. For example, Mercedes-Benz gained the top position in categories such as "the most valuable global luxury car," "the most valuable German brand," and "the most valuable global premium car brand."

THE BRIBERY ACCUSATIONS AND RESPONSES

On March 23, 2010, the *New York Times* revealed that Daimler was on the verge of settling a court dispute and planned to plead guilty to bribery charges and pay a total fine of $185 million (Savage, 2010, para. 1). The newspaper mentioned that the U.S. DOJ had launched a longtime investigation into Daimler's business practices that shed light on the corrupt business practices that Daimler engaged in and that brought the company a profit of about $1.9 billion.

The *New York Times* provided insights into the court filing stating that the corporation "made hundreds of improper payments worth tens of millions of dollars to foreign officials" who, in turn, secured contracts with their government for purchasing Daimler's cars (Savage, 2010, para. 3).

Daimler resorted to bribing officials in 22 countries over a period of 10 years. More specifically, the company made use of foreign accounts to transfer the bribes to government officials and engaged its employees to serve as "cash desks"—a term used to refer to the sums of money the employees withdrew in order to bribe officials. Some other bribery cases Daimler was accused of concerned the business practices that the corporation enacted in countries such as China and Russia. For example, in Russia, Daimler overcharged invoices and later transferred the money to governmental officials: for a car with a cost of approximately $508,000, Daimler transferred a sum of $79,000 to the governmental representatives (Savage, 2010, para. 3). Additional charges brought against Daimler concerned bribing the wife of a government official from China who was negotiating the selling of contracts for Mercedes-Benz vehicles, paying for luxury holidays, and giving expensive gifts to an official from Turkmenistan (Reuters, 2010, para. 4). In Russia, in return for the bribes, Daimler obtained contracts for the Special Purpose Garage that provided cars for the president and the prime minister of the country as well as for dignitaries who made official visits to the Kremlin (Kramer, 2010, para. 6). Contacted by the *New York Times* to provide a response to the situation, Daimler's spokesman, Han Tjan, preferred to make no comments.

At the court hearing that took place on April 1, 2010, Daimler pleaded guilty to bribery and agreed to pay a criminal fine of $96.3 million and a civil fine of $91.4 million. Additionally, Daimler's subsidiaries in China and Russia entered a deferred prosecution agreement that would allow them to avoid indictment if, during the following 2 years, they implemented legal business practices. The judge Louis J. Freech, a former FBI director, was appointed to monitor the two subsidiaries for a period of about 2 years.

The judge of the U.S. District Court in Washington, D.C. regarded Daimler's agreement as a "just resolution." However, a principal deputy in the Justice Department's criminal division made harsh remarks regarding Daimler's corrupt business practices:

> Using offshore bank accounts, third-party agents, and deceptive pricing practices, these companies saw foreign bribery as a way of doing business. (Reuters, 2010, para. 4)

The company's responses to the accusations of bribery and its subsequent settlements emerged only after the court hearing. They revealed that Daimler intended to transform the crisis into an opportunity of improvement of its policies and business practices. For example, Dieter Zetsche, the chairman of Daimler's board asserted the following:

> We have learned a lot from the past experience. . . . Today, we are a better and a stronger company, and we will continue to do everything we can to maintain the highest compliance standards.

As shown, the chairman mentioned that Daimler would "continue to maintain the highest standards of compliance." Hence, his official statement fails to admit to any kind of wrongdoing and excludes a display of concern or remorse (Reuters, 2010, para. 5). Nonetheless, Zetsche's response is the only official statement that Daimler made during the period of the scandal. Daimler did not interact with the media, and one single press release was posted on Daimler's website after the court hearing of April 1, 2010. However, it was removed from the website a few months afterward. The press release provided detailed information on the settlement that Daimler reached with the DOJ and assured stakeholders that enough finances were available to pay for the civil and criminal fines that amounted to $185 million. Additionally, the press release stated that the corporation had collaborated with the DOJ during the past investigation and that compliance had a high priority at Daimler.

According to the press release, some of the future steps that Daimler planned to take to discourage the practice of bribery included the appointment of local compliance managers in all its business units who would report to a chief compliance officer and regular training seminars and conferences on the compliance rules. Daimler also planned to establish a consultation desk on compliance whose purpose was to answer the questions that employees may have in this regard. Daimler's press release was addressed mainly at its stakeholders, subsidiaries, and affiliates and revolved around the corrective action that Daimler planned to enact to avoid similar situations in the future. Yet the press release made no references to bribery nor did it admit to any kind of wrongdoing. Daimler failed to address its internal stakeholders, the employees whose vision of the company and values may have altered after the bribery crisis and, more precisely, the employees whose subsidiaries operated in the United States and who, because they were not involved in the bribery cases, may have heard about the crisis from a third source. Surprisingly, Daimler's online press release contained an endnote that mentioned the circumstances under which the company could not commit to the aforementioned measures:

> This document contains forward-looking statements that reflect our current views about future events. The words "anticipate," "assume," "believe," "estimate," "expect," "intend," "may," "plan," "project," "should" and similar expressions are used to identify forward-looking statements. These statements are subject to many risks and uncertainties, including a lack of further improvement or a renewed deterioration of global economic conditions, in particular a renewed decline of consumer demand and investment activity in Western Europe or the United States, or a downturn in major Asian economies . . . changes in laws, regulations and government policies, particularly those relating to vehicle emissions, fuel economy and safety, the resolution of pending governmental investigations and the outcome of pending or threatened future legal proceedings; and other risks and uncertainties. . . . If any of these risks and uncertainties materialize, or if the assumptions underlying any of our forward-looking statements prove incorrect, then our actual results may be materially different from those we express or imply by such statements. We do not intend or assume any obligation to update these forward-looking statements. Any forward-looking statement speaks only as of the date on which it is made. (Press Information, 2010, p. 5)

It is relevant to note that Daimler's bribery case was not singular but rather it emerged in a business environment that had been shaken by cases of corporations that engaged in bribing government officials in exchange for contracts. For example, the German telecommunication giant Siemens pled guilty in a U.S. court in 2008 and paid civil and criminal fines that amounted to $1.6 billion. In addition, HP underwent court investigations after providing computer equipment for the general offices of Russia's chief prosecutor. What makes the situation of Daimler, Siemens, and HP similar is the 1977 FCPA under which they were charged for bribery. The law prohibits American and international companies that operate in the United States to engage in acts of bribery in any parts of the world. Considered to reflect the democratic and capitalistic values of America, the law was also criticized for failing to make allowances for the local cultures and political systems in which multinational corporations operate. The FCPA will be further discussed in more detail for a better understanding of how the ethical tensions regarding corporate bribery play out.

THE BRIBERY LAW AND ITS IMPLICATIONS

Following the Watergate scandal, the questionable contributions of American corporations to the reelection campaigning of President Nixon, and evidence that over 400 U.S. international corporations had been bribing government officials abroad, the U.S. Congress enacted the FCPA. The purpose of this law was to compel corporations to adhere to certain international rules of ethics (Hines, 1995; Murphy, 2005; Wayne, 2000). According to the FCPA, American companies and international companies that operated in the United States were prohibited from engaging in bribery in any countries they conducted business. From the beginning, the law entailed connotations of ethics and morality. For example, some of the congressional statements of that time pointed to the importance of promoting the American democratic values abroad:

> The payment of bribes to influence acts or decisions of foreign officials, foreign political parties or candidates for foreign political office is unethical . . . it is counter to the moral expectations and values of the American public.
>
> I think what is at stake here is really, in a number of significant respects, the reputation of our own country, and I think that we have an obligation to set a standard of honesty and integrity in our business dealings not only at home but also abroad which will be a beacon for the light of integrity for the rest of the world. (Murphy, 2005, p. 3)

Because corrupt business practices characterize political systems in transition to democracy (Weinstein, 1971), the law was regarded as enabling corporations to perform the role of agents of change by enacting democratic and Western values in the countries in which they operated. In other words, the ethical business practices could ultimately lead to a quicker transition to a better political, economic, and social system of the developing countries.

The law also emphasized the moral responsibility that the U.S. corporations have in promoting abroad American values such as justice, freedom, and democracy. In this vein, one of the congressmen who contributed to the 1977 law asserted the following:

> What is at stake ultimately is confidence in, and respect for, American businesses, American corporations, American principles—indeed, the very democratic political values and free competitive economic system which we view as the essence of our most proud heritage and most promising future.
>
> The interference in democratic ideals with corporate gifts undermines everything we are trying to do as a leader of the free world. (Murphy, 2005, p. 3)

Contrary to the belief that the democratic values embedded in the FCPA would allow corporations to make positive changes in the political systems in which they operated, there was much criticism about the dwindling of the American business abroad. For example, studies pointed out that while bribery cases in developing countries slightly decreased after the bribery law was enacted in 1977 American businesses reduced their investments abroad. Additionally, it was predicted that foreign companies might stop investing in the United States and move their headquarters to milieus that were more conducive to business such as China, for example (Hines, 1995; Murphy, 2005; Wayne, 2000). Moreover, critics of the FCPA denounced the law for its ignorance of cultural discrepancies and for the law's failure to set distinct lines between bribery as a corrupt act and bribery as a token of gratitude and gift giving. Critics of the law also pointed out that the FCPA lacked a proper definition of the term *bribery* (Murphy, 2005). While the FCPA stated that bribery was wrong and immoral, it did not provide an exact explanation as to why it was a wrongful act. Apart from the economic explanations that focused on how bribery negatively affected the efficiency of the market and how it deteriorated international commercial relations, the law omitted any explanations regarding culturally related aspects (Murphy, 2005).

Whether viewed as a means for corporations to become agents of change in developing countries or as an act through which the United States was trying to impose its own business ethics on other countries (Murphy, 2005), the FCPA compelled corporations like Daimler, Siemens, and HP to face jurisdiction and pay millions of dollars in criminal and civil fines. At the same time, the FCPA endangered their reputation.

Several ethical dilemmas arise in situations similar to Daimler's that concern the business strategies that transnational corporations should enact in countries where bribery is a business requirement and where gifts are a symbol of gratitude meant to compensate for salaries below the poverty line.

ETHICAL DILEMMAS: TENSIONS IN BUSINESS PRACTICES AND CRISIS RESPONSE

Daimler's situation is no different from the crises that HP and Siemens faced in the past for breaking the American anti-bribery legislation: Daimler also engaged in corrupt business practices with the purpose of ensuring contracts. Business strategies of this kind are proof that companies still engage in cost-benefit analysis and try to measure and predict the financial risks they expose themselves to by going against the international legislation. Such an approach to business fails to consider possible alternatives of practices that may positively impact the bottom line of the organizations in the long term.

Since today there is no more clear distinction between the personal and the corporate sphere, corporations can consider the possibility of aligning their organizational values with those of their various stakeholders. In this vein, finding a common ground with regard to values would allow corporations to educate their employees and perform their role as agents of change. Bribery acts negatively affect countries in transition to democracy by impeding their economic development and undermining the efficiency of the market (Wayne, 2000). Additionally, bribery crises that involve government officials perpetuate the distrust of the citizens when it comes to politicians. This, in turn, could lead to low self-efficacy, political disengagement, and low voter turnout. By contrast, multinational corporations that operate in developing countries could lose their place in the market if they do not adhere to common business practices such as bribery.

Daimler's crisis raises also an ethical question of transparency from both the perspective of its business practices and the ways in which the company communicated during the crisis.

Showing transparency during times of crisis helps a corporation recover more quickly, and it minimizes the damage that the crisis may have on its reputation and brand (Benoit, 1995; Coombs, 2007; Hearit, 2006). Some famous well-managed crises of the past during which corporations engaged in dialogic communication and transparency were faced by Pepsi and Johnson & Johnson. Their engagement with the affected stakeholders, the transparency that they displayed when communicating with the media, along with the ethical measures they took to put an end to the crises, helped them to recover quickly and reduced the damage of their reputation and their financial losses.

Daimler's communication about the crisis showed concern toward the stakeholders to the extent to which the company reassured them that there were enough financial resources to cover the criminal and the civil fines. Surprisingly, despite its lack of transparency, Daimler was declared one of the most powerful brands in the world 1 year after the crisis. Thus, Daimler's case raises the question of whether strong brands in general and luxury brands in particular should engage in dialogic communication and transparency if their brand is too strong to be affected by scandals.

In sum, Daimler's crisis reveals the ethical tensions that corporations face when conducting business abroad as well as the way in which organizations should communicate with their stakeholders in times of crisis. While corporations need to adapt to the cultural and societal norms of various countries, international legislation restricts their business practices. Conversely, the purpose of restrictive laws such as the FCPA is to promote Western values that would help developing countries in their transition to democracy and economic prosperity.

DISCUSSION QUESTIONS

1. From the perspective of foundational and situational ethics, what are the tensions that multinational corporations face when they operate in a different political and social environment?

2. Apart from bribery, what aspects of a developing country compel international corporations to face ethical dilemmas vis-à-vis the business practices they should engage in?

3. Apart from Daimler, Siemens, or HP, can you think of other multinational corporations that operate in countries in development? What cultural issues are they facing?

4. Do you think that adaptation to the business environment of a developing country is easier for corporations from a specific industry? If yes, which one?

5. What measures should an international corporation take to contribute to the transition of a country to democracy and economic prosperity?

6. What role do employees (natives of that specific country) from entry levels (e.g., the customer service department, the sales department) play in helping a country's transition to democracy?

7. What are the short-term and the long-term negative effects that lack of transparency in crisis communication could cause to a company?

8. What are some other American laws that guide international corporate practice?

REFERENCES

Anthonissen, P. F. (2008). *Crisis communication.* London: Kogan Page.

Benoit, W. (1995). *Accounts, excuses, and apologies: A theory of image restoration strategies.* Albany: State University of New York Press.

Coombs, W. T. (2007). *Ongoing crisis communication. Planning, managing, and responding.* Thousand Oaks, CA: Sage.

Gatti, C. (2010, March 29). Alstom at center of web of bribery inquiry. *New York Times.* Retrieved from http://www.nytimes.com/2010/03/30/business/global/30alstom.html

Hearit, K. M. (2006). *Crisis management by apology. Corporate response to allegations of wrongdoing.* Mahwah, NJ: Lawrence Erlbaum.

Hines, H. R. (1995). *Forbidden payment: Foreign bribery and American business after 1977.* Unpublished working paper.

Jonsen, A. R., & Toulmin, S. (1988). *The abuse of casuistry: A history of moral reasoning.* Berkeley: University of California Press.

Kramer, A. E. (2010, April 29). Russia slow to pick up the lead in bribery cases. *New York Times.* Retrieved from http://www.nytimes.com/2010/04/30/business/global/30ruble.html

Murphy, A. G. (2005). The migratory patterns of business in the global village. *NYU Journal of Law & Business, 229,* 1–25.

Press Information. (2010, April, 1). *Daimler Press Release.* Retrieved from http://www.daimler.com/dccom/downloads/en

Reuters. (2010). Daimler bribery settlement is approved. *New York Times.* Retrieved from http://www.nytimes.com/2010/04/02/business/02daimler.html

Savage, C. (2010, March 23). Daimler is said to settle bribing charges. *New York Times*. Retrieved from http://www.nytimes.com/2010/03/24/business/24daimler.html?scp = 1&sq = daimler%20is%20 said%20to%20settle%20bribing%20charges&st = Search

Ulmer, R. R., Sellnow, T. L., & Seeger, M. W. (2007). *Effective crisis communication: Moving from crisis to opportunity*. Thousand Oaks, CA: Sage.

Wayne, H. (2000). Bribery in international business transactions and the OECD Convention: Benefits and limitations. *Business Economics*. Retrieved from http://www.allbusiness.com/human-resources/employee-development-employee-ethics/686469-1.html

Weinstein, M. (1971). *Systematic political theory*. Columbus, OH: Charles E. Merrill Publishing Company.

PART V

Accountability

The Deepwater Horizon Disaster

Challenges in Ethical Decision Making

Elaine M. Brown

This case explores the complexities involved in ethical decision making in organizations. Using the British Petroleum (BP) oil spill as an example, the case suggests that complex interorganizational structures involved with oil drilling make accountability complicated. In such an environment, decision makers must consider a range of tensions, including people versus profits and short- versus long-term benefits in order to account for multiple decisions points and diverse stakeholders.

We are committed to the safety and development of our people and the communities and societies in which we operate. We aim for no accidents, no harm to people and no damage to the environment.

—BP (2009)

In Revelations it says the water will turn to blood. That's what it looks like out here—like the Gulf is bleeding. This is going to choke the life out of everything.

—P. J. Hahn, director of coastal zone management for Louisiana's Plaquemines Parish (quoted from NBC, MSNBC.com, and News Services, 2010)

Companies today often proclaim to have their stakeholders' best interests in mind. They may stress a "triple bottom line" of people, planet, and profits; emphasize being good corporate citizens within their communities; or accentuate the goal of sustainability by protecting long-term assets such as employees and the environment. However, the promising rhetoric, *even if it is sincere,* cannot be fulfilled without an accumulation of strategic and daily decisions that reflect this discourse of corporate social responsibility. Decisions (including not only what is decided but also what issues are determined to be opportunities for decisions in the first place) are where the rubber meets the road—where rhetoric becomes reality, or not.

Ethical decision making, however, is a complicated matter. Very few issues are clear-cut, organizational structures and routines often obfuscate who is responsible for a decision, and organizational culture may define certain actions as common sense and thus don't require a decision. In addition, decisions are often between competing "goods" such as short-term versus long-term best interests, innovation versus tried-and-true status quo, or minimizing different types of risks. This case study, which explores the 2010 Deepwater Horizon oil rig explosion and Macondo well blowout, provides a clear example of the complexities involved in ethical decision making in organizations. Who, or what, was responsible for the worst oil spill in history? What decisions made the catastrophe inevitable? Why did those decisions make sense to the decision makers at the time? When were actions taken out of habit or "common sense" instead of as a result of conscious decisions? The sequence of actions (and inactions) that led to the disaster illustrate the challenges entailed in ethical decision making within the daily, time-pressured environment of a complex, multicompany organizational site. After a brief overview of the event and its impact, this case study will explore the disaster by explaining the key actors involved, highlighting problematic decisions that may have contributed to the catastrophe and considering important factors in how and why those decisions may have been made.

THE BLOWOUT AND ITS AFTERMATH

On April 20, 2010, soon after the completion of a cement job that was supposed to seal the Macondo exploratory well to prepare it for later use as a production well, leaking hydrocarbons (gas and oil) from the well reached the Deepwater Horizon oil drilling rig nearly a mile overhead and caused an explosion. The pressure of the escaping hydrocarbons, in addition to the loss of control of the drilling rig and its operations caused by the explosion, created a blowout of the well. The explosion killed 11 individuals, injured 16 others, and left the remaining 99 survivors traumatized. The "blowout," the term used for the sudden and continuous surge of oil and gas from a well, resulted in nearly 5 million barrels of oil discharged over a period of 87 days. During those days, there were a variety of techniques attempted to stop the flow including the use of remotely operated vehicles (ROVs) to shut the well by closing the blowout preventer, placing a "cofferdam" over the end of the riser and using "kill mud" and "junk shot" to try to plug the hole. However, the flow was not stopped until July 15 when the riser was successfully capped. Later, a deepwater intercept, or relief, well, which had been started on May 2, was finally completed and ensured that the Macondo well was "dead."

BP (the official operator of the well), the U.S. Coast Guard, and a number of other public and private agencies were tasked with cleanup both during and after the spill. "At its peak, efforts to stem the spill and combat its effects included more than 47,000 personnel; 7,000 vessels; 120 aircraft; and the participation of scores of federal, state, and local agencies" (Mabus, 2010, p. 2). Millions of feet of boom were used to contain the oil and keep it from shore. Private boats were recruited and outfitted to skim off the oil. Oil patches on the ocean's surface were burned. Dispersants were used to break down and change the distribution of the oil. By August, these efforts, as well as the capture of oil from the insertion tube, accounted for the fate of just over one third of the escaped oil. An additional 40% of the oil has evaporated, dissolved, or been dispersed naturally, leaving approximately one quarter of the oil remaining in the water and along the shore (National Commission, 2011b).

The consequences of this disaster are tragic and extensive. The first cost of the accident, of course, was the immediate loss of life. Amidst the enormity of this catastrophe in which we heard numbers in the thousands and millions (millions of barrels of oil, millions of gallons of dispersants, millions of feet of boom, thousands of square miles of closed fishing waters, thousands of miles of coast, etc.), 11 may seem like an almost insignificant number. Yet, when we remember that Jason Anderson, Dale Burkeen, Donald Clark, Stephen Curtis, Roy Kemp, Gordon Jones, Karl Dale Kleppinger, Blair Manuel, Dewey Revette, Shane Roshto, and Adam Weise (National Commission, 2011a) each had loved ones and futures that can no longer be realized, we begin to appreciate how significant the loss of 11 human beings really is.

Other, less immediate but equally troubling outcomes of the disaster have to do with the impact of the oil (and dispersants) on wildlife, human health, and the economy of the area. The oil that was discharged into the Gulf was "a combination of many different chemicals, a number of which are harmful to people" (Mabus, 2010, p. 50) and the environment. Pictures showed the immediate effects of the crude: oil-covered pelicans and sea turtles, dead dolphins and whales, gooey marshlands. But the effects of the spill on wildlife and the environment are more complex than pictures can show. "Rescue workers can clean and treat oiled birds and other relatively large animals that come ashore. But how do you deal with de-oiling plankton?" (Sylvia Earle, quoted in Dell'Amore, 2010). The food chain may be continuing the negative impacts of the oil as larger animals feed on smaller, affected organisms. In addition, although the 1.84 million gallons of dispersant used to break up the oil and keep it from coming ashore were not as toxic as the oil it treated, there is currently no dispersant available that is completely nontoxic (National Commission, 2011c). Because dispersants had never been used on such a scale and in the same ways before, no one knows its long-term impact. It may be years before the full impact on wildlife of both oil and dispersant is identified.

Negative effects on humans were both immediate and also more insidious through long-term consequences. Cleanup workers felt the first of the health effects because of direct contact with the oil and other toxins. "In Louisiana in the early months of the oil spill, more than 300 individuals, three-fourths of whom were cleanup workers, sought medical care for constitutional symptoms such as headaches, dizziness, nausea, vomiting, cough, respiratory distress, and chest pain" (Solomon & Janssen, 2010, p. 1118). Long-term effects may or may not be from direct contact. As an example of indirect effects, consider that just as the food chain may affect animals, there is also the possibility that humans who eat seafood from the Gulf may ingest "trace amounts of cadmium, mercury, and lead" (Solomon & Janssen, 2010, p. 1118). In addition, there are behavioral health issues involved. Past disasters, including oil spills, have been associated with a rise in mental health issues, substance abuse, and family dysfunction (Mabus, 2010; Solomon & Janssen, 2010). This disaster brings with it the same problems.

In addition to health effects, the spill brought with it negative economic consequences. The spill "caused the closure of 88,522 square miles of federal waters to fishing" (Mabus, 2010, p. 2). Both this closure and continuing concerns over the safety of Gulf seafood has severely interfered with commercial (and recreational) fishing. The loss in gross revenue to Louisiana's fishing industry through 2013 is estimated to be $115 million to $172 million (White, 2010). The travel and tourism industry in the Gulf was hard hit as well. A recent study by Oxford Economics (2010) estimates the loss of visitor spending in Louisiana through 2013 to be $295 million. The economies of other Gulf states have been similarly affected with dollar losses translating into the loss of thousands of jobs.

When put in terms of the consequences, especially consequences this severe, it is obvious that the decisions leading up to this catastrophe were *ethical* decisions—decisions that had considerable consequences for the organization, the community, and the environment. However, the ethical nature of individual decisions may or may not have been clear at the time those decisions were made. As we consider the key actors in this catastrophe as well as the decisions individuals faced, we must consider to what extent decision makers may or may not have felt that their decisions were ethical in nature (as opposed to simply technical) and how (or if) they took into account the possible consequences of their actions.

WHO IS TO BLAME?

Although many critics have argued that the blowout was ultimately BP's responsibility, the complex interorganizational structure involved with oil drilling makes accountability much more complicated. The underwater canyon in which the Macondo oil well was located was leased through the Minerals Management Service (MMS) to a group of three companies: (1) BP (who owned 65% of the lease), (2) Anadarko Petroleum (25%), and (3) MOEX Offshore (10%). BP was designated as the lease operator and thus the primary actor in the drama that unfolded.

BP determined it would drill an exploratory well (Macondo) to learn more about the geology of the canyon and to confirm that there was a large enough oil and gas reservoir to merit a full production well. In order to drill, they needed a partner: Transocean. Transocean's drilling rig, the Deepwater Horizon (as well as its operations), was contracted by BP for approximately $500,000 per day. Although BP personnel were on board the rig for coordination and oversight, most of the rig personnel were Transocean. Within this contractual arrangement, liability (and accountability) has come into question. Tony Hayward (2010), CEO of BP, stated the following in an early interview with CNN:

> The responsibility for safety on the drilling rig is Transocean. It is their rig, their equipment, their people, their systems, their safety processes. . . . The systems processes on a drilling rig are the accountability of the drilling rig company.

However, the contract between BP and Transocean indicates that, as the operator of the well, BP is ultimately responsible:

In the event any well being drilled hereunder shall blowout, crater or control be lost from any cause, company shall bear the entire cost and expense of killing the well or of otherwise bringing the well under control and shall protect, release, defend, indemnify, and hold harmless contractor from and against all claims, suits, demands, and causes of action for costs actually incurred in controlling the well. (quoted in Phillips, 2010)

The question of who is liable is still being investigated and may be argued in courts for years.

Contractors, hired for specialized jobs, were also part of the drill operations and as such were potential actors. Mud engineers, ROV technicians, tank cleaners, evaluation teams, and others were part of the operations required for the drilling project. As the cement contractor, Halliburton became a major figure in the Macondo disaster as well. As noted earlier, the exploratory stage of the Macondo well was wrapping up. In order to close the well, cement is pumped in to seal the space between the casing and the wellbore, preserving the drill shaft and prohibiting the escape of hydrocarbons. When a well is later reopened as a production well, crews punch holes in the casing and cement and allow oil and gas to flow into the well. Problems with the cement job are likely to have been a contributing factor in the catastrophe, making Halliburton a key actor.

In addition to culpability within the oil industry, many critics have pointed to the U.S. government as partially to blame for the Deepwater catastrophe. Through its dual roles of leasing agent and regulator the MMS, a governmental agency, was also a key organizational actor. Critics maintain that oversight to ensure the safety of drilling operations was compromised by carelessness and even corruption within MMS.

A final actor, pointed to by many as complicit in the disaster even without direct contact, is us. "Why was a corporation drilling for oil in mile-deep water 49 miles off the Louisiana coast? To begin, Americans today consume vast amounts of petroleum products—some 18.7 million barrels per day—to fuel our economy" (National Commission, 2011a, p. viii). How much of a factor is pressure from consumers? How much do our demands for (cheap) fuel drive potentially risky ventures? Can we in any way be held accountable for mistakes and shortcuts made by others?

The actors previously listed (with the exception of the American people) are organizations. However, even though we may be able to point to organizations as responsible, the culture within those organizations may have led to certain decisions making more "sense" than others, and it was generally individuals who made the call at key decision points. Individuals, or small groups of people, within each of the previously listed organizations were faced with problems that needed solutions. Many of the choices that were made between possible alternatives contributed to the eventual catastrophe.

WHAT WENT WRONG?

Deepwater oil drilling is an extremely complex, often dangerous, enterprise. The technological advances needed for drilling miles below the ocean's surface has been compared to those required for exploring outer space (National Commission, 2011a, p. viii). Systems, processes, and materials must be coordinated perfectly for production and safety. In the case of the Macondo well, problems in all three were present. However, it was the decision making involved in choosing to use certain processes or particular materials that has come under scrutiny as the key factor leading to the blowout. "Available evidence and testimony indicates that there were multiple (10 or more) major decisions and subsequent actions that developed in the days before the blowout that in hindsight (hindsight does not equal foresight) led to the blowout" (Deepwater Horizon Study Group, 2010, p. 7). Decisions about well design, materials selection, and determining how to evaluate job success marked some of the key choice points in the chain of events that followed. These decisions were made by various key actors and were typically not between "good" and "bad" alternatives but rather were made within complicated contexts in which an array of factors influenced choices.

Because of the physical results of the explosion and blowout and the fact that the scene is a mile below the surface of the ocean, the evidence that would shine light on the exact cause of the accident is not available. We may never know exactly what happened to allow the flow of hydrocarbons. However, there are many factors that investigators have pointed to as problematic and that (may have) played at least some part in the disaster.

One of these factors was the well design. There are alternatives involved in the selection of various aspects of well design. These selections are based on industry best practices as well as concerns about the surrounding environment. For the Macondo well, there were (at least) two design choices that have been implicated in the ensuing disaster. First, BP's design team chose to use a "long-string" casing instead of a more complex "liner" that would have been "easier to cement into place at Macondo" (National Commission, 2011a, p. 95). Although a standard industry design, early computer models showed that the long-string casing was unreliable for the cementing job needed in the particular surroundings at Macondo. However, it was attractive because the alternative, a liner, "would result in a more complex—and theoretically more leak-prone—system over the life of the well" (National Commission, 2011a, p. 95). The dilemma for decision makers was one of short-term versus long-term reliability and the possible risks involved in sacrificing that reliability. To reconsider the risk involved with the long-string casing, the computer models (run by Halliburton with BP interaction) that showed the need for the liner system were questioned. An in-house BP expert was brought in, inputs were "corrected," and the new calculations confirmed that the long-string system could be used after all. Although there is no evidence that this particular choice led to the instability that caused the blowout, it has been flagged in hindsight as problematic.

Another key issue with well design was the decision of the number of "centralizers" used for the well. Centralizers hold the casing string in place and ensure that it hangs in the center of the well bore. This centering is necessary to make sure that cement flows evenly and there are no spaces where drilling mud is caught and ends up compromising the integrity of the cement. The original BP design called for 16 centralizers. Halliburton engineers advised at least that many be used. However, when the time came to implement the design, only six of the type called for in the design were available from the supplier. When substitute centralizers were sent to replace the missing centralizers, the onboard team believed that they were the "stop collar" slip-on type that had been responsible for recent problems in another Gulf of Mexico operation. These centralizers brought with them the risk of slipping as they were put into place, thereby damaging components and adding debris to the mix (BP, 2010, p. 63). The BP on-rig engineer decided that, because the wellbore was nearly vertical, the risks involved with using the stop collar centralizers were greater than the risks of not using them. To confirm this decision, he e-mailed a drilling engineer on shore who disagreed about the number needed but told him, "but who cares, it's done, end of story, [we] will probably be fine" (National Commission, 2011a, p. 116). The time needed to find more acceptable centralizers or even to come to agreement about the wisest course of action was not taken. Again, no one knows if this choice directly led to disaster, but it is one more suspect in the eventual cement failure.

Another suspect is the choice of the cement composition itself. The Macondo well was a "nightmare well" that had many problems, not least of which was the possibility of "lost returns," which is the loss of mud, cement, or hydrocarbons through the fracturing of the surrounding rock formation. On April 9, "pressure exerted by the drilling mud exceeded the strength of the [deepwater rock] formation" (National Commission, 2011a, p. 91) causing fracturing. Although the cracks were able to be filled, it was determined that drilling had gone as deep as possible because of the risk of continued fracture and resulting loss. Losing returns became the "No. 1 risk" (National Commission, 2011a, p. 99) and the pressure that cement would place on the fragile formation was evaluated very carefully. To lessen the pressure of the cement, BP and Halliburton chose to use a "nitrogen foam cement" in which an even distribution of tiny bubbles create a strong but light cement. If the bubbles combine, however, this mixture can become unstable and create unequal distribution and possible fracture sites. Repeated testing of the cement mixture showed that because of environmental factors in the area the mixture would not be stable at Macondo. There is some evidence that suggests that these test failures were not communicated to BP (National Commission, 2011a, p. 101). Other indications suggest that these results were simply not emphasized:

> The Halliburton and the BP Macondo well team's technical reviews of the cement slurry design appeared to be focused primarily on achieving an acceptable circulating density during cement placement to prevent lost returns. Other important aspects of the foam cement design, such as foam stability, possible contamination effects and fluid loss potential did appear to have been critically assessed. (BP, 2010, p. 34)

For whatever reason, cement which was predicted to fail was nonetheless used to seal the well.

There was a process in place to evaluate the success of the cement job after it had been completed to make sure it had not failed. However, "success" and therefore failure were based on the criteria of having no lost returns—no loss of oil or fluids because of additional fracturing of the rock. In order to evaluate this success a decision tree had been created to assess the outcome and to establish whether further tests were needed. Because there had been full returns throughout, the job was determined to have gone well, everyone was congratulated on a job well done, and the contract evaluation team on hand to perform additional testing on the cement was deemed unnecessary and sent home. Further testing by this team may very well have found the problems with the cement job in time to be able to address them without further incident.

Later in the day, one additional required test was conducted on the cement job that could have challenged earlier assurances if it had been believed. A negative pressure test determines if the well is sealed by reducing pressure in the well to zero, sealing it with the blowout preventer, and waiting to see if the pressure remains zero or rises. Rising pressure indicates that there is a leak and hydrocarbons are entering the well. An initial negative pressure test failed—pressure continued to rise. This result, however, was explained away. A drilling expert on board the rig explained that it could be a result of a "bladder effect." This explanation was not questioned. It was easier to believe the initial findings of success and look for confirmation of it than to believe a negative result. Therefore, a second test was conducted to confirm nothing was wrong. The second test was conducted on the "kill line," a smaller parallel line to the original "drill line" that had been tested earlier. Theoretically, testing either of the two would give the same results. The test on the kill line passed. The discrepancy between the first failing and the second passing was never questioned and investigated. The second test was simply accepted as successful. In hindsight, it is clear that hydrocarbons *were* leaking into the well and the initial failed negative pressure test was accurate. Decisions about what types of tests were needed and what they indicated played a significant role in realizing too late that there were problems.

The decisions, and decision points, that were previously described represent only a portion of those flagged by investigators as problematic. There were a variety of other pivotal decisions as well as oversights and potential negligence that may have also contributed to the blowout. Space limitations make it impossible to fully lay out all that may have gone wrong on the Deepwater Horizon. Additionally, it is still somewhat unclear which factors ultimately caused the catastrophe. Nonetheless, "the most significant failure at Macondo" according to the National Commission's (2011a) final report to the president, "was a failure of industry management . . . [and the] management of decision-making processes within BP and other companies" (p. 122). Choice points, such as how many centralizers to use or what to do (or believe) about a test failure, came at every juncture.

THE COMPLEXITIES OF DECISION MAKING

So why were certain decisions made? What were the decision makers thinking? In what ways were ethics considered, or not? The most simplistic explanations about how or why decisions are made focus on costs versus benefits. Determining decision criteria helps decision makers prioritize and weigh their options rationally. In the Macondo case, time, money, productivity, and risk were obvious criteria. Operations cost nearly $1,000 per minute and thus time was of the essence. Additionally, individuals had to determine whether an option would actually work. Computer models and experience (both firsthand and the stories of others) gave information about how likely an alternative was to be productive. Risk was another consideration. As noted earlier, there are different types of risk. In hindsight we automatically think about safety risks. However, because of the problems with this particular well, the most prominent risk in the minds of the decision makers was the risk of damaging the well through fracturing the rock formation.

Imagining that decision makers based their decisions objectively on these (and potentially other) criteria, however, assumes the use of purely rational, well-informed choice. Based on this view of decision making, it would seem that the inclusion of ethics as an important decision criterion would have led to more ethical decisions. The reality, however, is simply not that straightforward. We must realize that decision makers are "bounded" (Simon, 1979)—they cannot be perfectly rational because of a number of factors, not least of which are the limitations of time and information.

In the case of the decisions in the Macondo blowout, there was a lack of information available to decision makers because of poor communication. "Each individual decision may have made some sense in isolation from the others. But together, they created a time bomb" (Barton, 2010). Because departments and/or organizations did not necessarily communicate with each other, decision makers were often not aware of the context of their decisions.

> Information appears to have been excessively compartmentalized at Macondo as a result of poor communication. . . . As a result, individuals often found themselves making critical decisions without a full appreciation for the context in which they were being made (or even without recognition that the decisions *were* critical). (National Commission, 2011a, p. 123)

For instance, people interpreting the first failed negative pressure test may have taken it more seriously if they had known that there was a strong possibility that there would be problems with the cement. The organizational complexity of interdependent companies—and even different departments within the same organization—created an environment in which the bigger picture may have been lost as individual, department-specific decisions were being made.

Time and distraction also limited decision makers. Not only was time a criterion in decision making but pressure was as well: There was very little (or no) time to carefully consider all the options. The expense of the operations cast an overall urgency to all decision processes. Dialogic communication and participation in decision making help to ensure better, more ethical choices. However, these practices take time and therefore would have been very difficult to carry out within the urgency felt by all involved with the Deepwater Horizon.

In addition, daily distractions and the need to multitask were very much a part of organizational life. For example, on the day that the explosion occurred on the Deepwater Horizon, there was a "management visibility tour" going on, a change of shift, and the wrapping up of operations at the end of the exploratory stage. The rig was hopping. Four VIPs, two from BP and two from Transocean, had come in on a helicopter that day in order to tour the rig and celebrate the success of its operations. The tour (the four VIPs along with the guides from the rig) passed through the drill shack where the negative pressure test was being conducted. In addition, since it was 5:00 p.m., the shift was about to change, and people from both shifts were squeezed into the space. This chaos may very well have led to the easy acceptance of the explanation of a "bladder effect" instead of a careful investigation into possible problems. Distraction and the tyranny of multiple urgent tasks was a very real component of organizational life.

Besides the limitations involved in making a rational decision there are also ways in which conscious decisions are not made but are instead assumed. Some alternatives and options may never come up for a formal decision; the action to be taken is "common sense." What happens is based on a collective context as informal discussions occur and a common view emerges (Mintzberg & Waters, 1990). "Decisions" are simply a rubberstamping of what has been worked out in local interactions beforehand and are thus based in organizational culture and discourse (Boden, 1994).

As noted by those appointed to study the disaster, no one made a *conscious* decision to sacrifice safety (Broder, 2010; Deepwater Horizon Study Group, 2010). However, BP's *organizational culture* was brought up time and again in the congressional hearings about the disaster. BP, according to many, was not safety conscious and the willingness to cut corners and take risk was part of its DNA. Local, daily interactions as well as strategic decisions upheld and reinforced the company's value for production over safety. BP's history of disasters, especially the 2005 Texas City refinery explosion and the 2006 Alaska oil spill, was raised as evidence of a continued "indifference to risk" (Committee on Energy and Commerce, 2010). This culture was destined to lead to (another) disaster: "When the culture of a company favors risk-taking and cutting corners above other concerns, system failures like this oil spill disaster result without direct decisions being made or tradeoffs being considered" (Edward Markey, quoted in Broder, 2010). Decisions that were made (or decision points that were ignored) occurred within a culture that valued some things more than others and made those valuations seem natural. Thus, for *ethical* decision making to be a regular occurrence within an organization, ethics must be integral within the culture of that organization.

Finally, one additional nondecision technique that should be discussed was the abdication of decision-making responsibility to bureaucratic processes and regulatory bodies. As noted earlier, a decision tree was used to determine whether or not further evaluation of the cement job was necessary. Decision trees can be very helpful, but they may not be sufficient. In this case, the underlying assumptions were faulty. The criteria used were inadequate. By using the tool, however, those making the call did not have to make a real decision; they simply had to follow the code. Following MMS regulations sometimes worked the same way. As federal regulators, MMS was charged with determining the requirements for drilling, supposedly using worker safety and environmental concerns as key criteria. Thus, when BP met the requirements they could (and did) point to regulations and/or permission as the reason for their actions. Bureaucracy took (at least some of) the responsibility out of the hands of BP personnel and put it into the regulatory system. A major flaw in this, however, was the multitude of problems with the MMS and its system of regulation. All too often, the MMS simply rubberstamped whatever BP (or others in the oil industry) proposed due to lack of personnel and resources as well as potentially inappropriate ties to the oil industry. Thus, the regulations being followed by BP did not include satisfactory safeguards. In following those requirements, BP was assured of nothing except the ability to say they had followed the rules.

ETHICS: AN INTEGRAL PART OF DECISION MAKING

Decisions are the cornerstone of ethics, but values are not always the most obvious factor in the daily, time-pressured environment of the corporate world. Decisions are complicated and contextual. Decision makers draw on available information and common understandings to choose best alternatives. In order to make better, more ethical decisions, communication must be improved and common (potentially less-than-ethical) understandings inherent in an organization's culture must be challenged. It is not until decision (and nondecision) points are recognized as *ethical* in nature and decisions become more value-oriented that companies that profess to care about their stakeholders will truly be able to walk the talk.

Prior to the Macondo blowout, BP's public discourse was one of responsibility and safety. Safety was supposedly a "top priority" at BP, and when Tony Hayward took over as CEO in 2007 he promised a "laser focus on safety" (Committee on Energy and Commerce, 2010). The company has proclaimed, "Our goals are simply stated—no accidents, no harm to people, and no damage to the environment" (Browne, 1996). This statement, from one of the earliest iterations of BP's website, has been repeated (in one form or another) every year as BP has declared its commitment to sustainability and ethical actions. Yet the Deepwater Horizon disaster (as well as previous disasters and safety violations) make cynics out of even the most trusting of onlookers. Talk is not enough. Ethical values *must* be integral in the daily decisions that determine the actions taken by an organization in order for the organization to be truly responsible.

DISCUSSION QUESTIONS

1. Although the resulting catastrophe made it evident that the decisions described in this case study had ethical implications, many did not appear to be clearly ethical choices at the time. Even though they may not have been obvious, however, ethical perspectives may have provided a foundation for some choices. What ethical perspectives, if any, did actors use as they made critical decisions?

2. How might transparency and dialogic communication have prevented the catastrophe?

3. There were many actors involved in the project. What is the appropriate level of responsibility for each of them? Should one company be fully (or partially or not at all) responsible because of its position as principal and coordinator? What is the responsibility of each partner/contract organization in making sure that the primary company is doing what is right?

4. Bureaucratic forms led, in this case, to the abdication of moral responsibility for particular decisions. Can bureaucracy ever help make our decisions more ethical? How or how can it not?

5. Acknowledging that many "decisions" are simply a reflection of common understandings and organizational culture, how can we encourage better, more ethical decision making within our own organizations?

6. Within a complex organizational structure like the one described in this case study, how would you suggest improving communication, especially with regard to providing the context necessary for decision makers to make the best decisions?

REFERENCES

Barton, J. (2010, June 17). *Opening statement of the Honorable Joe Barton, ranking member, Committee on Energy and Commerce, Subcommittee on Oversight and Investigations Hearing on the role of BP in the Deepwater Horizon explosion and oil spill.* Retrieved from http://republicans.energycommerce.house.gov/News/PRArticle.aspx?NewsID = 7942

Boden, D. (1994). *The business of talk: Organizations in action.* London: Polity Press.

BP. (2009). *Sustainability review 2009: Operating at the energy frontiers.* Retrieved from http://www.bp.com/liveassets/bp_internet/globalbp/STAGING/global_assets/e_s_assets/e_s_assets_2009/downloads_pdfs/bp_sustainability_review_2009.pdf

BP. (2010). *Deepwater Horizon accident investigation report.* Retrieved from http://www.bp.com/liveassets/bp_internet/globalbp/globalbp_uk_english/incident_response/STAGING/local_assets/downloads_pdfs/Deepwater_Horizon_Accident_Investigation_Report.pdf

Broder, J. M. (2010, November 8). Investigator finds no evidence that BP took shortcuts to save money. *New York Times.* Retrieved from http://www.nytimes.com/2010/11/09/us/09spill.html

Browne, J. (1996, November 1). *BP's commitment to health, safety and environmental performance.* Retrieved from http://web.archive.org/web/19970127223645/www.bp.com/health.html

Committee on Energy and Commerce: Subcommittee on Oversight and Investigations. (2010, June 17). *Hearing on "The role of BP in the Deepwater Horizon explosion and oil spill"* [video]. Retrieved from http://democrats.energycommerce.house.gov/index.php?q = hearing/hearing-on-the-role-of-bp-in-the-deepwater-horizon-explosion-and-oil-spill

Deepwater Horizon Study Group. (2010, November 24). *Letter to the National Commission on the BP Deepwater Horizon Oil Spill and Offshore Drilling.* Retrieved from http://www.oilspillcommission.gov/sites/default/files/documents/DHSG % 20letter % 2011 % 2024 % 2010.pdf

Dell'Amore, C. (2010, May 4). Gulf oil spill a "dead zone in the making"? *National Geographic News.* Retrieved from http://news.nationalgeographic.com/news/2010/05/100504-science-environment-gulf-oil-spill-dead-zone/

Hayward, T. (Interviewee). (2010, April 28). BP CEO outraged over oil spill [video]. *CNN.* Retrieved from http://edition.cnn.com/video/#/video/us/2010/04/28/tsr.intv.todd.hayward.cnn

Mabus, R. (2010). *America's Gulf Coast: A long term recovery plan after the Deepwater Horizon oil spill.* Retrieved from http://www.oilspillcommission.gov/sites/default/files/documents/Mabus_Report.pdf

Mintzberg, H., & Waters, J. (1990). Studying deciding: An exchange of views between Mintzberg, Waters, Pettigrew, and Butler. *Organization Studies, 11*(1), 1–16.

National Commission on the BP Deepwater Horizon Oil Spill and Offshore Drilling. (2011a). *Deepwater: The Gulf oil disaster and the future of offshore drilling: Report to the president.* Retrieved from http://www.oilspillcommission.gov/final-report

National Commission on the BP Deepwater Horizon Oil Spill and Offshore Drilling. (2011b). *The amount and fate of the oil: Staff working paper no. 3.* Retrieved from http://www.oilspillcommission.gov/sites/default/files/documents/Updated % 20Amount % 20and % 20Fate % 20of % 20the % 20Oil % 20Working % 20Paper.pdf

National Commission on the BP Deepwater Horizon Oil Spill and Offshore Drilling. (2011c). *The use of surface and subsea dispersants during the BP Deepwater Horizon oil spill: Staff working paper no. 4*. Retrieved from http://www.oilspillcommission.gov/sites/default/files/documents/Updated%20Dispersants%20Working%20Paper.pdf

NBC, MSNBC.com, & News Services. (2010, June 4). Obama lashes out at BP on Gulf visit. *MSNBC*. Retrieved from http://www.msnbc.msn.com/id/37463005/ns/disaster_in_the_gulf/

Oxford Economics. (2010, December). *Tourism economics: The impact of the BP oil spill on visitor spending in Louisiana*. Retrieved from http://www.crt.state.la.us/tourism/research/Documents/2010-11/OilSpillTourismImpacts20101215.pdf

Phillips, D. (2010, August 19). *It's BP vs. Transocean in a colossal fight over liability for the Gulf oil spill*. Retrieved from http://www.bnet.com/blog/sec-filings/it-8217s-bp-vs-transocean-in-a-colossal-fight-over-liability-for-the-gulf-oil-spill/513?tag = content;drawer-container

Simon, H. A. (1979). Rational decision making in business organizations. *The American Economic Association, 69*(4), 493–513.

Solomon, G. M., & Janssen, S. (2010). Health effects of the Gulf oil spill. *The Journal of the American Medical Association, 34*(10), 1118–1119.

White, J. (2010, October 15). BP oil spill may cost Louisiana fishing industry $172 million. *Times-Picayune*. Retrieved from http://www.nola.com/business/index.ssf/2010/10/bp_oil_spill_may_cost_louisian.html

Outsourcing U.S. Intelligence

Hamilton Bean

This case examines the role of private sector contractors who conduct intelligence operations and other "inherently governmental" activities, including those affecting the life, liberty, or property of private persons. It explores the ethical paradoxes of outsourcing U.S. intelligence, considering the tension between the efficacy and ethics of such practices. Finally, it questions whether the ethics of intelligence operations should be codified as a set of normative guidelines or understood as context-specific and, therefore, situational.

The *New York Times* reported on March 14, 2010, that Michael D. Furlong, a senior U.S. Defense Department official, had "under the cover of a benign government information-gathering program" developed a network of private sector contractors to help track and kill suspected militants in Afghanistan and Pakistan (Filkins & Mazzetti, 2010). Specifically, in 2008, Furlong oversaw a $24 million Lockheed Martin program called Capstone that used subcontracted firms to gather information about Afghanistan's political and tribal cultures. Former CIA, Psychological Operations (PSYOPs), and Special Forces operatives staffed some of the subcontracted firms, including Strategic Influence Alternatives, Inc.; American International Security Corporation; and International Media Ventures. Additionally, business partners Eason Jordan (a former CNN executive) and Robert Young Pelton (author of *The World's Most Dangerous Places*) indirectly participated in Capstone through the development of a subscription news service and database geared toward U.S. military personnel: *AfPax Insider*. According to the Pentagon, officials used some of the information gathered under Capstone to plan lethal strikes against militants (Mazzetti, 2010c). The CIA's station chief in Kabul alerted the Pentagon to the possible illegality of Capstone in December 2009; however, the program continued until May 2010—2 months after the *New York Times* initially broke the story.

Executive orders, institutional memoranda, and the U.S. Code generally prohibit private sector contractors from conducting intelligence operations and other "inherently governmental" activities, including those affecting the life, liberty, or property of private persons (Chesterman, 2008; DeYoung, 2010; Ignatius, 2010; Office of the Director of National Intelligence [ODNI], 2009). Therefore, in his response to the alleged "off-the-books" intelligence operation, U.S. Defense Secretary Robert Gates directed a top aide, Michael Decker, to investigate whether U.S. policy or legal guidelines were ignored (Mazzetti, 2010a). Decker's 15-page classified report, reviewed by the Associated Press, accused Furlong of overstepping his authority and concluded that rules governing intelligence needed to be more clearly defined (Mazzetti, 2010c). Additional Pentagon and Air Force investigations into Capstone were underway as this case study was going to print.

Intelligence outsourcing represents an ethical quandary—Furlong referred to himself as "the king of the gray areas" (Mazzetti, 2010b). In the case of Capstone, the ethicality (and legality) of the program hinges on interpretations of the concepts of "intelligence" and "information." The ethical norms underlying military "intelligence collection" differ from private sector "information gathering." This situation demonstrates how "two different norms, both claiming sovereignty over ethics in their own context of application, may clash when enacted together" (Clegg, Kornberger, & Rhodes, 2007, p. 112). Organizational communication scholars have recently turned their attention to how such discursive clash generates associated tensions, paradoxes, and dilemmas (Grant, Hardy, Oswick, & Putnam, 2004). Controversies surrounding Blackwater's operations in Iraq, alleged abuse by Titan and CACI employees at Abu Ghraib prison, and contractor participation in waterboarding CIA detainees (Gorman, 2008) underscore that market-based government[1] can pit the values of efficiency and effectiveness against countervailing concerns for lawfulness, transparency, and accountability (Adams & Balfour, 2010). Despite questions surrounding the ethicality of private sector intelligence gathering, the industry's main trade association—the Intelligence and National Security Alliance—currently provides no ethical guidelines or codes of conduct for its 100 corporate members.

THE ETHICAL AMBIGUITIES OF INTELLIGENCE OUTSOURCING

Contractors have always been an integral part of U.S. military operations; even George Washington's Continental Army made use of civilian contractors during the American Revolutionary War (Dies, 2007). However, the scope and scale of contracting increased dramatically during the Cold War, leading President Eisenhower to warn Americans in 1961 of the dangers of a permanent armaments industry (the "military-industrial complex"). While the post–Cold War "peace dividend" shrunk defense and intelligence budgets by more than 30%, the proliferation of new threats and conflicts (e.g., Somalia, Haiti, and Bosnia) stretched tight resources. As a result, agencies increasingly turned to contracting and outsourcing[2] to supplement their efforts. After the September 11, 2001, terrorist attacks in the United States, contracting with or outsourcing to private sector corporations soared to an estimated 70% of overall U.S. intelligence spending on goods, services, and personnel (Shorrock, 2008).

---

[1] Market-based government refers to contracting, outsourcing, competitive sourcing, privatizing, and engaging in public–private partnerships (Adams & Balfour, 2010).

[2] According to Lahneman (2003), "outsourcing" within the Intelligence Community "refers to the practice of . . . turning over entire business functions to an outside vendor that ostensibly can perform the specialized tasks in question better and less expensively than it can" (p. 573). "Contracting," by contrast, refers to the process of integrating a company's employees into a government agency's existing staff and normal operations as a way to gain needed expertise and skill sets. In practice, however, the term contracting out is often synonymous with outsourcing.

The outsourcing of U.S. intelligence vividly illustrates the "corporate colonization" of national security (Deetz, 1992). Indeed, the ODNI acknowledged in 2009 that private sector contractors constitute nearly one third of the U.S. intelligence community's workforce (ODNI, 2009). The estimated $40 billion private intelligence sector consists of major defense contractors including Lockheed Martin, Booz Allen Hamilton, BAE Systems, Northrop Grumman, and SAIC, among many others (Shorrock, 2008) as well as smaller, specialized intelligence "shops" (Harris, 2005).

In "Outsourcing the IC's [Intelligence Community's] Stovepipes?" intelligence scholar William Lahneman (2003) speculated whether outsourcing might actually improve agencies' efficiency and effectiveness. Lahneman noted that intelligence agencies resemble large corporations in three ways: (1) both are secretive, (2) both maintain subunits that compete for scarce resources while simultaneously promoting the organization as a whole, and (3) both must "contract, partner, or outsource to other organizations for specific expertise" (p. 575). An ostensible benefit of outsourcing includes the ability to rapidly secure specialized skills on a temporary basis (but often at a higher cost than were the government to hire employees "in-house"). Lahneman noted that intelligence agencies and corporations differ in that the latter are compelled to maximize profit and are able to exit markets when business conditions are unfavorable. U.S. intelligence agencies, by contrast, must maximize *performance* by anticipating/preventing harm to national interests, and agencies must continually acquire information about adversaries despite extreme risk and cost. As a result, Lahneman argued that setting strategic priorities for intelligence agencies, as well as assembling and disseminating intelligence products[3] in order to inform U.S. national security policy, are inherently governmental functions and should not be outsourced. The "vast majority" of intelligence *collection* activities and "many" *analytical* tasks are nevertheless "good candidates" for outsourcing, according to Lahneman (pp. 583–589). In summary, although intelligence agencies differ from corporations in their fundamental purpose, according to Lahneman, agencies would do well to outsource intelligence collection and analysis in pursuit of efficiency and effectiveness.

Philosophy professor Christopher Caldwell (2010) opposes Lahneman's position and argued, "The use of private businesses to gather intelligence for the purposes of national security . . . constitutes a serious moral wrong" (p. 32). For Caldwell, when corporations pursue profit in an environment with scant regulatory oversight, it is likely that those corporations will act unethically: "Whereas a government has pressure to uphold international laws and human rights, a business has a direct economic incentive to disregard these if it is helpful to gather more information to increase profitability" (p. 41). For Caldwell, the democratic values of life and liberty may too easily become subjugated to the value of profit in a privatized intelligence system. Even when corporations are caught circumventing rights to liberty (e.g., contractor-generated "no-fly" lists that erroneously include the names of law-abiding citizens on them), those corporations are often shielded from official accountability because they are not responsible to citizens in the same way as government agencies.

Philosopher James Roper (2010) agreed with Caldwell, stating, "In general, it would be unethical to use private corporations to conduct intelligence activities for national security

---

[3] Intelligence "products" refer to documents and presentations such as the President's Daily Brief (PDB) and the National Intelligence Estimate (NIE).

purposes" (p. 47). Roper's argument rests on the differing social functions of business and government, with the latter required to give all citizens a voice, protect rights and liberties, balance numerous societal functions (security, public health, social services, etc.), and ensure "socially optimal" balances among competing priorities. Roper concluded, "'Contracting out' anything but the most trivial aspects of [intelligence] is tantamount to contracting out our national defense. . . . doing this is tantamount to changing the very nature of our nation" (p. 66). Roper did not indicate whether he considers collection and analysis "trivial" intelligence activities.[4]

While Lahneman invokes the values of efficiency and effectiveness in support of the ethicality of intelligence outsourcing, Caldwell and Roper invoke the ideals of life and liberty to assert that outsourcing intelligence is generally *unethical*. Instead of seeking a definitive answer, the perspective developed here views the following:

> the ethical theorist [as] an "interpreter" rather than a "legislator" . . . of practice, with a concern for how ethical systems come to bear on concrete practices of managing and decision-making, and how the potentially different ethical systems of different stakeholders interact with and, at times, come into conflict with each other. (Clegg et al., 2007, p. 118)

Organizational communication scholarship makes a unique contribution to the study of ethics through analysis of how speech and writing *mediate* conflicting ethical discourses in specific organizational situations requiring moral agency (Grant et al., 2004; Kuhn, 2009).

ETHICS AS PRACTICE

The academic subfield of *intelligence ethics* (Goldman, 2006) is more or less focused on one central question: Are individual ethics and the practices of intelligence agencies commensurable? The goal of this subfield is to establish "[an ethical] framework that can transcend the intelligence community" and "enable [intelligence] practitioners to define their responsibilities, provide guidance, inspire, motivate, raise awareness and consciousness, as well as improve the quality and consistency of the work they perform" (p. xiii). This conception of ethics rests on "a theoretical normativism that assumes that the ethical distinction between 'right' and 'wrong' can be codified and then applied in order to ascertain whether certain actions or behaviors are deemed ethical or unethical" (Clegg et al., 2007, p. 109).

By contrast, *ethics as practice* is a theoretical perspective that goes beyond concerns for idealized, control-oriented frameworks and rule-bound codes of conduct to "situations of ambiguity where dilemmas and problems will be dealt with without the comfort of consensus or certitude" (Clegg et al., 2007, p. 109). An ethics as practice perspective also goes

---

[4] According to the ODNI's "Key Facts About Contractors" (2009), "The Intelligence Community does not condone or permit contract personnel to perform inherently governmental intelligence work, as defined by OMB Circular A-76 revised, and reinforced recently in Intelligence Community Directive 612. Core contract personnel may perform activities such as collection and analysis; however, it is what you do with that analysis, who makes that decision, and who oversees the work that constitute the 'inherently governmental' functions."

beyond utilitarian maxims (e.g., "the greatest good for the greatest number") to investigate what people actually do vis-à-vis ethics at work, directing awareness "not towards models that define, predict or judge ethics in and of themselves, but rather towards an examination of how ethics are differentially embedded in practices that operate in an active and contextualized manner" (pp. 110–111). Importantly for this case, Clegg et al. (2007) pointed to how people use ethical discourses opportunistically:

> It is not that [ethical] codes produce people's social actions but that skilled social actors will from time-to-time use codes to accomplish those actions that they seek to bring off. Organizational members engage with such formulations as a potential instrument of power that can be used to legitimize one's own and delegitimize another's standpoint in power relations. (p. 113)

Within this perspective, ethical uncertainties, contradictions, and incoherencies are accounted for rather than dismissed as inconsistent with transcendental moral models, principles, and prescriptions. However, ethics as practice does not require "a slide into relativism"; instead, it encourages people to see how the moral principles that guide our actions need to be continually open to questioning and revision—not abandonment (Clegg et al., 2007, p. 118).

Ethics as practice focuses on the multiple discourses that retrospectively organize, categorize, make sense of, and judge behaviors. The "revolving door" between government and industry and the similarities between institutional and corporate cultures within the intelligence sector (Keyton, 2005) ensure that actors have "ready-at-hand" several convincing discursive resources to persuade themselves and others of the virtue of outsourcing within the national security arena (Kuhn, 2009, p. 698). Analyzing the situated judgments and discursive resources of intelligence stakeholders is extremely difficult given the institutional strictures of secrecy. Nevertheless, organizational communication scholar Timothy Kuhn (2009) provides a way of examining judgments by analyzing actors' "accounts" of them. For Kuhn, "Accounting involves an individual responding to an explicit or implicit accusation, providing a . . . commentary that can reveal the discourses acting upon, and sanctioning, particular subject positions" (p. 684). Such accounts involve the strategic use of discursive resources—that is, "concepts, expressions, or other linguistic devices that, when deployed in talk, present explanations for past and/or future activity that guide interactants' interpretation of experience while molding individual and collective action" (Kuhn, 2006, p. 1341). These accounts "reveal the discourses acting upon, and sanctioning, particular identities while also exposing rules for appropriate activity" (p. 1341). Discourses, in turn, "constitute the substrate for organizing by providing sets of representations, statements, narratives, images, and codes that produce ways of seeing objects and events" (p. 1342). The remainder of this case draws on interview material contained in news reports to describe the discursive resources that actors involved in Capstone used to account for their own and others' actions.[5]

---

[5] According to Kuhn (2009), "if researchers seek to comprehend the forces shaping workplace subjectivities and practices, examining the discursive resources deployed in interview responses makes methodological sense" (p. 696).

DISCOURSE AS A STRATEGIC (ETHICAL) RESOURCE

Capstone was first conceptualized in July 2008 after 200 Taliban insurgents ambushed U.S. forces in Wanat, Afghanistan (DeYoung, 2010). In responding to the event, then-commander of U.S. forces in Afghanistan General David McKiernan called for an information service that would use regional experts to establish better situational awareness—"ground truth"—for U.S. forces (Ignatius, 2010). The U.S. military's frustration with the quality of intelligence it was receiving about Afghanistan surfaced publically in January 2010. A report from NATO's senior intelligence official, Major General Michael Flynn, declared the following:

> Eight years into the war in Afghanistan, the U.S. intelligence community is only marginally relevant to the overall strategy. Having focused the overwhelming majority of its collection efforts and analytical brainpower on insurgent groups, the vast intelligence apparatus is unable to answer fundamental questions about the environment in which U.S. and allied forces operate and the people they seek to persuade. (Flynn, Pottinger, & Batchelor, 2010, p. 7)

The report concluded that intelligence analysts "must embrace open-source, population-centric information as the lifeblood of their analytical work. They must open their doors to anyone who is willing to exchange information, including Afghans and NGOs as well as the U.S. military and its allies" (Flynn et al., 2010, p. 23).

Within this context, Eason Jordan and Robert Young Pelton proposed AfPax to General McKiernan. The subscription service would use employees and informants to interview local officials, including militia leaders, and provide reports on the general situation in the provinces (Stein, 2010). The subscription service would be open to almost anyone, but the bulk of the funding and subscribers would come from the U.S. military (which would also obtain exclusive access to a specialized database). General McKiernan endorsed Jordan and Pelton's proposal and introduced the two men to Furlong to help arrange funding and contract management. General David Petraeus, then-Commander of U.S. Central Command (CENTCOM), wrote a January 2009 letter endorsing the proposed program, and a CENTCOM legal opinion stamped "Secret" approved it—adding specific language that it should not carry out "inherent intelligence activities" (Mazzetti, 2010b).

Furlong—who had previously run psychological operations and propaganda programs for the U.S. military in Bosnia, Kosovo, and Iraq—also used other Capstone subcontractors to gather information about Afghan tribal structures and the workings of militant groups (Chatterjee, 2010). In the process, these subcontractors would occasionally glean detailed information about "suspected militants and the location of insurgent camps" (Chatterjee, 2010). Officially, Furlong worked in strategic communications for General Petraeus, but instead of focusing on strategic communications' core task of "deliberately . . . communicating and engaging with intended audiences" (The White House, 2009, p. 2), Capstone reports fed directly into the military operations center in Kabul and were transmitted to high-ranking Pentagon and CIA officials for "possible lethal action in Afghanistan and Pakistan" (Filkins & Mazzetti, 2010).

In June 2009, Jordan and Pelton were abruptly told that their services were no longer needed: Rear Admiral Gregory Smith, the U.S. military's director for strategic communications in Afghanistan, said the following:

> He did not need what Mr. Pelton and Mr. Jordan were offering and that the service seemed uncomfortably close to crossing into intelligence gathering—which could have meant making targets of individuals. "I took the air out of the balloon," [Admiral Smith] said. (Filkins & Mazzetti, 2010)

Furlong, however, continued to advocate for AfPax. Admiral Smith responded, "I finally had to tell him, 'Read my lips, we're not interested'" (Filkins & Mazzetti, 2010). Furlong then turned to International Media Ventures (which, because of arcane subcontracting processes, had provided start-up funds to AfPax) and American International Security Corporation to gather information with the remaining Capstone funds.

Furlong speculated that Jordan and Pelton—angered at being cut out of the program— eventually tipped off the CIA and the media to Capstone's activities (Contreras, 2010). Pelton has denied the accusations (Masters, 2010). Nevertheless, in an August 2009 assessment, General Stanley McChrystal, by then the top U.S. commander in Afghanistan, wrote that Capstone subcontracts "should be supported as these will significantly enhance . . . monitoring and assessment efforts" (Chatterjee, 2010). Given these ambiguities, the *New York Times'* exposé prompted Capstone participants to persuade audiences of their ethicality using two overarching discursive resources: what I term (1) *oscillation* and (2) *strategic ambiguity.* The possibility of criminal prosecution, ostracism, and/or being excluded from future contracting opportunities precluded a simple strategy of denial or avoidance.

Managing Ethics Via Discursive Oscillation

Following the *New York Times'* initial story, Pelton asserted that he had repeatedly told Furlong that AfPax was not to be used to bolster intelligence operations in the region. Pelton claimed that it was "a constant battle with Furlong," who was "trying to push us in that direction [intelligence gathering for lethal strikes]" (O'Connor, 2010). Pelton claimed to have told Furlong that "'kinetic action' (i.e., drone strikes) were incompatible with 'the now accepted counter-insurgency strategy'" that relied on awareness of wider sociocultural and political conditions in the region. Colleagues told Pelton that video images that he had posted on AfPax had been used for a strike in the South Waziristan region of Pakistan (Filkins & Mazzetti, 2010). Pelton told *CorpWatch* that after he learned about Furlong's "real intentions," AfPax opted out of the Capstone program: "When we suspected [what Furlong] was doing . . . we protested. That moral stand cost us millions" (Chatterjee, 2010). However, the *Washington Post* reported on May 25, 2010, that AfPax was shuttered not because of any moral stand but because the *New York Times'* story potentially placed the organization's network of informants in harm's way. Jordan and Pelton feared that AfPax employees "could be branded as spies and killed because of the publicity" (Stein, 2010).

To persuade audiences of his morality, Pelton relied on a strategy of identifying with national security norms while distancing himself from the symbolically tainted categories of "spy" and "contractor." He declared that he and Jordan were "'not spies and not contractors, but open-source information providers' who got caught in the middle of what might be 'a CIA Frankenstein'" (O'Connor, 2010). Pelton even persuaded the *New York Times* to amend its initial March 14 story: "An earlier version of this story and an accompanying picture caption misstated the occupation of Robert Young Pelton. He is a writer, not a government contractor" (Stein, 2010). Pelton explained, "The narrative has become Blackwater-like. . . . The unstated assumption is that we are the same sort of 'contractors' as Blackwater" (O'Connor, 2010).

However, Pelton's identification with accepted ethical principles regarding the role of contractors in intelligence operations was selective. He explained the following during an interview with commentator Ian Masters (2010):

> We provided . . . interviews with Taliban leadership in which we inserted questions from [U.S.] commanders on the ground essentially creating a dialogue between the Taliban and the U.S. military. We provided transcripts for . . . radio mullahs . . . details of the squabbling going on inside the Taliban leadership, etc., etc. It's all good stuff.

However, Pelton incongruously asserted during the interview: "We're no different than if you hired *The New York Times* to do a story." Pelton tried to emphasize the value of AfPax to the U.S. military while simultaneously distancing AfPax from the realm of intelligence:

> I don't say that Mike Furlong was a bad person for trying to kill terrorists. I really have no problem with that. I just didn't want him to use our contract vehicle to do that with. And keep in mind, we were actually the "white hat" guys: If you wanted to meet a member of the Taliban, we would go do that on your behalf or introduce you in a meeting. And one of our strengths was that we were able to sit at the "General" level—set up a meeting in a restaurant with Taliban commanders inside Kabul—and they could discuss whatever they wanted to discuss, and no one would be the wiser. So, we were a fairly interesting asset that the military used. (Masters, 2010)

Pelton's comments indicate how he strategically oscillated between commercial and national security discourses to account for the ethicality of his practices. Capstone participants appealed to the values of efficiency and effectiveness in response to explicit or implicit questions regarding the appropriateness of having private sector organizations conduct work that could be construed as intelligence operations. For example, Pelton commented, "The CIA operates in Pakistan, and the DoD [Defense Department] can't, and they're [the CIA] fairly ineffective inside Afghanistan, so we [AfPax] embarrassed the agency [the CIA]" (Masters, 2010). Pelton suggested that the CIA's embarrassment might have spurred the agency to terminate Capstone:

> The problem is that the General [McChrystal] needed what we were providing. So that got sandbagged [by either Furlong or the CIA], and instead this haphazard

"Jason Bourne" operation flourished . . . so, now what is happening is that people like Major General Flynn don't have the basic information they need to make decisions. (Masters, 2010)

Pelton implied that the U.S. military was incapable of making decisions in the absence of his company's services, which he hoped would be recontracted: "We hope that the end result of all this publicity is that people realize that there are cheap and effective ways to find out what's going on on-the-ground in Afghanistan," he said (Masters, 2010). Furlong similarly appealed to the values of efficiency and effectiveness, telling the *San Antonio Express-News*: "[Capstone] is not about anything but providing the best force protection we can provide all of those 20-somethings in foxholes . . . It's about saving lives" (Contreras, 2010). During this interview, Furlong attempted to concatenate the values of "effectiveness" and "life" while simultaneously asserting Capstone's benign nature: The collection teams that Furlong supervised did not "go around 'kicking in doors' and killing people" (Contreras, 2010). Furlong constructed an image of immoral mercenaries to emphasize that Capstone was not involved in such practices—and therefore, ethically sound. In summary, oscillation between the discourses of national security and commerce enabled Capstone participants to opportunistically account for the ethicality of their practices in the face of implicit and explicit charges of immorality.

Managing Ethics Via Strategic Ambiguity

Organizational communication scholar Eric Eisenberg (1984) described how managers may use ambiguous messages to preserve their privileged positions and deflect blame. Strategic ambiguity "takes advantage of the diverse meanings that different people can give to the same message"; when under pressure, words that seem to mean one thing can be asserted to mean something else (Eisenberg, Goodall, & Trethewey, 2007, pp. 32–33). For example, Tom Johnson, a former chairman and chief executive of CNN and a mentor to Eason Jordan, remarked the following to a reporter:

> There is a bright red line between information gathering for open source reporting and information gathering for classified use by intelligence agencies. . . . I said repeatedly to Eason that he was getting into a zone of significant risk to his reputation . . . Eason told me . . . his organization gathered information for open source use and that he did not violate my guidance. (Stein, 2010)

Furlong similarly asserted that the role of Capstone contractors was to "collect information that is openly available, such as banter at markets or bazaars that might contain information about potential attacks on U.S. interests" (Contreras, 2010). Furlong claimed that he would "take stuff in open source and throw it into the intelligence pipeline. . . . I don't take this information and go directly to a kill" (Contreras, 2010). Capstone participants thus attempted to differentiate between open source information and intelligence in ways that supported the ethicality of their practices. This discursive strategy may be problematic in that other government officials and corporate executives have sought to *equate* open source information and intelligence. For example, an objective of the ODNI's Open Source Center is to "redefine 'open source' as one of the 21st Century's [sic] most important sources of intelligence."[6]

An ethics as practice perspective encourages investigators to locate the specific vocabulary that stakeholders use to justify their actions. In the case of Capstone, that vocabulary includes the concepts of "force protection" and "atmospherics." While paying private sector corporations to gather "intelligence" appeared objectionable, paying them to gather defensive "force protection" information was not. Additionally, "atmospheric collection" regarding the general workings of militant groups and tribal structures was not rhetorically equivalent to "intelligence." Furlong told the *Express-News* that Capstone produced "more than 260 'atmospheric protection reports' and that their work helped thwart the assassinations of Afghan allies" (Thompson & Mazzetti, 2010). In practice, stakeholders apparently used these vague terms "to skirt military restrictions on intelligence gathering" (Mazzetti, 2010b). According to unnamed Defense Department officials, Capstone contractors themselves did as follows:

> regarded the contract as permission to spy. . . . one of the contractors reported on Taliban militants massing near American military bases east of Kandahar. Not long afterward, Apache gunships arrived at the scene to disperse and kill the militants. (Mazzetti, 2010b)

General McKiernan, however, said in an interview with the *New York Times:*

> [McKiernan] never endorsed hiring private contractors specifically for intelligence gathering. Instead, he said, he was interested in gaining "atmospherics" from the contractors to help him and his commanders understand the complex cultural and political makeup of the region. "It could give us a better understanding of the rural areas, of what people there [are] saying, what they were expressing as their needs, and their concerns," he said. "It was not intelligence for manhunts," he said. 'That was clearly not it, and we agreed that's not what this was about." To his mind, he said, intelligence is specific information that could be used for attacks on militants in Afghanistan. (Mazzetti, 2010b)

Here, McKiernan's use of strategic ambiguity shifted blame to Capstone participants: McKiernan depicted himself as simply interested in gaining vague-yet-useful "atmospherics"— not the "intelligence" that Capstone participants gathered to target and kill militants.

In summary, in this case, advocates of market-based government used the discursive resources of oscillation and strategic ambiguity to opportunistically manage the ethical tensions generated when national security norms collide with commercial imperatives. The use of these two discursive resources enabled Capstone participants to deflect accusations of immorality, shift blame, preserve their expertise and authority, and demonstrate their ethicality.

---

[6] Open Source Center, https://www.opensource.gov/

SUMMARY

Critics of market-based government have focused on the ethical conflict between profit maximization and countervailing commitments to lawfulness, transparency, and accountability (Adams & Balfour, 2010). A communication perspective is useful for explaining how stakeholders discursively encourage or discourage corrective reforms in the face of persistent corporate abuses (Conrad, 2004). Specifically, by pinpointing how actors strategically and opportunistically draw on discursive resources to persuade themselves and others of the ethicality of their practices, communication appears to be the conceptual bridge needed to understand how advocates of market-based government are able to successfully dismiss or refute charges of immorality. Clegg et al. (2007) would encourage readers of this book to "refrain from generalizing judgments [about ethics] and focus on local meaning and sensemaking practices that constitute ethics" (p. 119). Along these lines, this case provided readers with a glimpse of how intelligence stakeholders leveraged national security and commercial discourses to their advantage. The blurring boundaries among government agencies, commercial firms, and the concepts of intelligence and information created conditions rife with ethical ambiguities. The ongoing struggle over the meanings of and relationships among these concepts ensures that determining the ethicality of intelligence outsourcing will remain an elusive task.

DISCUSSION QUESTIONS

1. How do American cultural values promote outsourcing/contracting within the U.S. national security arena?

2. Are some national security activities inherently governmental functions that should not be outsourced or contracted to private-sector corporations? Why or why not?

3. How do trade-offs among the values of transparency, accountability, efficiency, and effectiveness generate ethical tensions in the U.S. national security arena?

4. Would a financial penalty for errors force government contractors to be more accountable? What might be the consequences of such a requirement?

5. This case identified two discursive resources that stakeholders used to manage ethical tensions surrounding intelligence outsourcing. Can you identify other discursive resources used in other areas of government?

6. How does an "ethics as practice" perspective differ from other conceptualizations of ethics presented in this book?

REFERENCES

Adams, G. B., & Balfour, D. L. (2010). Market-based government and the decline of organizational ethics. *Administration & Society, 42*, 615–637.

Caldwell, C. M. (2010). Privatized information gathering: Just war theory and morality. *International Journal of Intelligence Ethics, 1*(2), 32–45.

Chatterjee, P. (2010, March 16). Afghanistan spy contract goes sour for Pentagon. *CorpWatch*. Retrieved from http://www.corpwatch.org/article.php?id = 15550.

Chesterman, S. (2008). "We can't spy . . . if we can't buy!": The privatization of intelligence and the limits of outsourcing 'inherently governmental functions'. *European Journal of International Law*, *19*, 1055–1074.

Clegg, S., Kornberger, M., & Rhodes, C. (2007). Business ethics as practice. *British Journal of Management*, *18*, 107–122.

Conrad, C. (2004). The illusion of reform: Corporate discourse and agenda denial in the 2002 "corporate meltdown." *Rhetoric & Public Affairs*, *7*, 311–338.

Contreras, G. (2010, March 18). Info-gathering office defended. *San Antonio Express-News*, p. 01A.

Deetz, S. A. (1992). *Democracy in an age of corporate colonization: Developments in communication and the politics of everyday life*. Albany: State University of New York Press.

DeYoung, K. (2010, March 19). Defense official says Afghan program was authorized. *Washington Post*. Retrieved from http://www.washingtonpost.com/wp-dyn/content/article/2010/03/18/AR2010031805447.html

Dies, H., Jr. (2007, July 1). Guide to the proper use of civilian intelligence contractors in the War on Terrorism. *Military Intelligence Professional Bulletin*. Retrieved from http://findarticles.com/p/articles/mi_m0IBS/is_3_33/ai_n31128427/

Eisenberg, E. M. (1984). Ambiguity as strategy in organizational communication. *Communication Monographs*, *51*, 227–242.

Eisenberg, E. M., Goodall, H. L., Jr., & Trethewey, A. (2007). *Organizational communication: Balancing creativity and constraint*, 5th ed. New York: Bedford/St. Martin's.

Filkins, D., & Mazzetti, M. (2010, March 14). Contractors tied to effort to track and kill militants. *New York Times*, p. A1.

Flynn, M. T., Pottinger, M., & Batchelor, P. D. (2010). *Fixing intel: A blueprint for making intelligence relevant in Afghanistan*. Washington, DC: Center for a New American Security.

Goldman, J. (Ed.) (2006). *Ethics of spying: A reader for the intelligence professional*. Lanham, MD: The Scarecrow Press, Inc.

Gorman, S. (2008, February 8). CIA likely let contractors perform waterboarding. *Wall Street Journal*, p. A3.

Grant, D., Hardy, C., Oswick, C., & Putnam, L. (Eds.). (2004). *The Sage handbook of organizational discourse*. Thousand Oaks, CA: Sage.

Harris, S. (2005, May 15). Intelligence incorporated. *Government Executive Magazine*, *37*, 40–47.

Ignatius, D. (2010, March 18). When the CIA's intelligence-gathering isn't enough. *Washington Post*. Retrieved from http://www.washingtonpost.com/wp-dyn/content/article/2010/03/16/AR2010031602625.html

Key facts about contractors. (2009). Retrieved from www.dni.gov/content/Truth_About_Contractors.pdf

Keyton, J. (2005). *Communication and organizational culture: A key to understanding work experiences*. Thousand Oaks, CA: Sage.

Kuhn, T. (2006). A "demented work ethic" and a "lifestyle firm": Discourse, identity, and workplace time commitments. *Organization Studies*, *27*, 1339–1358.

Kuhn, T. (2009). Positioning lawyers: Discursive resources, professional ethics and identification. *Organization*, *16*, 681–704.

Lahneman, W. J. (2003). Outsourcing the IC's stovepipes. *International Journal of Intelligence and CounterIntelligence*, *16*, 573–593.

Masters, I. (2010, March 15). *Robert Young Pelton & Ian Masters Pt 1—15 March 2010*. Retrieved from http://www.youtube.com/watch?v = Gr9AXRowUbY.

Mazzetti, M. (2010a, April 27). U.S. begins inquiry on spy network in Pakistan. *New York Times*, p. A9.

Mazzetti, M. (2010b, May 15). U.S. is still using private spy ring, despite doubts. *New York Times,* p. A1.

Mazzetti, M. (2010c, October 28). Inquiry finds U.S. official set up spy ring in Asia. *New York Times,* p. A10.

O'Connor, R. (2010, May 18). International media mis-adventures: The Pentagon's private and secret spy ring. *Huffington Post.* Retrieved from http://www.huffingtonpost.com/rory-oconnor /international-media-mis-a_b_580304.html

Office of the Director of National Intelligence. (2009). *Key facts about contractors.* Retrieved from www.dni.gov/content/Truth_About_Contractors.pdf

Roper, J. E. (2010). Using private corporations to conduct intelligence activities for national security purposes: An ethical appraisal. *International Journal of Intelligence Ethics, 1*(2), 46–73.

Shorrock, T. (2008). *Spies for hire: The secret world of intelligence outsourcing.* New York: Simon & Schuster.

Stein, J. (2010, May 25). Setting the record straight on "contractor" spies. *Washington Post.* Retrieved from http://voices.washingtonpost.com/spytalk/2010/05/times_corrects_spy_contractor. html

The White House. (2009). *National framework for strategic communication.* Retrieved from www.fas .org/man/eprint/pubdip.pdf

Thompson, G., & Mazzetti, M. (2010, March 25). U.S. official defends contractors' mission. *New York Times,* p. A6.

Silence in the Turmoil of Crisis

Peanut Corporation of America's Response to Its Sweeping Salmonella Outbreak

Alyssa Grace Millner and Timothy L. Sellnow

This case explores how organizations should engage in crisis communication, seeking to balance open communication with the public and self-interest. It addresses the ethical dilemma between a desire for open disclosure and the realistic threat of legal repercussions to such disclosure. Finally, it also considers the degree to which different interest groups—the company, the industry, consumer advocacy groups, and government regulators, among others—are responsible for identifying problems and alerting the public.

Organizational crisis communication literature consistently calls for prompt, open, and honest responses by organizations facing crises (Seeger, 2006). In direct contrast, organizations' legal counsels frequently recommend limited responses, fearing detailed communication will work against the organization in legal battles stemming from the crisis. Hearit (1995) explained, "Corporate rhetors that admit responsibility virtually invite lawsuits" (p. 13). Organizations connected with public crises struggle with the tension between open communication and self-protection. Indeed, many debates arise inside corporate headquarters as leaders prepare their crises responses (Coombs, 2007). Thus, the tension between a desire for open disclosure and the realistic threat of legal repercussions to such disclosure creates an ethical dilemma for organizations. Peanut Corporation of America (PCA) leaders faced this communication dilemma when they found themselves at the heart of a salmonella outbreak the U.S. Department of Agriculture (USDA) referred to as "one of the largest food safety recalls ever in the United States" (Wittenberger & Dohlman, 2010, p. 1).

Salmonella is a common cause of food poisoning. In fact, salmonella is America's leading source of food poisoning (Brumback & Alonso-Zaldivar, 2009). Salmonella is spread when humans consume foods contaminated with animal feces (Centers for Disease Control and Prevention [CDC] 2009). Frequently salmonella-contaminated foods are of animal origin, but any food product can become tainted with salmonella, as was the case in Blakely, Georgia. Also, Severson (2009) reported that salmonella bacteria can survive for an extended period of time in peanut butter products.

As is often the case with food poisoning, those who suffer the most in cases of salmonellosis are the very young and the very old. The CDC (2009) explained the following:

> Salmonellosis is an infection with bacteria called *Salmonella*. Most persons infected with *Salmonella* develop diarrhea, fever, and abdominal cramps 12 to 72 hours after infection. The illness usually lasts 4 to 7 days, and most persons recover without treatment. . . . The elderly, infants, and those with impaired immune systems are more likely to have a severe illness. (para. 1)

Though reports of salmonella illnesses began in the fall of 2008, PCA did not make its first public recall announcement until early 2009. PCA neglected to communicate remorse, explanation, or informational updates to stakeholders *throughout* the crisis, despite increasing reports of salmonellosis (Millner, Veil, & Sellnow, 2011). The company's refusal to publicly accept responsibility limited consumers' understanding of the unfolding crisis. Nilsen (1966) argued that humans are free to the degree that they are able to act independently and think for themselves; an assault against free will and informed decision making is an infringement on significant choice. In other words, when individuals aren't provided with enough accurate information to make an informed decision, then the ethic of significant choice has been violated.

PCA is a peanut manufacturer responsible for processing approximately 2% of the industry's peanuts and peanut by-products (Chapman & Newkirk, 2009). PCA "produced blanched, split, granulated, and roasted peanuts. Peanut meal, peanut butter, and peanut paste were also produced" (Wittenberger & Dohlman, 2010, p. 17). The Food and Drug Administration (FDA) investigators reported that, in 2009, PCA's salmonella-tainted peanut products were unwittingly used in more than 3,900 other food items (Wittenberger & Dohlman, 2010), leading to 714 salmonellosis cases and nine deaths in 43 states (CDC, 2009). In addition, the FDA released nearly a dozen different Georgia state and federal inspection reports citing PCA's Blakely plant for unclean premises and food manufacturing protocol violations. PCA's Plainview, Texas, location was also tested for salmonella on the premises and in manufactured products; final reports explained that the Plainview plant tests were "99% positive for salmonella [but] in *this* case the tainted products did *not* make it to consumers" (Stark & Banner, 2009). Ultimately, the Blakely plant was identified as the primary manufacturing location for one of the largest food recalls the world has ever seen (Odom, 2009).

In this case, we outline the unusual aspects of the PCA salmonella contamination and explain how these factors escalated the outbreak's intensity. First, the case is overviewed with a timeline narrative highlighting the key points contributing to the case's burgeoning impact. Second, we address effective organizational communication's importance as it relates to PCA's sanitation practices, the nature of the contaminated by-products, and communication reticence. These factors created compounding problems for PCA, an array of other organizations in the food industry, and several government agencies. We conclude with closing observations and questions for discussion.

TIMELINE NARRATIVE

Peanut paste is used in everyday foods such as crackers and cookies. Wittenberger and Dohlman (2010) wrote the following:

> Recalled products containing [PCA] peanut ingredients include brownies, cakes, pies, many types of candy, cereals, cookies, crackers, donuts, dressings and seasonings, prepared fruit and vegetable products, ice creams, peanut butter and products, pet foods, pre-packaged meals, snack bars, snack mixes, and toppings. (p. 4)

The contamination of commonly consumed food items made this an acute crisis because of its far-reaching impact. This crisis reached catastrophic dimensions, due in large part to PCA's history of unclean plant management. In fact, congressional testimony dates salmonella's presence at PCA's Blakely plant "as far back as 2006" (Alonso-Zaldivar & Blackledge, 2009, para. 6), with repeated Georgia state health code violations from 2006 to 2008 (Boudreau, 2009). Georgia health department records highlight PCA's chronic unhygienic production and allude to unethical business practices.

According to ABC's Hartman and Barrett (2009), the first peanut-related incident occurred in 1990 when the FDA cited a Virginia plant for shipping products with toxins. In 2001, the FDA found the same toxins in peanut products at another plant; the FDA also documented improper compliance and poor equipment (Hartman & Barrett, 2009). On September 4, 2007, inspectors from the Georgia Department of Agriculture examined the Blakely plant and discovered uncovered products, damaged equipment, and unsanitary conditions (Hartman & Barrett, 2009). The Blakely, Georgia, plant experienced regular mandated state inspections. Reports of recurring sanitation citations and unethical manufacturing practices depict PCA as the liable organization following the peanut food crisis. Repeated offenses are meaningful because they illustrate an organization's true colors. Next, the following timeline outlines the major peanut butter-related occurrences of 2008 and 2009.

Peanut Corporation of America Case Facts in 2008

On April 11, 2008, a Canadian-owned distributing company refused a PCA shipment of chopped peanuts because the product contained pieces of metal (Hartman & Barrett, 2009). Two months later, the FDA conducted a weeklong inspection of the Blakely plant, citing it for unsanitary conditions (Hartman & Barrett, 2009). In 2008, "Seven tests performed for the company were positive for salmonella. In each case, after a retest is negative, the product is shipped" (Associated Press, 2009b, para. 4).

By September 2008, the CDC began reporting illnesses (Associated Press, 2009b; Hartman & Barrett, 2009). On October 23, the Blakely plant was again cited for unsanitary premises and improper equipment maintenance (Hartman & Barrett, 2009). Salmonella reports triggered a governmental response on November 25. CDC partnered with state and local officials to assess cases of salmonellosis reported in over a dozen states (Associated Press, 2009b). At the end of December, PCA operators were charged with their first salmonella-related death (Associated Press, 2009b). Salmonellosis deaths throughout the nation were reported in late 2008 and into early 2009, with allegations that PCA's contaminated peanut paste was the cause. Overall, 2008 marked the beginning of the peanut salmonella crisis, but the process of source identification and mass salmonellosis outbreak accelerated greatly in 2009.

Peanut Corporation of America Case Events in 2009

The FDA is responsible for examining all food crisis cases in an effort to assess the level of neglect or wrongdoing. On January 7, 2009, the FDA launched an institutional food service investigation (Hartman & Barrett, 2009). After several federal inspection visits and FBI raids, PCA ceased production at its Blakely plant (Associated Press, 2009b). Recalls started January 10, beginning with the King Nut label, a company that used PCA as its manufacturer and distributor (Associated Press, 2009b). According to USDA's Wittenberger and Dohlman (2010), "On January 10, an opened 5-pound container of King Nut peanut butter tested positive for the outbreak strain of salmonella" (p. 3). Three days later, PCA recalled all of its products made at the Blakely plant "on or after July 1, 2008, because of possible salmonella contamination" (Associated Press, 2009b, para. 13). Marler Clark, legal expert in foodborne illness cases, filed lawsuits on behalf of salmonella victims as early as January 20, 2009 (Bronstad, 2009). On January 23, the USDA released a statement warning that possibly tainted products had been unknowingly distributed to food and nutrition programs (Hartman & Barrett, 2009). The USDA's Food and Nutrition Service functions to educate school children about healthy eating practices.

Next, federal officials stumbled across interesting news at the end of January. During 2007 and 2008, after finding salmonella in some of its products, PCA sent samples of the same products to another laboratory for testing. The contracted laboratory's secondary tests regularly came back negative for salmonella, at which point PCA sold the products to food manufacturers and distributors (Cohen, 2009; Hartman & Barrett, 2009). In late January, FDA found internal records from the Blakely plant showing a dozen instances in 2007 and 2008 of the company identifying salmonella in its products. FDA also reported cockroaches, mold, and leaks at the plant (Hartman & Barrett, 2009). On January 28, PCA again extended its peanut paste recall, reclaiming products made after January 1, 2007. That same day, CDC reported that over 500 people had contracted salmonellosis to date, eight of whom died (Associated Press, 2009b; Hartman & Barrett, 2009). January concluded with the U.S. Department of Justice (DOJ) promising a criminal investigation (Associated Press, 2009b).

February began with an announcement by President Obama that the FDA would undergo a comprehensive review as a result of the peanut salmonella outbreak (Associated Press, 2009b). On February 3, 2009, reports surfaced of a Plainview, Texas, PCA manufacturing plant that "operated for years uninspected and unlicensed by government health officials" (Associated Press, 2009b, para. 28). The FDA suspended PCA from doing business with the federal government for at least 1 year (Sylvester, 2009).

February was a tumultuous month for many reasons, including damaging ice storms in Kentucky and Arkansas. Almost 200,000 emergency meal kits were sent to Kentucky and Arkansas in response to their disasters. The meal kits were recalled because they contained possibly tainted peanut butter (Associated Press, 2009b). By February 5, the CDC had counted 575 cases of salmonellosis in 43 states (Associated Press, 2009b; Schiavoni, 2009). The same day, government officials and a salmonellosis victim's mother testified before a Senate subcommittee about the outbreak (Hartman & Barrett, 2009). This congressional hearing was a particularly significant event because it was the first time investigators, regulatory agencies directors, and PCA salmonellosis victims came together simultaneously to discuss the outbreak.

The FBI raided the Blakely plant on February 9 (Hartman & Barrett, 2009). By February 11, estimates projected that over 1,500 products had been recalled, nearly 600 people had been sickened in 44 states, and 9 had died from the salmonella-tainted peanut by-products (Hartman & Barrett, 2009; Schiavoni, 2009). The Plainview plant announced it had voluntarily suspended operations during the investigation (Hartman & Barrett, 2009). On February 13, PCA declared bankruptcy (Marler Clark, 2009). By mid-March, the CDC had confirmed almost 700 cases of salmonellosis in the United States. These key events uncovered a pattern of unsafe, unprofessional, unpredictable, and unethical business practices. The next section will further delve into PCA's poor organizational management and stakeholder communication throughout the peanut crisis.

KEY MANAGEMENT ISSUES

Three management issues complicated the outbreak crisis for PCA: (1) previous decisions the company made about plant cleanliness, (2) the fact that the company sold an ingredient rather than an end product, and (3) the company's choice to remain largely silent. Each of these intensified the crisis. We discuss each of these compounding factors next.

Compounding "Mistakes" in Plant Cleanliness

The U.S. Public Health Service Act requires that all companies adhere to food safety practices. PCA—disregarding federal requirements, human morality, and financial common sense—failed to follow high ethical standards in its food production processes. The state of Georgia has records citing PCA's Blakely plant for repeated violations in 2006, 2007, and 2008 (Boudreau, 2009). The FDA found Blakely plant internal records showing a dozen instances of unsanitary production and of bacteria in shipped peanut by-products (Schmit, 2009). Though peanut butter is considered a low-risk food product for contracting salmonella bacteria (Associated Press, 2009a), PCA's poor sanitation and upkeep at the Blakely and Plainview plants resulted in a national outbreak of salmonellosis. At least 12 times from 2007 through 2009, PCA "*knowingly* shipped products that initial tests showed were contaminated with salmonella" (Boudreau, 2009). In fact, PCA products were tested for salmonella, and laboratory results regularly came back positive. PCA then had its product retested by an alternate, contracted laboratory. Once the secondary laboratory provided a negative test result, the products were shipped (Cohen, 2009; Hartman & Barrett, 2009). In short, PCA compounded its failure by maintaining unsanitary plant conditions and by knowingly shipping tainted products. The calculated decision to ship contaminated products illustrates that PCA placed more value on profit than the health and safety of its consumers.

Compounding Impact on the Food Industry

PCA's contamination crisis was *not* the result of one or two tainted products manufactured by a singular company. Rather, PCA's peanut paste was used in a countless number of food products around the world. Estimates declare that somewhere between 3,500 and 4,000 different food products were recalled because of the PCA contamination (Schmit, 2009; Wittenberger & Dohlman, 2010). PCA's peanut paste was also used in a handful of animal foods, leading to sick canines and pet food and feed-grade peanut butter recalls (Marler, 2009). The fact that PCA's peanut paste was an ingredient, not an end product, makes it a unique case. Typical recalls affect single product types such as eggs or ground beef, where only the distribution date is needed to identify and return or discard the product. PCA's peanut paste, however, found its way into hundreds of different products manufactured by dozens of different organizations. Thus, the recall volume swelled as the raw ingredient was found in product after product.

Compounding Communication Issues

PCA offered minimum communication in response to the crisis. For example, PCA offered no public statements about its product recall until January 13, 2009, months after salmonellosis cases had been linked to the company in the fall of 2008. Hallman and Cuite (2010) noted that confusion can arise when consumers have too little information about contaminated products. They explain that if consumers "cannot successfully distinguish affected from unaffected products, they are likely to either under-react by assuming that they do not own any of the recalled products or over-react by discarding or avoiding the purchase of anything that resembles it" (Hallman & Cuite, 2010, p. 4). It should be noted that PCA's reticence was likely prompted by a desire for corporate protection. It is probable, we argue, that PCA executives did not take adequate responsibility (or participate in apologia) because they valued their own right to self-protection over open communication or consumer right to significant choice. Competing values lead to ethical dilemmas, as exemplified by this peanut paste food crisis.

Despite rising consumer anxiety, PCA maintained its silence. During the February 2009 congressional hearing, PCA's owner and the Blakely plant manager both pled the Fifth Amendment, allowing them to legally resist answering any questions. PCA's silence created an information void during the crisis, denying consumers the regular updates they needed in order to make informed decisions about how to protect themselves and their families during the outbreak. News networks sought to fill the information void by providing what Veil and Ojeda (2010) described as adjusting information. They explained, "The media can assist in providing adjusting information and . . . can be used to convey instructions to the public" during a crisis (p. 415). During the peanut paste crisis, third-party organizations such as government agencies and peanut industry leaders used media sources to provide critical updates about the growing cascade of recalled products.

Again, PCA's silence and lack of transparency introduced an information vacuum—a void in which consumers knew very little about the evolving recall. During a crisis, absence of information is simply unacceptable. Therefore, throughout the peanut salmonella crisis, government agencies and peanut industry leaders shared messages with consumers about (1) which products were safe, (2) what to do with contaminated products, and (3) where to seek medical help. For example, the FDA repeatedly announced (through local news and global news channels) that jarred peanut butter was safe (Carey, 2009). Similarly, the Federal Emergency Management Agency (FEMA) instructed ice storm victims and other consumers to throw away emergency meal kits and counseled anyone who had eaten potentially contaminated products to contact a local health official or the CDC (Hensley, 2009).

Government agencies were instrumental in providing stakeholders with crisis information. Peanut industry leaders also shared pertinent information with consumers. For example, Martin and Robbins (2009) of the *New York Times* observed the following:

> Many consumers, apparently disregarding the fine print of the Salmonella outbreak and food recall . . . are swearing off all brands of peanut butter, driving down sales by nearly 25 percent. The drop-off is so striking that brands like Jif are taking the unusual step of buying ads to tell shoppers that their products are not affected. (para. 1–2)

Similarly, a CNN broadcast explained how Jif and Peter Pan "started costly ad campaigns to reassure the public" that their peanut products were 100% safe (Phillips, 2009). Clearly, government agencies and peanut industry leaders utilized various media channels in an effort to provide updates about the developing peanut paste contamination. Millner et al. (2011) characterized third-party communication of this nature as proxy communication. Proxy communicators must often speak on behalf of an entire industry in circumstances where organizations afflicted with crisis choose silence. Millner et al. (2011) noted that "proxy communicators actually speak *in place of* the liable organization/crisis event to provide the needed information" (p. 75). In the PCA crisis, organizations like the FDA, FEMA, the CDC, Peter Pan, and Jif communicated messages of self-protection and clarification to consumers in an effort to counter PCA's negligence and silence. For the most part, these messages did not critique PCA. Instead, proxy communicators provided messages designed to clarify the situation and empower consumers to protect themselves. In this case, proxy communicators acted as ethical agents; their efforts enabled the flow of information during a crisis that reinstated the ethic of significant choice.

SUMMARY

The PCA case remains one of the largest and most complex in history. This chapter depicted a case laden with the ethical implications—competing values and goals, unethical decision making and production practices, compounding industry issues and crises, significant choice, organizational accountability, and duty via proxy communicators. For nearly 2 years, Americans were unsure what to do with peanut butter and peanut by-products, because the surge of contaminated products created considerable uncertainty and alarm for consumers. The complexity of this crisis created a number of communication challenges for PCA and the food industry in general. PCA's lack of communication fostered uncertainty and heightened anxiety throughout the contamination crisis. Also, PCA's decision to remain silent through much of the crisis prompted others to compensate for the vacuity of information. Proxy communicators emerged as the first line of defense for consumers anxious to learn more about the recall and how to avoid illness.

DISCUSSION QUESTIONS

1. To what extent did ethical lapses in PCA's manufacturing practices lead to a large-scale, organizational communication failure during the crisis?

2. To what extent was PCA justified in remaining largely silent during the crisis? To what extent was PCA forced into silence?

3. To what extent were the proxy communicators justified in stepping forward to communicate during the crisis?

4. Were all of the organizations and agencies described in the case equally justified in assuming the role of proxy communicator?

5. What are the potential ethical complications for proxy communicators in crises?

6. If PCA had decided to communicate during the crisis, what messages of communication would have been most important to stakeholders? What messages would have been most helpful for consumers?

REFERENCES

Alonso-Zaldivar, R., & Blackledge, B. J. (2009, February 11). Stewart Parnell, Peanut Corp owner, refuses to testify to confess in salmonella hearing. *Huffington Post*. Retrieved from http://www.huffingtonpost.com/2009/02/11/stewart- parnell-peanut-co_n_166058.html

Associated Press. (2009a, January 27). In peanut checks, gaps for salmonella sneak by: Federal regulators rely on states, who rely on companies to police selves. *MSNBC*. Retrieved from http://www.msnbc.msn.com/id/28880214/

Associated Press. (2009b, February 9). Timeline of events in salmonella outbreak. *Fox Atlanta*. Retrieved from http://www.myfoxatlanta.com/dpp /news/Event_Timeline_in_Salmonella_Outbreak_020909

Boudreau, A. (Reporter). (2009, February 7). *CNN special investigations unit* [Television broadcast]. Atlanta: CNN.

Bronstad, A. (2009, January 20). First suit tied to peanut butter-related salmonella outbreak is filed. *The Law Journal*. Retrieved from http://www.marlerclark.com/case_news/detail/ first-suit-tied-to-peanut-butter-related-salmonella-outbreak-is-filed

Brumback, K., & Alonso-Zaldivar, R. (2009, January 16). Peanut butter probe expands, salmonella contamination confirmed at Georgia plant. *Huffington Post*. Retrieved from http://www .huffingtonpost.com/2009/01/16/peanut-butter-probe-expan_n_158689.html

Carey, R. (Reporter). (2009, January 19). *CNN headline news, prime time* [Television broadcast]. Atlanta: CNN.

Centers for Disease Control and Prevention. (2009, November 16). *Salmonellosis*. Retrieved from http://www.cdc.gov/nczved/divisions/dfbmd/diseases/salmonellosis/

Chapman, D., & Newkirk, M. (2009, February 08). Blakely plant part of firm with humble start: Company of hardworking Lynchburg, Va., CEP has faced trouble before. *Atlanta Journal-Constitution*. Retrieved from http://www.ajc.com/services/content/news/stories /2009/02/08/ peanutcorp0208.html

Cohen, E. (Reporter). (2009, February 11). *CNN senior medical correspondent* [Television broadcast]. New York: CNN.

Coombs, W. T. (2007). *Ongoing crisis communication: Planning, managing, and responding* (2nd ed.). Thousand Oaks, CA: Sage.

Hallman, W. K., & Cuite, C. L. (2010). *Food recalls and the American public: Improving communications*. New Brunswick, NJ: Rutgers, The State University of New Jersey, Food Policy Institute.

Hartman, B., & Barrett, K. (2009, February 10). Timeline of the salmonella outbreak: Track the chain of events in the recall of more than 1,550 peanut products. *ABCnews*. Retrieved from http:// abcnews.go.com/Health/story?id = 6837291&page = 1

Hearit, K. M. (1995). "Mistakes were made": Organizations, apologia, and crises of social legitimacy. *Communication Studies, 45*(1, 2), 1–17.

Hensley, T. (Reporter). (2009, February 5). *WTVQ 38 local news* [Television broadcast]. Lexington, KY: American Broadcasting Company.

Marler, B. (2009, January 19). Update—does Peanut Corporation of America supply peanut butter for dog biscuits? *The Marler Network*. Retrieved from http://www.marlerblog.com/case-news/update---does-peanut-corporation-of-america-supply-peanut-butter-for-dog-biscuits/

Marler Clark. (2009, February 18). Marler Clark files salmonella lawsuit on behalf of Las Vegas child sickened by peanut butter. *The Marler Network*. Retrieved from http://www.marlerclark. com/press_releases/view/marler-clark-files-salmonella-lawsuit-on-behalf-of-las-vegas-child-sickened/

Martin, A., & Robbins, L. (2009, February 6). Fallout widens as buyers shun peanut butter. *New York Times*. Retrieved from http://www.nytimes.com/2009/

Millner, A. G., Veil, S. R., & Sellnow, T. L. (2011). Proxy communication in crisis response. *Public Relations Review, 37*(1), 74–76.

Nilsen, T. R. (1966). *Ethics of speech communication*. Indianapolis: The Bobbs-Merril Company, Inc.

Odom, A. (2009, January 28). Blakely plant is sole source of salmonella. *Herald-Gazette*. Retrieved from http://www.barnesville.com/archives/178-Blakely-plant-is-sole-source-of-Salmonella.html

Phillips, K. (Reporter). (2009, February 10). *CNN newsroom* [Television broadcast]. Atlanta: CNN.

Schiavoni, L. (Reporter). (2009, February 7). *Lou Dobbs tonight* [Television broadcast]. New York: CNN.

Seeger, M. W. (2006). Best practices in crisis communication: An expert panel process. *Journal of Applied Communication Research, 34*, 234–244.

Severson, K. (2009, January 22). List of tainted peanut butter items points to complexity of food production. *New York Times*. Retrieved from http://www.nytimes.com/2009/01/23/health/23scare. html?_r = 1

Schmit, J. (2009, April 28). Broken links in food-safety chain hid peanut plants' risks. *USA Today*. Retrieved from http://www.usatoday.com/money/industries/food/2009-04-26-peanuts-Salmonella-food-safety_N.htm

Stark, L. (Reporter), & Banner, J. (Producer). (2009, February 10). *ABC world news* [Television broadcast]. Blakely, GA [On-location]: American Broadcasting Company.

Sylvester, L. (Reporter). (2009, February 11). *Lou Dobbs tonight* [Television broadcast]. Washington DC: CNN.

Veil, S. R., & Ojeda, F. (2010). Establishing media partnerships in crisis response. *Communication Studies, 61*(4), 412–429.

Wittenberger, K., & Dohlman, E. (2010, February). *Peanut outlook: Impacts of the 2008-09 foodborne illness outbreak linked to Salmonella in peanuts*. Retrieved from http://www.ers.usda.gov/Publications/OCS/2010/02Feb/OCS10A01/ocs10a01.pdf

Patrolling the Ethical Borders of Compassion and Enforcement

Kendra Dyanne Rivera and Sarah J. Tracy

This case examines the role of government agents to patrol the U.S. border and the challenges they face to follow the law and to uphold their personal values. It explores the dilemmas of employees who confront conflicting views of what is right and wrong about their jobs, both within their organization and among members of the public. These tensions create a range of ethical dilemmas that pit individuality versus community and herald deeply intertwined notions of honor, justice, patriotism, mercy, and compassion.

INTRODUCTION: WORKING ON THE BORDER

The U.S. Border Patrol plays an important governmental role in immigration, narcotics deterrence, and national security. Border Patrol agents often face critiques that they do either too much or too little in preventing immigrants, narcotics, and potential terrorists from entering the nation through its more than 6,000 miles of land borders with Canada and Mexico and over 2,000 miles of coastal sea borders. Controversial immigration laws, such as Arizona's State Bill 1070 that allows police to arrest people who they suspect to be in the country without legal documentation, have caused many to publicly question whether the Border Patrol is effectively accomplishing its job (e.g., Cooper & Myers, 2010; McCombs, 2010). Popular news stories often portray Border Patrol Agents as incompetent (e.g., Steinhauer, 2009; Surdin, 2009) or as brutal, uncontrolled, and uncaring (e.g., Holstege, 2008; White, 2008). Immigrant rights activist groups such as the National Council for La Raza (NCLR) have called for a stop to agent brutality (Demo, 2004), and regularly hold public protests demanding the restriction of Border Patrol activity.

Meanwhile, civilian militia groups such as the Minutemen Civil Defense Corps assert that the Border Patrol is not doing *enough* to secure the national borders against "the unlawful and unauthorized entry of all individuals, contraband and foreign military" (www .minutemanhq.com). Even social media sites such as Youtube.com reflect the nation's conflicted views of the Border Patrol, with some videos mocking agents, others depicting agent abuse of power, and still others framing agents as national heroes.

In sum, Border Patrol agents work in an environment with multiple conflicting notions about what is right or wrong about their job. Although some Americans may feel that they understand the Patrol because of what they see, hear, and read in the media, few are aware of the work agents actually do on a day-to-day basis. Most do not understand the wide range of emotions agents experience or what it's like for agents to face such an array of critiques from so many different "audiences" and "clients." In any given situation, agents must consider conflicting messages from the individual perspectives involved—the agent, the citizen of the community, and the immigrant. At the same time, agents must keep up with the ambiguous web of collective "patriotic duty" expectations emerging from the Border Patrol organization, the American government, and the local community. These tensions create a perfect storm of ethical dilemmas that pit individuality versus community and herald deeply intertwined notions of honor, justice, patriotism, mercy, and compassion.

This case study offers a glimpse into the dilemmas faced by Border Patrol agents as they confront the ethical tensions of compassion to immigrants and the community versus their sworn duty to enforce the laws of the United States. Based on more than 165 hours of ethnographic fieldwork, this case study encapsulates stories gathered across the data set, including direct quotes taken from recorded interviews and "in situ" recordings of trainings and events and the first author's observations of agents in the field. Although the names have been changed to protect the identities of participants, this case study reflects the complex nexus of ethical tensions experienced by Border Patrol agents.

PART ONE: PATROLLING THE DESERT

It was a cold desert night. Agent Aaron pulled his green Border Patrol coat around his broad shoulders and stepped out of the truck. He reached for the flashlight in his belt, shifting the weight of his holstered radio, baton, pepper spray, and gun. Switching the light on, he scanned the desert in front of him: low shrubs, saguaro cactus, Joshua trees, and sand spread out as far as he could see.

The call had come over the radio just a few minutes ago. Motion sensors embedded in the ground near the border with Mexico were triggered, alerting the Patrol that someone was roaming in land where they probably shouldn't be. Someone, or probably a group of people, had crossed the border without documentation, hoping to make it safely into the United States under the cover of darkness.

Agent Aaron had been taught to track footprints in the dirt and look for broken branches or litter along a trail. This tracking activity is what the Border Patrol calls "cutting sign," and Aaron was proud of the fact that after 2 years at the Patrol, he knew exactly what to look for in order to track someone in the desert. Tracking was fun, but he knew that finding the immigrants was when the tough part of the job kicked in. That's when he sometimes wondered if he had made the right decision by joining the Patrol. In cases like this, Aaron felt the stirrings of a familiar dilemma—the duty to arrest but the desire to be humane.

He walked quietly through the bushes, blazing his flashlight back and forth low to the ground, eyes keen for anything that looked out of place. When tracking, he turned up the volume in his ears to loud, hyperaware of the sounds around him. He knew the difference between the noise of the wind in the shrubs, a bird shifting in its nest, and the sound of human breathing—steady, fast and shallow with the fear of being caught.

It wasn't long before he saw them—a scattering of footprints in the sand. Some were bigger, with deep tread and expansive gaps between strides. Aaron knew these were probably the tracks of bigger, heavier men. He also saw some smaller, shuffling footprints near the edges, as though a younger boy were following behind the group. Aaron grabbed his radio and called in his find, asking for backup and letting the dispatcher know his location.

"I'm proceeding on foot," he said in a low, hushed voice. Sliding the radio back into its holster, Aaron pointed the flashlight back at the footprints and began to follow them. Tracking would be easier and quicker now that he had found their trail. He just had to move quickly enough to cover ground more quickly than the group so that he could catch up.

Aaron reached the bottom of a hill and noticed that the footprints began to scatter in several different directions. This was a pretty common practice for groups of undocumented immigrants or drug smugglers, as they spread out to try and confuse or distract Border Patrol agents. He knew the change in footprints meant that the group was probably aware that they were being followed. Aaron took a couple of minutes to examine the difference in the way the tracks moved, noting that most of the heavier tracks seemed to continue up onto the hill. Looking up toward the top of the hill, Aaron thought he could see movement next to a saguaro cactus standing tall against the starry sky. He quickly began hiking up the hill, radioing in his position and his plan to follow the tracks up the hill.

Aaron kept a steady pace, taking long strides. Switching off his flashlight, he would have a better chance at some element of surprise. He kept his breathing shallow and quiet, stepping as lightly as his 6-foot-tall body would allow. In a matter of minutes, he had scaled the hill and was just steps away from the saguaro.

A crackling of branches on his right was all the warning he needed.

"U.S. Border Patrol!" he shouted. "Stop and come here!" "Alto! Ven aquí!" he repeated in Spanish. His heart raced, and a small voice in his head wondered if he should have waited for backup. Shaking off the momentary misgiving, he quickly stepped toward the bushes, knowing he was trained for this very scenario and had successfully accomplished apprehensions many times.

"Come out!" he repeated, the baton in one hand and his other on the holster of his gun. Apprehending a group in the desert was always potentially dangerous, but he knew that most immigrants were far more afraid of him than he was of them. Still, he needed to follow procedure.

Suddenly, a body emerged from the darkness of a bush. One small, solitary figure moved hesitantly into the pathway in front of the looming patrol officer.

She was only about 5 feet tall and could not have weighed more than 100 pounds. Agent Aaron recognized her youth—probably no more than about 19 years old. Her gray T-shirt worked like camouflage in the night haze, but he could see that she was shivering, struggling to hold on to the sweatshirt wadded up in her arms.

"Put your hands up!" he ordered her. "Where are the others?" he gave commands and asked questions in rapid succession. She simply shook her head.

"Put your hands above your head!"

"Poner sus manos sobre la cabeza!" Agent Aaron ordered again in Spanish, but she shook her head again. Now he was getting frustrated. He wondered if she was from somewhere other than South America and didn't understand either English or Spanish. Agent Aaron took a step closer and saw tears streaming down her face.

"They all left me because I couldn't walk fast enough," she sobbed.

"Put your hands up where I can see them," Agent Aaron repeated a third time.

"I can't," she told him.

Aaron moved to reach for the woman's arms to put them behind her back. One of the first things they learned at the Border Patrol Academy is that you always have to be able to see the hands of the person you're apprehending. Otherwise, they could be holding a weapon. Agent Aaron's instincts told him that the woman wasn't a threat, but he still needed to follow procedure—again that all-too-familiar dilemma. She might be small, but with a gun, she could end his life in just seconds.

The woman was shivering so badly that she seemed to be rocking in the breeze. Agent Aaron wondered why she wasn't wearing the sweatshirt she was holding. "I will ask you one more time," he said firmly. "Put your hands above your head, where I can see them." Agent Aaron took another step toward her, his baton elevated in a defensive position.

"I can't," she repeated, lifting the sweatshirt in her arms. "I'm holding my baby."

The bundle unfolded to reveal an infant, only a couple of months old, wearing nothing but a dirty diaper. The whiteness of the diaper shone in the moonlight, just before the baby gasped in the chill of the night air and let out a small but painfully pitiful cry.

PART TWO: THE CALL OF DUTY

Aaron had become accustomed to the unpredictability of his job. Serving as a Border Patrol agent wasn't exactly what he had thought it would be. There were still moments when he was surprised—when he found that his training hadn't prepared him for situations he encountered in the field. These unpredictable moments were the ones that he carried home with him after his shift, when he sat reclined in his old La-Z-Boy chair staring at the television screen but still seeing the images from his time at work. He had always considered himself an ethical person, but negotiating the multiple tensions he now faced as an agent caused him new and often confusing dilemmas that required more decision making than he thought the job would require.

When Aaron returned from his tour of duty in Iraq, he knew he wanted out of the military. He liked his life in uniform but didn't want to risk being sent off to war again. One of his friends told him that the Border Patrol was hiring. Aaron didn't know much about the Patrol. Even though he grew up in a Southwestern American town and had taken several quick trips down to Mexico to shop as a kid—and later to party as a young man—he had never really thought about the officers in green who stopped the car to ask if everyone was a U.S. citizen. Still, his friend insisted that it was a good job with good pay. Plus he could continue to serve his country.

Aaron decided to check out the Border Patrol's website. He read about how the Border Patrol has tripled in size since the 9/11 terrorist attacks in 2001 and how protecting the nation's borders is a key emphasis for the Department of Homeland Security.[1] According to the website, "The priority mission of the Border Patrol is preventing terrorists and terrorists' weapons, including weapons of mass destruction, from entering the United States."[2] The emphasis on protecting America from terrorists made a lot of sense to Aaron, particularly since he'd just come home from fighting the war in Iraq. Although terrorism and weapons of mass destruction weren't part of what he normally thought about when he pictured the Border Patrol, he liked the idea of continuing to fight a war against terror within the borders of the United States.

Aaron examined the photos and the videos on the Border Patrol's website. While the website said less than he expected about immigrants, he liked what he saw. One video in particular really made sense to Aaron. In it, the man said, "As Americans we have a duty to serve our country. The question is, how will you serve?" In the next scene, the man wore a Border Patrol uniform and said, "I've made my choice. The U.S. Border Patrol."[3] Other video commercials showed images of men and women working together with weapons and riding around on ATVs, snowmobiles, jet skis, or on horseback. What was missing were photos of terrorists or immigrants or anyone else agents might work with.

The information on the website suggested that Border Patrol life would be similar to the military except with less danger and similar to being a cop—only he'd have fewer people to deal with. The job definitely looked like a lot more fun than fighting the war in Iraq. Aaron figured he'd have a leg up on most of the other new recruits because of his past military training. After doing his research, Aaron began to agree with his friend. Becoming an agent seemed like a perfect job for him.

Aaron dove headfirst into the 6-month-long process of filling out the Border Patrol application, taking the various physical and written tests, and completing the interviews and background checks to finally get accepted into the Border Patrol. Meanwhile, the voices of those who first encouraged him to apply faded away as voices questioning his decision to become an agent began coming at him fast and furious.

"Have you seen the stories on the news?" his mother asked him, her voice strained over the phone. "They say Mexico is the most dangerous place in the world right now!" she said, sounding as though she might start to cry. "I don't think I want you working with those people down there!"

His dad was a little more supportive. "Well," he said, "you're still serving your country. Just remember who you are and where you came from. Keep your honor."

---

[1] The U.S. Border Patrol has seen tremendous growth over the past decade. Information about the numbers of agents comes from personal communication with the public relations office at the Washington, D.C., headquarters and from the following Border Patrol documents:

   Customs and Border Protection. (2007). National Border Patrol strategy. Report from the Office of the Border Patrol. Retrieved from http://www.cbp.gov/xp/cgov/border_security/border_patrol/border_patrol_ohs/

   Customs and Border Protection. (2011). Customs and border protection, "Who we are and what we do." Retrieved from http://www.cbp.gov/xp/cgov/border_security/border_patrol/who_we_are.xml

[2] This "priority mission" quote comes from the home web page of the U.S. Border Patrol at www.cbp.gov. It is also reprinted on many organizational documents and webpages.

[3] Several commercials are posted on the Border Patrol's website. This commercial also has a transcript posted. You can obtain them at their website: http://www.cbp.gov/xp/cgov/careers/customs_careers/border_careers/bp_agent/videos/

Some of Aaron's friends also weighed in with their opinions. "How can you become a Border Patrol agent?" his friend Matt asked. "I mean, won't you feel guilty about arresting people who are just trying to pursue the American dream?" Monica had the complete opposite reaction, telling him, "Catch as many border crossers as you can. I don't want any criminals in my community, and I don't think it's fair that illegals don't pay taxes."

With all the contradictory messages of his family and friends still swirling in his head, Aaron reported for duty. Just hours after arriving at the "Welcome Meeting" his first day, he received standard instructions on benefits and payroll and signed a pile of forms. Then they got to the meat of the job, watching a slide show that featured everything from 12 border crossers crammed into a sedan, to packages of drugs smuggled into a tire, to Mexican gang member tattoo markings. The assistant chief of the sector—the regional office to which he was assigned—told the new agents, "You're about to begin what's probably the hardest and most important challenge of your life. The Border Patrol is challenging. We want to make sure that you have what it takes. We want guys who are willing to pull their own weight and then some." Aaron glanced around the room. Although the website had pictured some female agents, it was mostly guys in this orientation session. Still, Aaron wondered why the chief kept using "guys" when there were three women among the new recruits.

The assistant chief looked out across the nervous faces of the 21 recruits. "There's some advice I'll give you. It's a single word that you'll probably hear over and over at the academy and again when you get back here. That word is *integrity*. Integrity is something you either have before your training or you don't. So many agents get into trouble because they lack integrity, judgment." He continued, "From this point forward, continue to ask yourself, 'How is what I'm about to do going to affect me, my agency and my career, and others?' Think about the consequences. Think about your options. And make the right decision."

Aaron had listened to the assistant chief carefully and felt proud to be starting a job where integrity was so important. At the end of the day, when the recruits stood at attention and took the oath, he felt convinced of his decision. With his eyes focused on the U. S. flag in the front of the room, he pledged with the others, "I do solemnly swear. . . . That I will support and defend the Constitution of the United States, against all enemies, foreign and domestic. That I will bear true faith and allegiance to the same; that I take this obligation freely, without mental reservation or purpose of evasion, and that I will well and faithfully discharge the duties of the office of which I am about to enter, so help me God."

PART THREE: BECOMING BORDER ENFORCEMENT

When he graduated from the 3-month Border Patrol Academy, Agent Aaron felt mentally and physically prepared for the field. He had been right. The training was easier for him than some of the other recruits. One guy had quit within a week—he just couldn't handle the physical training. A woman had dropped out after about a month because she injured her knee, and two more recruits went home 2 weeks later because they feared failing the legal exam. One recruit was kicked out because he got caught driving drunk. Out of a total of 21 from his sector who had originally been deployed to their training site in Artesia, New Mexico, only 16 returned with Aaron to begin the "internship" as a trainee agent in the field. Still, upon graduation, Agent Aaron felt the academy had well prepared the recruits to watch for and apprehend undocumented immigrants, narcotics smugglers, terrorists, weapons, or whatever else they might encounter.

On his first day as an agent, Aaron was assigned a journeyman, or an experienced agent, with whom he would work and learn from until he became a full-time agent on his own. His journeyman, named Hank, was a former small town university cop who had been an agent for 10 years. After 9/11, Hank decided to join the Border Patrol, in part after hearing on the news that many of the terrorists had been in the United States without proper documentation. As Hank put it, "I welcome others to my country. But you gotta come in the right way. You gotta do it with all the right paperwork, and go through the proper channels. Otherwise, you're here illegally, and you've got to go."

A couple of weeks after he started working with Hank, Aaron got called to the "Welcome Back" meeting at the sector office. Reluctantly, Agent Aaron took a day off from his field training to attend the required meeting, where he signed another stack of paperwork and watched another slide show. At the meeting, Aaron was restless and bored. During the break, he got up and grabbed a cup of coffee, hoping the caffeine could provide a jolt of energy. Over break time snacks, he whispered to another recruit, Kat, saying, "I can't believe they pulled us out of the field for this crap!"

"No kidding," she replied. "I could be hanging out at the checkpoint, but instead I'm sitting here listening to stuff I already know." Agent Kat rolled her eyes and shook her head.

When break was over, the agents reluctantly returned to their seats for the next speaker.

"I'm the chaplain for this sector," the man introduced himself. "You may be thinking, 'Why does the Patrol even have a chaplain?' But I'm here to tell you, I'm here for you if you need me. I'm not gonna try to get you to believe any specific religion or anything like that. I'm just here to listen to your problems or to help you through a hard time in your life."

He cleared his throat and continued. "You all just returned from the academy. You got training in how to drive, how to shoot, how to speak Spanish, and to know the law." He took a step closer to the new agents. "You even learned how to take down another person with your own body strength. But not once"—he seemed to lock eyes with Agent Aaron for a second before looking away—"not once in all your training did you ever receive a lesson about how to handle the stress of this job." The chaplain paused and looked around the room.

Agent Aaron shifted in his seat.

"When you're in the field, you're gonna see things," the chaplain continued, "things you didn't expect to see, things that will break your heart. Kids and old people. Sick people. People just wanting a better life. And you're gonna bust their dreams. Eventually, all that stuff's gonna take a toll on you. And you will feel stressed."

Looking down the line of agents sitting at the tables, Aaron saw several of his peers squirming a bit. The tone of the chaplain was completely different than what they had heard in the rest of their training. *What is this guy talking about?* Aaron thought.

"In the year 2000, even before September 11th," the chaplain told the new agents, "163 law enforcement officers died in the line of duty. Even with all the training they received, just like you received, 163 law enforcement officers still died." He glanced down at his notes. "And yet, amidst all that training, no one ever got any suicide prevention training, or de-stress training. And that's why 418 law enforcement officers committed suicide in 2000. That's nearly three times as many law enforcement officers who took their *own* lives than those who were killed by the bad guys."

The chaplain took a moment to let the numbers sink in. More than 400 law enforcement suicides in a year.

"That's why I'm here," the chaplain concluded. "I'm here so that when you feel stressed out you have somewhere to go. You can come talk to me. We can work it out together so that you don't need to find a solution to your stress by taking your own life."

As the chaplain finished up, Aaron breathed a sigh of relief. He still felt pretty confused about what he'd just heard. The chaplain's comments seemed totally off topic. *Okay, so some crazy law enforcement officers committed suicide,* Aaron thought. *But that's not true for the Patrol, right?*

"O-kaaay," the next speaker said sarcastically as the chaplain left the room, holding the word until the door slammed shut. "Now maybe we can get back to the important stuff!" He laughed, and the new agents seemed happy to join in the lightness of this new speaker. "If any of you feel like you can't handle the job—or if this is just too much for you—now you know where to go!" The speaker smiled and laughed again. "For the rest of us, we'll man up and take care of the real business of protecting the country!" Agent Aaron joined the others in laughter.

But a few weeks later, Agent Aaron wasn't laughing.

He was holding the hand of an elderly man whom he and his journeyman Hank had found lying on the desert floor in 118-degree heat. Hank returned to the truck to call for the ambulance, leaving Aaron to deal with the undocumented immigrant, who was barely breathing. It seemed certain that by the time the ambulance arrived the man would certainly be dead. Aaron was acutely aware that his touch on the man's clammy and dirty skin was likely the last touch that the man would ever feel.

"I just want to see my daughter again," the man told Agent Aaron in broken English. "And send some money back home to my wife." Aaron looked into the man's blue eyes and wondered what country he was from. Although the only language Aaron learned at the academy was Spanish, he had gotten used to listening to all sorts of accents—from Romanian to Vietnamese to Ethiopian. The immigrants he encountered were more than just the stereotypical Mexicans. Despite their origin, almost every immigrant he encountered said they were in search of a better life. They were trying to "pick themselves up by their bootstraps" and find a way to live the American dream.

And so, Agent Aaron was quickly learning that being a Border Patrol agent entailed much more than patrolling the desert in a vehicle, more than stopping people at a checkpoint, and more than arresting "bad guys" who didn't deserve to be in the country. Being an agent also meant helping people who were dehydrated from the desert's searing sun. It meant giving directions to people who got lost on their vacation and helping ranchers herd their cattle back inside the fence. Being an agent meant serving as the *public face of immigration*—the person that everyone, whether supporters or haters, could either blame or praise for preventing undocumented immigrants from entering the United States.

A couple of months later, Agent Aaron's buddy Mike told him a story about stopping at a gas station to get a snack and a drink, saying, "When I came out, a day-old hot dog in one hand and an energy drink in the other, this woman is screaming! I mean, it took me a minute to even realize she was yelling at me. She was cussing about how Border Patrol agents are the devil and how we rape women and kill people in the desert and stuff like that." Mike was laughing again. "She was totally spitting in my face she was so close to me. And before I could decide whether to laugh at her, push her out of the way, or what, this other guy walks up and starts yelling back at her! And this guy," he continued, "he's yelling and cussing at the woman about how all immigrants are scum, and they're stealing Americans' jobs and ruining the health care system, and how the Patrol is just trying to clean up America for the people who pay their taxes. It was crazy, man!"

"So, what did you do?" Aaron asked, wondering what he would do if he encountered that situation.

"Well, it's honor first, man!"

Aaron and Mike both burst out in uncontrollable laughter. The motto "Honor First" was practically tattooed on agents' brains from the first day at the academy. The Border Patrol wanted agents to always act with integrity and honor, so the phrase "Honor First" was emblazoned across walls at the station, was standard in supervisors' signature lines in e-mails, and even hung on the back of the stall doors in the bathroom. But how to actually *enact* "honor first" in the field seemed vague to most agents, and they joked about the fact that, in the end, the only way to know if you lived up to the Border Patrol's requirement of honor first was if you avoided getting written up for making the wrong decision in the field. Write-ups equaled lost honor.

While in many ways they joked about the repeated use of the phrase, agents also took honor seriously, and all of Aaron's friends in the Patrol believed they were doing their jobs with integrity. However, because of the ambiguous way the Patrol used honor first, the new agents had difficulty defining or talking about it in a way that had real meaning in their work.

Aaron and Mike continued laughing for a moment, then Aaron shook his head.

"For real, Mike," Aaron repeated. "What did you do in response to those people at the gas station?"

"What else could I do?" Agent Mike asked. "I got into my truck and drove away. Ate my stale hot dog in peace and quiet!"

Later that night, Aaron pulled slowly into his driveway, turning over Mike's situation in his head. *How are we supposed to know how to handle all these different people?* he thought. He pulled the keys from the ignition, then let his head fall onto the steering wheel. He closed his eyes. He didn't want to go into his house. He didn't want to go back to work. He didn't seem to want to do anything.

Even with his eyes squeezed shut, Aaron could still see the faces he encountered at work: his supervisor, senior officers, and his journeyman, Hank—all who somehow made it at the Patrol and were trying to teach him how to be a good agent. He saw the little girl in the detention center whose face lit up when he handed her some juice. He saw fear in the eyes of the young undocumented lettuce cutter who told Aaron that he needed to work so that he could pay for his mother's surgery. He saw the dying old man who just wanted to see his daughter one last time.

These were the scenes that were curiously absent from the Border Patrol recruitment materials that Aaron had first encountered months ago. They were scenes that very few of his friends and family seemed to understand were a primary part of his job. Aaron began to reconsider the chaplain's words about stress in the Patrol. For the first time, it sank in that being a Border Patrol agent was as much or more about working with everyday people than it was with catching terrorists and drug dealers. His everyday clients were more likely to be sick and weak than to be armed and dangerous. The complexity of such a job was going to require a savvy balance of compassion and being on guard—a balance that came with a unique set of ethical dilemmas. He decided to approach them as best he could.

PART FOUR: MAKING ETHICAL DECISIONS

The wind began blowing harder through the desert. Agent Aaron shivered in his heavy coat, blinked hard, and looked away from the crying baby in the woman's arms.

What the hell is wrong with this woman? he thought. *How could she put her baby at risk like this? I know she wants a better life for herself and her family, but what was she thinking trying to cross the desert with so much danger!*

Clenching his jaw, Agent Aaron thought, *What am I supposed to do now?*

He reached out and covered the baby with the woman's sweatshirt so that the infant would at least have a bit more warmth. Aaron wondered whether the woman had begun the journey with more clothes, food, and diapers but already used it up or whether her comrades had taken off with the remaining gear, assuming she would either soon die or get caught by the Patrol.

Agent Aaron felt conflicted by his roles as a Border Patrol agent. On the one hand, he had taken an oath to do his duty to protect his nation. The Patrol had trained him in the correct procedures—to arrest the woman, handcuff her hands behind her back, and take the baby into custody. Officially, it was not his concern whether the woman or baby were warm, comfortable, or healthy.

On the other hand, Agent Aaron felt an ethical responsibility to be compassionate to the people in his custody. The woman and her baby were human beings. They were trying to find a better life, in search of the American dream. The baby didn't have a choice in making this journey at all. Aaron wanted to act with integrity, honor, and within his duty, yet he also wanted to respect human life.

How do I live up to the expectations and duties of the Patrol, while maintaining integrity and honor? Agent Aaron thought. *How do I treat the undocumented immigrants in my custody? And how do I abide by the organizational mandates to arrest and detain immigrants while still being caring and compassionate? Is it possible to do both at the same time?* Certainly, he could do this. However, he was less sure exactly *how* he would do so. . . .

DISCUSSION QUESTIONS

1. What should Agent Aaron do? What options does he have in this situation?

2. Who is owed an ethical response here? The woman, baby, agent, organization, nation, community? Is there a priority order of these groups?

3. Write out a potential course of action that would likely be well regarded for each of the following audiences. Is it possible to consider holding the "right/right" ethics in these different positions in "tension," given the fact that practical, real-world decisions must be made by agents in the field?

   a. the U.S. Border Patrol as a governmental organization
   b. an undocumented immigrant
   c. an anti-immigration activist (such as Minutemen)
   d. a pro-immigration activist (such as the NCLR)
   e. a Border Patrol agent

4. When you read the case study, did you assume Aaron was a certain race? If so, what race did you envision him? Why? In what ways does the ethnic or racial background of the agent matter, if at all?

5. In what ways does the gender of the agent matter, if at all? What challenges might a female agent face at the Patrol, given what you've just read about the job? In what ways might the ethical challenges shift for both the agent and the organization?

6. Some of the key words for the Border Patrol are duty, honor, and integrity.

   a. Create definitions for these words, then discuss how they overlap and interact or are separate and distinct from each other.
   b. How do these represent a "right/right" dilemma as discussed by Steve May in the opening of this book?
   c. Can acting with "honor" and "integrity" ever be unethical?

7. What types of ethical responsibilities do you think the organization has in terms of advertising the job, recruiting employees, and helping prepare agents for the emotion and stress of the job?

8. Outside research: Go to the U.S. Border Patrol website, and watch recruitment commercials (http://www.cbp.gov/xp/cgov/careers/customs_careers/border_careers/bp_agent/videos/). Make a list of what's there and what's missing. Then make recommendations about what the Border Patrol could add or change, based on a potential ethical responsibility to recruits.

   a. Extended research: Look up recruitment commercials and websites from other organizations and do the same exercise. Discuss the ethics of organizational representations of work.

REFERENCES

Cooper, J. J., & Myers, A. L. (2010). *How Arizona became the center of immigration debate.* Associated Press. Retrieved from http://hosted.ap.org/dynamic/stories/U/US_IMMIGRATION_WHY_ARIZONA?SITE = TXHAR&SECTION = HOME&TEMPLATE = DEFAULT

Demo, A. (2004). Sovereignty discourse and contemporary immigration politics. *Quarterly Journal of Speech, 91,* 291-311.

Holstege, S. (2008, December 5). Mistrial ends murder case against Ariz. border agent. *Arizona Republic.* Retrieved from http://www.azcentral.com/arizonarepublic/news/articles/2008/11/05/20081105corbett-verdict1105.html

McCombs, B. (2010). Experts go over SB 1070's key points. *Arizona Daily Star.* Retrieved from http://azstarnet.com/news/article_a9006f6b-f9b6-59db-87b4-d54a09b4b786.html

Steinhauer, J. (2009, May 13). Scouts train to fight terrorists and more. *New York Times,* p. A1. Retrieved from http://www.nytimes.com/2009/05/14/us/14explorers.html?_r = 2&th&emc = th

Surdin, A. (2009, March 17). Border Patrol requests Mexican music encore. *Washington Post.* Retrieved from http://www3.signonsandiego.com/stories/2009/mar/17/1n17border00132-border-patrol-requests-mexican-mus/?uniontrib

White, E. (2008, July 28). *Appeals court upholds prison for border agents.* Retrieved from http://www.dallasnews.com/sharedcontent/dws/news/texassouthwest/stories/072908dntexagents.409b4ca.html

PART VI

Courage

Google's Dilemma in China

Jane Stuart Baker and Lu Tang

This case explores whether we should use one set of universal ethics that is applicable to all cultures or multiple ethical standards situated in the diverse legal, cultural, and social contexts of various nation states. In an era of globalization, it raises questions about how global companies should deal with conflicting ethical views from divergent stakeholders around the world. The case also seeks to examine the dilemmas of aligning organizational values and practices in other parts of the world that may not share such ethics.

The process of globalization is fundamentally changing the ways corporations do business today (Castells, 1996). While there is a lack of consensus on the causes, conceptualization, and effects of globalization, Held, McCrew, Goldblatt, and Perraton (1999) identified the following four aspects as its defining characteristics: (1) the extensity of the networks that connect different countries, people, and organizations in the world; (2) the intensity of the interaction in these networks; (3) the speed with which information, capital, people, and products move around the globe; and (4) the impact of these trends on different communities.

Within the organizational realm, scholars have been examining two concurrent trends by which globalization has affected today's organizations: convergence and divergence (Stohl, 2001). The convergence approach emphasizes how the social, economic, and technological infrastructures of the global market lead organizations to operate and communicate similarly in the global context. On the other hand, the divergence perspective focuses on the heterogeneity of organizational practices that are brought about because of different cultures around the world. At the center of this tension is the dialectical relationship between globalization and localization. Great attention has been paid to examining how today's organizations globalize or localize their practices and communication to be successful in this new era of globalization.

As corporations are increasingly integrated into the global marketplace, stakeholders such as governments, international nongovernmental organizations, employees, and customers have scrutinized the ethics applied to their practices. The concept of ethics is problematized by globalization as different cultures bring different concepts of ethics (Scherer & Palazzo, 2008). What constitutes ethical practices for today's corporations? Should there be one set of universal ethics that is applicable to all cultures or multiple ethical standards situated in the different legal, cultural, and social contexts of different nation-states? How should global companies deal with conflicting ethics and requirements from their different stakeholders around the world? Should they adhere to their own ethical standards developed in the context of their home country and culture or adapt their ethical standards to meet the local social and legal environments?

Caught in this dilemma is Google, the largest search engine in the world. Google has no doubt influenced our use of the Internet as a source of information. According to market research source Experian Hitwise (2010), Google accounted for over 70% of total Internet searches in the United States during June 2010. Along with the success of its business, Google has presented itself as a highly ethical company. Its corporate philosophy features the statement, "You can make money without doing evil" (Google, 2011).

Despite Google's official stance toward this philosophy, the company's behavior—specifically, the 2006 launch of its China-based search engine, Google.cn—has drawn skepticism from human rights organizations and the U.S. government. Since the launch, Google has conceded to China's censorship laws by agreeing to filter out politically sensitive terms, such as *Falun Gong, democracy,* and *Tiananmen,* from its search results. Human rights activists and political leaders have, in turn, accused Google of betraying its espoused ethical standards by ignoring the value of freedom of expression and information access. In the years that have followed, Google has responded in various ways, shifting its rhetorical strategies as it has attempted to address changing needs.

Google has not faced such ethical challenges alone. Technology firms such as Yahoo!, Microsoft, Cisco Systems, and Sun Microsystems have all faced similar criticisms by congressional leaders and human rights organizations, who criticized the technology companies for lacking integrity and urging them to take a stand for human rights when doing business abroad. While the ethics of any of these companies would be worth further examining, Google presents a particularly interesting case because the company has staunchly defended its business practices as ethical in spite of opposition by some stakeholders. This case introduces the controversy around Google's China-based search engine Google.cn and how Google and different stakeholders have addressed and negotiated this controversy. Excerpts from Google's official statements, such as company blogs and testimonies before the U.S. Senate and Congress, are presented to bring to light the ethical dilemmas the company has faced between 2006 and 2010.

THE LAUNCH OF GOOGLE.CN

On January 27, 2006, Google published a blog explaining that Chinese users of Google.com were experiencing slow and often unavailable service. The blog stated that Google was not proud of the service it was able to provide and argued for the need to create a local search engine, Google.cn, based in China. The company acknowledged that Chinese law would require that search results on this local version of Google be censored, which would violate the company's commitment to free information access. Nonetheless, Google used the blog as a forum for aligning the decision to launch Google.cn with the fulfillment of its corporate mission:

We ultimately reached our decision by asking ourselves which course would most effectively further Google's mission to organize the world's information and make it universally useful and accessible. Or, put simply: how can we provide the greatest access to information to the greatest number of people?

Filtering our search results clearly compromises our mission. Failing to offer Google search at all to a fifth of the world's population, however, does so far more severely. Whether our critics agree with our decision or not, due to the severe quality problems faced by users trying to access Google.com from within China, this is precisely the choice we believe we faced. By launching Google.cn and making a major ongoing investment in people and infrastructure within China, we intend to change that. (McLaughlin, 2006)

On February 15, shortly after the official launch of Google.cn, the Committee on International Relations of U.S. Congress held a hearing in which private companies, scholars, and government leaders were invited to make statements regarding Internet freedom in China and the roles to be played by American technology firms. Eliot Schrage, Google's vice president for corporate communication and public affairs, presented a testimony that further rationalized Google's decision to launch the China-based search engine. Schrage (2006) first defended Google's interest in maintaining a business relationship with China and explained that Google had lost market share in China because of its commitment to maintaining the uncensored Google.com for Chinese users:

Operating without a local presence, Google's slowness and unreliability appears to have been a major—perhaps the major—factor behind our steadily declining market share. According to third-party estimates, Baidu has gone from 2.5% of the search market in 2003 to 46% in 2005, while Google has dropped to below 30% (and falling).

However, Schrage (2006) also acknowledged that the company's desire to compete with its Chinese counterparts like Baidu created an ethical dilemma:

There is no question that, as a matter of business, we want to be active in China. . . . It would be disingenuous to say that we don't care about that because, of course, we do. We are a business with stockholders, and we want to prosper and grow in a highly competitive world. At the same time, acting ethically is a core value for our company, and an integral part of our business culture. Our slowness and unreliability has meant that Google is failing in its mission to make the world's information accessible and useful to Chinese Internet users. Only a local presence would allow Google to resolve most, if not all, of the latency and access issues. But to have a local presence in China would require Google to get an Internet Content Provider license, triggering a set of regulatory requirements to filter and remove links to content that is considered illegal in China.

Schrage (2006) then framed Google's dilemma in terms of two choices:

[1] stay out of China, or [2] establish a local presence in China—either of which would entail some degree of inconsistency with our corporate mission. In assessing these options, we looked at three fundamental Google commitments:

a. Satisfy the interests of users,
b. Expand access to information, and
c. Be responsive to local conditions.

Based on the previous considerations, Schrage presented Google's decision, which entailed three parts. First, the company had opted to launch Google.cn and censor the search results according to Chinese law. Second, Google had begun to disclose the fact that it was filtering the results "in a step toward greater transparency." Third, Google had promised not to launch a Chinese version of Gmail and Blogger so that the company would not be faced with requests by China's government to release private and confidential information sent and posted by users.

Despite Google's attempts to align its business practices and ethical standards, representatives of human rights organizations presented a very different picture of Internet access in countries such as China. Timothy Kumar of Amnesty International directly accused technology companies of complying with foreign governments' censorship laws at the expense of human rights:

Several international companies provide Internet services in China, and many have headquarters within the United States. Some of these companies, including Cisco Systems and Sun Microsystems, have helped to build the infrastructure that makes Internet censorship possible while others, including Yahoo!, Microsoft, and Google are increasingly complying with government demands to actively censor Chinese users by limiting the information they can access. (Kumar, 2006)

Speaking directly to Google, Kumar drew attention to the recent launch of the company's Chinese search engine. Quoting Secretary General Irene Khan, Kumar pointed out discrepancies between Google's practices in China and its stated commitment to free information access:

Whether succumbing to demands from Chinese officials or anticipating government concerns, companies that impose restrictions that infringe on human rights are being extremely short-sighted. The agreements the industry enters into with the Chinese government, whether tacit or written, go against the IT industry's claim that it promotes the right to freedom of information of all people, at all times, everywhere. (Kumar, 2006)

Tom Malinowski, representative for Human Rights Watch, another influential human rights organization, also protested the actions of technology companies. In Malinowski's

(2006) testimony, he presented common arguments made by the Internet corporations in defense of censorship and then attacked them:

> [An] argument made by some companies is that censorship is acceptable if Chinese Internet users are honestly told what is happening. This is the argument that Google is making, because the Chinese Google site includes a disclaimer at the bottom informing users that some information is being censored. But is Google really being honest and open about what it is doing? Google is not disclosing a crucial piece of information—it is not saying how its censorship system works. It is not telling users what material—what sites, words, and ideas—the Chinese government is telling it to block. [Another] argument that companies, including Google, make is that the sites they remove from their search engine results are in any case blocked by the Chinese government, and thus that their Chinese users are not being denied anything to which they previously had access. But this is not entirely true. If you punch in the words "human rights" on Google, you will find links to literally millions of websites, from the home pages of NGOs, to government sites, to newspapers, universities, and blogs in scores of countries around the world.

THE END OF CENSORSHIP?

Despite the challenging remarks made by human rights organizations at the hearing, Google went about business as usual until 2010, when an attack on Gmail accounts of human rights activists in China forced executives to change strategies. On January 12, Google's senior management published a blog entry in response to these attacks, announcing the company's plan to end the censoring of search results. David Drummond, senior vice president of corporate development, stated, "We have decided we are no longer willing to continue censoring our results on Google.cn" and indicated that Google would exit China if the Chinese government would not agree to loosen its Internet censorship and filtering requirements (Drummond, 2010a).

On March 2nd, at the U.S. Senate hearing on Global Internet Freedom and the Rule of Law, Nicole Wong, vice president and deputy general counsel of Google, redefined the relationship between business and ethics. While in the 2006 testimony, business and ethics were framed as contradicting each other, at least in the context of Google's operation in China, Google's 2010 testimony positioned the two as indispensable to one other. Censorship could indeed hurt business and human rights simultaneously:

> The debate on Internet censorship is, of course, not only about human rights. At issue is the continued economic growth spurred by a free and globally accessible Internet. . . . When a foreign government pursues censorship policies in a manner that favors domestic Internet companies, this goes against basic international trade principles of non-discrimination and maintaining a level playing field. Local

competitors gain a business advantage, and consumers are deprived of the ability to choose the best services for their needs. And when a government disrupts an Internet service in its entirety—e.g., blocking an entire website because of concerns with a handful of user-generated postings—the government is restricting trade well-beyond what would be required even if it had a legitimate public policy justification for the censorship. (Wong, 2010)

Wong (2010) also reiterated Internet censorship as a global problem and called for the collaboration of the U.S. government and corporations in promoting an international code of conduct to respond to foreign governments who demanded censorship:

Ultimately, governments that respect the right to online free expression should work together to craft new international rules to better discipline government actions that impede the free flow of information over the Internet. We need forward-looking rules that provide maximum protection against the trade barriers of the new technology era. On the multilateral human rights front, enforcing and supporting the mechanisms of the International Covenant on Civil and Political Rights and others under the UN system (e.g., the UN Human Rights Committee) to demand accountability from governments for Internet censorship is helpful. At the very least, these mechanisms can be better used to shine light on government abuses.

Beginning March 23rd, Google.cn visitors were automatically redirected to the uncensored Google.com.hk. Drummond commented on this new approach:

We believe this new approach of providing uncensored search in simplified Chinese from Google.com.hk is a sensible solution to the challenges we've faced—it's entirely legal and will meaningfully increase access to information for people in China. We very much hope that the Chinese government respects our decision, though we are well aware that it could at any time block access to our services. We will therefore be carefully monitoring access issues, and have created this new web page, which we will update regularly each day, so that everyone can see which Google services are available in China. (Drummond, 2010b)

Various human rights organizations, such as Human Rights Watch, now praised Google for its stance on censorship and freedom of expression and urged other Internet companies to follow in Google's footsteps. Human Rights Director Arvind Ganesan declared the following:

Google's decision to offer an uncensored search engine is an important step to challenge the Chinese government's use of censorship to maintain its control over its citizens. . . . This is a crucial moment for freedom of expression in China, and the onus is now on other major technology companies to take a firm stand against censorship. (Human Rights Watch, 2010)

However, other commentators were less optimistic that Google's decision would have any real impact on improving human rights regarding information access. Cynthia Wong, an attorney at the Center for Democracy and Technology in Washington responded, "Google's move is really commendable but I don't think it will have a major impact on China's system of filtering" (Farrell, 2010).

A REVISED APPROACH

In a June 28, 2010, blog, Google announced that it was rescinding on its strong position toward redirecting users of Google.cn to Google.com.hk. Believing that the renewal of its operating license was at stake, representatives posted a blog explaining that the company had relaxed its policy and that instead of automatically redirecting users to Google.com. hk, they would be taken to a landing page, at which time they would be given the option to continue on to the censored Google.cn or opt for the uncensored Google.com.hk:

> It's clear from conversations we have had with Chinese government officials that they find the redirect [to the uncensored Google.hk] unacceptable—and that if we continue redirecting users our Internet Content Provider license will not be renewed . . . we have started taking a small percentage of [users] to a landing page on Google.cn that links to Google.com.hk . . . which we can provide locally without filtering. This approach ensures we stay true to our commitment not to censor our results on Google.cn and gives users access to all of our services from one page. (Drummond, 2010c)

Google updated its blog on July 9, 2010, to announce that the Chinese government had indeed granted its request for a renewal of the Internet content provider (ICP) license based on the condition that users would not automatically be directed to Google.com.hk but would be given the choice between the Hong Kong version of Google and the censored Google.cn.

MOVING TOWARD A THEORETICAL APPROACH OF CORPORATE SOCIAL RESPONSIBILITY

Google's move demonstrates its attempt to be accountable to multiple stakeholders simultaneously. The company's initial decision to launch the China-based search engine can be interpreted as the company's attempt to be accountable to its shareholders. However, when this practice attracted criticism from other stakeholders, such as the general public in the United States, human rights organizations, and the U.S. government, the company adapted both its business and rhetorical strategies to respond to these stakeholders. How about Google's users in China? What has the company done to be accountable to them?

In examining Google's practices and rhetoric regarding Internet censorship, the company appeared to face several dilemmas. Carroll (1991) proposed a widely used model describing corporations' social responsibility. At the most basic level, the corporation should focus on economic goals: maximizing profits, minimizing losses, and streamlining for efficiency. At the legal level, corporations are ensuring that while they are maximizing profits they are also abiding by local, state, and national laws and working cooperatively with regulatory agencies to avoid engaging in practices that society considers wrong. At the legal level, the business is fulfilling its contract with society but going no further. The third level focuses on the corporation's ethical responsibilities to its stakeholders and to society to produce goods and services that do not cause harm and that are produced through fair and just means. At this level, the corporation chooses not to engage in certain practices even though they may be legal if doing so would cause societal harm. Carroll's model depicts the highest set of goals as philanthropic pursuits. These transcend mottos such as Google's well-known "Don't be evil" mantra and actually improve society, the community, or the environment in ways that transcend the core service or goods that the business provides. In managing the controversy around Internet censorship, Google addressed several levels of social responsibility in Carroll's model, namely economic responsibility, legal responsibility, and ethical responsibility.

One challenge Google faced was how to make compatible its economic, legal, and ethical goals. In particular, Google sought to increase profits by exploiting the vast market in China but also felt bound by the ethical responsibility of adhering to values such as human rights and freedom of expression. Another dilemma that Google faced was deciding how best to manage the contradiction between its ethical standards for Internet freedom with calls for censorship from the Chinese government.

Google has clearly faced ongoing difficulties during its tenure in China. No choice has been straightforward, and with every decision the company has made, it has risked alienating one group of stakeholders in order to satisfy another. The case highlights the importance of attending to multiple definitions of ethical responsibility simultaneously and the inherent difficulties in doing so. Moreover, organizations face new obstacles when seeking to apply ethical standards from their local culture in an international setting, as such standards are not always held universally. Organizations such as Google must be mindful of these challenges not only because of how they might affect their reputation and business but also in the ways they impact the people they purport to serve through their corporate missions.

DISCUSSION QUESTIONS

1. Did Google make the right choice initially—to launch Google.cn and censor the search results?

2. How has Google's rhetoric regarding ethics, human rights, and business changed over time?

3. What perspective(s) on ethics form the basis for Google's decisions?

4. Does Google's rhetoric match its behavior? What implications does this have for Google? For Chinese users of its services?

5. What responsibilities do companies like Google have in promoting human rights internationally?

6. Is it ethical for Google to base its decision regarding censorship on what competitors like Yahoo! and Microsoft are doing?

7. How important is it for an organization to stand by its values, even when they clash with the local values of a foreign nation in which the organization is operating?

REFERENCES

Carroll, A. B. (1991). The pyramid of corporate social responsibility: Toward the moral management of organizational stakeholders. *Business Horizons, 34*, 39–48.

Castells, M. (1996). *The rise of the network society*. Malden, MA: Blackwell.

Drummond, D. (2010a, January 12). A new approach to China. [Weblog comment]. Retrieved from http://googleblog.blogspot.com/2010/01/new-approach-to-china.html

Drummond, D. (2010b, March 22). A new approach to China: An update. [Weblog comment]. Retrieved from http://googleblog.blogspot.com/2010/03/new-approach-to-china-update.html

Drummond, D. (2010c, June 28). An update on China. [Weblog comment]. Retrieved from http://googleblog.blogspot.com/2010/06/update-on-china.html

Experian Hitwise. (2010). *Experian Hitwise reports Bing share of searches increases 7 percent for June 2010* [Data file]. Retrieved from http://www.hitwise.com/us/press-center/press-releases/google-searches-jun-10/

Farrell, M. B. (2010, March 25). Google China move puts pressure on Microsoft, Yahoo. *Christian Science Monitor*. Retrieved from http://www.csmonitor.com/USA/2010/0325/Google-China-move-puts-pressure-on-Microsoft-Yahoo

Google. (2011). Our philosophy: Ten things we know to be true. Retrieved from http://www.google.com/corporate/tenthings.html.

Held, D., McGrew, A., Goldblatt, D., & Perraton, J. (1999). *Global transformations: Politics, economics, and culture*. Stanford, CA: Stanford University Press.

Human Rights Watch. (2010, March 22). *China: Google decision shows government intransigence.* Retrieved from http://www.hrw.org/en/news/2010/03/22/china-google-withdrawal-shows-government-intransigence.

Kumar, T. (2006, February 15). *Testimony of Amnesty International before the Subcommittee on Asia and the Pacific, and the Subcommittee on Africa, Global Human Rights, and International Operations.* Committee on International Relations, United States House of Representatives.

Malinowski, T. (2006, February 15). *Testimony of Human Rights Watch before the Subcommittee on Asia and the Pacific, and the Subcommittee on Africa, Global Human Rights, and International Operations.* Committee on International Relations, United States House of Representatives.

McLaughlin, A. (2006, January 27). *Google in China.* [Weblog comment]. Retrieved from http://googleblog.blogspot.com/2006/01/google-in-china.html

Scherer, A. G., & Palazzo, G. (2008). Globalization and corporate social responsibility. In A. Crane, A. McWilliams, J. Moon, & D. S. Siegel (Eds.), *The Oxford handbook of corporate social responsibility* (pp. 413–431). New York: Oxford University Press.

Schrage, E. (2006, February 15). *Testimony of Google Inc. before the Subcommittee on Asia and the Pacific, and the Subcommittee on Africa, Global Human Rights, and International Operations.* Committee on International Relations, United States House of Representatives.

Stohl, C. (2001). Globalizing organizational communication. In F. M. Jablin & L. Putnam (Eds.), *The new handbook of organizational communication: Advances in theory, research, and methods* (pp. 323–378). Thousand Oaks, CA: Sage.

Wong, N. (2010, March 22). *Testimony of Google, Inc. United States Senate Hearing on Global Internet Freedom and the Rule of Law.* Retrieved from http://judiciary.senate.gov/pdf/10-03-02Wong%27sTestimony.pdf

Speaking Up Is Not an Easy Choice

Boat Rocking as Ethical Dilemma

Ryan S. Bisel and Joann Keyton

This case explores the challenges in our current health care system, which often pits provider costs against patient access. In this case, a community-based provider of in-home health care services must balance economic, bottom-line interests with those of patients. As employees see the quality of care erode, they must decide whether to remain loyal to their employer or to speak up and raise concerns.

HOSPICE CARE, INC

Health care in the United States is changing. Emotional and contentious debates about access, cost, insurance, and quality permeate political forums and talk shows. These debates often pit morally charged premises like the need to provide for the *least among us* against economic concerns about policies' potential to undermine businesses' viability. In actual practice, these complex issues tend to unfold in unexpected ways. For instance, this case explains the story of how one community-based provider of in-home health care services, Hospice Care, Inc., was forced to stop providing care to patients who could not pay when the organization failed to adapt to federal changes to the Medicare system. Ironically, changes to the Medicare system were initially designed to streamline payouts, enhance provider accountability, and improve patient care. However, for Hospice Care, the policy change resulted in a need to stop providing care to the dying indigent in the community it was created to serve.

Hospice Care specializes in caring for dying patients and their families, while allowing patients to maintain quality of life by receiving care in their own homes. Medicare insurance, private donations, and the city's taxpayers fund the organization. Major changes to Medicare's billing system and payout rules slowly depleted the organization's financial reserves. Hospice Care failed to respond to these changes quickly and suffered the consequences: Within 6 years, the organization's budget deficit exceeded hundreds of thousands of dollars. The city threatened to pull its support if the organization did not improve its financial condition. Hospice Care's board of directors responded by replacing the executive director, firing 10% of the staff, changing billing software, and no longer admitting patients who could not pay for services. These dramatic changes had the desired effect: The organization achieved a budget surplus in a little less than a year and retained the city's financial support.

In the years since these major changes, Hospice Care employees explain that their organization is different than it once was. One employee, a nurse, explained, "We used to be a close-knit family type deal, a place with heart. Now, we're all about the 'metrics' as they [management] call it. More money, less time, bill, bill, bill! I used to feel like I got to build relationships with my patients. Now, I'm out the door, off to the next billable visit" (Bisel & Barge, 2011). The tumultuous period of change made many employees wary of management. They experienced strong emotions associated with the uncertainty of their organization's near-failure: They felt a sense of heartache at seeing their coworkers' jobs terminated and a sense of purposelessness at no longer working for an organization that helped the poor in their community. Taken together, many employees felt like Hospice Care had lost its way.

RIGHT/RIGHT DILEMMA: LOYALTY OR OBEDIENCE?

While workers maintained a certain reservation about management's decisions, daily work–life eventually regained a mundane quality. Management had not implemented any new large changes for some time. However, similar to years past, Hospice Care was again struggling financially. This time Hospice Care was not receiving enough referrals from local doctors to create much-needed revenue.

Referrals and Physical Therapy Staff

Typically, Hospice Care gains new patients through referrals. Here is how it works: Physicians advise patients and their families to contact Hospice Care. Then, hospital staff calls Jan, the intake nurse, at Hospice Care. In turn, Jan makes insurance arrangements and then contacts her immediate supervisors, Lisa and Claire, who decide which health care skill sets and disciplines are needed to meet patients' needs. Hospice Care employs registered nurses, nurse's aides, social workers, ministers, and physical therapists. Any combination of these professionals may be sent to care for patients in their own homes. Recently, the executive director (and the highest-ranking decision maker), Tina, made the decision to fire two of the organization's three physical therapists as a means of reducing expenses—a move Tina justified by citing Hospice Care's declining referrals over recent months.

Just 2 weeks after these physical therapists were fired, Jan noticed that intake calls were increasing. However, many of the referrals included requests for physical therapy (PT). The one remaining physical therapist was quickly overbooked and the point came when Jan had to turn away referrals. Knowing Hospice Care's long battle with financial instability, Jan reacted to turning away referrals by alerting Lisa, Claire, and Tina by e-mail. The following is a record of their e-mail interaction:

TABLE 22.1   E-Mail Exchange Among Jan (Intake Nurse), Lisa, and Claire (Immediate Supervisors) With Tina (Executive Director) Copied in the First Message

Initial Message:

From: Jan

Sent: Wednesday, March 17, 3:27 pm

To: Lisa, Claire

Cc: Tina

Subject: Referrals not taken

FYI: Just to keep you in the know . . . we have lost at *least* 10 referrals due to limited PT staff. All but two were from [local, partnering hospital]. There are likely more we would have gotten, but the hospital is starting to call other agencies w/o even asking us.

Response Message:

From: Lisa

Sent: Wednesday, March 17, 4:54 pm

To: Jan

Cc: Claire

Subject: PTs we are not taking

Jan—let's plan for you to touch base with Claire and I at the end of the day to see where we are with PT referrals (not taking due to coverage . . .) then Claire and I will let Tina know.

Jan's Perspective as Frontline Worker

displacement

Jan's initial e-mail message was motivated by a concern for and loyalty to Hospice Care and the disadvantaged persons it used to serve. She worked for the home health care provider for nearly 20 years and took great pride in being the *voice* of the organization to incoming callers. Despite the dramatic changes over recent years and that many of her personal friends were fired from their positions with Hospice Care, she still remained deeply committed to the service Hospice Care contributed to its community. Past financial woes seemed to be the fault of past executive directors and top-level managers who did not react to changes in the organization's work and cash flows. Jan felt she was observing the onset of yet another management failure. If Hospice Care's current financial trouble was the result of declining numbers of billable visits, then, Jan reasoned, turning away referrals would only make the problem worse. Jan believed that, by firing all but a single physical therapist, Tina created a scenario in which Hospice Care's money issues would go from bad to catastrophic. Jan's message was intended to make it clear that Tina's decision to fire PT staff was brash and that the two PT staff should be rehired urgently.

Jan did not expect the response she received from Lisa and Claire, her immediate supervisors. Their response seemed hard to explain; it was as though Lisa and Claire were more concerned that Tina was copied on her e-mail than about the content of the e-mail. From

Jan's perspective, it appeared her immediate bosses just wanted more control over what she was reporting to the executive director. Jan was dumbfounded. Lisa did not seem to be responding to Jan's urgent plea for more PT help; rather, Lisa seemed more concerned that Tina was copied on the e-mail. Now, given her boss's reply e-mail, Jan felt she would be insubordinate to Lisa's directive if she told Tina the bad news about referrals.

Lisa and Claire's Perspectives as Middle Managers

Both Lisa and Claire worked at Hospice Care for many years. Each started with the organization as hospice nurses and was promoted to their current jobs of managing teams of health care professionals. These two teams were designed to mirror one another and serviced separate geographic areas of the city. When one team was overbooked, the other would often help. As a part of the major changes implemented by Hospice Care's board of directors, Lisa and Claire were promoted to their current middle management positions. They were tasked with overseeing the clinical aspects of Hospice Care's services, which included assigning health care professionals to patient cases and evaluating the quality of their work. In addition, they were tasked with reporting directly to the executive director, Tina. Lisa and Claire were initially excited about their promotions.

Lisa and Claire soon learned, however, that being a middle manager required a different set of skills than the ones they honed as hospice nurses. Political games permeated the job. They discovered that if a social worker felt like he was being assigned too few—or too many—patients, then sooner or later Lisa or Claire would receive complaints. Sometimes those complaints came from the social worker, sometimes from the social worker's teammates, and sometimes they received complaints from the executive director herself. Employees would complain directly to Tina, and when that happened, Tina followed up with Lisa and Claire. These experiences gave Lisa and Claire a certain perspective, which they explained as "Leave Tina out of the loop by taking care of problems yourself." They reasoned that approach was the best way to maintain a positive impression with Tina and maintain their jobs.

Tina's Perspective as Executive Director

Tina, the executive director, was hired at a time when Hospice Care was in a state of flux. The organization was failing financially, and the board of directors was making sweeping changes to curb those troubles. Tina was a dynamic leader and the kind of person who actually relished the challenge of helping an organization weather crisis. She believed past executive directors were often too hands-off, uninvolved, and timid. Tina reasoned that it was past leaderships' passivity that was ultimately responsible for Hospice Care's financial woes. She promised herself and the board of directors to be more engaged and active in her management style: She would make tough decisions quickly to keep Hospice Care financially viable. When the number of referrals dwindled, Tina discussed current patient care needs with Lisa and Claire. They explained to Tina that PT work seemed to be dropping and one of the three PT staff was working less than part-time due to the lack of referrals requiring physical therapy care. Tina went into action and fired two of the three PT staff as a means of reducing personnel expenses.

COMMUNICATING BAD NEWS UPWARD

Seen from an organizational communication perspective, Jan's e-mail message is somewhat unexpected, while Lisa's response to Jan is not so surprising. Researchers observed and documented a particular dynamic in supervisor–subordinate communication, which might be described as the contamination of power relationships on information sharing: Workers avoid—or tend to be reluctant to provide—bad news to their supervisors for fear of retribution and being associated with hurt feelings (Bisel, Messersmith, & Kelley, in press; Milliken, Morrison, & Hewlin, 2003; Ploeger, Kelley, & Bisel, in press). These fears create a constraint on the upward transmission of bad news in hierarchy. Transmitting bad news up the hierarchy has been labeled *boat rocking* (Redding, 1985) by organizational communication scholars to distinguish the communication situation from whistle-blowing—a process that occurs when an organizational member reveals organizational guilt to external agencies (e.g., calling a federal agency to report illegal activity). Just as few workers will ever be whistle-blowers, surprisingly few workers engage in boat rocking, especially when the bad news involves labeling behavior as unethical (Bisel, Kelley, Ploeger, & Messersmith, 2011). The constraint on information sharing up the command structure often results in top-level managers being unaware of the task-related and moral challenges faced by frontline workers—and even the organization itself.

For example, when AIG CEO Martin Sullivan was accused of mismanaging AIG, he claimed he was unaware of the now infamous derivatives contracts. Furthermore, he explained, "I was receiving reports, but they didn't indicate any problems with the portfolio" (Clark, 2010, para. 4). While such an explanation may seem incredulous, the reluctance to deliver bad news to one's boss could have underpinned Sullivan's ignorance of the scope of AIG's problems. Of course, it is also likely Sullivan did not or would not have wanted to hear about the details of such bad news whether or not employees were forthcoming with such information. To date, the U.S. Securities and Exchange Commission (SEC) as well as the U.S. Justice Department decided not to file charges against Sullivan, perhaps in part due to the difficulty of identifying exactly what information Sullivan knew and when (Krisher, 2010).

Perhaps it seems unusual that subordinates are reluctant to communicate bad news to their bosses. Milliken and colleagues (2003) interviewed employees about their experiences with communicating bad news to their supervisors. Interestingly, 85% of participants reported that "on at least one occasion, they had felt unable to raise an issue or concern to their bosses even though they felt the issue was important" (p. 1459). There may in fact be situations in which subordinates are probably *rewarded* for holding back. Research suggests that workers who engage in managing their boss's impressions of them by showing deference to and agreeing with their boss tend to achieve higher pay and promotions. Theorists argue that the effect is likely indirect: When subordinates engage in these relationship-maintenance strategies, their bosses evaluate them and their job performance more favorably because supervisors see them as trusted in-group members; in turn, those favorable job performance appraisals increase the likelihood that subordinates will receive bigger salaries and more frequent advancement opportunities (Bolino, 1999; Wayne & Kacmar, 1991).

Jan's Moral Courage and Duty

Given these common workplace dynamics, we can see how Jan's e-mail message to her immediate supervisors and the executive director embodies moral courage. Jan reported the fact that Hospice Care has "lost at *least* 10 referrals due to limited PT staff." Since Tina fired the PT staff, the e-mail message can be read as Jan's indictment of her boss's decision making and actions. Such a move boldly threatens Tina's public image (Brown & Levinson, 1987) and demonstrates how messages do not merely communicate factual information but also relational and political information as well. Despite the risks of being associated with negative or hurt feelings, Jan prioritized her loyalty to Hospice Care, and those the organization was designed to serve, over her concern for her own standing with her supervisors. Thus, for Jan, when the concern for self conflicted with concern for her organization, she spoke up courageously to promote her collective's well-being, even at the risk of retribution. We may interpret her message as motivated by an ethic of duty to her organization—invested in her by her position because as the intake nurse she had special access to important information that needed to be shared with top-level decision makers.

Lisa's Disqualification of Jan's Right to Speak

Within organizations, the moral right to speak is unequally distributed. Certain organizational members become sanctioned as an *author*-ized source to speak on behalf of the collective. Owners, proprietors, chief executives, and the like are imbued with the ability to represent their organizations in ways that frontline workers often cannot. This process is similar to disqualification, or the way in which organizational members are silenced. Disqualification occurs when authorized members (like management) engage in the "denial of the right of expression . . . through rendering the other unable to speak adequately" (Alvesson & Deetz, 2000, p. 178). While situated in seemingly polite language, Lisa responded to Jan's initial message by disqualifying her right to send Tina this bad news directly. She wrote, "Let's plan for you to touch base with Claire and I . . . *then Claire and I* will let Tina know" (emphasis added). Lisa's directive set up a situation in which Jan would have to choose between obeying her supervisor and remaining loyal to the operational success of Hospice Care. If Jan obeyed Lisa, her immediate supervisor, then Jan's firsthand knowledge of lost referrals is disqualified and Jan would lose the opportunity to demonstrate her organizational loyalty by bringing the referral problem to Tina's attention. On the other hand, if Jan disobeyed Lisa, she would circumvent the chain of command, an action that would likely harm her relationship with her supervisor (Kassing, 2007).

CONNECTION TO SYSTEMS APPROACH

This case also illustrates a systems approach to the study of organizational communication. From a systems approach, organizations are metaphorically likened to biological organisms. Those biological systems that adjust and adapt well to their environmental challenges *survival of the fittest*

survive and thrive; those systems that fail to adapt to environmental challenges die. In other words, it is better to be a cactus in the desert than an oak tree. In this case, system dynamics like permeability, entropy, corrective feedback, and requisite variety are apparent. Like all organizations, Hospice Care functions with a certain degree of permeability in that materials and information flows into and out of its boundaries. In this health care organization, a frontline worker—not the supervisors or the executive director—knew the critical explanation of why referrals were rapidly declining because of her access to information flowing across this boundary. From a systems perspective, getting such bad news communicated from below (as well as the intake system itself) is essential to Hospice Care's ability to recover from a possible misstep in their staffing choices. If Jan did not communicate this information to her bosses then entropy, or decay and dissipation, may quickly take hold of the organization. Closed systems never last for long. If Jan did communicate the critical nature of this information to top-level decision makers, despite Lisa's directive, she would be providing a valuable systems function: corrective feedback. Successful systems locate and change missteps and deviations that make them less capable of meeting environmental challenges (Weick, 2001; Weick & Sutcliffe, 2007). In this case, the firing of staff that made Hospice Care unable to deal with the influx of incoming patients with physical therapy needs appears to be a misstep that must be located and changed.

In a similar sense, Hospice Care is dangerously close to failing to achieve requisite variety with its environment or matching internal system complexity to environmental complexity (Weick, 2001). If the staffing problem is left unaddressed, the inability to serve new physical therapy patients could kick off a number of related system failures: Without enough new patients, billable hours will dwindle. Without enough billable hours, other types of clinicians (e.g., social workers) will likely need to be fired. Without a critical mass of clinicians (and, thus internal complexity), Hospice Care will not be able to provide enough types of care to encourage future patients to seek Hospice Care's services over other hospice providers. Clearly, the interdependence of systems within systems helps us to see the ways in which a seemingly ordinary e-mail message is part and parcel of overall organizational functioning. Therein, we see how the real challenge of management is to cultivate quality information sharing despite the cooling effect power relationships tend to have on subordinates' willingness to provide supervisors with corrective feedback (Bisel et al., in press).

WHAT SHOULD JAN SAY NOW?

The ethical nature of Jan's communication dilemma is made more striking by the relatively small amount of upward feedback—when compared to downward feedback—typical of hierarchical organizations (Hargie, Tourish, & Wilson, 2002). Unfortunately, when crucial corrective feedback needs to flow from subordinates to their supervisors, those upward messages are often "systematically distorted, constrained and eliminated" (Tourish & Robson, 2003, p. 162) by the very supervisors the messages were intended to help or inform. Constraining upward communication from subordinates creates a bind or paradox for employees in that some may be left to interpret their situation as *I am damned if I speak up and damned if I don't.* Whether Jan decides to comply with her supervisor's wishes or not, there will be repercussions for her *and* her organization either way. What would you do if you were Jan?

DISCUSSION QUESTIONS

1. In what ways does this case demonstrate how moral courage might be needed to help your organization achieve its goals?

2. Is disqualifying employees' right to speak always unethical?

3. How do the qualities of openness and willingness to listen from the relationship perspective of ethics take on new meanings for you when you consider these qualities from Tina's, Lisa's, and Jan's perspectives?

4. If you were Lisa, having just read this chapter, how might you change your e-mail response to Jan?

5. Suppose you are Tina, having just read this chapter. Write an e-mail (or e-mails) to Lisa, Jan, and Claire that attempt to correct some of the ethical and communication problems that are emerging.

REFERENCES

Alvesson, M., & Deetz, S. (2000). *Doing critical management research.* Thousand Oaks, CA: Sage.

Bisel, R. S., & Barge, J. K. (2011). Discursive positioning and planned change in organizations. *Human Relations, 64,* 257–283.

Bisel, R. S., Kelley, K. M., Ploeger, N. A., & Messersmith, J. (2011). Workers' moral mum effect: On facework and organizational ethics. *Communication Studies, 62,* 153–170.

Bisel, R. S., Messersmith, A. S., & Kelley, K. M. (in press). Supervisor-subordinate communication: Hierarchical mum effect meets organizational learning. *Journal of Business Communication.*

Bolino, M. C. (1999). Citizenship and impression management: Good soldiers or good actors? *Academy of Management Review, 24,* 82.

Brown, P., & Levinson, S. C. (1987). *Politeness: Some universals in language usage.* Cambridge, UK: Cambridge University Press.

Clark, A. (2010, June). US politicians amazed as ex-AIG boss Martin Sullivan pleads ignorance: Former AIG boss accused of being asleep at the wheel. *The Guardian.* Retrieved from http://www.guardian.co.uk/business/2010/jun/30/us-lawmakers-amazed-at-aig-boss-ignorance

Hargie, O., Tourish, D., & Wilson, N. (2002). Communication audits and the effects of increased automation: A follow-up study. *Journal of Business Communication, 39,* 414–436.

Kassing, J. W. (2007). Going around the boss: Exploring the consequences of circumvention. *Management Communication Quarterly, 21,* 55–74.

Krisher, T. (2010, May 22). AIG executives won't face criminal charges, lawyers say. *Huffington Post.* Retrieved from http://www.huffingtonpost.com/2010/05/22/aig-executives-no-criminal-charges_n_586203.html

Milliken, F. J., Morrison, E. W., & Hewlin, P. F. (2003). An exploratory study of employee silence: Issues that employees don't communicate upward and why. *Journal of Management Studies, 40,* 1453–1476.

Ploeger, N. A., Kelley, K. M., & Bisel, R. S. (in press). The hierarchical mum effect and degrees of dissent: A new investigation of organizational ethics. *Southern Communication Journal.*

Redding, W. C. (1985). Rocking boats, blowing whistles, and teaching speech communication. *Communication Education, 34,* 245–258.

Tourish, D., & Robson, D. (2003). Critical upward feedback in organizations: Processes, problems and implications for communication. *Journal of Communication Management, 8,* 150–167.

Wayne, S. J., & Kacmar, M. K. (1991). The effects of impression management on the performance appraisal process. *Organizational Behavior and Human Decision Processes, 48,* 70–88.

Weick, K. E. (2001). *Making sense of the organization.* Malden, MA: Blackwell.

Weick, K. E., & Sutcliffe, K. M. (2007). *Managing the unexpected: Resilient performance in an age of uncertainty.* San Francisco: Jossey-Bass.

- Unethical use of power
- whistle blowers
- boat rocking
- false information or no information being shared w/ exec. dir.

- Jan was disqualified as an authority

- organizations rely on spokespeople as a "face" of the company

The Aftermath of Scandal

Picking Up the Pieces of a Shattered Identity

Elizabeth A. Williams

This case examines the tensions that employees felt as they coped with the demise of their organization as a result of misconduct. In the midst of the scandal, employees had to decide whether to remain loyal to the organization, frame the scandal in a positive light, or accept the truth that the organization had acted unethically. In addition, employees who accepted that the organization engaged in unethical and illegal behavior had to consider whether a few individuals or the collective, as a whole, were responsible.

I identified my personal worth as being a partner in Arthur Andersen.

—Vincent[1] (30 years at Arthur Andersen)

I was proud to be part of Arthur Andersen. Proud to be part of a national and international network of people. It meant a lot to get the experience and be part of a group of people that were experiencing worldwide clients and large companies, that . . . carried some kind of weight in our profession of accounting. So, I was very proud to be a part of that.

—Brian (2 years at Arthur Andersen)

I was proud. I think that because it was a Big 5 public accounting firm. It was reputable.

—Sarah (1 year at Arthur Andersen)

---

[1] Quotations throughout this chapter are taken from interviews with individuals who were employees of Arthur Andersen when the firm collapsed. Pseudonyms are utilized to protect the anonymity of these individuals.

I met a lot of great people who I thought had high integrity and did good work and enjoyed what they did and had a zest, if you will, for what they were doing. I have never experienced anything like that elsewhere and it's a shame. I was lucky to have my time there.

—Cedric (1 year at Arthur Andersen)

I loved the firm . . . it was a great organization. I felt lucky that I had chosen that [organization].

—Drew (2 summers interning at Arthur Andersen)

At the beginning of the new millennium, Arthur Andersen seemed to be a company to model. It was considered one of the "Big Five" accounting firms (Squires, Smith, McDougall, & Yeack, 2003), had a reputation of hiring only the best (Brewster, 2003), and as suggested by the quotations that were previously offered by former employees, Arthur Andersen was an excellent place to work. Then things spiraled out of control for the company. At the end of 2001, Arthur Andersen was linked with one of the largest Wall Street scandals in U.S. history—the accounting practices and eventual bankruptcy of Enron (Brewster, 2003).

The purpose of this case study is not to examine the ethical decisions that led to Arthur Andersen's involvement in the Enron debacle (for a thorough analysis, see Brewster, 2003; Squires et al., 2003) but rather this case examines the tensions Arthur Andersen's employees felt as they coped with the demise of their organization. For example, as the news of the scandal broke, individuals were faced with the choice of remaining loyal to the organization, finding ways to explain the scandal that positively framed the organization, or accepting the truth that the organization had committed misdeeds—a decision between loyalty and truth. Furthermore, employees who acknowledged that the organization engaged in unethical and even illegal behavior were left to consider whether these actions could be attributed to a single individual or if there were larger systemic issues that had allowed these activities to occur—a decision to attribute responsibility at the individual level or the collective level.

Indeed, as this chapter will show, Arthur Andersen employees were a group of individuals who were highly connected to the company and the failure of their organization affected them deeply. This case study first provides a historical context of how Arthur Andersen became entangled in the Enron controversy and eventually went out of business. It then utilizes existing scholarship on identification to explore how individuals were connected with the organization and the dilemmas they faced when their organization became embroiled in scandal. Finally, this case study examines how some Arthur Andersen employees came to terms with their organization's ethical shortcomings and the implications of their identification with the organization.

THE COLLAPSE OF ARTHUR ANDERSEN

Before its collapse, Arthur Andersen had "almost 350 offices in major cities throughout 84 countries, with 85,000 worldwide employees serving 100,000 clients, including governments and multinational corporations" (Squires et al., 2003, p. 5). Indeed, it had been compared to the Titanic—an "unsinkable" company (Squires et al., 2003, p. 4). However, just as the Titanic met its fate, so did Arthur Andersen. Retrospective accounts of the scandal leading to Enron's collapse point to three key moments that resulted in Arthur Andersen's collapse: (1) its connection and response to the Enron scandal, (2) previous penalties for questionable accounting practices, and (3) finally an indictment by the federal government.

Enron, an energy trading company, was recognized as the seventh largest corporation in the United States before its collapse (Brewster, 2003, p. 240). However, Enron was engaged in some "oblique" accounting practices, including negotiating "what qualifies as revenue, when revenue should be recorded, where debt can be hidden, and so forth" (Brewster, 2003, pp. 230–231). Arthur Andersen was Enron's auditor, and David Duncan was the partner who was leading the Arthur Andersen team at Enron. Duncan overruled instructions from the firm's professional standards committee on how to handle Enron's accounting processes (Brewster, 2003). Then in 2001, Enron faced financial losses and was forced to restate financial statements from several of the previous years (Brewster, 2003). Arthur Andersen employees working on the Enron account were instructed to enact the firm's "document retention policy" and began shredding documents (Brewster, 2003, p. 242). The shredding stopped when the company was subpoenaed for documents related to Enron, but news of the shredding certainly was not well received and made Arthur Andersen look as if it were guilty of wrongdoing.

This was not the first time that Arthur Andersen had been connected to auditing failures. The company had been fined for its role in an accounting fiasco at Waste Management shortly before the Enron scandal hit (Brewster, 2003, p. 246). Indeed, Arthur Andersen would be linked to many of the large accounting scandals of the early 2000s—besides Enron and Waste Management, the company was also linked to Sunbeam, Global Crossing, Qwest, and WorldCom (Brewster, 2003, p. 246).

As a result of their destruction of documents, Arthur Andersen was indicted by the Department of Justice (DOJ) for obstruction of justice (CBS News, 2008). The indictment essentially spelled disaster for the firm as most of its clients left (Brewster, 2003). The company was convicted of the obstruction of justice charge in June 2002, but the U.S. Supreme Court unanimously overturned the conviction in 2005 (CBS News, 2008; Greenhouse, 2005). While the reversal of the conviction was seen as justice for those who had worked at Arthur Andersen, it was too late for the firm, as they had sold their various business units to other accounting firms when the company was indicted and began to lose its clients (Greenhouse, 2005).

IDENTIFICATION WITH ORGANIZATIONS

Identity and Identification

Individual identity "constitutes what is somehow core to my being, what compromises the consistently traceable thread that is 'me' over time, and what somehow distinguishes me idiosyncratically from a myriad of other people" (Gioia, 1998, p. 19). Identity can be viewed as the substance that makes each person unique. The differentiation between individuals is an important aspect of identity, but social identity theory tells us that identity also is about connections to others (Tajfel & Turner, 1979). That is, part of an individual's identity comes from those people or groups with whom individuals associate themselves. Conversely, the choices people make as to with whom they surround themselves are influenced by how they see their identity (Tajfel & Turner, 1979).

Whereas identity may define the core of our being, identification is the *process* through which people link to others. Identification is the process by which humans choose the organizations and individuals with whom they want to be affiliated and how they go about forging those relationships (Cheney, 1983a). These choices of with what or whom to identify hold important consequences for how people perceive the world around them and the actions that they take. To clarify, organizational *identification* can be described as the act of creating our identity in an organization by internalizing organizational values and using those values to make decisions, whereas *identity* can be described as how we define ourselves in terms of the organizations or social structures with which we choose to align and the values we use when determining what actions to take or not to take (Scott, Corman, & Cheney, 1998).

Inducements and Decisions to Identify

Identity and identification play a pivotal role in modern organizations. Many organizations devote large amounts of time and financial resources to invoke identification with organizational goals and values. Most of these attempts to induce identification occur through organizational rhetoric, which is communicated through a variety of different corporate communication channels, such as vision statements, strategic plans, newsletters, face-to-face communication, etc. (Cheney, 1983a; DiSanza & Bullis, 1999).

In Cheney's (1983b) foundational piece, he examined the rhetoric of various organizations and how language is used to induce identification. Cheney relied on a threefold scheme when he examined various strategies that organizations use to foster identification, including the common ground technique, identification by antithesis, and the assumed "we." The common ground technique refers to rhetoric that makes individuals feel as one with the organization (e.g., the title of Arthur Andersen's in-house publication was *The People of Arthur Andersen* [Cheney, 1983b, p. 150]). Identification by antithesis is the reliance on pointing out those things that members of the organization can unite against (e.g., regulation by the government [Cheney, 1983b, p. 153]). And the assumed "we" includes the use of inclusive pronouns in organizational rhetoric (e.g., former chairmen of Arthur Andersen stated, "We all recognize the importance of timely and informative communications and we hope that, no matter what our size, we will be able to retain togetherness so that we can obtain our combined objectives" [Cheney, 1983b, p. 154]). As seen in the examples given, one organization that Cheney used as an example was Arthur Andersen. Throughout Cheney's article, readers can see that Arthur Andersen employed all of the aforementioned strategies. Indeed, as evidenced in the quotations at the beginning of this chapter, former Arthur Andersen employees reported being highly identified with the organization.

So far, the discussion has focused on the role the organization plays in encouraging employees to identify; however, this focus does not portray the complete picture. Individuals also play a role in the identification process. They are not unwilling subjects but rather *active* participants (see Connaughton, 2005; Tompkins & Cheney, 1985). Individuals are "actively identifying themselves with various targets," and organizations are "influencing the identifications of members" (Scott, Corman, & Cheney, 1998, p. 310). One factor that may influence an individual's choice to identify is the organization's image.

ORGANIZATIONAL IMAGE

Image has been defined as "attributes members believe people outside the organization use to distinguish it" (Dutton & Dukerich, 1991, p. 547); this was later termed "construed external image" (Dutton, Dukerich, & Harquail, 1994). That is, the perceptions that individuals have about how others view them and their organization can be referred to as the organization's image. The way the organization's image is perceived by those in the organization can influence how organizational members define their identities and with what they identify. For example, individuals often want to be members of prestigious organizations (i.e., they choose to identify with these organizations). Likewise, if an individual is a member of a prestigious organization, it may be a large part of their identity because of the reputation associated with it.

Organizational members monitor how outsiders view their organization (i.e., its image) because the organization's image also reflects on them. According to Dutton and Dukerich (1991), "deterioration of an organization's image is an important trigger to action as each individual's sense of self is tied in part to that image" (p. 520). In other words, changes in the image of organizations, especially negative changes, may create dissonance in individuals. Therefore, Arthur Andersen employees not only had the foundation of their identity, those values with which they identified (e.g., integrity), called into question but also saw the image of the company for which they worked fall into disrepair. Some may have felt that this reflected on them as individuals. That is, as the organization's image was negatively affected, individuals may have experienced conflict over their personal identity. As mentioned previously, individuals are active participants in the identification process, and these individuals had chosen to identify with this organization whose image was now tarnished. Some of these employees may have also felt that their own image (i.e., how others perceive them personally) was tarnished.

The scandals that led to the collapse of one of America's premier accounting firms not only shook the accounting profession but it also left organizational members to deal with a threat to their personal identity. In many cases, the activities in which the organization was accused of participating violated the values upon which the employees' organizational identification was based. Indeed, nearly 20 years after Cheney's initial study examining how Arthur Andersen fostered identification through a focus on its values, the organization collapsed and its integrity was called into question. Understanding the eventual fate of Arthur Andersen, we are left to wonder how organizational members, who had been encouraged to strongly identify with the firm, coped with the collapse of their organization. After all, these individuals had experienced the rhetoric of identification and had come to have certain expectations when it came to the values and the direction of the organization. Likewise, they had made an active choice to identify with the organization and, as a result, the organization also reflected on them as individuals. Highly identified employees of Arthur Andersen were left struggling between the obligations they felt to the organization and a need to preserve a sense of self. How would they explain the scandal? Where would they assign blame for the organization's actions? How would they move forward? Wrestling with these questions was not easy for Arthur Andersen employees. Indeed, the scandal left them questioning their obligations to others (i.e., what duty did they have to remain loyal to the organization?) as well as presented them with the challenge of navigating their changing relationships with other employees and with the organization as a whole.

COMING TO TERMS WITH A SCANDAL

The individuals included in this case study all told similar stories of how they dealt with the collapse of their organization. We now turn to those stories.

Stories of Common Enemies

Cheney (1983b) pointed to identification by antithesis as one of the elements organizations use to encourage identification. Specifically, organizations sometimes point to external influences as adversaries. Similar to how organizations use common enemies to promote identification, former Arthur Andersen employees used common enemies to make sense of what happened to their organization.

Arthur Andersen employees often placed internal blame on one person or a small group. Sarah stated, "It basically boiled down to one person who didn't have integrity." Likewise, Cedric cited a "lack of integrity on part of management." When describing the actions of these individuals or small groups, most participants described their actions as being "ironic." They point to the fact that the actions of the few responsible for the collapse did not match what they had experienced within the firm's culture or the interactions that they had with other employees at Andersen.

The government and/or politics were also cited as major contributors to the collapse of Andersen. As Drew explained,

[Arthur Andersen] just kind of got shut down improperly by the federal government. . . . I think Andersen would still be here today if it wasn't for the indictment which made them not allowed to do their job. They said you can no longer do your job. I mean it's almost like they found them guilty without finding them guilty because just by indicting them for this, they were no longer allowed to do their job so they were forced to shut down.

Furthermore, in Drew's explanation (and others like it) he accused the government of making an example of Andersen even though all the other Big Five firms engaged in similar accounting practices. This was echoed by Brian, who worked at Andersen for 2 years: "Andersen was the one that was caught up in the poster board material as opposed to every other firm that was doing the same thing."

Brian also pointed to a systems failure in the accounting industry: "A lot of blame was placed on Andersen when it was really the lack of independence between consulting and clients." Vincent also pointed to industry-wide issues as one of the catalysts for the collapse. According to Vincent, there was immense pressure on auditing departments to "keep clients, to grow, to be profitable," all while cutting fees. He blamed these pressures for causing a select few to "lose sight of 'do what's right for the firm'"—the slogan that had always guided decision making at Arthur Andersen.

There was not a singular enemy but a multitude of common enemies on which blame could be placed for Andersen's downfall. These enemies varied from what has often been touted as "a few bad apples," to the government and politics, to a failure of the accounting industry as a whole. In each case, the locus of control for Andersen's destiny rested outside of the organization or at least outside of the relationships that existed within the organization with which Arthur Andersen employees so strongly identified. These employees did not place accountability on the organization or the culture that persisted within the organization. They did not question whether the practices in the organization aligned with the stated organizational values.

Stories of Opportunities Lost

While these employees placed blame for their organization's collapse outside of the organization, they still shared a sense of loss. The losses felt by these individuals were great. However, despite the losses, the individuals still felt "lucky" to have been a part of the organization.

Drew told a poignant story of interning with the organization for 2 years and the joy he felt at being chosen to be part of the "premier firm" that had the "most talented individuals in all of the Big Five at the time." He told of being "immersed in the culture even if it was just an internship because I mean I was ready to start there." Drew's story dramatically shifted, however, to one of lost opportunities as he was notified shortly before graduation that he no longer had a job. He explained the following:

I've lost a lot and now where it's taken my career; I'm at least a year behind where I would have been, if not two. But I mean I loved the firm. . . . I felt lucky that I had chosen that one at first out of the ones that I've seen.

Cedric, who was in his first year of employment at Andersen, expressed similar regret. Furthermore, he articulated a certain amount of frustration at not being able to find a similar experience elsewhere.

> I've worked for several companies since then, and none of them stimulate me or are anywhere near as fulfilling as my short time there. I have good feelings and memories about it, but at the same time it makes me sad to think of the opportunity that I lost.

Vincent, who was nearing the age of retirement at Andersen when it collapsed, spoke of both financial losses and a loss of his sense of self. When asked if being a partner at Andersen had been a significant part of his identity, he stated the following:

> I didn't realize this until it was gone. I identified my personal worth as being a partner in Arthur Andersen. And so there are two things: one is obviously that I lost that identity and second was that I lost millions. And believe it or not, losing my identity was worse than losing the money. It really didn't hit me for a year how deeply that disturbed me.

As we can see from their accounts, the sense of loss that former Andersen employees experienced was deeper than just the loss of their job.

Stories of Moving Forward: The Remnants of an Organization

Opportunities were lost, but perhaps more interesting is what remained for employees following the collapse of their firm. What continues to exist for these individuals are the relationships they formed and their sense that they were part of something "good." While Arthur Andersen may no longer exist as an organization, it is clear that the relationships built at Andersen are still thriving.

Brian pointed to the "silver lining" that he experienced after the collapse of Andersen when he was able to start his own company:

> It's kind of been a hidden blessing for me because they took all these contacts from Andersen and spilled them all out in the marketplace. Everyone went off in different directions, which allowed me and gave me confidence now . . . to start my own business kind of relying on those contacts. And who knows what it would have been like had that not happened.

It was Brian's relationships that he had formed within the firm that sustained him and continue to sustain him after the firm's demise.

Likewise, the lesson that Cedric took from Andersen was one of relationships. He stated the following:

> I saw a lot of people who maybe didn't build the kinds of relationships that I did with certain people and they . . . were let go. So I think that I've carried that on to my other endeavors and kind of made it a point to build quality working relationships with the people I work with. That's the biggest thing that I've taken away from it.

Cedric pointed out that relationships have become so important to him that he has left other firms because they lacked a social aspect.

Finally, Vincent pointed to the strong network that still exists. He spoke of "alumni reunions of Andersen people" and he further shared the following:

> There always was an incredible strong bond with the Arthur Andersen alumni when the firm was around. If anything, with the demise of the firm the bond has almost gotten stronger. Every client that I have here at [my current firm] that I've brought into the firm has some Andersen connection. You know either it was an Andersen client or somebody went to work there that was an Andersen alum.

So while Arthur Andersen may no longer exist as an organization, it is clear that the relationships built at Andersen are still thriving.

It became evident through their stories that employees relied on external factors to explain what happened to the organization. By placing the locus of blame outside of the organization, individuals were able to recognize their loss but still maintain their ties to the organization. These ties were evident through their expression of continued relationships despite their sense of loss. However, we are left wondering what lessons employees may have missed by attributing the cause of the scandal to forces outside of the organization's control. Would employees have been able to maintain their loyalty to the organization had they thought that the organization's values and overall practices were not in alignment? Had these employees not framed the actions of the auditing group working with Enron as being atypical of the organization, would they have felt as inclined to maintain strong relationships after the failure of the organization? And finally, what are ramifications of these employees' experiences at Arthur Andersen on their future identifications?

DISCUSSION QUESTIONS

1. One way that former Arthur Andersen employees made sense of the organization's downfall was to place blame externally. What organizational variables may these individuals be overlooking?

2. Cheney (1983b) identified three ways that organizations attempt to foster identification. Think about an organization of which you are a part and the communication within that organization. What examples do you see of these three tactics?

3. What are the benefits and dangers of having highly identified employees for an organization? What are the benefits and dangers of being a highly identified employee?

4. Dutton and Dukerich (1991) pointed to the role the organization's external image has on individuals' identification. What role do you think the public nature of the scandal played in how individuals responded to the scandal?

5. Reflecting on recent scandals in industry, how have employees of these organizations responded to the scandal?

REFERENCES

Brewster, M. (2003). *Unaccountable: How the accounting profession forfeited a public trust.* Hoboken, NJ: John Wiley.

CBS News. (2008). Timeline: Arthur Andersen. *CBS News.* Retrieved from http://www.cbsnews.com/htdocs/troubled_companies/framesource_andersen.html

Cheney, G. (1983a). On the various and changing meanings of organizational membership: A field study of organizational identification. *Communication Monographs, 50,* 342–362.

Cheney, G. (1983b). The rhetoric of identification and the study of organizational communication. *Quarterly Journal of Speech, 69,* 143–158.

Connaughton, S. L. (2005). *Inviting Latino voters: Party messages and Latino party identification.* New York: Routledge.

DiSanza, J. R., & Bullis, C. (1999). "Everybody identifies with Smokey the Bear": Employee responses to newsletter identification inducements at the U.S. Forest Service. *Management Communication Quarterly, 12*(3), 347–399.

Dutton, J. E., & Dukerich, J. M. (1991). Keeping an eye on the mirror: Image and identity in organizational adaptation. *Academy of Management Journal, 14*(1), 517–554.

Dutton, J. E., Dukerich, J. M., & Harquail, C. V. (1994). Organizational images and member identification. *Administrative Science Quarterly, 39,* 239–263.

Gioia, D. A. (1998). From individual to organizational identity. In D. A. Whetten & P. C. Godfrey (Eds.), *Identity in organizations: Building theory through conversations* (pp. 17–31). Thousand Oaks, CA: Sage.

Greenhouse, L. (2005, May 31). Justices unanimously overturn conviction of Arthur Andersen. *New York Times.* Retrieved from: http://www.nytimes.com/2005/05/31/business/31wire-andersen.html

Scott, C. R., Corman, S. R., & Cheney, G. (1998). Development of a structurational model of identification in the organization. *Communication Theory, 8*(3), 298–336.

Squires, S. E., Smith, C. J., McDougall, L., & Yeack, W. R. (2003). *Inside Arthur Andersen: Shifting values, unexpected consequences.* Upper Saddle River, NJ: Prentice Hall Financial Times.

Tajfel, H., & Turner, J. (1979). An integrative theory of intergroup conflict. In W. G. Austin & S. Worchel (Eds.), *The social psychology of intergroup relations* (pp. 38–43). Monterey, CA: Brooks/Cole Publishing.

Tompkins, P. K., & Cheney, G. (1985). Communication and unobtrusive control in contemporary organizations. In R. D. McPhee & P. K. Tompkins (Eds.), *Organizational communication: Traditional themes and new directions* (pp. 179–210). Beverly Hills, CA: Sage.

Casework and Communication About Ethics

Toward a Broader Perspective on Our Lives, Our Careers, Our Happiness, and Our Common Future

George Cheney

Philosophers often ask scholars in communication about what the field of communication studies offers to the discussion of ethics today. After all, if ethics are *grounded* in philosophical positions and then *applied* to various contexts—like work, science, and politics—what is the need for special attention to communication about ethics? Is that "just talk" or simply a vehicle for transmitting ideas? We know that talk is often cheap as when a promise is broken by a friend or a nation professes peace on the one hand and then acts militaristically on the other. Does the *expression* of an ethical position deserve attention as much as the position itself? The philosophers have a point in that except for occasional forays into ethics by scholars of rhetoric and persuasion, relatively little attention has been given to ethics in our field. As we see in most of our textbooks, ethics appears a bit like an afterthought: "Oh, and by the way, if we have time, we'll talk about this last chapter it's about ethics" (a major exception is of course Johanessen, 2002; see also Cheney, May, & Munshi, 2011).

Still, the studies of rhetoric and persuasion have shown us how ethics are implied by the very capacity for choice and the "framing" of choice in language and other symbols has an inherent ethical dimension. As just one example, consider how commercial advertising and political campaigns often create what some call "the illusion of two alternatives" by presenting the reader, listener, or viewer with a "choice" framed like this: "If you don't buy this facial cream or support this candidate, really bad things are going to happen." Thus, the very definition of a situation, as any debater knows, really makes a difference in the course of a discussion—and helps to define not only practical choices but what we consider things of value or goodness.

So when I'm teaching ethics and communication, I ask students to consider both cases where the role of communication is obvious—as in issues of lying, or professional confidentiality, or the sharing of information, or individual privacy—but also the ways communication is central to discussions of material–ethical issues such as genetic modification, global warming, or the end of life. For instance, just shifting terminology from "global warming" to "climate change" in public discourse can suggest less urgency and, therefore, affect public perceptions and ultimately public policy. Words matter.

HOW TO CONNECT THESE CASES WITH BROADER ISSUES

This book has offered you an array of current cases, ranging from responses to food contamination to the transformation of care in a hospice after organizational transformation. Contemporary issues include migration and border enforcement, the ethics of marketing and advertising regarding corporate social responsibility, ghostwriting for medical journals, the outsourcing of intelligence, and various forms of organizational integrity. Importantly, many of these cases implicate more than one major sector of society. Further, the analyses presented here are nuanced in considering the broader social, economic, and political contexts for many organizational dilemmas and decisions. Thus, both the range and depth of cases here invite the reader to consider not only specific ethical issues but also to explore ways we can do and be better. In that effort, communication-based analyses can play enormous roles, as the contributors here have demonstrated in their careful examinations of definitions, frames, rhetorical strategies, patterns of discourses, series of interactions, and mediated as well as nonmediated networks.

REVISITING ETHICAL THEORY IN LIGHT OF CONTEMPORARY CASES

Applied ethics has certainly come a long way in recent years, as you can see not only with this book but also from the many practical discussions of the relevance of fields as diverse as engineering and interactive media. Until roughly 1990, there were not a lot of "middle-level" discussions of applied or practical ethics that bridged the abstract theories of, say, Aristotle, Kant, John Stuart Mill, and others with day-to-day pressures, concerns, and decisions of all of us. What's more, writings on applied ethics—especially in business—tended either to sound so idealistic as to set unattainable standards or be uninspired in their treatment of ethical practice as simply a matter of working within the boundaries of the law. This made "business ethics"—jokingly called an oxymoron—easy to dismiss from either a philosophical or a management perspective. Today, there is a much wider range of writings, videos, and speeches that offer us realistic and inspiring assessments of ethical practice. For making stronger linkages between cases and theory, we can thank feminist ethicists, notably, Carol Gilligan (1982); ethicists concerned with democracy, community, and difference like Selya Benhabib (1996); and environmental ethicists such as Andrew Light (Light & Rolston, 2003). I mention these three perspectives in particular because of the ways they are helping us to grapple with how today's ethical dilemmas are both timeless and distinctive. Environmental ethicists, for instance, aid us in rethinking our place in the world, our goals for the world, and our relations to other creatures and the entire biosphere. These discussions are valuable, regardless of what conclusions any of us may draw. In addition, when we start taking the environment, aspects of difference, and democracy seriously, we can see how very specific issues like the types of people favored in typical executive recruitment (or the type of policies perpetuated by them) can be cast broadly.

THE NEED FOR BROADER REFLECTION

In the late 1990s, I was teaching an executive MBA seminar in New Zealand on leadership to a group of middle-high level Chinese executives. As I was presenting both traditional and new conceptions of leadership to the class, one of the managers raised his hand and hesitatingly asked, "Professor Cheney, we appreciate hearing about all these ideas, and we do want to cover them at some point. But I was talking to some of my colleagues on the break. And what we most want today is a chance to talk about ethical dilemmas and work and how to deal with them. You see, we have very few people to confide in, and our work schedules don't give us the time to think and talk about these things." At that moment, I put down my notes, sat down in a circle with the students, and we began discussing the cases that they each were facing. I was reminded about the need to be flexible with pedagogy (or teaching philosophy and strategy) as the need for an open space of reflection was pressed upon me.

I have found much the same need for reflection by my students at home, and it comes to the foreground every time I teach a class on quality of work–life or on communication ethics. This is why I have revised my classes over the years from a largely deductive (theory → principle → application) model to one where theoretical discussions arise out of consideration of cases as much as they come out of the foundational readings by Aristotle and others. But the conversation doesn't end there because an individual case doesn't mean very much until it is tied to other cases and we talk about wider lessons. To demystify theory a bit, just remember that it is all about speaking across cases and situations. And whether you realize it or not, you already have lay or implicit theories of important matters like work, love, family, friendship, power, money, and probably also career, success, and productivity. These "theories" almost always suggest ethics even when we're not paying attention to that side of things. For example, if we buy the maxim that "Time is money," this may mean that we evaluate many or all activities in terms of very specific notions of efficiency and worth. But, what are the blind spots associated with this saying and its associated worldview (Cheney, Lair, Ritz, & Kendall, 2010)? How do our notions of career manifest their own limitations as well as focused energies (e.g., Buzzanell & Goldzwig, 1991)? And how do we talk about ethical responsibilities and practices writ large?

BRINGING ETHICS TO LIFE: FOR US AS INDIVIDUALS, FOR OUR SOCIETY

What does it mean, then, to bring ethics to life—and to work? In a recent discussion in my communication ethics class, the students offered insights on why the term *morality* is more compelling than "ethics" to the U.S. public today. They explained how the latter term seems dry, abstract, without passion, and removed from our most cherished concerns. On the other hand, "morality" seems full of life and passion, and it relates to both religious and secular perspectives that are being hotly debated in politics and the media today. For my students, as well as for many leaders today, the phrase *moral values* carries with it a lot of significance, emotion, and concern. This is an interesting observation. Not only does it highlight the importance of language, of communication, but also it reminds us that people want very much to engage questions of "the good." So I suggest that we bring ethics out of its little box, in our classes, our textbooks, and our lives. Ethics should not be something that involves only abstract general rules or guidelines but something that connects what is "the good" with living "the good life" (Solomon, 1999).

TOWARD NEW UNDERSTANDINGS OF CAREER, SUCCESS, PRODUCTIVITY, AND HAPPINESS

One topic that I am coming to include in nearly every one of my classes these days is the transformation of the citizen to the consumer over the past century. Now why would this topic deserve so much attention? And what does it have to do with communication, work, and ethics? Why should we care? I begin with the connotations and practices associated with each of these terms and how it is that the word *consumption* has come to have a very different cluster of meanings at the beginning of the 21st century than it did at the start of the 20th. In 1900, consumption referred to use, waste, and to the disease of tuberculosis. It had both neutral and negative connotations. Today, consumption is elevated as a principal goal of individuals and our society: We see this in seemingly innocuous things such as the bumper sticker that says, "I'd rather be shopping" to the treatment of China in the news mainly as an emerging market of 1.25 billion consumers. "Consumer" has a very different ring than "citizen," and curiously, the term *citizen* now sounds out of date to many of my students just as it does to larger publics in North America, Europe, East Asia, Australasia, and beyond. Many members of our society readily announce, "But I *am* a consumer!" Of course, you and I are. But the problem with "the consumer" is that the term and the role do not readily suggest responsibilities; the emphasis is on rights and demands. Typically, when we hear the word *consumer,* we think mainly of what we want from and not what we might give to society. This means that we're less likely to think about ethical issues when we are thinking or acting with our consumer "hats" on than when we consider ourselves first of all as citizens (e.g., Cheney, 2005).

A *New Yorker* cartoon (Stevens, 1997) captures the problem perfectly. It shows one political leader seated beside another, saying, "My government is concerned about your government's torture and maiming of potential consumers." We laugh at such a frame because it sounds odd, but underlying the irony is the fact that when we think about the consumer role, responsibility, political engagement, and ethical choices often seem to disappear. This is true even for many people who consider themselves "socially responsible": While they may consciously choose to buy a car that gets good gas mileage, they will at the same time not even think about where their investments are directed. All of us—and I do mean all of us—compartmentalize, or contain, our ethical positions and our values in certain ways.

With the consumer in mind, I then move into issues of the market and happiness. Recent research on happiness and the consumer society is telling. Some surveys of life satisfaction in the United States show that happiness may have peaked in the year 1957! Understandably, this is disheartening to many of today's college students. Another study shows that when the *Forbes* 100 richest U.S. citizens were compared with a random sample from metropolitan phonebooks, the rich group came out only slightly happier on average than the randomly selected group. Finally, international surveys of more than 100 countries show that after a certain level of income—adjusted to about US$10,000—increased affluence does not yield increased happiness (see Hamilton, 2003). The title of one book that summarizes this kind of research makes the point well: the loss of happiness in market democracies (Lane, 2000). So what's going on?

When I ask students to write vision statements of their ideal careers in the quality of work–life class or their main ideals, or values, in the ethics class, there's an interesting convergence. Upon reflection, they realize that our consumer society doesn't necessarily deliver what it promises. While it pretends to be purely democratic in "giving 'em what they want," in some ways it diverts people from the things that really make them happy, beyond material subsistence: satisfying relationships with family and friends, meaningful work, and transcendent goals (Gilbert & Wilson, 2000; cf. Cheney, Zorn, Planalp, & Lair, 2008). So it may be that living "the good life" is not the same as living "a good life"—at least as we typically define things like wealth and success and being productive in our society. When many of us begin to reflect deeply on these things, we find that what advertising presents as solid and sure—a new car or a promotion is the path to happiness—is actually pretty fleeting.

BACK TO THE WAY WE TALK AND THE WAY WE ARE

This is why I spend so much time in class on aphorisms or maxims like "Get a real job" (see Clair, 1996), "Act like a professional" (Cheney & Ashcraft, 2007), and "It's just business" (Cheney, 1998). These sayings express deep commitments of our culture that often go unquestioned. For example, by proclaiming, "It's just business," a person is basically saying that certain activities—including harmful ones—shouldn't be evaluated by ethical standards "outside" of commerce as a justification in itself. This is part of the illusion of an *a*moral market, based on a faulty interpretation of Adam Smith's 1776 book *Wealth of Nations* (Smith, 1976; Werhane, 1991). In fact, Smith never imagined a market without emotions and values such as sympathy, compassion, and justice. Making these kinds of assumptions obvious or transparent can lead to some productive reflections on who we are, what we really want, and how we can make a better society.

Interestingly, it was Aristotle (1980), more than 2,400 years ago, who linked "the good life" and "a good life." His concept of *eudaimonia* was until fairly recently translated into English from the ancient Greek simply as "happiness." But now scholars agree that he meant something more than that: the idea of "flourishing," which takes into account not just individual life satisfaction but also one's role in the world. In other words, true happiness involves something much more than individual life satisfaction: the upgrading of one's audio equipment, the bigger house, or the status associated with a high-end brand. Ethics are ultimately not things we keep in a box but have woven throughout our lives. But this is not usually how ethics are taught or discussed or imagined, especially when it comes to business and professional activities (Cheney, 2004; Cheney et al., 2010; Seeger & Kuhn, 2011).

WHERE NOW?

As you reflect on the cases and issues discussed in this book, try to make connections not only to other cases and to foundational theories of ethics (such as discussed in the introduction) but also to your life commitments and life path. While you may not have to face certain issues—say, whether to report malfunctioning O-rings—you will inevitably face ethical choices about what kind of professional and what kind of person you want to be. And it is better to think about that consciously at various points than to wonder later, "How did I get here?"

REFERENCES

Aristotle. (1980). *The Nicomachean ethics* (D. Ross, Trans.). Oxford: Oxford University Press.

Benhabib, S. (Ed.). (1996). *Democracy and difference*. Princeton, NJ: Princeton University Press.

Buzzanell, P., & Goldzwig, G. (1991). Linear and non-linear career models: Metaphors, paradigms and ideologies. *Management Communication Quarterly, 4*, 466–505.

Cheney, G. (1998). "It's the economy, stupid!" A rhetorical-ethical perspective on today's market. *Australian Journal of Communication, 25*(3), 25–44.

Cheney, G. (2004). Bringing ethics in from the margins. *Australian Journal of Communication, 31*, 25–40.

Cheney, G. (2005, March 15). *The United States of consumers. Or, is there a citizen in the house?* Annual Humanities Lecture, University of Utah.

Cheney, G., & Ashcraft, K. L. (2007). The meanings and practices of professionalism. Considering "the professional" in communication studies: Implications theory and practice within and beyond the boundaries of organizational communication. *Communication Theory, 17*, 146-175.

Cheney, G., Lair, D. J., Ritz, D., & Kendall, B. E. (2010). *Just a Job? Communication, ethics and professional life*. New York: Oxford University Press.

Cheney, G., May, S., & Munshi, D. (Eds.). (2011). *The International Communication Association handbook of communication ethics*. New York: Routledge.

Cheney, G., Zorn, T. E., Jr., Planalp, S., & Lair, D. J. (2008). Meaningful work and personal/social well-being: Organizational communication engages the meanings of work. In C. Beck (Ed.), *Communication Yearbook, 32*, 137–186.

Clair, R. P. (1996). The political nature of the colloquialism "a real job": Implications for organizational socialization. *Communication Monographs, 63*, 249–267.

Gilbert, D. T., & Wilson, T. D. (2000). Miswanting. In J. P. Forgas (Ed.), *Feeling and thinking* (pp. 178–197). New York: Cambridge University Press.

Gilligan, C. (1982). *In a different voice*. Cambridge, MA: Harvard University Press.

Hamilton, C. (2003). *Growth fetish*. Sydney: Allen & Unwin.

Johanessen, R. (2002). *Ethics in human communication* (5th ed.). Prospect Heights, IL: Waveland Press.

Lane, R. E. (2000). *The loss of happiness in market democracies*. New Haven, CT: Yale University Press.

Light, A., & Rolston, H., III. (2003). *Environmental ethics: An anthology*. Malden, MA: Blackwell.

Seeger, M., & Kuhn, T. (2011). Communication ethics and organizational contexts: Divergent values and moral puzzles. In G. Cheney, S. May, & D. Munshi (Eds.), *The handbook of communication ethics* (pp. 166–189). New York: Routledge.

Smith, A. (1976). *Wealth of nations*. Oxford: Oxford University Press. (Original work published 1776)

Solomon, R. (1999). *A better way to think about business: How personal integrity leads to corporate success*. New York: Oxford University Press.

Stevens, M. (1997, July 21). My government is concerned about your government's torture and maiming of potential consumers. *New Yorker.*

Werhane, P. (1991) *Adam Smith and his legacy for modern capitalism*. New York: Oxford University Press.

Author Index

Subject Index

About the Editor

Steve May (PhD, University of Utah, 1993) is Associate Professor of Communication Studies at the University of North Carolina at Chapel Hill. Professor May's research focuses on the relationship between work and identity, as it relates to the boundaries of public/private, work/family, and labor/leisure. Most recently, he has studied the challenges and opportunities for organizational ethics and corporate social responsibility, with particular attention to ethical practices of dialogic communication, transparency, participation, courage, and accountability. His edited books include *The Handbook of Communication Ethics, The Handbook of Communication and Corporate Social Responsibility, The Debate Over Corporate Social Responsibility, Case Studies in Organizational Communication: Ethical Perspectives and Practices*, and *Engaging Organizational Communication Theory and Research: Multiple Perspectives*. His current book project is *Corporate Social Responsibility: Virtue or Vice?* He is a Leadership Fellow at the Institute for the Arts and the Humanities and an Ethics Fellow at the Parr Center for Ethics. He was recently named a Houle Engaged Scholar by the University of North Carolina at Chapel Hill and a Page Legacy Scholar by Pennsylvania State University. In addition, he serves as an Ethics Advisor for the Ethics at Work program at Duke University's Kenan Institute for Ethics. He is a past Editor of *Management Communication Quarterly* and Associate Editor of *The Journal of Applied Communication Research* and *The Journal of Business Communication*.

About the Contributors

Michelle Amazeen (MS, University of Illinois, 1992) is a doctoral student in the Mass Media and Communication program at Temple University and is currently an instructor in the Department of Advertising where she teaches a course on advertising ethics. Her dissertation research involves political communications—specifically, the role of misinformation in political advertising. Her research has appeared in the *Journal of Business Ethics* and the *Pennsylvania Communication Annual*.

Jane Stuart Baker (PhD, Texas A&M University, 2009) is Assistant Professor in the Department of Communication Studies at the University of Alabama. Her work has been featured in several books, including *Research Methods for Studying Difference: A Behind-the-Scenes Guide* (in press), *Reframing Difference in Organizational Communication Studies* (2010), and *Handbook of Crisis Communication* (2010). Her research focuses on organizational discourse, diversity, dialectics, and group communication in organizational contexts.

Hamilton Bean (PhD, University of Colorado at Boulder, 2009) is Assistant Professor at the University of Colorado Denver. His research intersects the fields of organizational communication and national security. His research appears in *Rhetoric & Public Affairs* and *Intelligence and National Security*.

Ryan S. Bisel (PhD, University of Kansas, 2008) is Assistant Professor of Organizational Communication at the University of Oklahoma. His primary research interests include supervisor-subordinate communication and organizational culture change. His work is published with *Management Communication Quarterly*, *Communication Theory*, and *Human Relations*.

Edward C. Brewer (PhD, Bowling Green University, 1995) is Professor of Communication Studies at Appalachian State University. His research interests include the relationship of personality to effective organizational and managerial communication, time and probability issues in organizational and interpersonal management issues, and organizational culture. Brewer has published articles concerning organizational communication and free speech issues in the *Journal of Business Communication, The Archive of Marketing Education, Business Quest, The Free Speech Yearbook, The Journal of Public Advocacy, Iowa Journal of Communication, Ohio Communication Journal, Kentucky Journal of Communication,* and the *Journal of Religion and Popular Culture*. Before he received his PhD, he worked in sales and banking and served as a pastor for 10 years.

Elaine M. Brown (MS, North Carolina State University, 2007) is a doctoral student in the Department of Communication Studies at the University of North Carolina at Chapel Hill. Her research focuses on the discourse and practice of corporate social responsibility.

Paula Cano is an independent scholar in New York City.

George Cheney (PhD, Purdue University, 1985) is Professor of Communication Studies at Kent State University. Previously, he was the John T. Jones Centennial Professor of Communication Studies at the University of Texas at Austin. He has also been Professor in the Department of Communication, Director of Peace and Conflict Studies, and Director of the Tanner Human Rights Center, all at the University of Utah. Also, he is Adjunct Professor in Management Communication at the University of Waikato, Hamilton, New Zealand. His interests include organizational communication, quality of work-life, professional ethics, employee rights and participation, organizational identity, power in organizations, the marketization of society, issues in globalization, and dissent and peacemaking. Recognized for both teaching and research, he has published over 90 journal articles and book chapters, along with eight books—many in collaborated efforts. He has lectured in North America, Western Europe, and Latin America. He is at work on three books, treating the topics of alternative organizations, the rhetoric of war and peace, and distinctive approaches to qualitative methods.

Teresa L. Clounch is Associate Dean of Students at Baker University.

Charles Conrad (PhD, University of Kansas, 1980) is Professor of Communication at Texas A&M University. He teaches courses in organizational communication; organizational rhetoric; and communication, power, and politics. His research currently focuses on the symbolic processes through which organizations influence popular attitudes and public policies. His most recent book is *Organizational Rhetoric: Resistance and Domination,* and he is writing a "close comparison" of organizational rhetoric and healthcare policy making in the United States and Canada.

Megan Dortch was an undergraduate student at Texas A&M University when the case study was written.

Jeanette Wenig Drake (PhD, Bowling Green State University, 2004) is Associate Professor of Communication at the University of Findlay. Prior to teaching, she managed strategic communications for various organizations in Columbus, Ohio. Her scholarship focuses on the influences of framing on public dialogue about food and farming and subsequently on public policy. Recent publications regarding organizational ethics include *The Public Relations Strategist, Ohio Communication Journal*, and K. M. Carragee and L. R. Frey's (Eds.) *Communication Activism* (Vol. 3).

Sarah B. Feldner (PhD, Purdue University, 2002) is Assistant Professor in the Diederich College of Communication at Marquette University. In her research, she focuses on the ways in which organizations establish and communicate identities both internally and externally. In particular, she has published work that looks at the ways in which organization mission impacts individual organization members, the role of dialogue in engaging publics, and the management of multiple identities in the context of active stakeholder involvement.

Carl E. Fischer is retired from the U.S. Army and now serves as Senior Military Analyst at System Studies and Simulation, Inc.

Rachel Gordon was an undergraduate student at Texas A&M University when the case study was written.

Loril M. Gossett (PhD, University of Colorado Boulder, 2001) is Associate Professor of Communication Studies and Organizational Science at the University of North Carolina at Charlotte. Her research interests primarily involve the study of nonstandard work arrangements (outsourced/contract labor, temporary workers, part-timers, volunteers, etc.). She examines how these alternative work relationships impact what it means to be or communicate as an organizational member—specifically with respect to issues of member identification, organizational power, and managerial control. Dr. Gossett's research has been published in journals such as *Management Communication Quarterly*, *Communication Monographs*, *National Association for the Practice of Anthropology Bulletin,* and *Communication Yearbook*.

Catherine Howard is a faculty member in the College of Business and Leadership at Fort Hayes State University.

Joann Keyton (PhD, Ohio State University, 1987) is Professor of Communication at North Carolina State University. Her current research examines the process and relational aspects of interdisciplinary teams, the role of training and influence of culture in organizational interventions, and how messages are manipulated in sexual harassment. In addition to publications in scholarly journals and edited collections, she has published three text-books for courses in group communication, research methods, and organizational culture in addition to coediting an organizational communication case book. Keyton was Editor of the *Journal of Applied Communication Research* (Vols. 31–33) and Founding Editor of *Communication Currents* (Vols. 1–5). Currently, she is Editor of *Small Group Research*. She is a founder and Vice-Chair of the Interdisciplinary Network for Group Research.

John Llewellyn (PhD, University of Texas, 1990) is Associate Professor at Wake Forest University. His research interests include organizational rhetoric, rhetorical criticism, public relations, urban legends, and sport communication. His work has appeared in *The Debate Over Corporate Social Responsibility*, *Society*, *Case Studies in Sport Communication, American Communication Journal, Research in Corporate Social Performance and Policy, Public Relations Quarterly, Journal of Communication,* and *Political Communication and Persuasion.*

Alexander Lyon (PhD, University of Colorado Boulder 2003) is Associate Professor at The College at Brockport, SUNY. His research interests include culture, ethics, and power in organizations. His work has appeared in journals such as *Communication Monographs*, *Management Communication Quarterly*, and *Journal of Applied Communication Research*, among others.

Roxana Maiorescu (MA, Virginia Tech, 2009) is a doctoral student in the Department of Communication at Purdue University. Her research interests include crisis management, corporate social responsibility, PR and social media, and critical theory in organizational communication.

Caryn E. Medved (PhD, University of Kansas, 1998) is Associate Professor of Communication Studies at Baruch College with the City University of New York. Her research focuses on nontraditional intersections between work and family communication practices and structures. She is Editor of the *Journal of Family Communication*. Her research has been funded by the Sloan Foundation and the Ohio University Research Council. Professor Medved's work has appeared in *Management Communication Quarterly*, *Journal of Family Communication*, *Communication Yearbook*, *Communication Studies*, *Journal of Applied Communication*, *the Sloan Work and Family Encyclopedia*, *Journal of Marriage and Family*, and *Women's Studies Quarterly*.

Rebecca J. Meisenbach (PhD, Purdue University, 2004) is Assistant Professor at the University of Missouri in Columbia, Missouri. Her research addresses issues of ethics and identity, particularly in nonprofit and gendered contexts. Current projects address stigma management in organizational contexts and the experiences of working moms as they return to paid work after a maternity leave. Her work has been published in outlets such as *Communication Monographs*, *Journal of Applied Communication Research*, *Management Communication Quarterly*, and *Sex Roles*.

Alyssa Grace Millner (MA, University of Arkansas at Little Rock, 2008) is a doctoral candidate at the University of Kentucky. Since early 2007, Millner has been involved in food crisis communication research funded by the National Center for Food Protection and Defense. Her collaborative research explores strategies for effective national crisis communication during food contaminations or adulteration disasters.

Rahul Mitra (MA, Bowling Green State University, 2009) is a doctoral student at Purdue University. His research interests include the evolving roles/ meanings of corporate responsibility and sustainable business, leadership, careers and meaningful work, and gender/ sexuality in organizations. His research has been published in *Communication, Culture & Critique*, *Journal of International and Intercultural Communication*, *Journal of Broadcasting & Electronic Media*, and *Journal of Communication Inquiry*.

Dean E. Mundy (PhD, University of North Carolina at Chapel Hill, 2010) is Assistant Professor at Appalachian State University. His research explores the communication strategies of advocacy organizations in the lesbian, gay, bisexual, and transgender (LGBT) movement. His dissertation researched the communication practices of state-based LGBT advocacy organizations—the organizations that do the lion's share of the work in the movement with only a fraction of the funding and attention. He is in the process of submitting articles from his dissertation and plans to continue studying how state-based advocacy can inform public relations, organizational communication, and social movement theory.

Natalie Nelson-Marsh (PhD, University of Colorado at Boulder, 2006) is Assistant Professor in the Department of Communication at Boise State University. Her main research interests include the study of nontraditional organizing such as virtual organizing, organizational culture, information and communication technologies, and organizational stability and change. She has published various journal articles in *Management Communication Quarterly* and *New Media and Society* as well as a book chapter in *Virtual and Collaborative Teams: Process, Technologies, and Practice.*

David R. Novak (PhD, Ohio University, 2006) is Assistant Professor at Erasmus University Rotterdam. His research centers on participatory organizing for social change. Specifically, he uses qualitative research methods, including visual methods to research participation, democracy, and community as they relate to homelessness and poverty. His research has appeared in the *Journal of Applied Communication Research*, *Communication Methods and Measures,* and *Visual Communication.*

Mark Ricci (MA, The College at Brockport, SUNY, 2009) is Adjunct Professor at The College at Brockport, Monroe Community College, and St. John Fisher College. His research focuses on critical and ethical perspectives on organizations, particularly the business of sports and pharmaceutical companies.

Kendra Dyanne Rivera (PhD, Arizona State University, 2010) is Assistant Professor in the Department of Communication Studies at Texas Tech University. She is an organizational communication scholar who is interested in employees' identities at work and the communication of emotion, burnout, engagement, and wellness in the workplace. She is particularly focused on the intersections of race, class, and gender and issues of social justice. Her research has been published in *Management Communication Quarterly*, and forthcoming articles will appear in the *Journal of Applied Communication Research*, *Women and Language*, and *Qualitative Inquiry.*

Katherine Russell was an undergraduate student at Texas A&M University when the case study was written.

Timothy L. Sellnow (PhD, Wayne State University, 1987) is Professor and Associate Dean for Graduate Studies at the University of Kentucky. Sellnow's primary research and teaching focus is on risk and crisis communication. He currently serves as theme leader for the risk communication research team at the National Center for Food Protection and Defense, a Center of Excellence sponsored by the Department of Homeland Security. Sellnow is the coauthor of three books on crisis and risk communication and past Editor of the *Journal of Applied Communication Research.*

Lu Tang (PhD, University of Southern California, 2007) is Assistant Professor at the Department of Communication Studies, University of Alabama. Her research examines the impact of globalization on communication practices within and across organizations, such as knowledge management, corporate culture, networks, and corporate social responsibility. Her research has been published in the *Journal of Business Ethics, Public Relations Review,* and *Journal of Health Communication.*

Sarah S. Topp is Assistant Professor of Speech and Drama and Director of Debate at Trinity University. She teaches classes on argumentation, social movements, persuasion, and political communication. Her research focuses on the rhetoric of social movement organizations.

Sarah J. Tracy (PhD, University of Colorado Boulder, 2000) is Associate Professor and Director of The Project for Wellness and Work-Life in the Hugh Downs School of Human Communication at Arizona State University at Tempe. Her scholarly work focuses on issues of emotion and work-life wellness within organizations and qualitative methodology. Her research can be found in outlets such as *Management Communication Quarterly, Communication Monographs, Communication Theory, Journal of Management Studies,* and *Qualitative Inquiry.* She is currently writing a book titled *Qualitative Methodology Matters: Creating and Communicating Qualitative Research With Impact.*

Anna Turnage (PhD, North Carolina State University, 2010) is Assistant Professor of Communication Studies, Bloomsburg University of Pennsylvania. Her research interests include rhetorical criticism, critical interpretive organizational communication, communication ethics, and the philosophy and theory of communication technology. Her dissertation, *Identification and Disidentification in Organizational Discourse: A Metaphor Analysis of E-mail Communication at Enron,* explores discourse in e-mails from Enron Corporation, analyzing how employees used metaphors to bridge dialectical tensions of power and resistance. She has published articles in *Southern Journal of Communication, Journal of Computer-Mediated Communication,* and *Communication Review.*

Shari R. Veil (PhD, North Dakota State University, 2007) is Director of Risk Sciences and Assistant Professor of Communication at the University of Kentucky College of Communications and Information Studies. Her research interests include organizational learning in high-risk environments, community preparedness, and communication strategies for crisis management. Her research has been funded by the U.S. Department of Agriculture (USDA), the Department of Homeland Security's National Center for Food Protection and Defense, and the National Center for Risk and Economic Analysis of Terrorism Events. Her work has been published in venues such as the *Journal of Applied Communication Research, Journal of Contingencies and Crisis Management, Journal of Business Ethics, International Journal of Technology and Human*

Interaction, Journal of Communication Management, Journal of Business Communication, International Journal of Strategic Communication, Communication Studies, and *Public Relations Review,* among others.

Elizabeth A. Williams (PhD, Purdue University, 2011) is Assistant Professor at Colorado State University. Her research interests include identification and leadership in a variety of organizational contexts, including distributed teams, multiteam systems, organizations experiencing change, and health organizations. Her work has been published in the *Journal of Communication, Journal of Health Communication, Health Communication,* and various edited volumes. She has conducted communication workshops in a variety of corporate and academic settings, has been recognized for excellence in teaching, and in 2007 was awarded Purdue University's College of Liberal Arts Distinguished Master's Thesis Award.

Aimei Yang is a PhD candidate in the Gaylord College of Journalism and Mass Communication at the University of Oklahoma. Her research interests include the study of civil organizations' transnational communication and advocacy and the structure and functions of virtual communication networks. Her work has been published in venues such as *Mass Communication and Society, Journal of Intercultural Communication,* and *Public Relations Review,* among others.

⊙SAGE research methods online

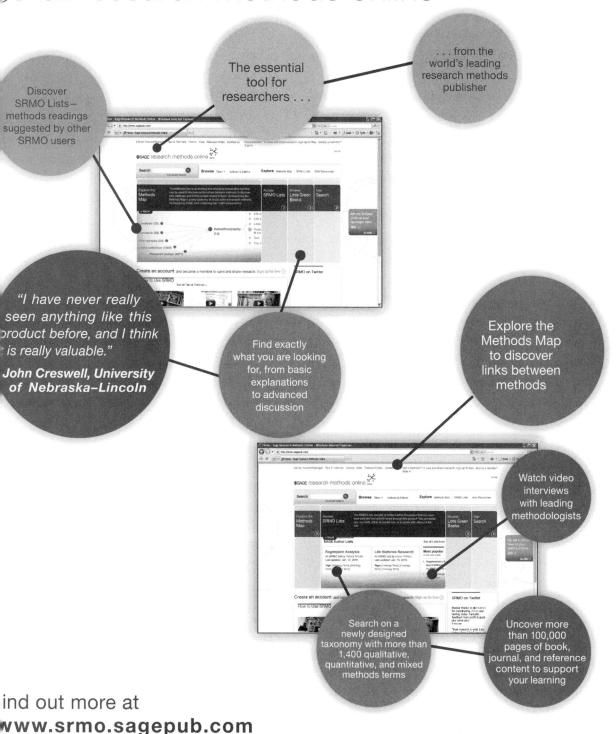

... from the world's leading research methods publisher

The essential tool for researchers ...

Discover SRMO Lists—methods readings suggested by other SRMO users

"I have never really seen anything like this product before, and I think it is really valuable."

John Creswell, University of Nebraska–Lincoln

Find exactly what you are looking for, from basic explanations to advanced discussion

Explore the Methods Map to discover links between methods

Watch video interviews with leading methodologists

Search on a newly designed taxonomy with more than 1,400 qualitative, quantitative, and mixed methods terms

Uncover more than 100,000 pages of book, journal, and reference content to support your learning

Find out more at
www.srmo.sagepub.com